OYAYUBIHIME
INFINITY

Volu

By Toru Fujieda

OYAYUBIHIME INFINITY

Volume: 2

READ MAIL
(SUBJECT)
CONTENTS
(MESSAGE BODY)

Chapter 6:
Searching for Thumbs (or, "The Fellowship of the Thumb")
... 3

Chapter 7:
The Secret of the Thumb
... 37

Chapter 8:
Betrayal
... 75

Chapter 9:
The Vision Mayu Saw
... 115

Chapter 10:
Escape (or, How I Really Feel)
... 153

THE STORY SO FAR

KANOKO AND MAYU ARE THE DAUGHTERS OF A FAMOUS ACTRESS. TO HELP HER BIG SISTER BECOME A STAR, KANOKO CREATES AN ALTER EGO FOR HER NAMED "MAYA." THOUGH THEIR FATHERS ARE DIFFERENT, BOTH KANOKO AND MAYU SHARE THE SAME BIRTHMARK ON THEIR THUMBS. AND THEN, ONE DAY, THE MOST POPULAR GUY IN SCHOOL, TSUBAME, NOTICES KANOKO'S BIRTHMARK, AND WON'T STOP BOTHERING HER ABOUT BEING HIS "DESTINED LOVE."

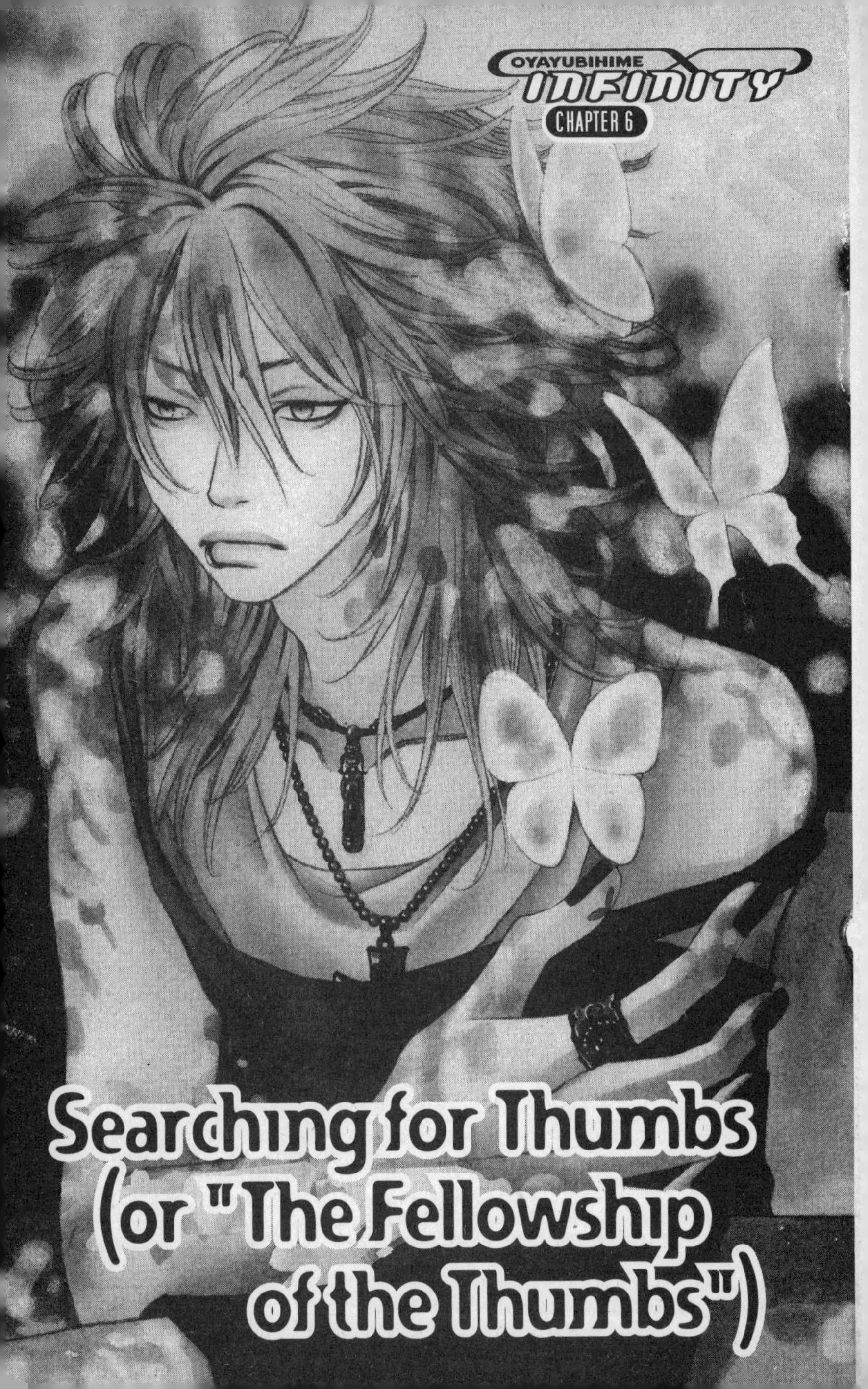
OYAYUBIHIME INFINITY
CHAPTER 6
Searching for Thumbs (or "The Fellowship of the Thumbs")

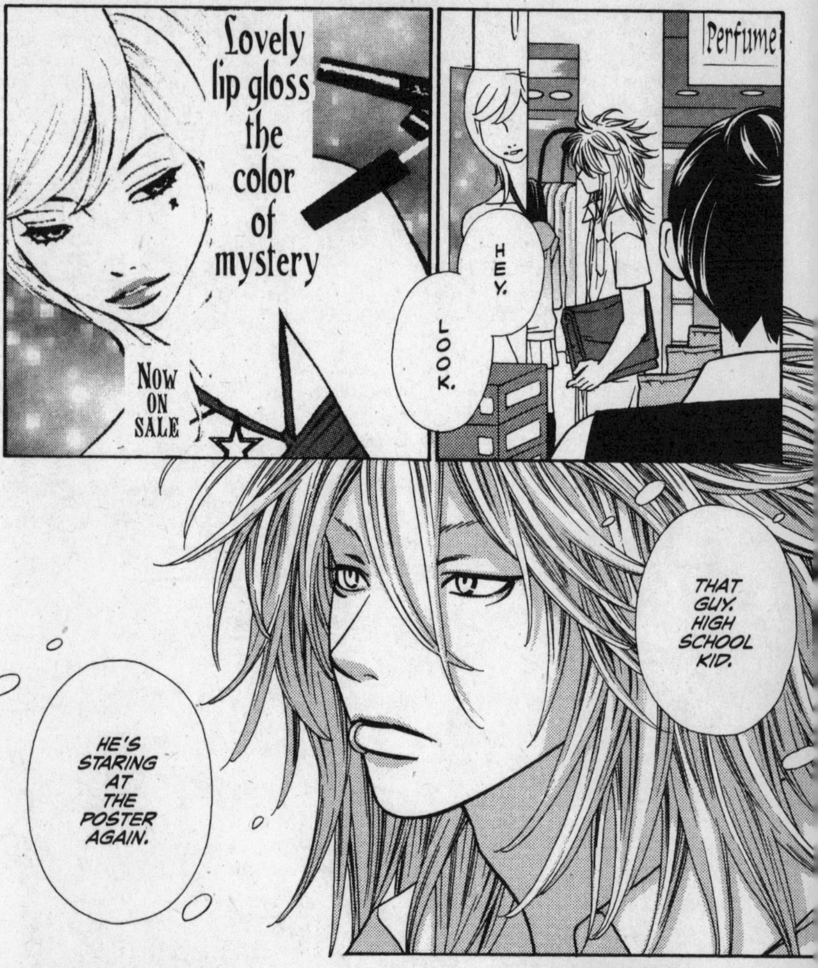
Perfume
HEY. LOOK.
Lovely lip gloss the color of mystery
Now ON SALE
THAT GUY. HIGH SCHOOL KID.
HE'S STARING AT THE POSTER AGAIN.

Character Guide: 3

Kanoko Himemiya

Birthday: 9/30

Blood Type: O

The most absolutely boring and ordinary character ever drawn by Toru Fujieda. She is so plain and ordinary that the publisher said, "You expect readers to like her?" Oh, little do they know what's going to happen...very soon. Oh yes, very soon!!

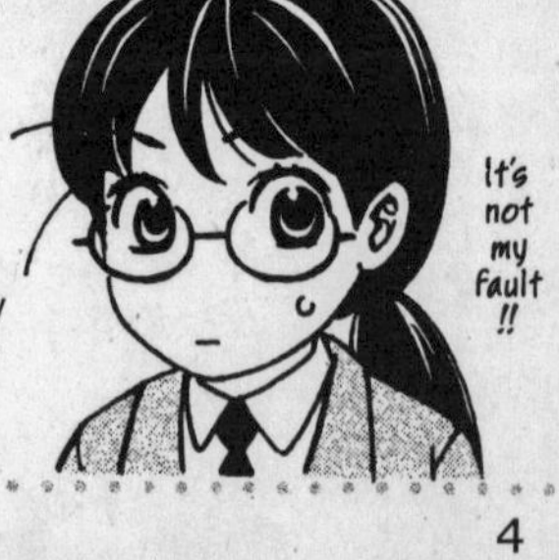
It's not my fault!!

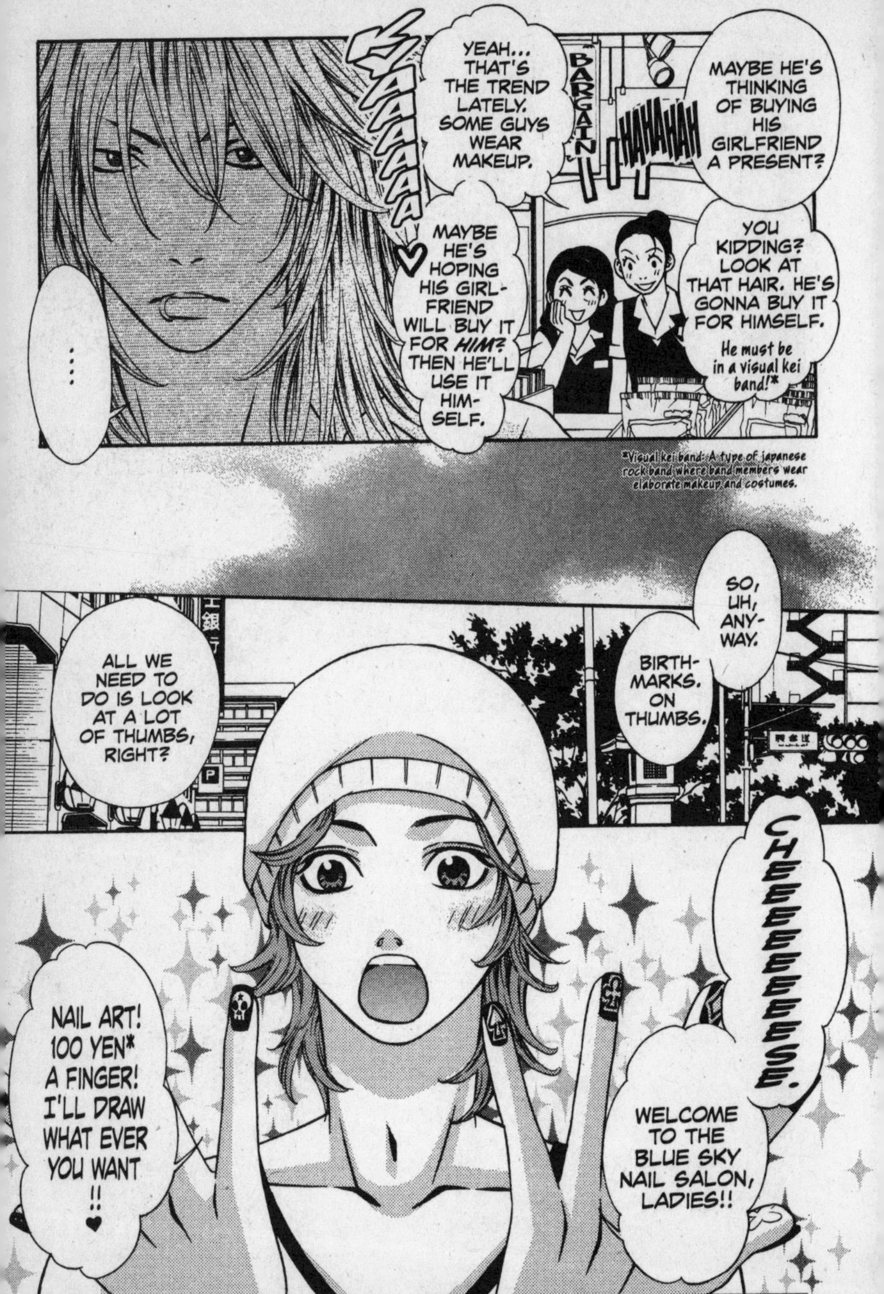
MAYBE HE'S THINKING OF BUYING HIS GIRLFRIEND A PRESENT?
HAHAHAH
BARGAIN
YEAH... THAT'S THE TREND LATELY. SOME GUYS WEAR MAKEUP.
YOU KIDDING? LOOK AT THAT HAIR. HE'S GONNA BUY IT FOR HIMSELF.
He must be in a visual kei band!*
MAYBE HE'S HOPING HIS GIRL-FRIEND WILL BUY IT FOR *HIM*? THEN HE'LL USE IT HIM-SELF.
....
*Visual kei band: A type of japanese rock band where band members wear elaborate makeup and costumes.
SO, UH, ANY-WAY.
BIRTH-MARKS. ON THUMBS.
ALL WE NEED TO DO IS LOOK AT A LOT OF THUMBS, RIGHT?
CHEEEEEEEESE.
WELCOME TO THE BLUE SKY NAIL SALON, LADIES!!
NAIL ART! 100 YEN* A FINGER! I'LL DRAW WHAT EVER YOU WANT !!♥
*100 YEN=APP.$0.85 U.S.

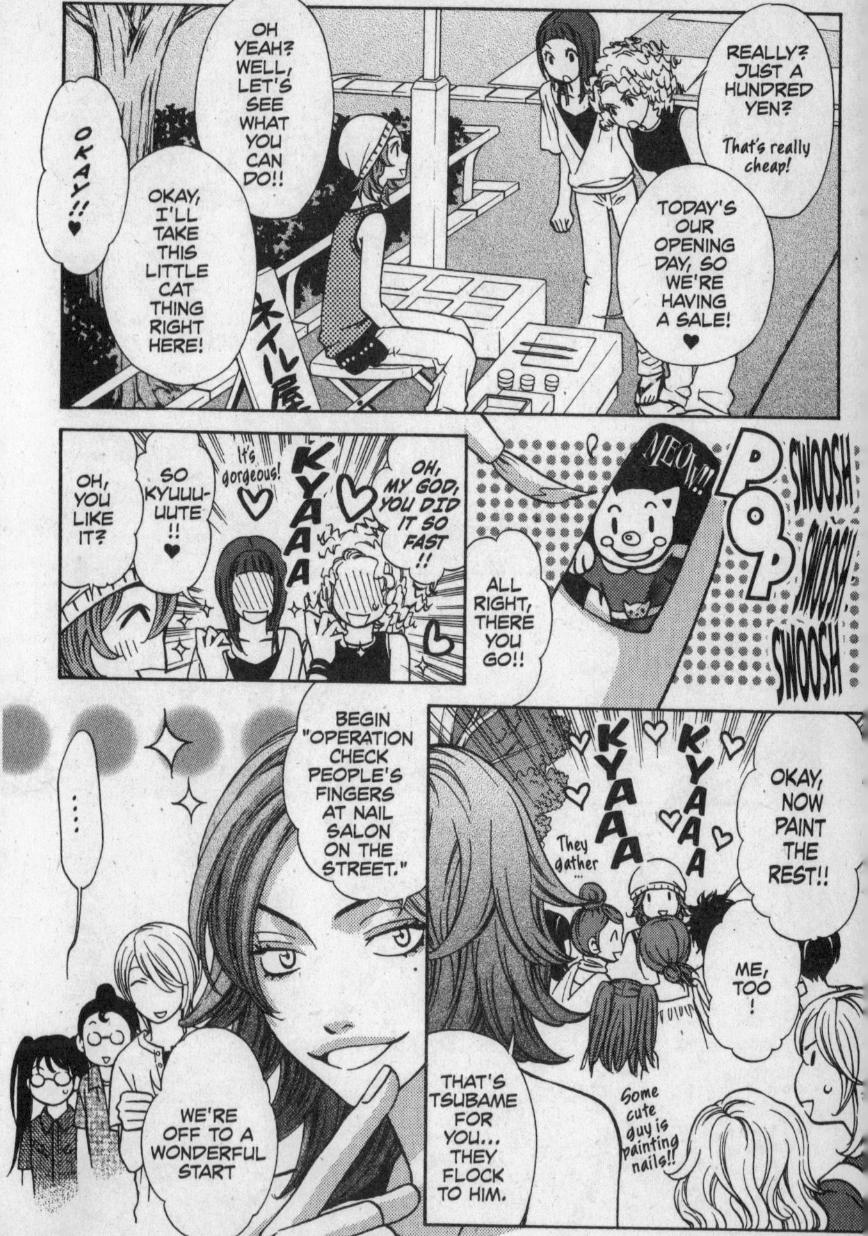

REALLY? JUST A HUNDRED YEN?
That's really cheap!
TODAY'S OUR OPENING DAY, SO WE'RE HAVING A SALE! ♥
OH YEAH? WELL, LET'S SEE WHAT YOU CAN DO!!
OKAY!! ♥
OKAY, I'LL TAKE THIS LITTLE CAT THING RIGHT HERE!
SWOOSH SWOOSH SWOOSH
POP
MEOW!!
ALL RIGHT, THERE YOU GO!!
OH, MY GOD, YOU DID IT SO FAST!!
KYAAAA
It's gorgeous!
SO KYUUUUTE!! ♥
OH, YOU LIKE IT?
OKAY, NOW PAINT THE REST!!
KYAAAA
KYAAAA
ME, TOO!
They gather...
Some cute guy is painting nails!!
THAT'S TSUBAME FOR YOU... THEY FLOCK TO HIM.
BEGIN "OPERATION CHECK PEOPLE'S FINGERS AT NAIL SALON ON THE STREET."
....
WE'RE OFF TO A WONDERFUL START

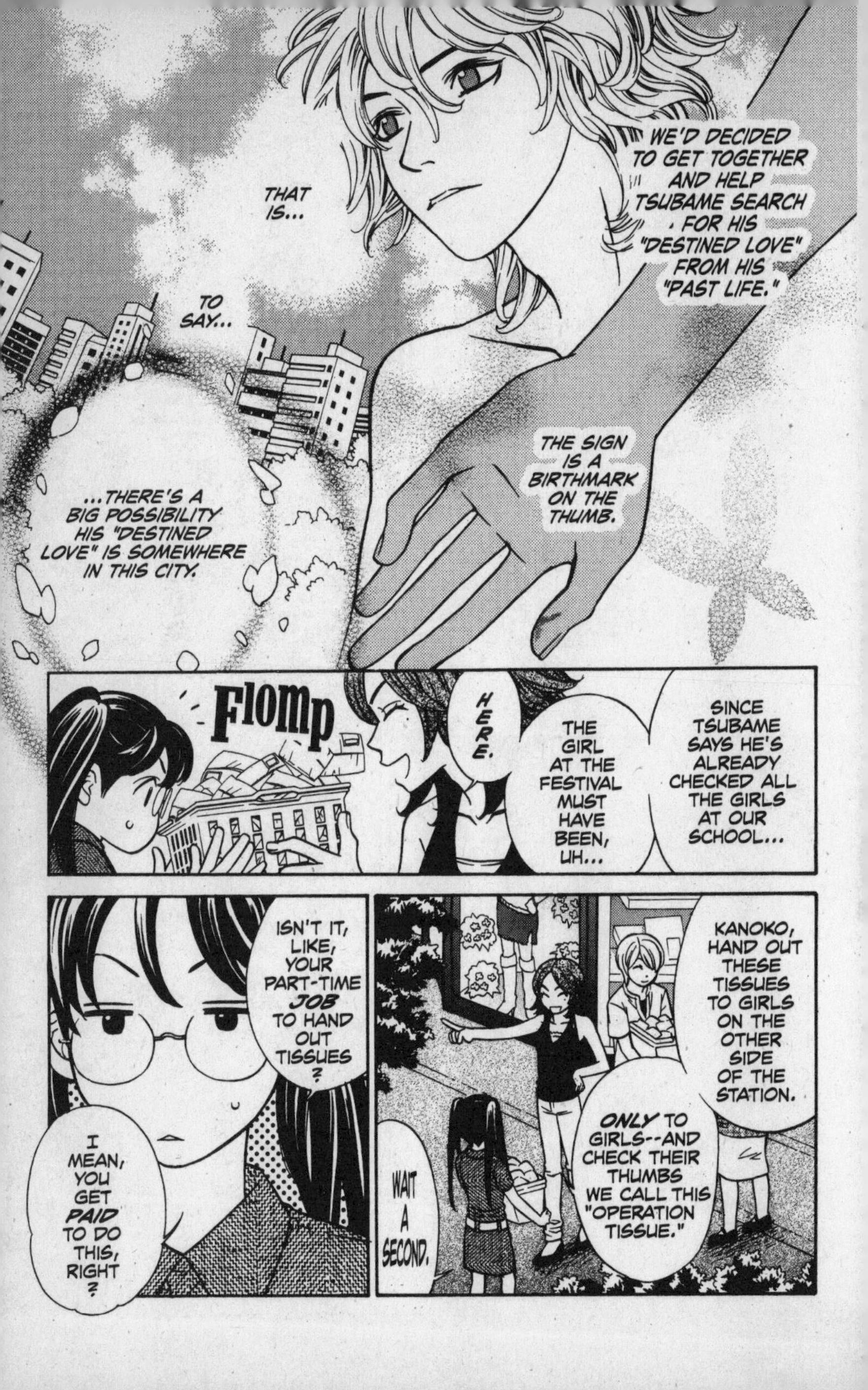
WE'D DECIDED TO GET TOGETHER AND HELP TSUBAME SEARCH FOR HIS "DESTINED LOVE" FROM HIS "PAST LIFE."
THAT IS...
TO SAY...
...THERE'S A BIG POSSIBILITY HIS "DESTINED LOVE" IS SOMEWHERE IN THIS CITY.
THE SIGN IS A BIRTHMARK ON THE THUMB.
SINCE TSUBAME SAYS HE'S ALREADY CHECKED ALL THE GIRLS AT OUR SCHOOL...
THE GIRL AT THE FESTIVAL MUST HAVE BEEN, UH...
HERE.
FLOMP
KANOKO, HAND OUT THESE TISSUES TO GIRLS ON THE OTHER SIDE OF THE STATION.
ONLY TO GIRLS--AND CHECK THEIR THUMBS WE CALL THIS "OPERATION TISSUE."
WAIT A SECOND.
ISN'T IT, LIKE, YOUR PART-TIME JOB TO HAND OUT TISSUES?
I MEAN, YOU GET PAID TO DO THIS, RIGHT?

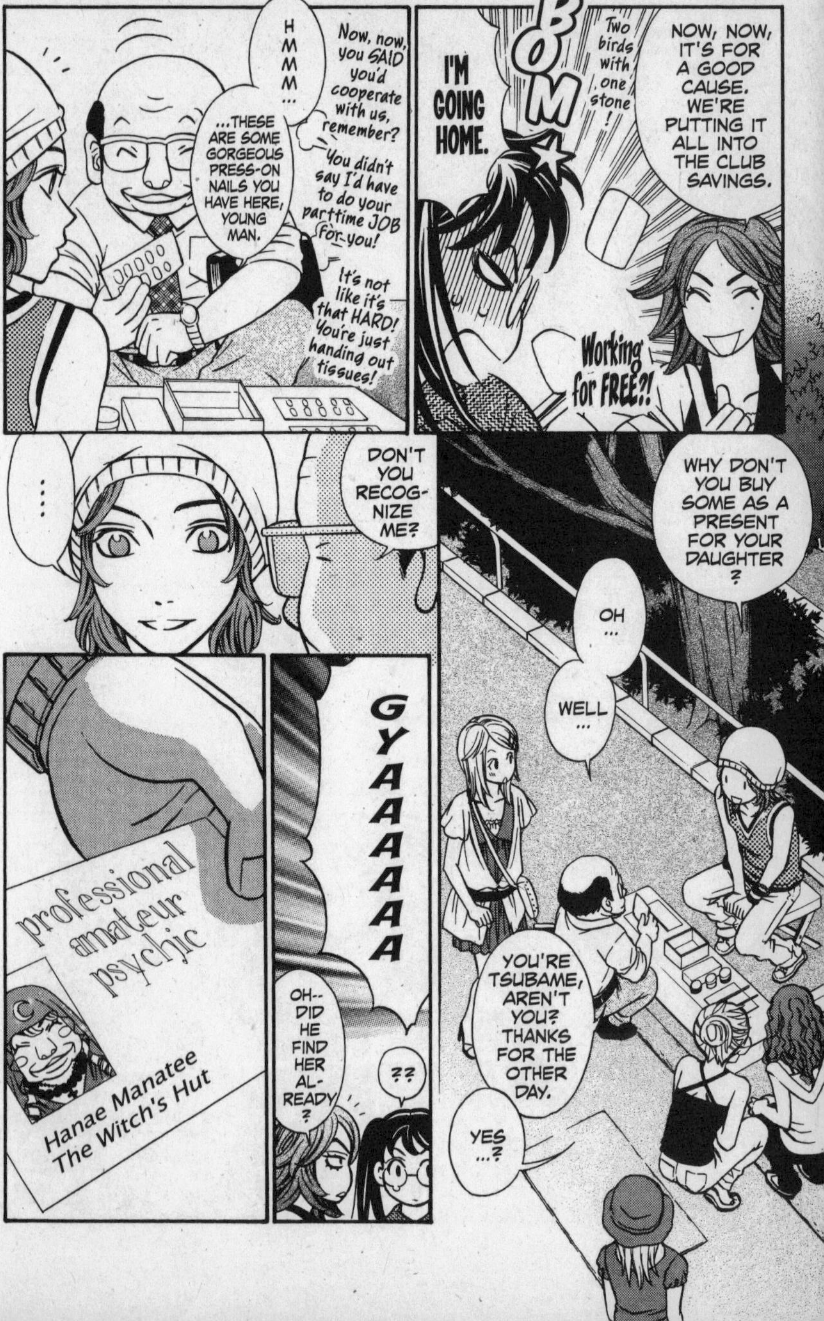
NOW, NOW, IT'S FOR A GOOD CAUSE. WE'RE PUTTING IT ALL INTO THE CLUB SAVINGS.
Two birds with one stone!
BOM
I'M GOING HOME.
Working for FREE?!
Now, now, you SAID you'd cooperate with us, remember?
HMMM...
...THESE ARE SOME GORGEOUS PRESS-ON NAILS YOU HAVE HERE, YOUNG MAN.
You didn't say I'd have to do your parttime JOB for you!
It's not like it's that HARD! You're just handing out tissues!
WHY DON'T YOU BUY SOME AS A PRESENT FOR YOUR DAUGHTER?
OH...
WELL...
YOU'RE TSUBAME, AREN'T YOU? THANKS FOR THE OTHER DAY.
YES...?
DON'T YOU RECOGNIZE ME?
....
GYAAAAAAA
OH-- DID HE FIND HER AL-READY?
??
professional amateur psychic
Hanae Manatee The Witch's Hut

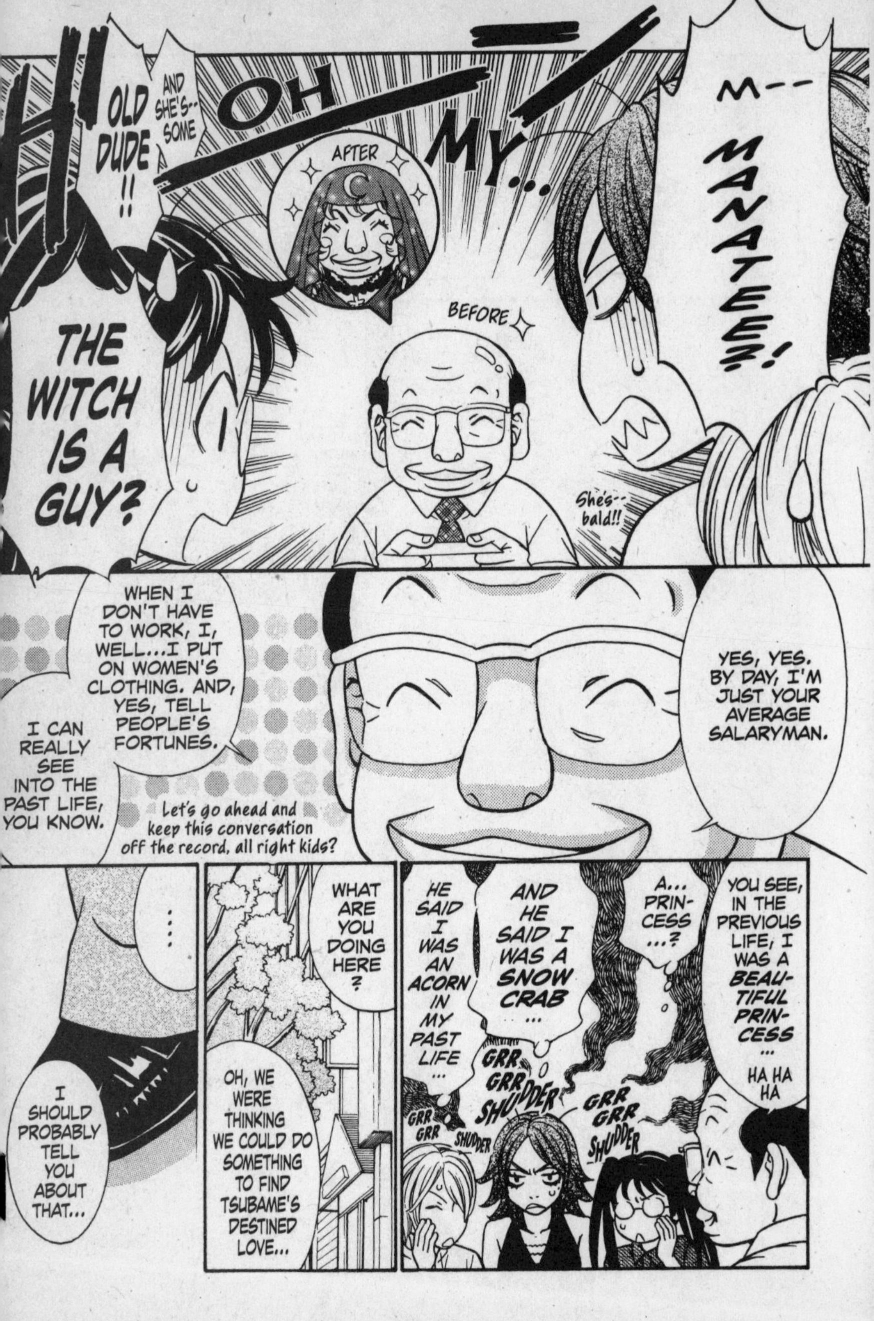
M-- MANATEE?!
OH MY...
AND SHE'S-- SOME OLD DUDE!!
AFTER
BEFORE
She's-- bald!!
THE WITCH IS A GUY?
YES, YES. BY DAY, I'M JUST YOUR AVERAGE SALARYMAN.
WHEN I DON'T HAVE TO WORK, I, WELL...I PUT ON WOMEN'S CLOTHING. AND, YES, TELL PEOPLE'S FORTUNES.
I CAN REALLY SEE INTO THE PAST LIFE, YOU KNOW.
Let's go ahead and keep this conversation off the record, all right kids?
YOU SEE, IN THE PREVIOUS LIFE, I WAS A BEAUTIFUL PRINCESS...
HA HA HA
A... PRINCESS...?
AND HE SAID I WAS A SNOW CRAB...
HE SAID I WAS AN ACORN IN MY PAST LIFE...
GRR GRR SHUDDER
GRR GRR SHUDDER
GRR GRR SHUDDER
WHAT ARE YOU DOING HERE?
OH, WE WERE THINKING WE COULD DO SOMETHING TO FIND TSUBAME'S DESTINED LOVE...
....
I SHOULD PROBABLY TELL YOU ABOUT THAT...

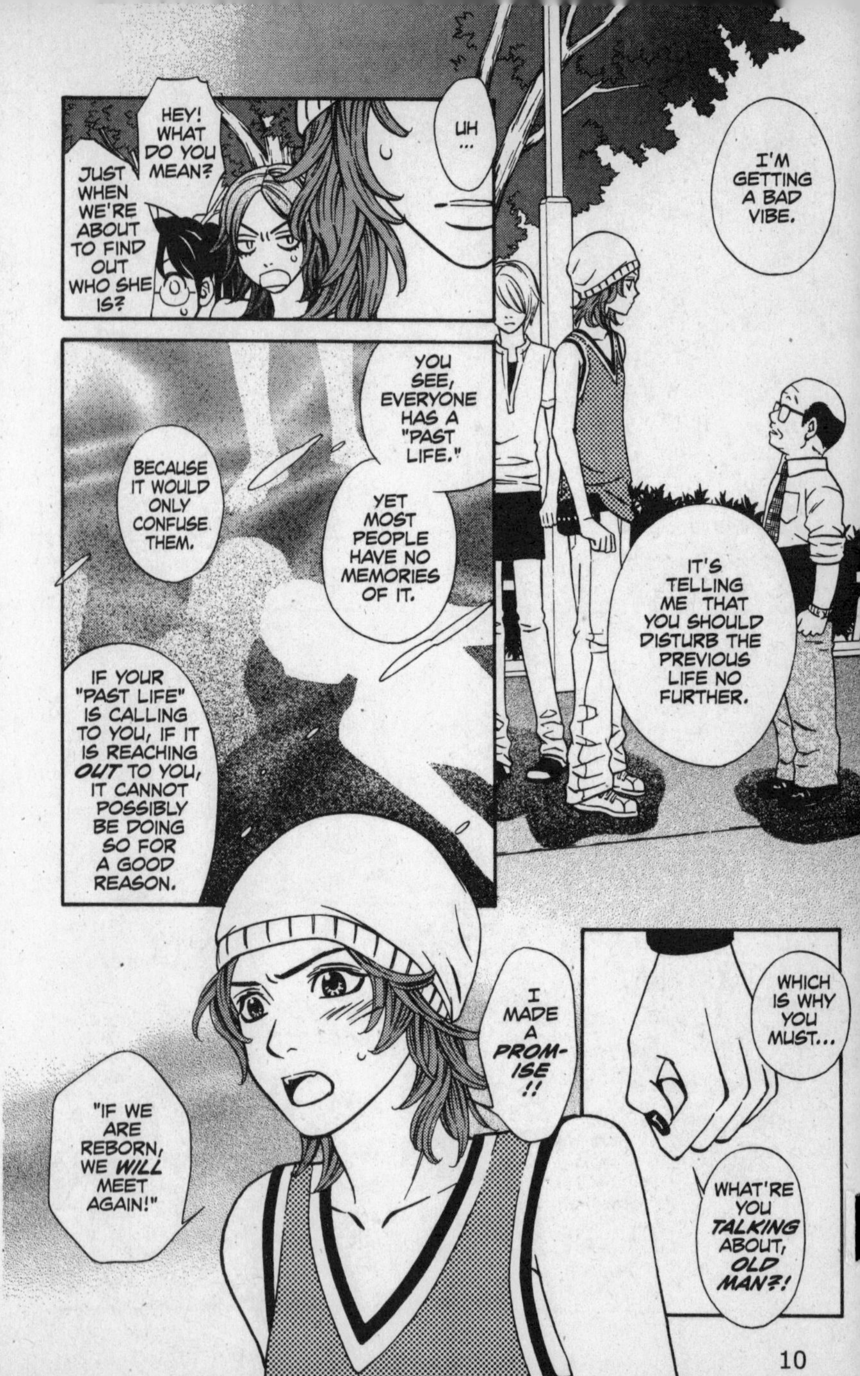
I'M GETTING A BAD VIBE.
IT'S TELLING ME THAT YOU SHOULD DISTURB THE PREVIOUS LIFE NO FURTHER.
UH ...
HEY! WHAT DO YOU MEAN?
JUST WHEN WE'RE ABOUT TO FIND OUT WHO SHE IS?
YOU SEE, EVERYONE HAS A "PAST LIFE."
YET MOST PEOPLE HAVE NO MEMORIES OF IT.
BECAUSE IT WOULD ONLY CONFUSE THEM.
IF YOUR "PAST LIFE" IS CALLING TO YOU, IF IT IS REACHING OUT TO YOU, IT CANNOT POSSIBLY BE DOING SO FOR A GOOD REASON.
WHICH IS WHY YOU MUST...
WHAT'RE YOU TALKING ABOUT, OLD MAN?!
I MADE A PROM-ISE!!
"IF WE ARE REBORN, WE WILL MEET AGAIN!"

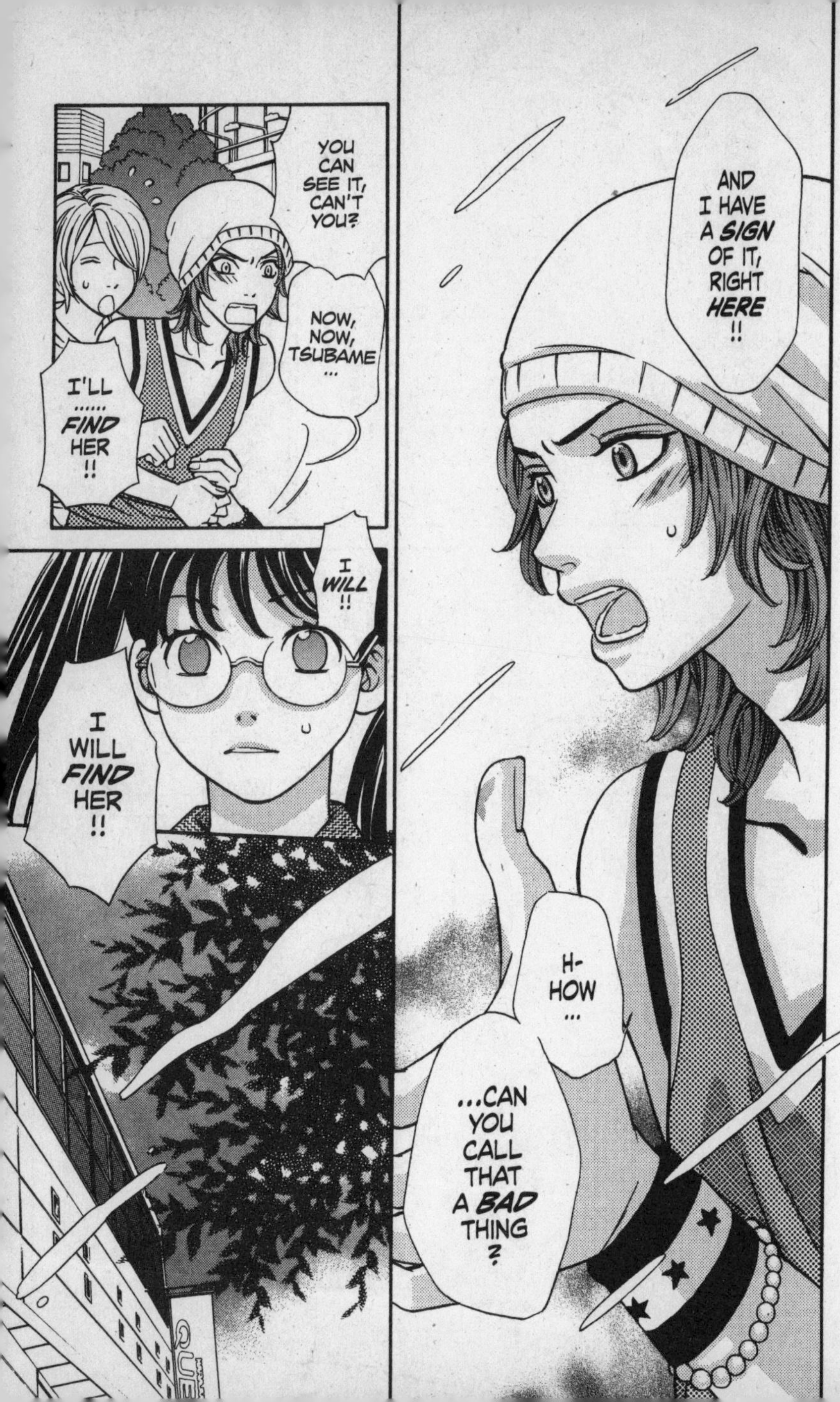
AND I HAVE A SIGN OF IT, RIGHT HERE !!
H-HOW ...
...CAN YOU CALL THAT A BAD THING ?
YOU CAN SEE IT, CAN'T YOU?
NOW, NOW, TSUBAME ...
I'LL ...... FIND HER !!
I WILL !!
I WILL FIND HER !!

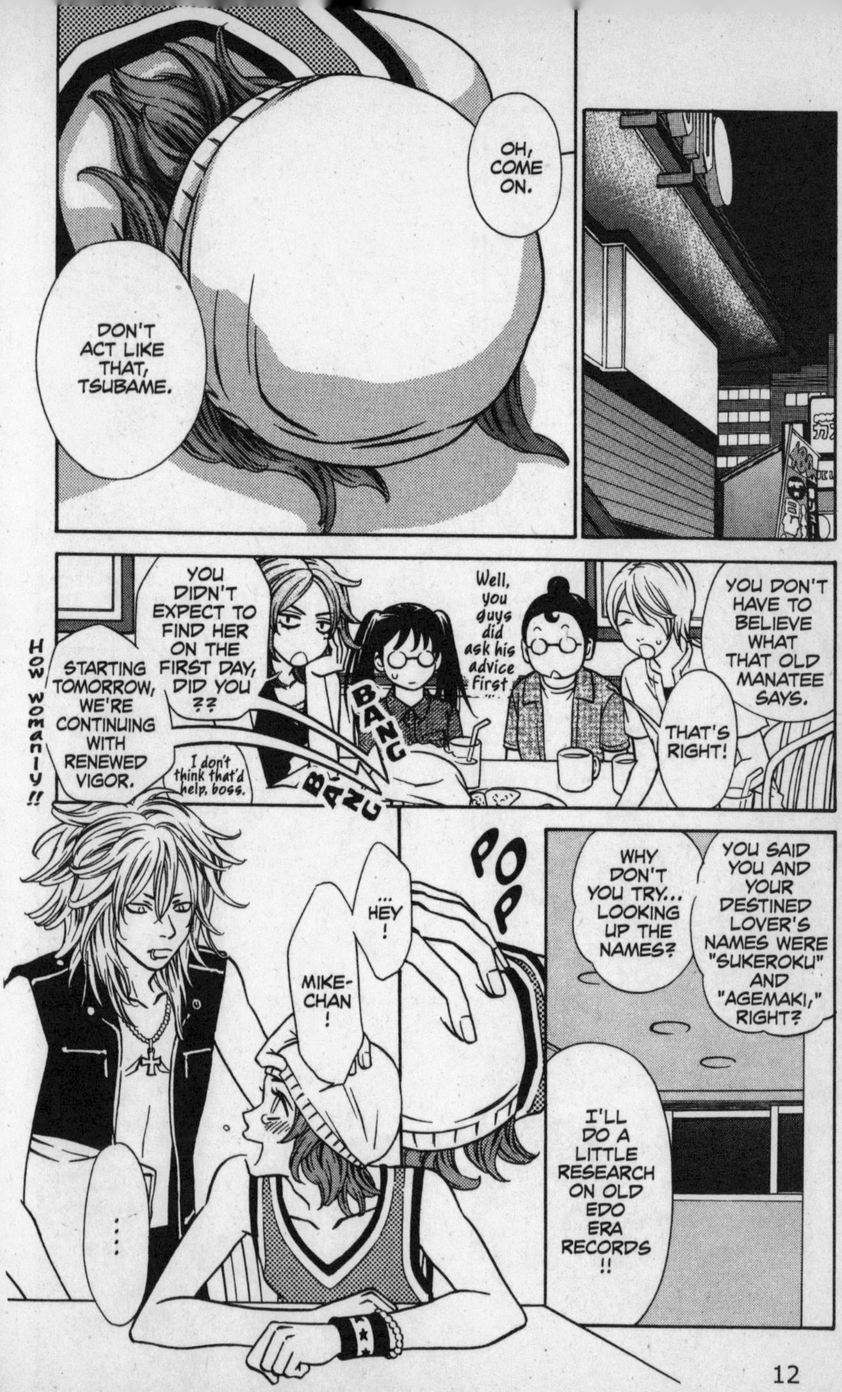
OH, COME ON.
DON'T ACT LIKE THAT, TSUBAME.
YOU DON'T HAVE TO BELIEVE WHAT THAT OLD MANATEE SAYS.
THAT'S RIGHT!
Well, you guys did ask his advice first...
BANG
BANG
YOU DIDN'T EXPECT TO FIND HER ON THE FIRST DAY, DID YOU??
STARTING TOMORROW, WE'RE CONTINUING WITH RENEWED VIGOR.
I don't think that'd help, boss.
How womanly!!
YOU SAID YOU AND YOUR DESTINED LOVER'S NAMES WERE "SUKEROKU" AND "AGEMAKI," RIGHT?
WHY DON'T YOU TRY... LOOKING UP THE NAMES?
I'LL DO A LITTLE RESEARCH ON OLD EDO ERA RECORDS!!
POP
...HEY!
MIKE-CHAN!
....

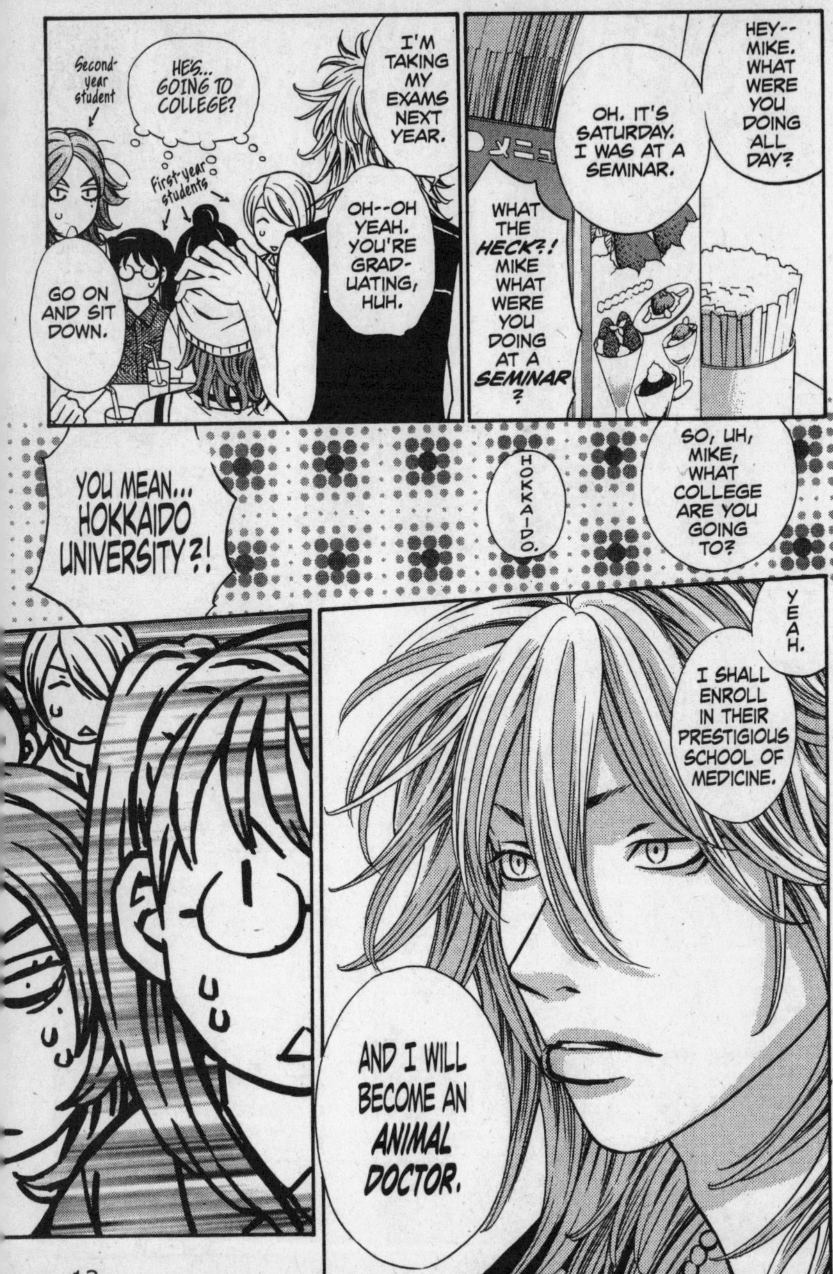
HEY-- MIKE. WHAT WERE YOU DOING ALL DAY?
OH. IT'S SATURDAY. I WAS AT A SEMINAR.
WHAT THE HECK?! MIKE WHAT WERE YOU DOING AT A SEMINAR?
I'M TAKING MY EXAMS NEXT YEAR.
OH--OH YEAH. YOU'RE GRADUATING, HUH.
HE'S... GOING TO COLLEGE?
Second-year student
First-year students
GO ON AND SIT DOWN.
SO, UH, MIKE, WHAT COLLEGE ARE YOU GOING TO?
HOKKAIDO.
YOU MEAN... HOKKAIDO UNIVERSITY?!
YEAH.
I SHALL ENROLL IN THEIR PRESTIGIOUS SCHOOL OF MEDICINE.
AND I WILL BECOME AN ANIMAL DOCTOR.

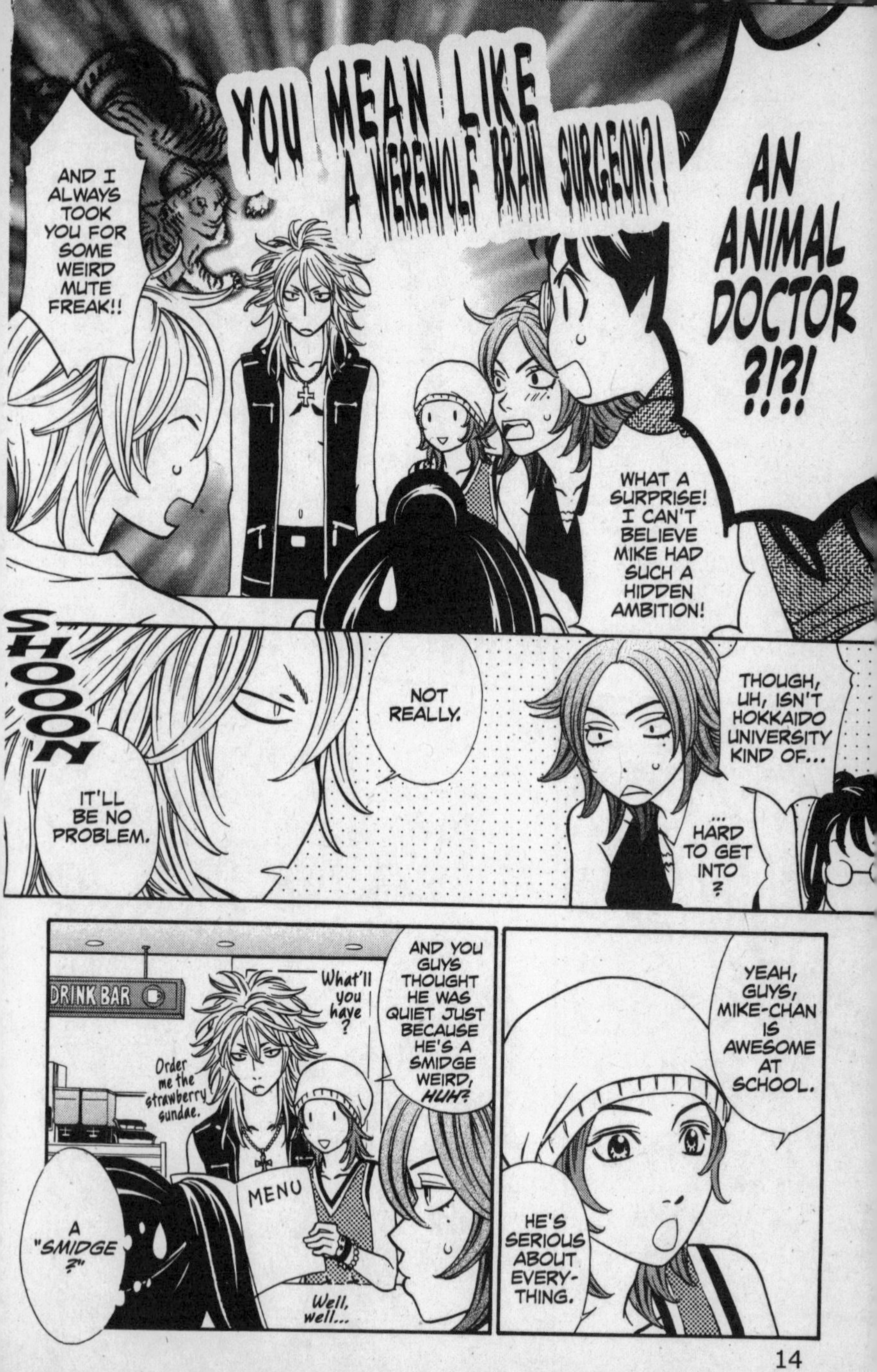
AN ANIMAL DOCTOR ?!?!
YOU MEAN LIKE A WEREWOLF BRAIN SURGEON?!
WHAT A SURPRISE! I CAN'T BELIEVE MIKE HAD SUCH A HIDDEN AMBITION!
AND I ALWAYS TOOK YOU FOR SOME WEIRD MUTE FREAK!!
THOUGH, UH, ISN'T HOKKAIDO UNIVERSITY KIND OF...
... HARD TO GET INTO?
NOT REALLY.
SHOOOON
IT'LL BE NO PROBLEM.
YEAH, GUYS, MIKE-CHAN IS AWESOME AT SCHOOL.
HE'S SERIOUS ABOUT EVERY-THING.
AND YOU GUYS THOUGHT HE WAS QUIET JUST BECAUSE HE'S A SMIDGE WEIRD, HUH?
What'll you have?
DRINK BAR
Order me the strawberry sundae.
MENU
A "SMIDGE?"
Well, well...

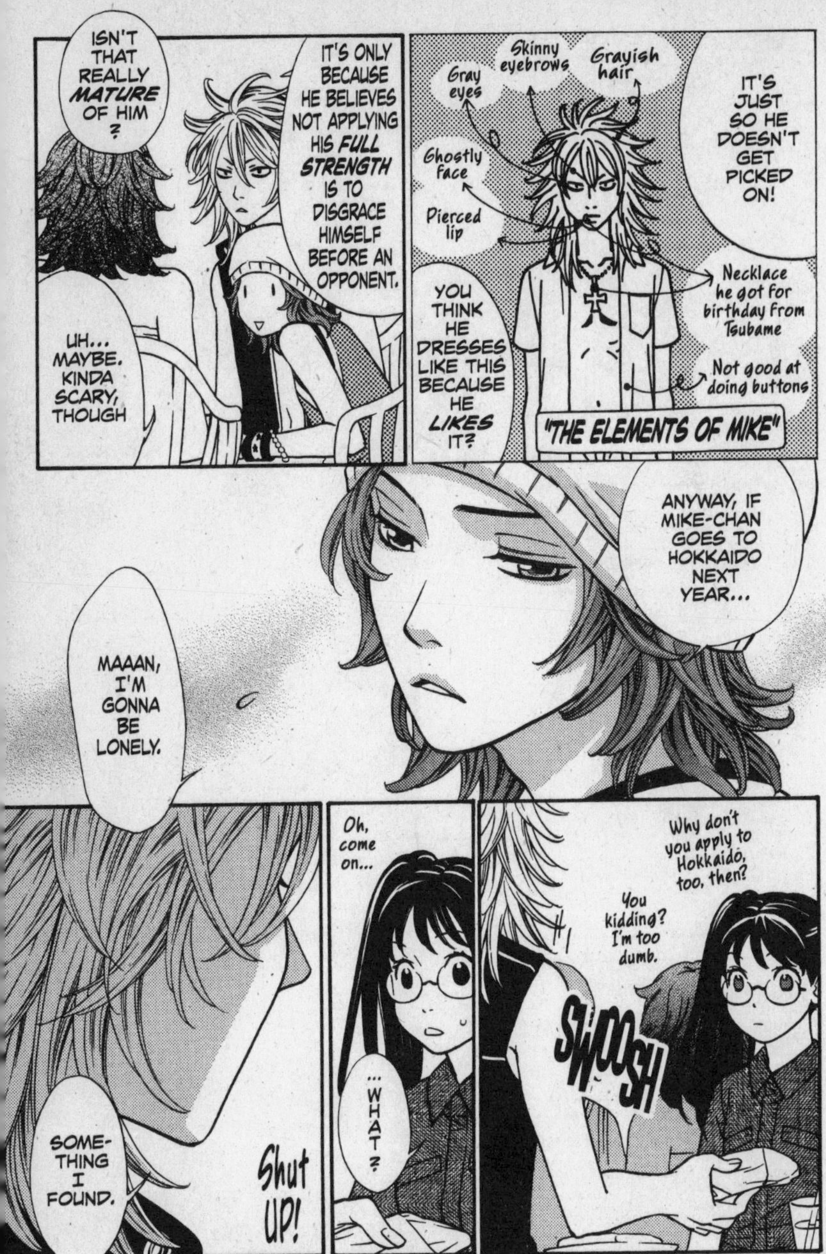

IT'S JUST SO HE DOESN'T GET PICKED ON!
Skinny eyebrows
Grayish hair
Gray eyes
Ghostly face
Pierced lip
Necklace he got for birthday from Tsubame
Not good at doing buttons
YOU THINK HE DRESSES LIKE THIS BECAUSE HE LIKES IT?
"THE ELEMENTS OF MIKE"
IT'S ONLY BECAUSE HE BELIEVES NOT APPLYING HIS FULL STRENGTH IS TO DISGRACE HIMSELF BEFORE AN OPPONENT.
ISN'T THAT REALLY MATURE OF HIM?
UH... MAYBE. KINDA SCARY, THOUGH
ANYWAY, IF MIKE-CHAN GOES TO HOKKAIDO NEXT YEAR...
MAAAN, I'M GONNA BE LONELY.
Why don't you apply to Hokkaido, too, then?
You kidding? I'm too dumb.
SWOOSH
Oh, come on...
...WHAT?
Shut UP!
SOME-THING I FOUND.

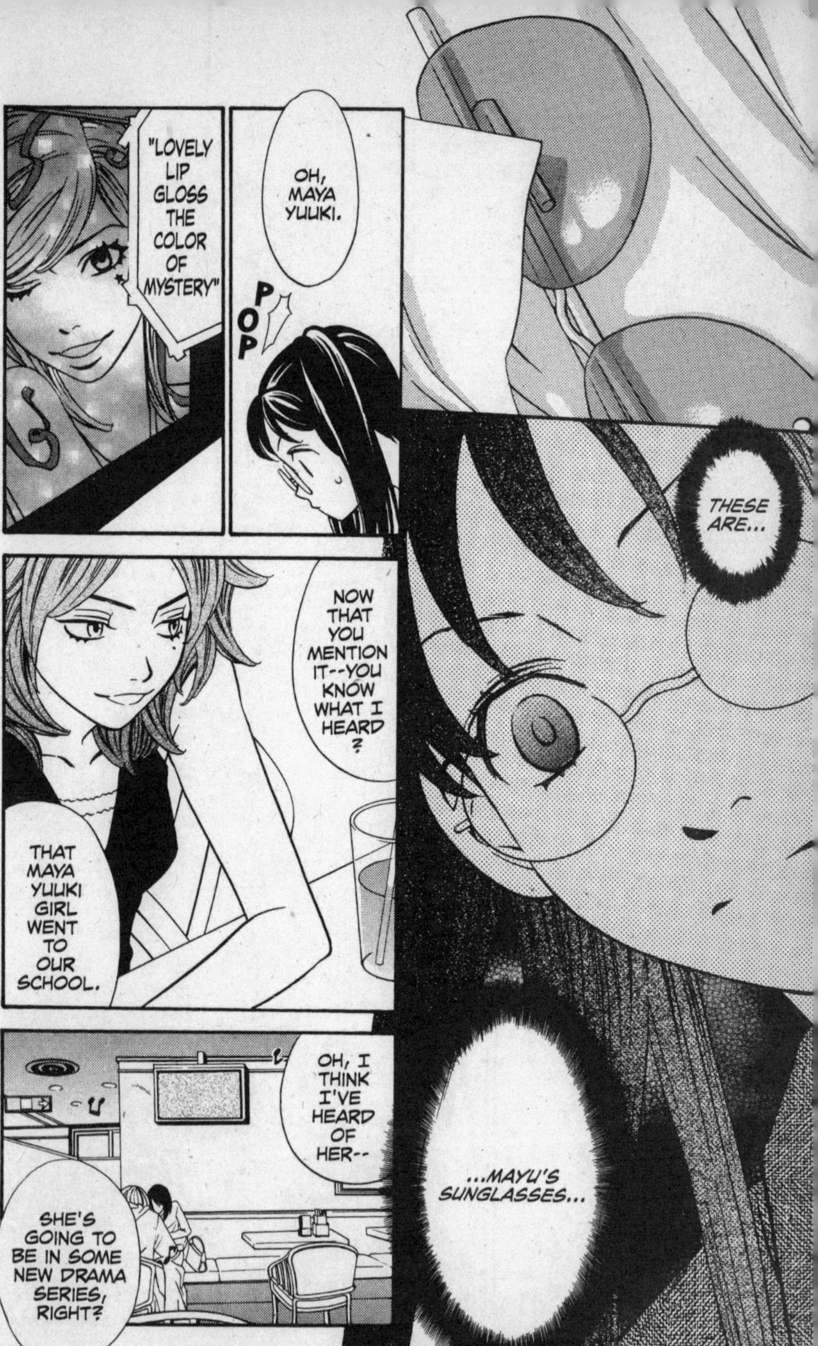
OH, MAYA YUUKI.
POP POP
"LOVELY LIP GLOSS THE COLOR OF MYSTERY"
THESE ARE...
...MAYU'S SUNGLASSES...
NOW THAT YOU MENTION IT--YOU KNOW WHAT I HEARD?
THAT MAYA YUUKI GIRL WENT TO OUR SCHOOL.
OH, I THINK I'VE HEARD OF HER--
SHE'S GOING TO BE IN SOME NEW DRAMA SERIES, RIGHT?

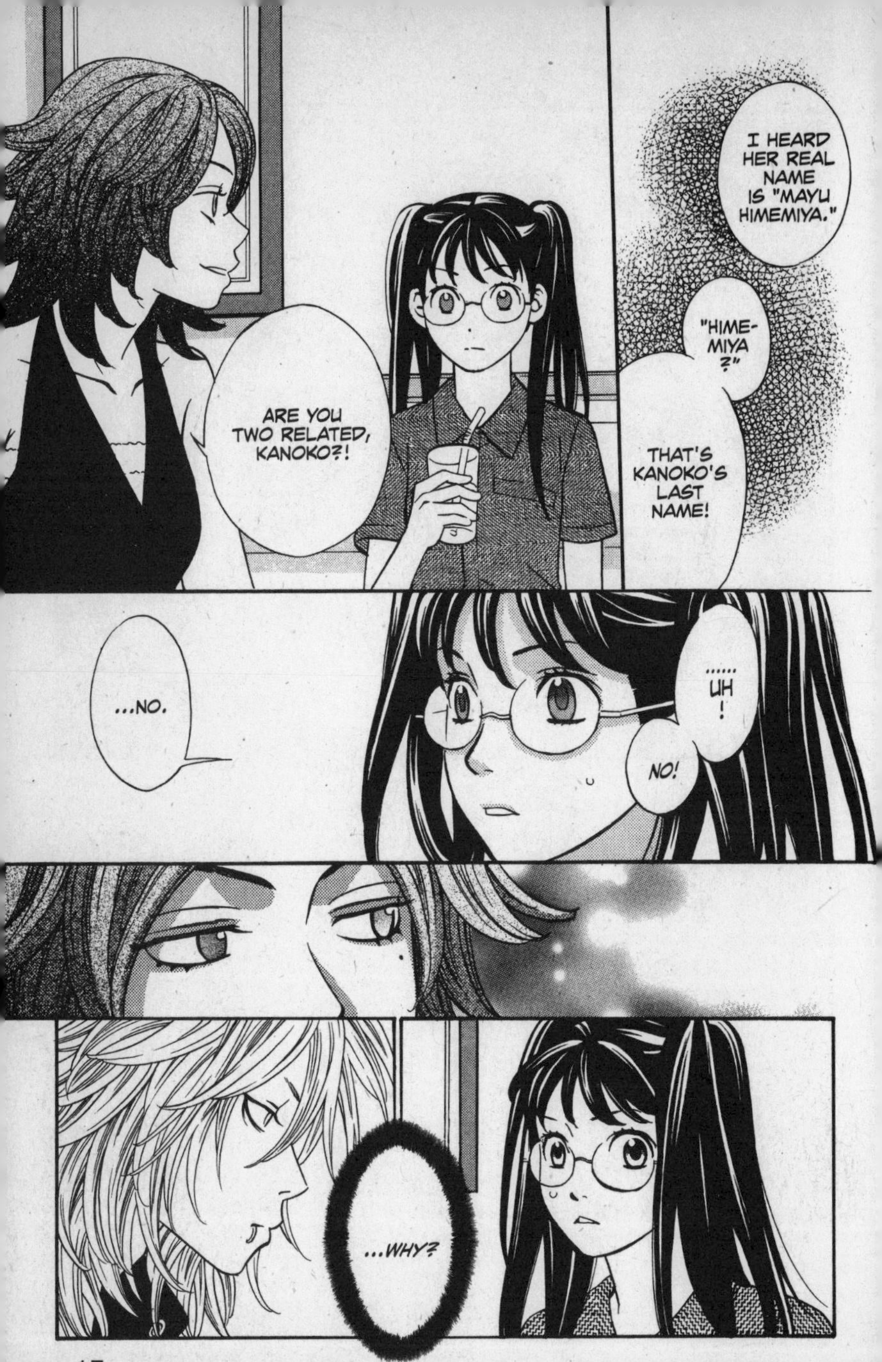
I HEARD HER REAL NAME IS "MAYU HIMEMIYA."
"HIME-MIYA?"
THAT'S KANOKO'S LAST NAME!
ARE YOU TWO RELATED, KANOKO?!
......UH! NO!
...NO.
...WHY?

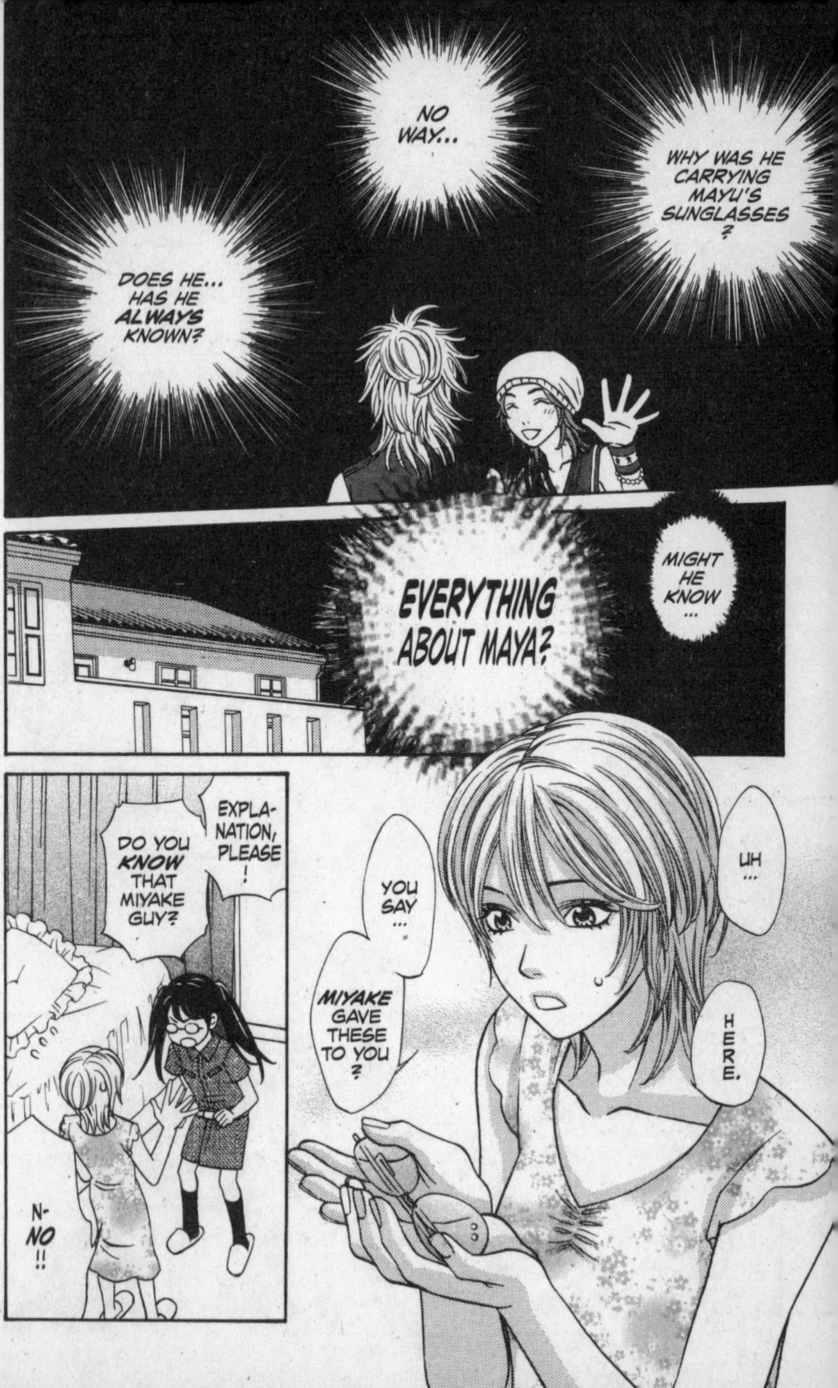
WHY WAS HE CARRYING MAYU'S SUNGLASSES?
NO WAY...
DOES HE... HAS HE ALWAYS KNOWN?
MIGHT HE KNOW ...
EVERYTHING ABOUT MAYA?
UH ...
HERE.
YOU SAY ...
MIYAKE GAVE THESE TO YOU?
EXPLANATION, PLEASE!
DO YOU KNOW THAT MIYAKE GUY?
N-NO!!

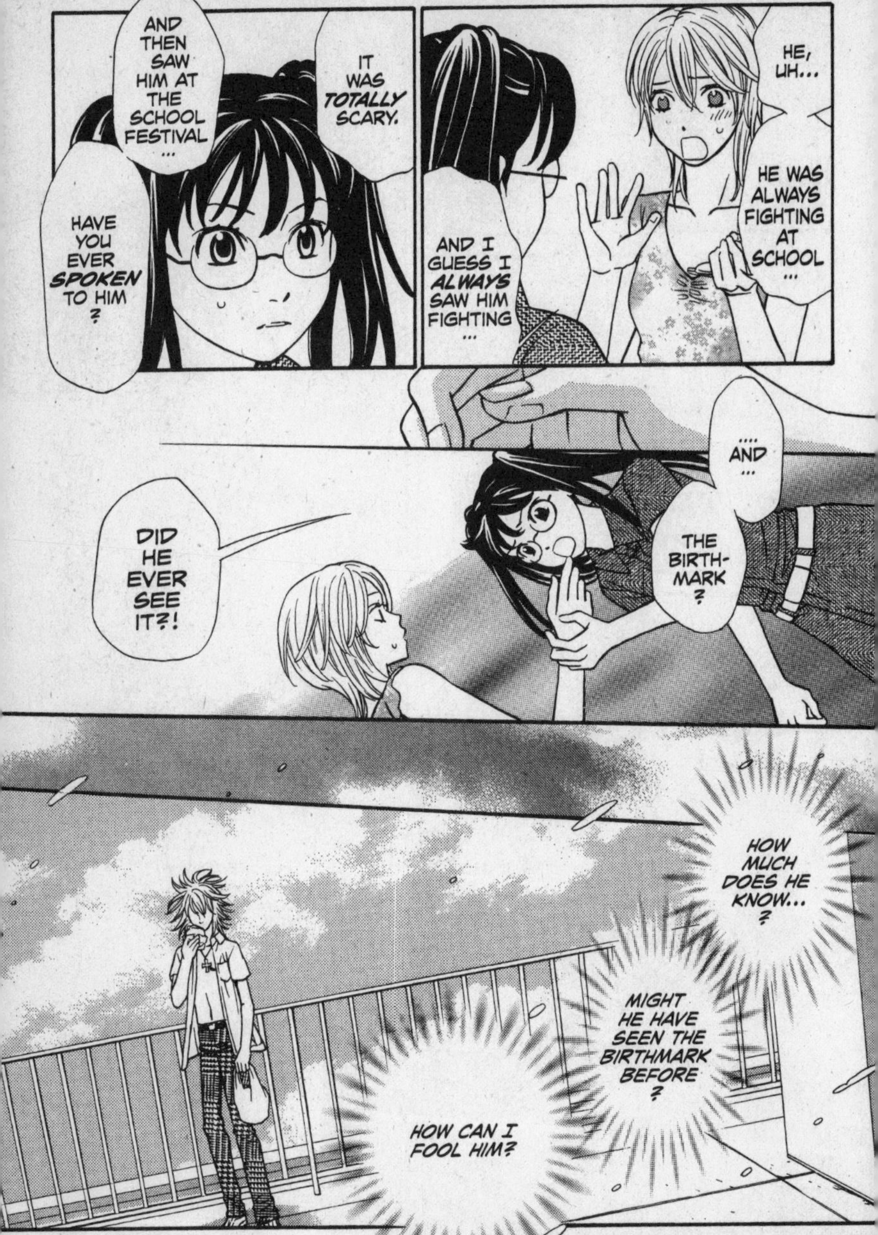
HE, UH...
HE WAS ALWAYS FIGHTING AT SCHOOL ...
AND I GUESS I ALWAYS SAW HIM FIGHTING ...
IT WAS TOTALLY SCARY.
AND THEN SAW HIM AT THE SCHOOL FESTIVAL ...
HAVE YOU EVER SPOKEN TO HIM?
.... AND ...
THE BIRTH-MARK?
DID HE EVER SEE IT?!
HOW MUCH DOES HE KNOW...?
MIGHT HE HAVE SEEN THE BIRTHMARK BEFORE?
HOW CAN I FOOL HIM?

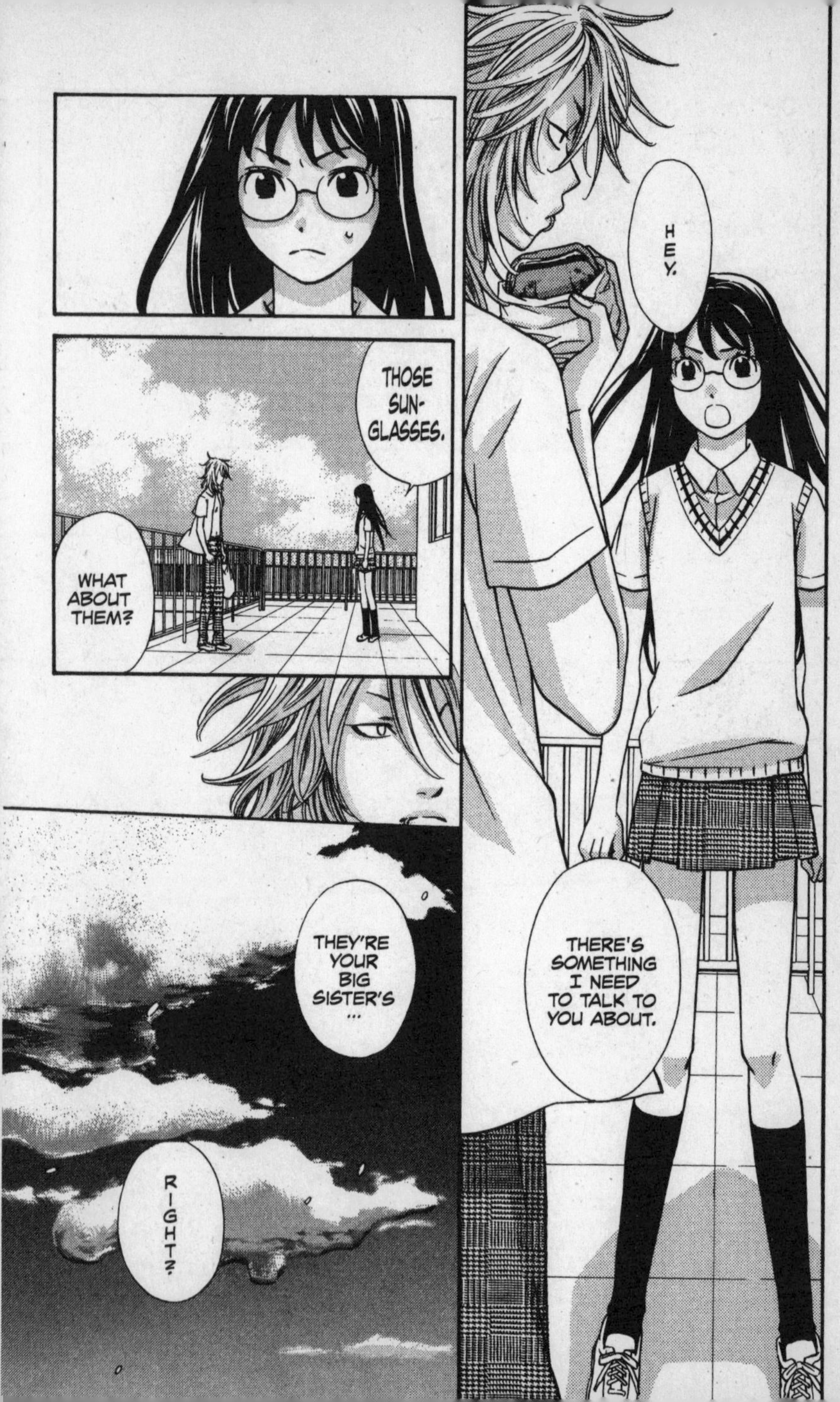
HEY.
THERE'S SOMETHING I NEED TO TALK TO YOU ABOUT.
THOSE SUN-GLASSES.
WHAT ABOUT THEM?
THEY'RE YOUR BIG SISTER'S ...
RIGHT?

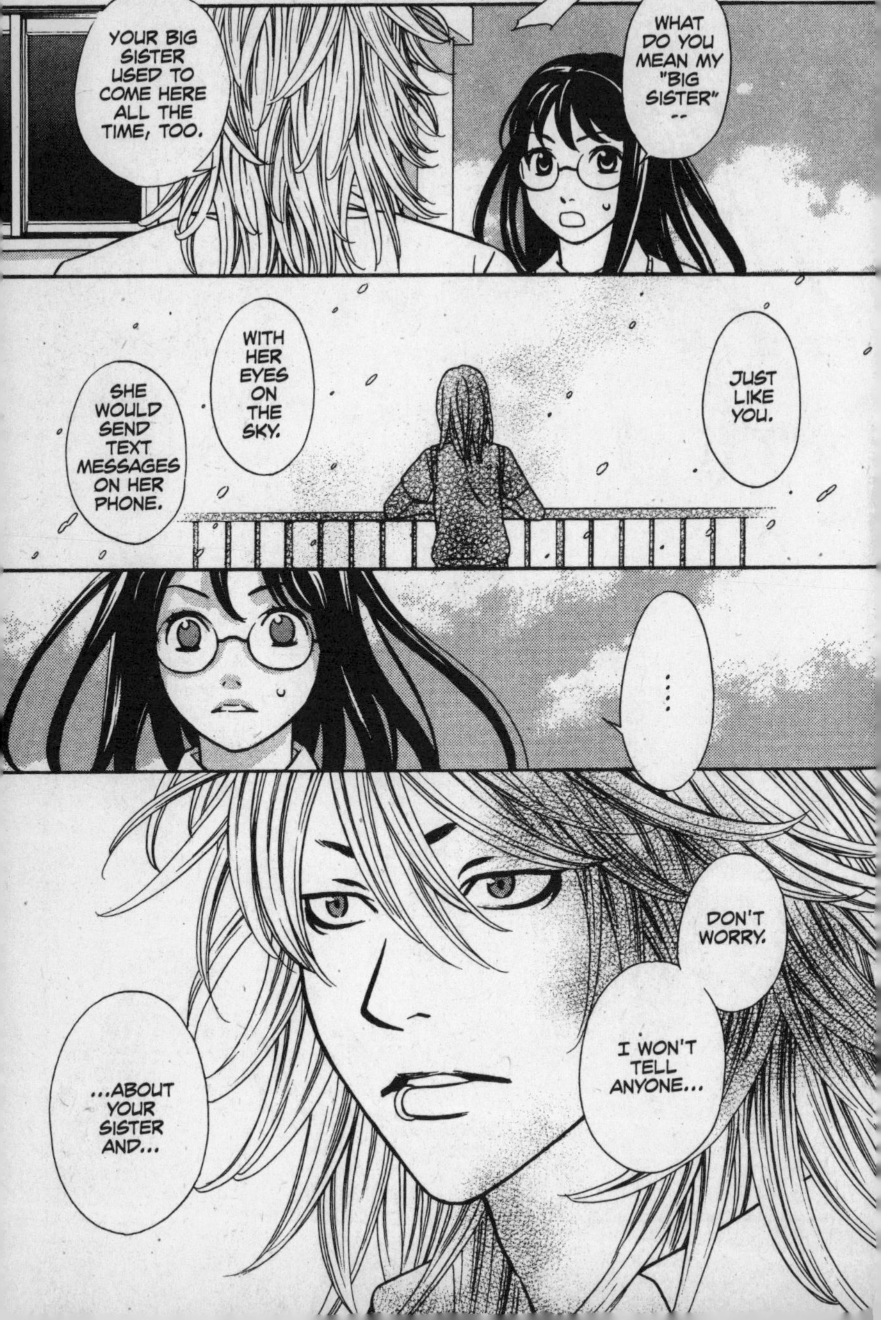
WHAT DO YOU MEAN MY "BIG SISTER" --
YOUR BIG SISTER USED TO COME HERE ALL THE TIME, TOO.
JUST LIKE YOU.
WITH HER EYES ON THE SKY.
SHE WOULD SEND TEXT MESSAGES ON HER PHONE.
....
DON'T WORRY.
I WON'T TELL ANYONE...
...ABOUT YOUR SISTER AND...

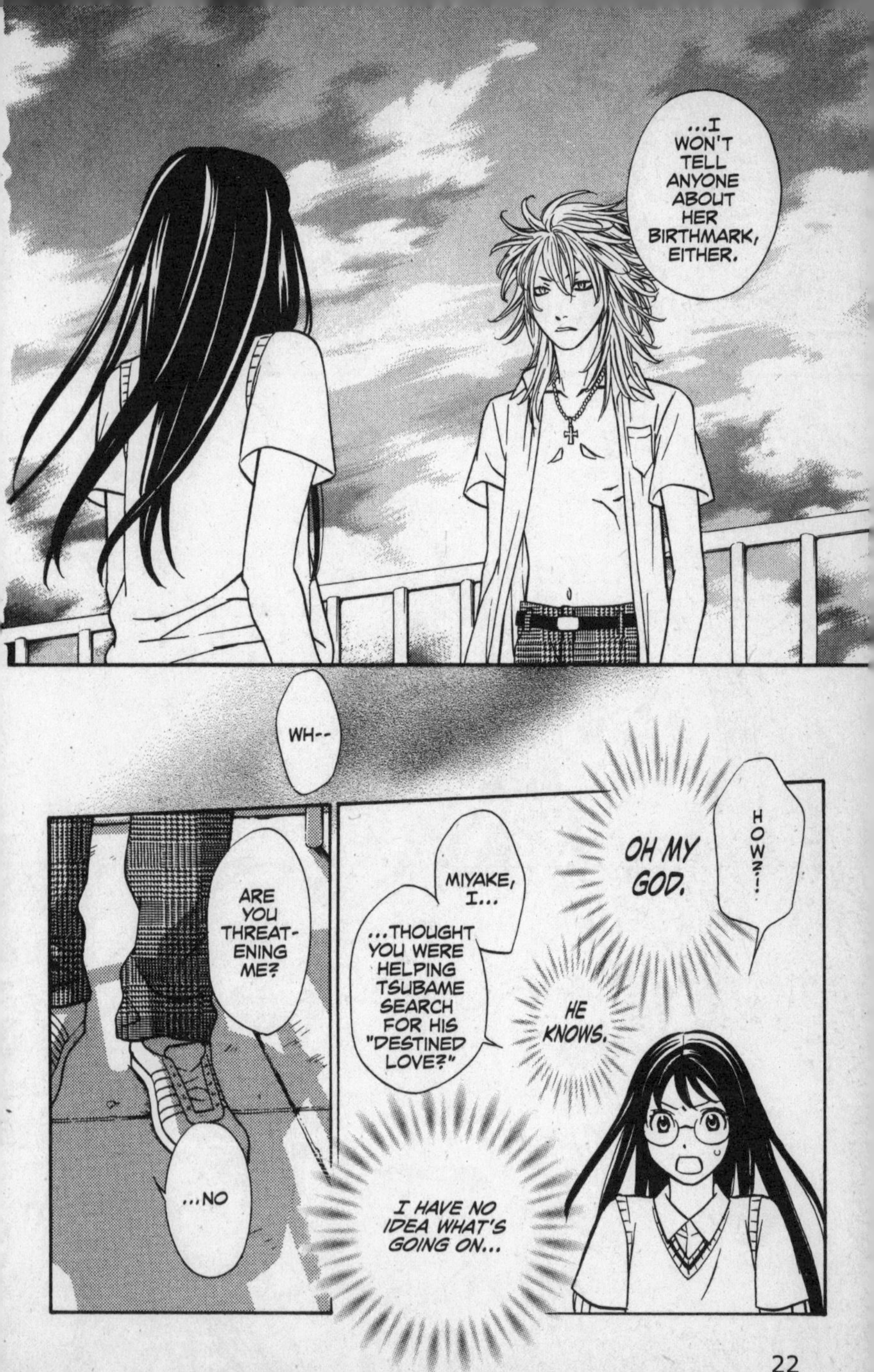
...I WON'T TELL ANYONE ABOUT HER BIRTHMARK, EITHER.
WH--
HOW?!
OH MY GOD.
MIYAKE, I...
...THOUGHT YOU WERE HELPING TSUBAME SEARCH FOR HIS "DESTINED LOVE?"
HE KNOWS.
I HAVE NO IDEA WHAT'S GOING ON...
ARE YOU THREAT-ENING ME?
...NO

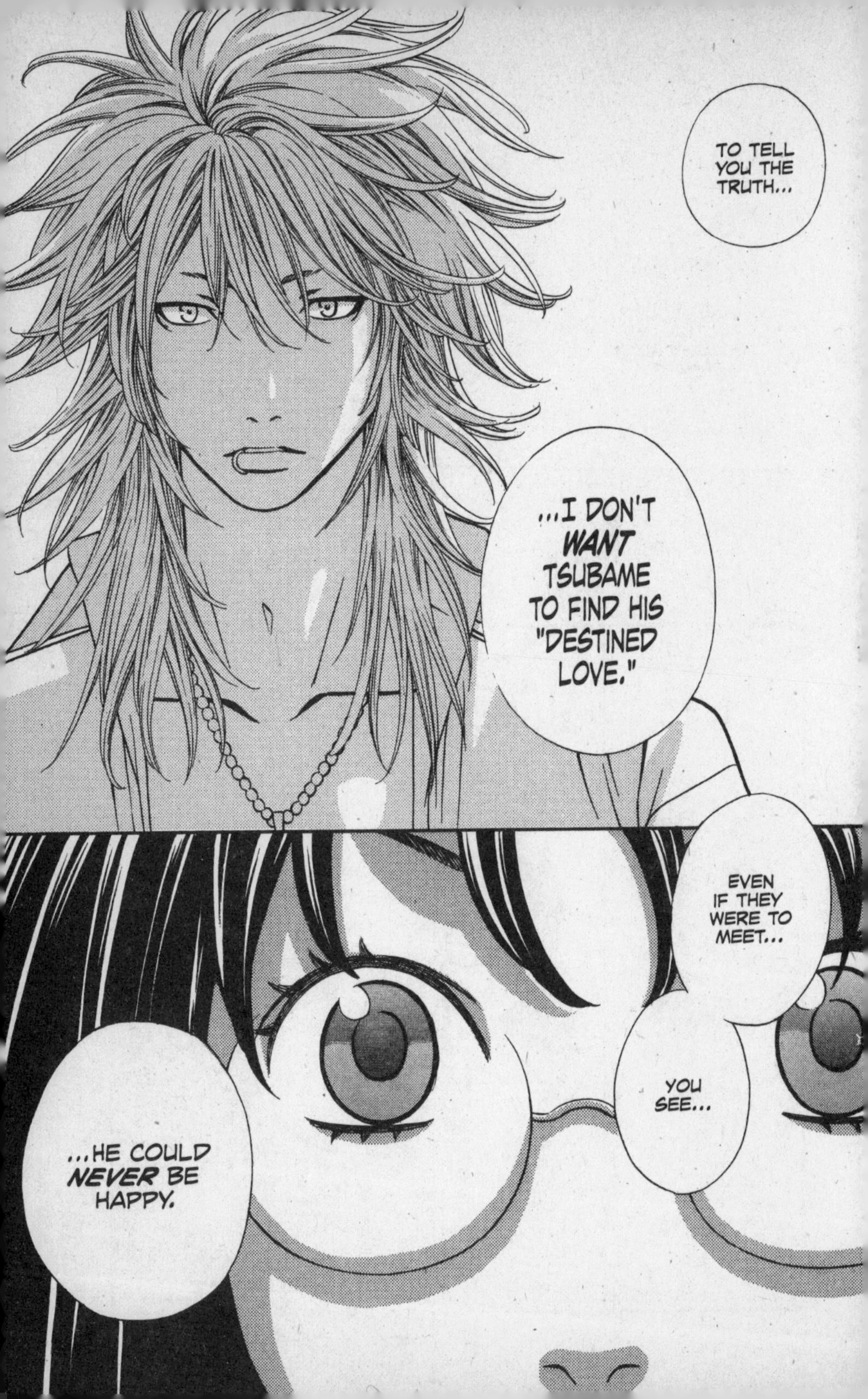
TO TELL YOU THE TRUTH...
...I DON'T *WANT* TSUBAME TO FIND HIS "DESTINED LOVE."
EVEN IF THEY WERE TO MEET...
YOU SEE...
...HE COULD *NEVER* BE HAPPY.

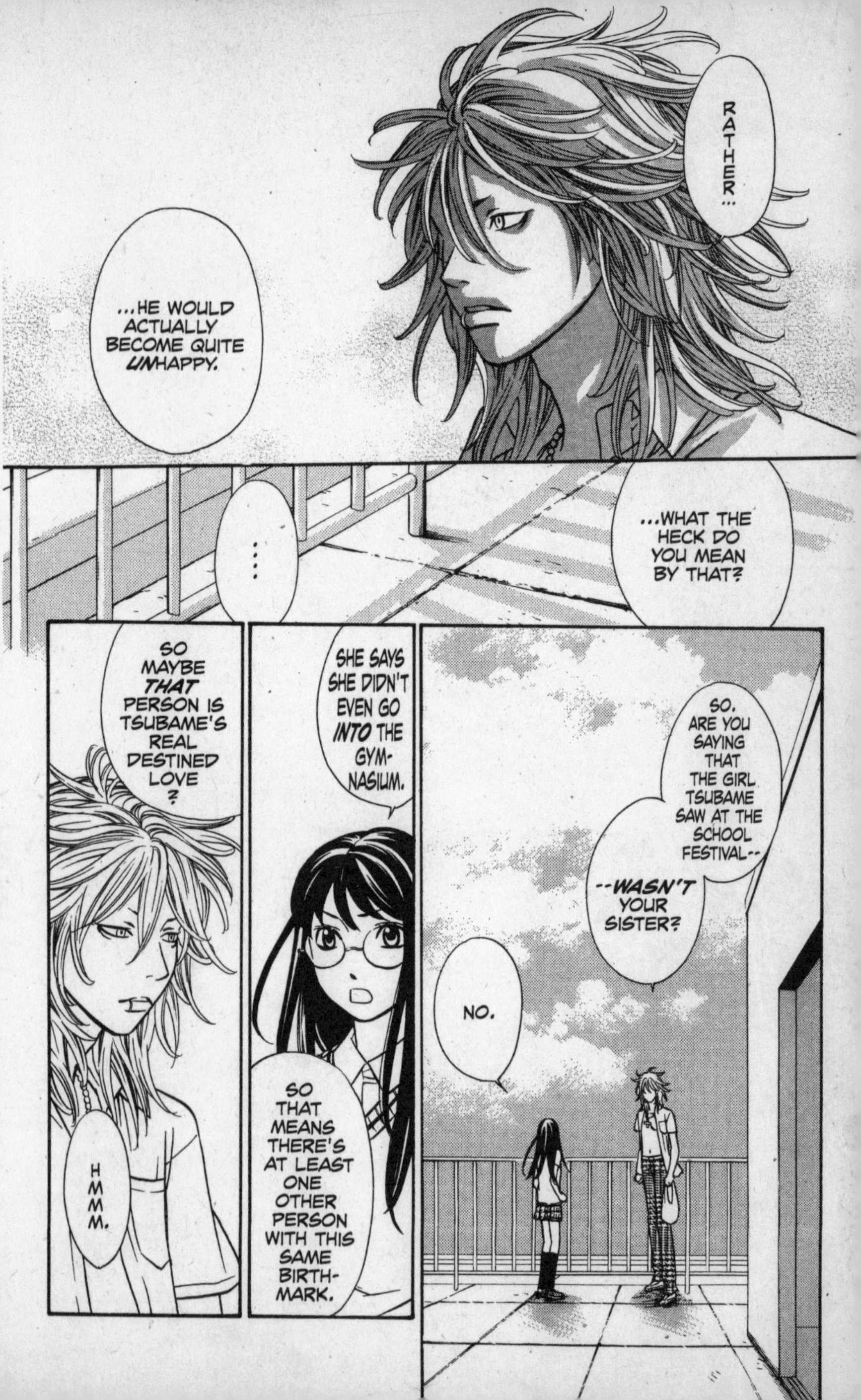
RATHER...
...HE WOULD ACTUALLY BECOME QUITE *UN*HAPPY.
...WHAT THE HECK DO YOU MEAN BY THAT?
....
SO. ARE YOU SAYING THAT THE GIRL TSUBAME SAW AT THE SCHOOL FESTIVAL--
--*WASN'T* YOUR SISTER?
NO.
SHE SAYS SHE DIDN'T EVEN GO *INTO* THE GYM-NASIUM.
SO THAT MEANS THERE'S AT LEAST ONE OTHER PERSON WITH THIS SAME BIRTH-MARK.
SO MAYBE *THAT* PERSON IS TSUBAME'S REAL DESTINED LOVE?
HMMM.

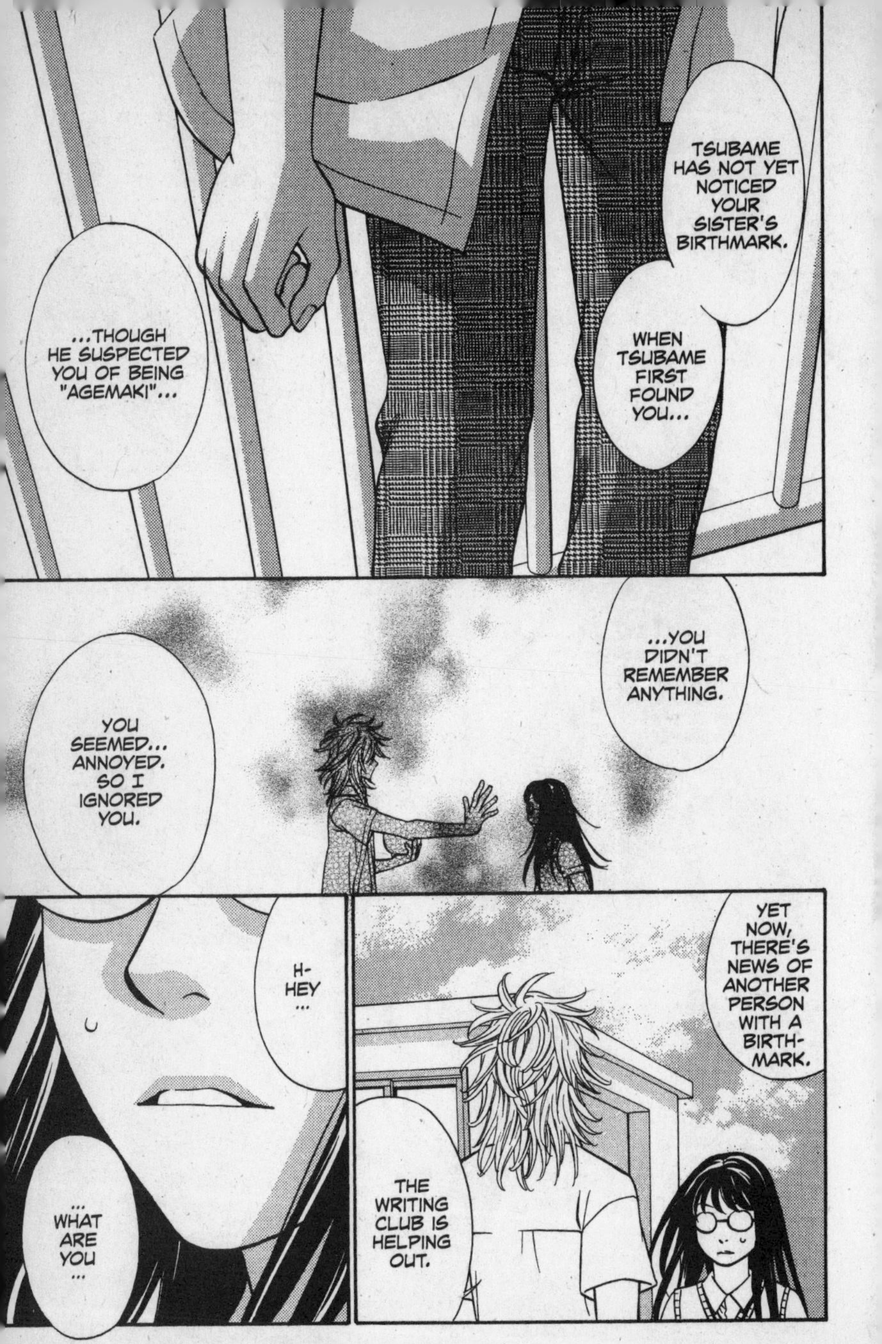
TSUBAME HAS NOT YET NOTICED YOUR SISTER'S BIRTHMARK.
WHEN TSUBAME FIRST FOUND YOU...
...THOUGH HE SUSPECTED YOU OF BEING "AGEMAKI"...
...YOU DIDN'T REMEMBER ANYTHING.
YOU SEEMED... ANNOYED. SO I IGNORED YOU.
YET NOW, THERE'S NEWS OF ANOTHER PERSON WITH A BIRTH-MARK.
THE WRITING CLUB IS HELPING OUT.
H-HEY...
...WHAT ARE YOU...

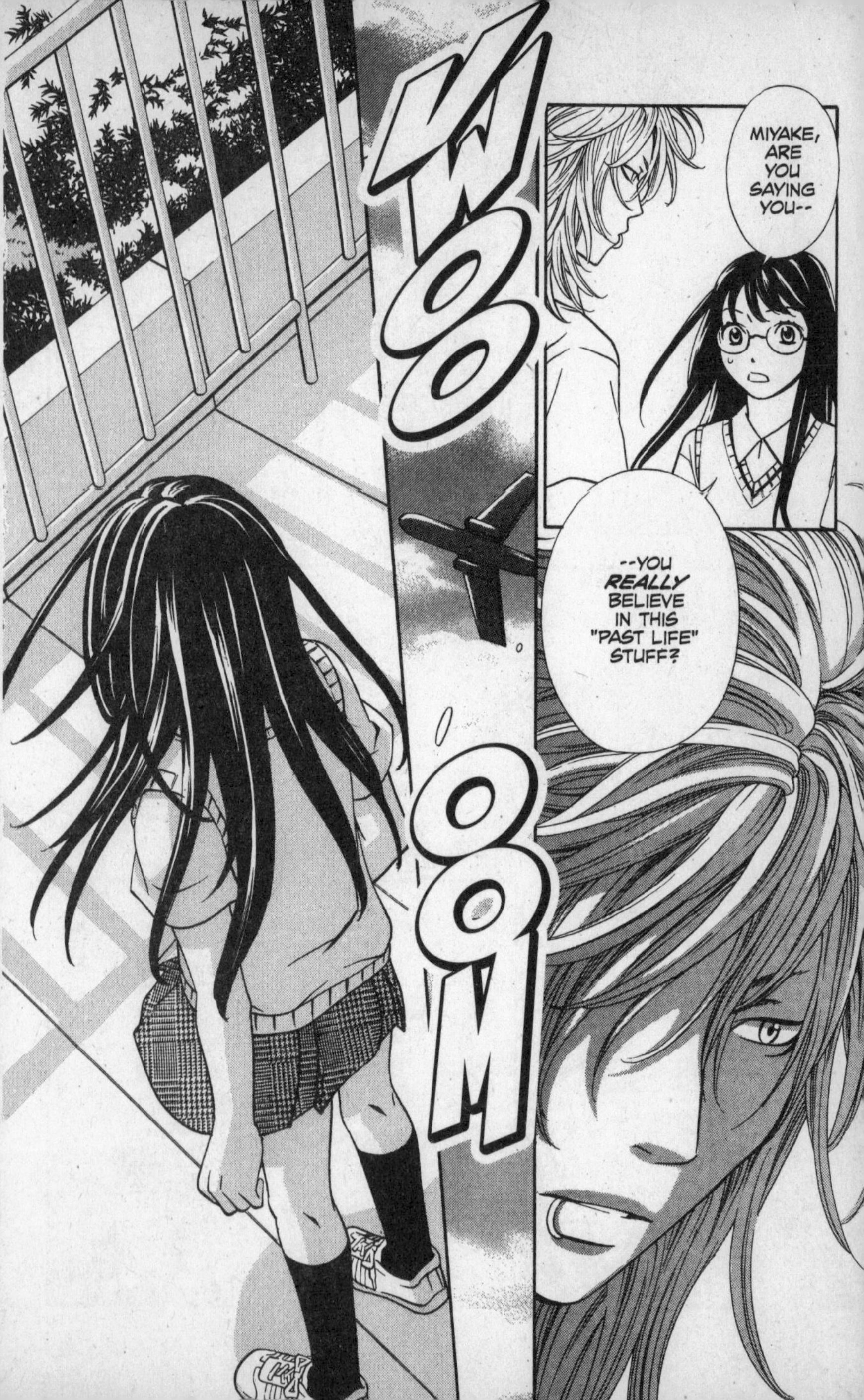
MIYAKE, ARE YOU SAYING YOU--
--YOU *REALLY* BELIEVE IN THIS "PAST LIFE" STUFF?
WOOOOOM

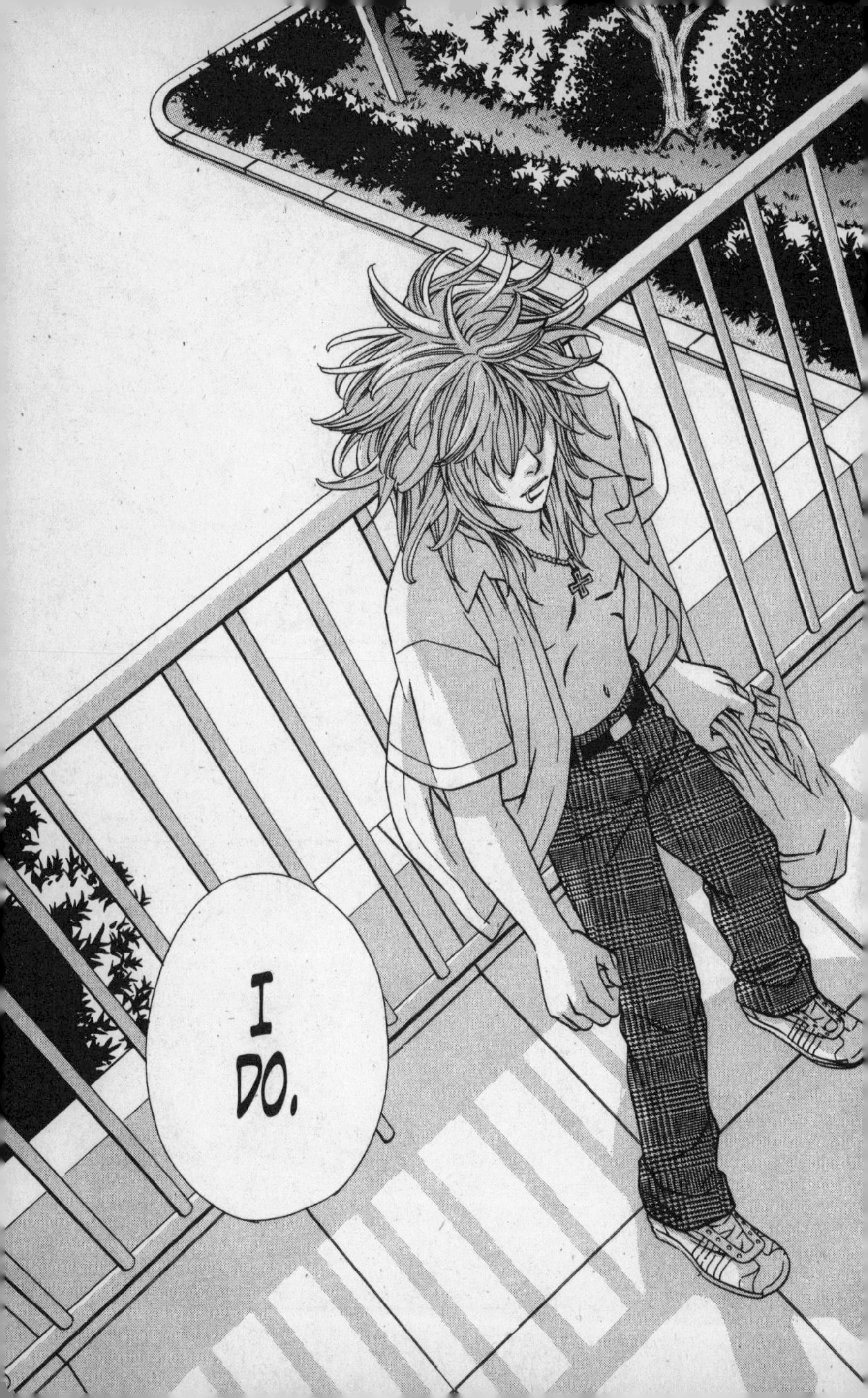
I DO.

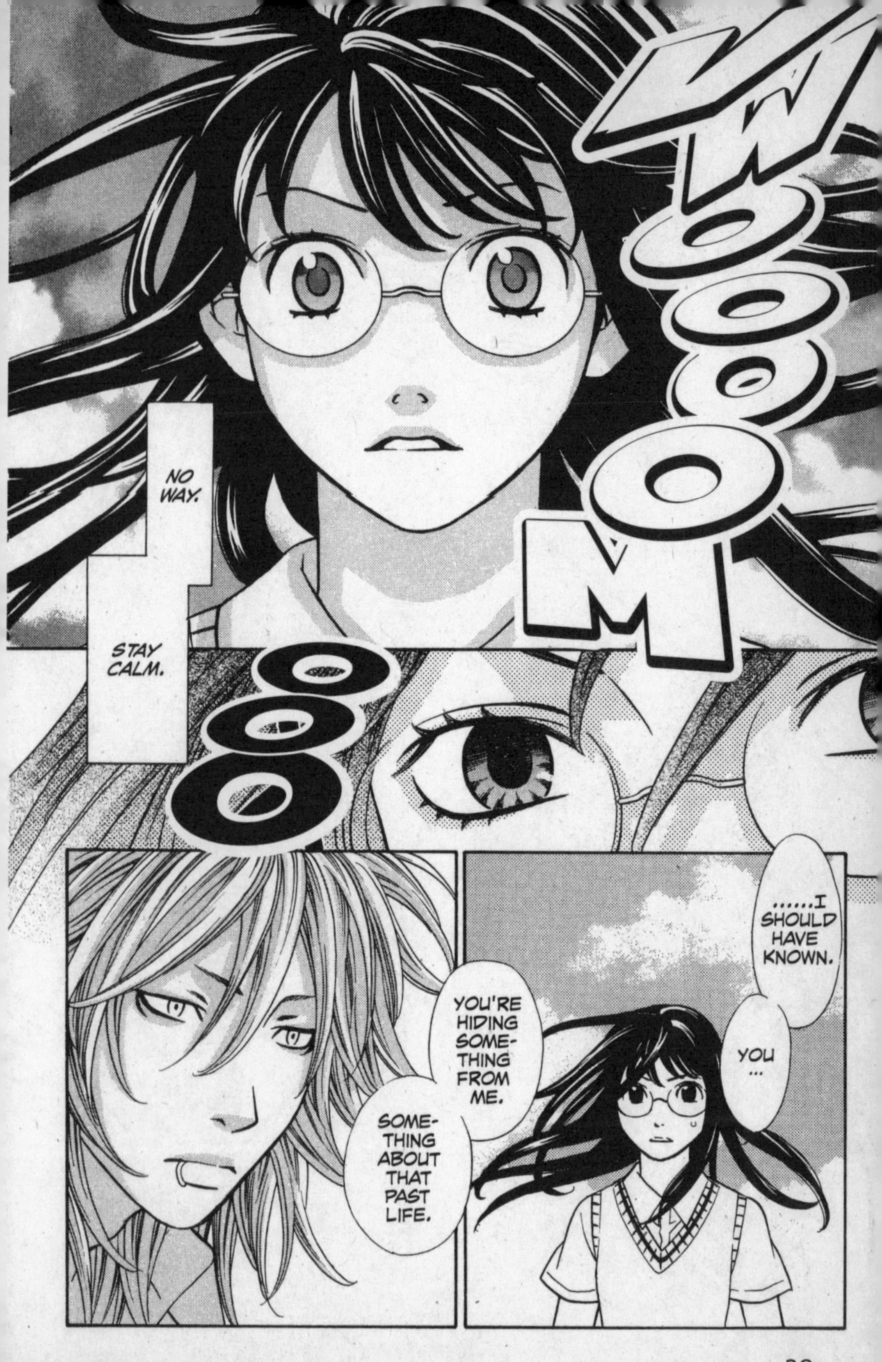
WOOOOOM
NO WAY.
STAY CALM.
OOO
......I SHOULD HAVE KNOWN.
YOU ...
YOU'RE HIDING SOMETHING FROM ME.
SOMETHING ABOUT THAT PAST LIFE.

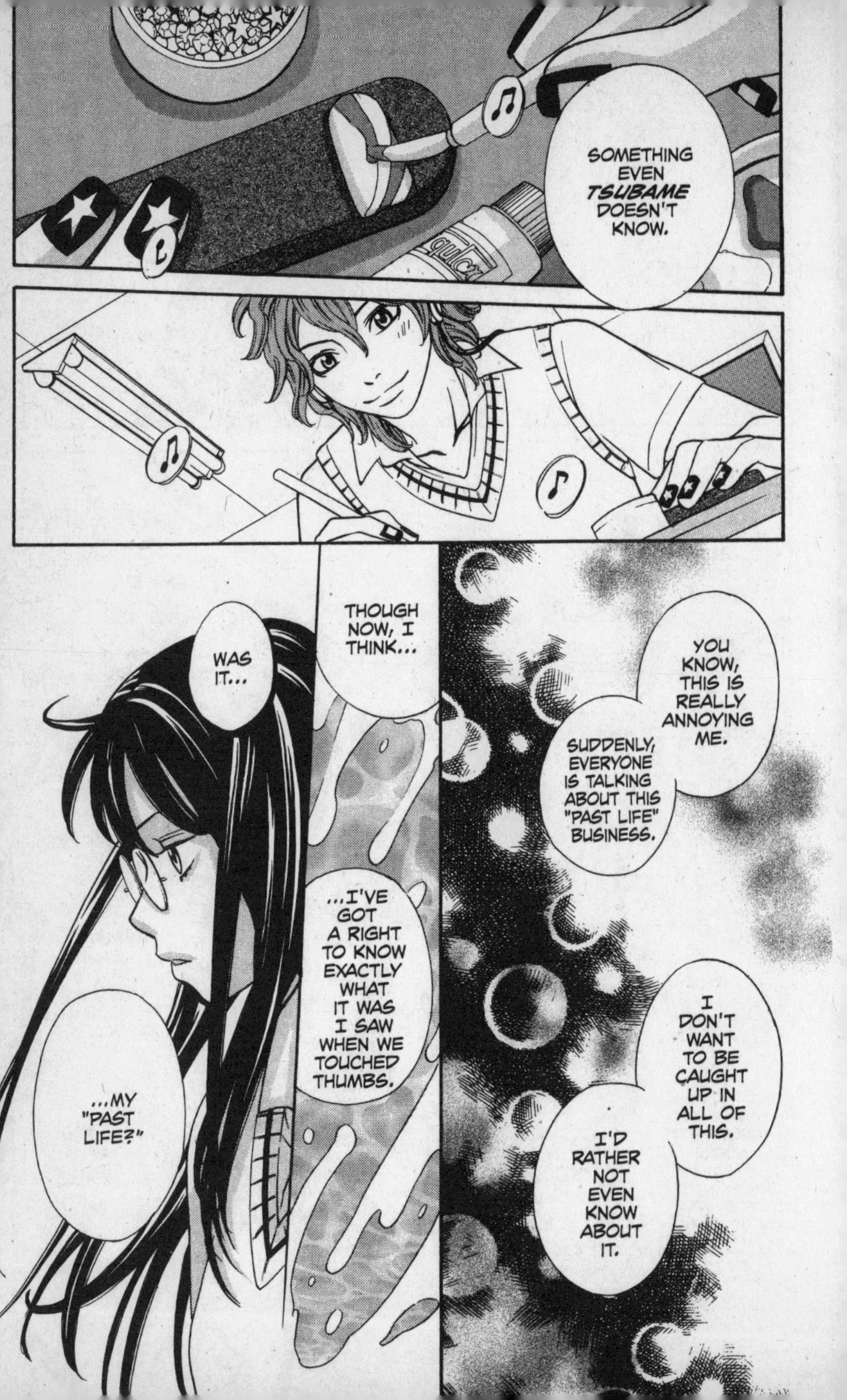
SOMETHING EVEN TSUBAME DOESN'T KNOW.
YOU KNOW, THIS IS REALLY ANNOYING ME.
SUDDENLY, EVERYONE IS TALKING ABOUT THIS "PAST LIFE" BUSINESS.
I DON'T WANT TO BE CAUGHT UP IN ALL OF THIS.
I'D RATHER NOT EVEN KNOW ABOUT IT.
THOUGH NOW, I THINK...
...I'VE GOT A RIGHT TO KNOW EXACTLY WHAT IT WAS I SAW WHEN WE TOUCHED THUMBS.
WAS IT...
...MY "PAST LIFE?"

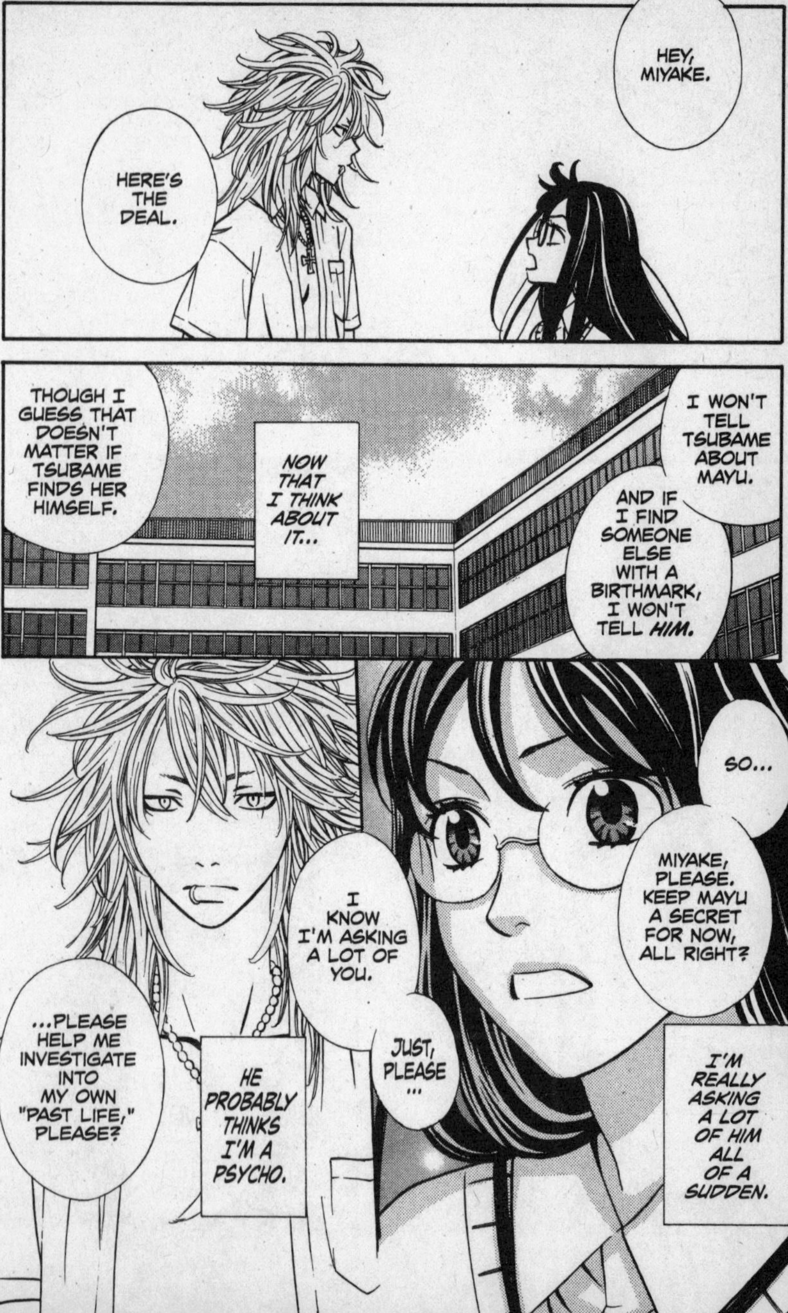
HEY, MIYAKE.
HERE'S THE DEAL.
I WON'T TELL TSUBAME ABOUT MAYU.
AND IF I FIND SOMEONE ELSE WITH A BIRTHMARK, I WON'T TELL *HIM*.
NOW THAT I THINK ABOUT IT...
THOUGH I GUESS THAT DOESN'T MATTER IF TSUBAME FINDS HER HIMSELF.
SO...
MIYAKE, PLEASE. KEEP MAYU A SECRET FOR NOW, ALL RIGHT?
I KNOW I'M ASKING A LOT OF YOU.
I'M REALLY ASKING A LOT OF HIM ALL OF A SUDDEN.
JUST, PLEASE ...
HE PROBABLY THINKS I'M A PSYCHO.
...PLEASE HELP ME INVESTIGATE INTO MY OWN "PAST LIFE," PLEASE?

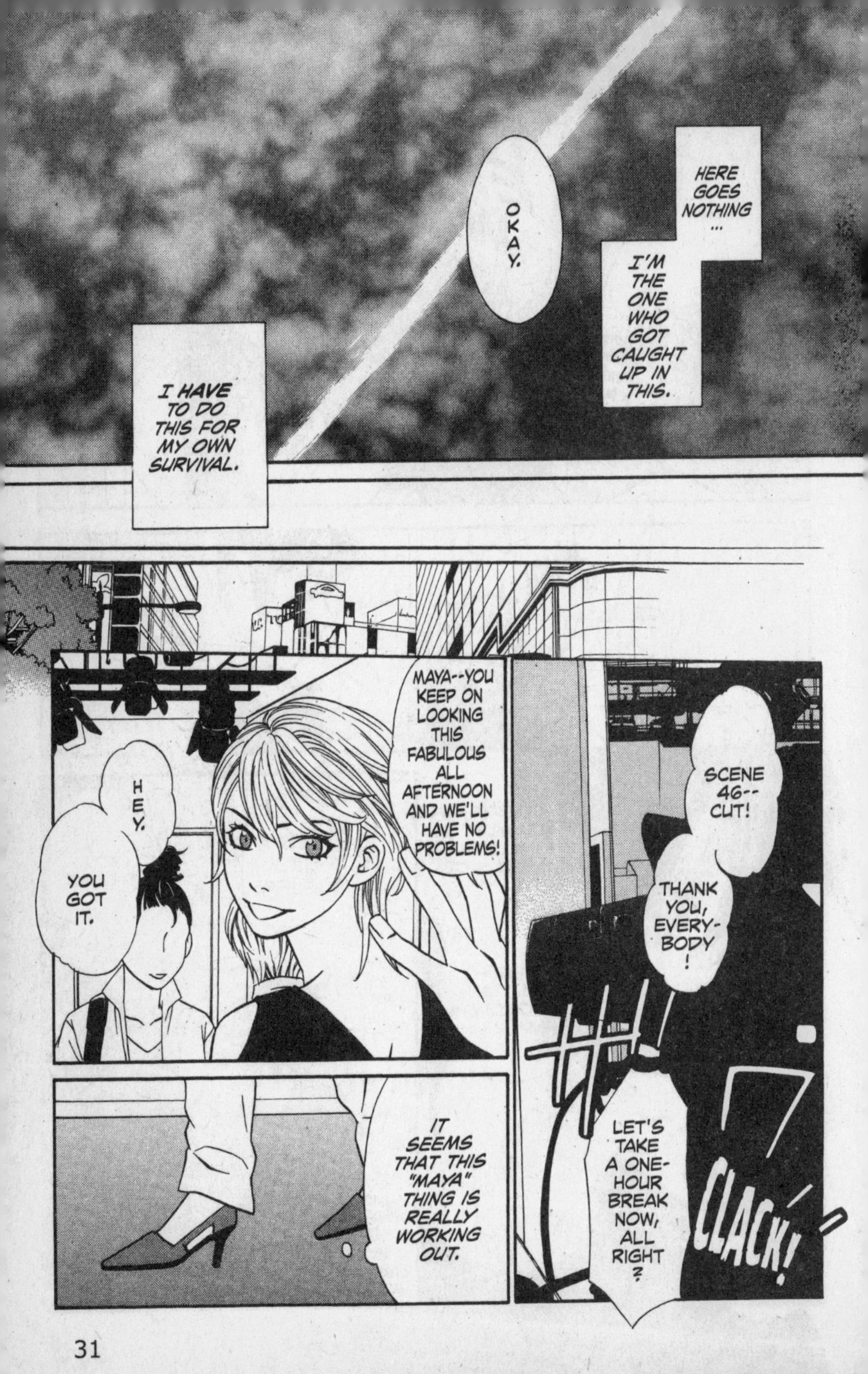
HERE GOES NOTHING...
I'M THE ONE WHO GOT CAUGHT UP IN THIS.
OKAY.
I HAVE TO DO THIS FOR MY OWN SURVIVAL.
SCENE 46--CUT!
THANK YOU, EVERYBODY!
CLACK!
LET'S TAKE A ONE-HOUR BREAK NOW, ALL RIGHT?
MAYA--YOU KEEP ON LOOKING THIS FABULOUS ALL AFTERNOON AND WE'LL HAVE NO PROBLEMS!
HEY.
YOU GOT IT.
IT SEEMS THAT THIS "MAYA" THING IS REALLY WORKING OUT.

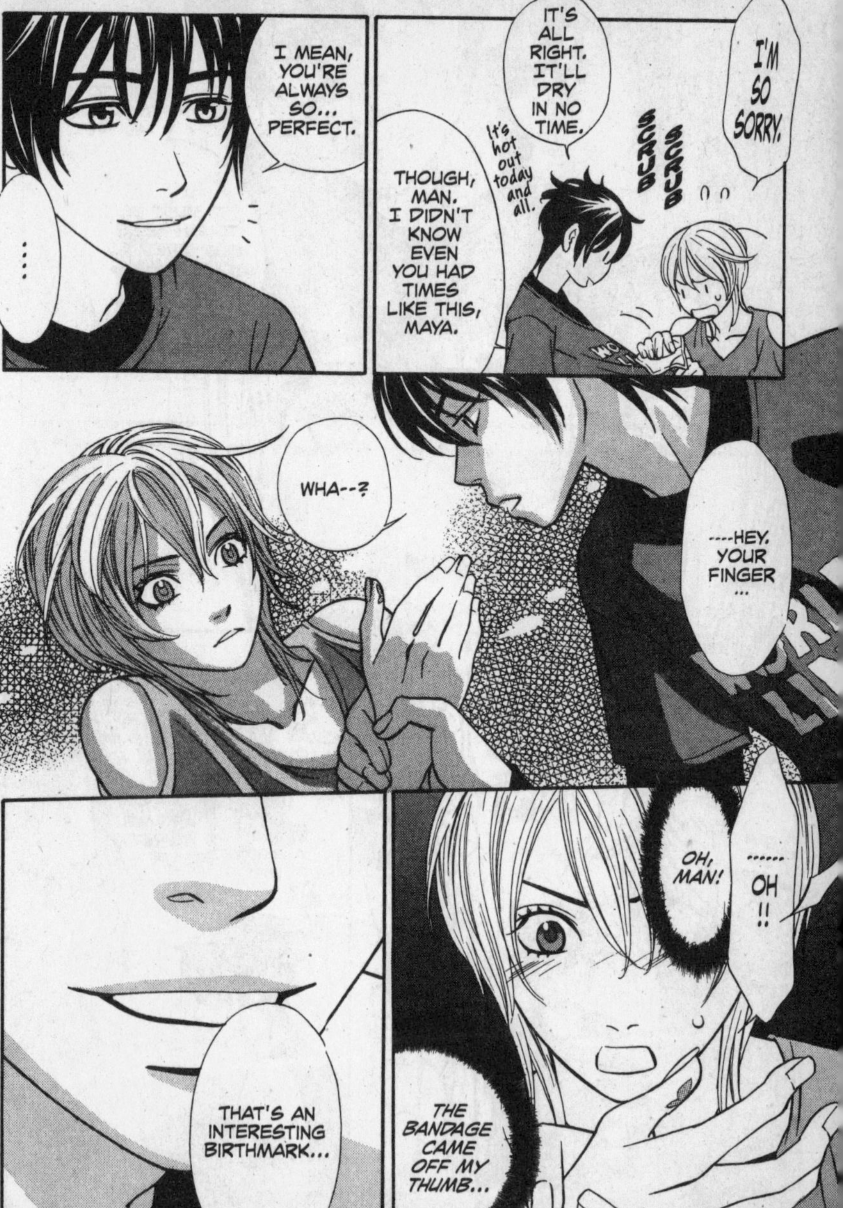
I'M SO SORRY.
SCRUB SCRUB
IT'S ALL RIGHT. IT'LL DRY IN NO TIME.
It's hot out today and all.
THOUGH, MAN. I DIDN'T KNOW EVEN YOU HAD TIMES LIKE THIS, MAYA.
I MEAN, YOU'RE ALWAYS SO... PERFECT.
.....
----HEY. YOUR FINGER...
WHA--?
......OH !!
OH, MAN!
THE BANDAGE CAME OFF MY THUMB...
THAT'S AN INTERESTING BIRTHMARK...

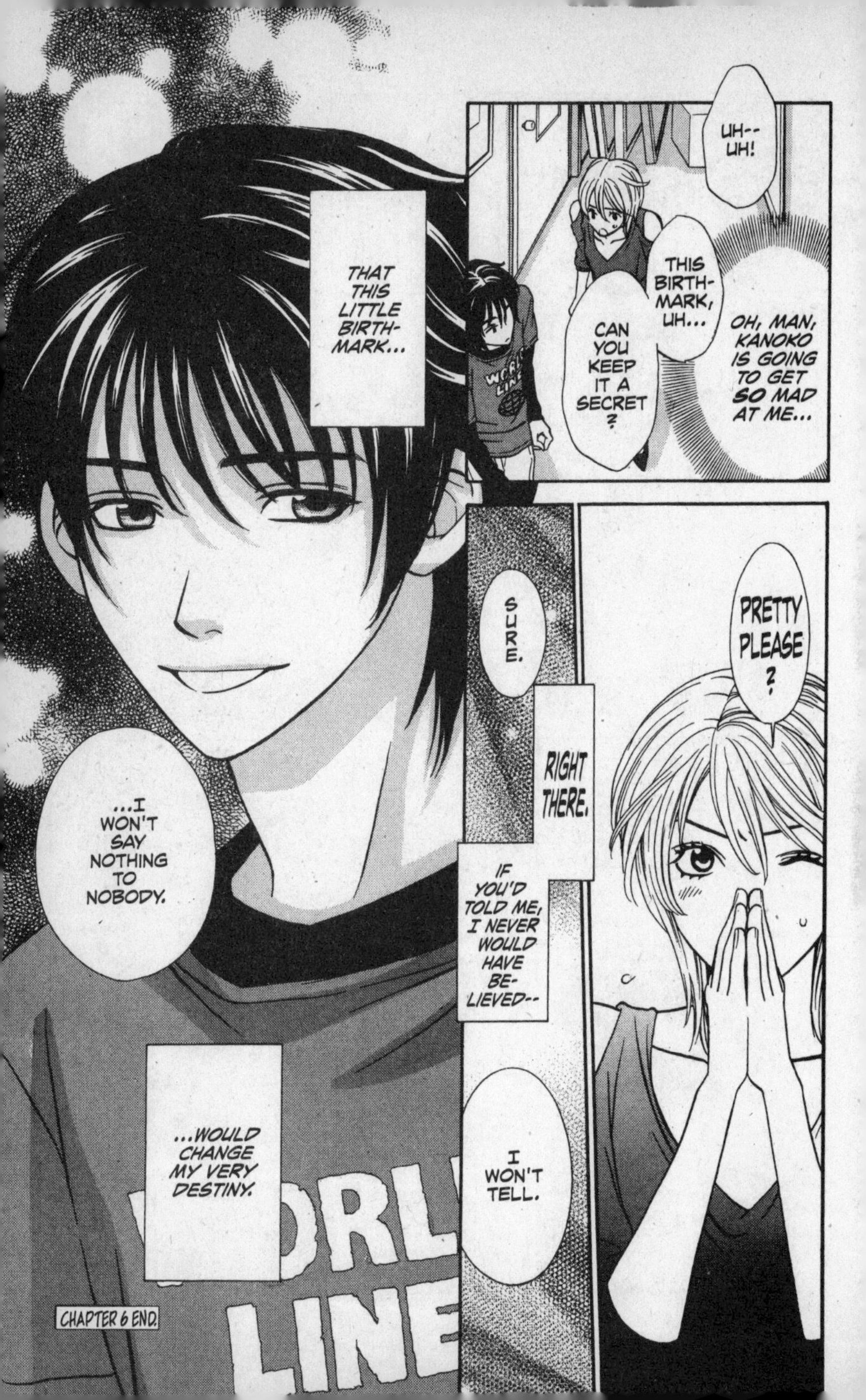

UH-- UH!
OH, MAN, KANOKO IS GOING TO GET SO MAD AT ME...
THIS BIRTH-MARK, UH...
CAN YOU KEEP IT A SECRET?
PRETTY PLEASE?
SURE.
RIGHT THERE.
I WON'T TELL.
IF YOU'D TOLD ME, I NEVER WOULD HAVE BE-LIEVED--
THAT THIS LITTLE BIRTH-MARK...
...I WON'T SAY NOTHING TO NOBODY.
...WOULD CHANGE MY VERY DESTINY.
CHAPTER 6 END.

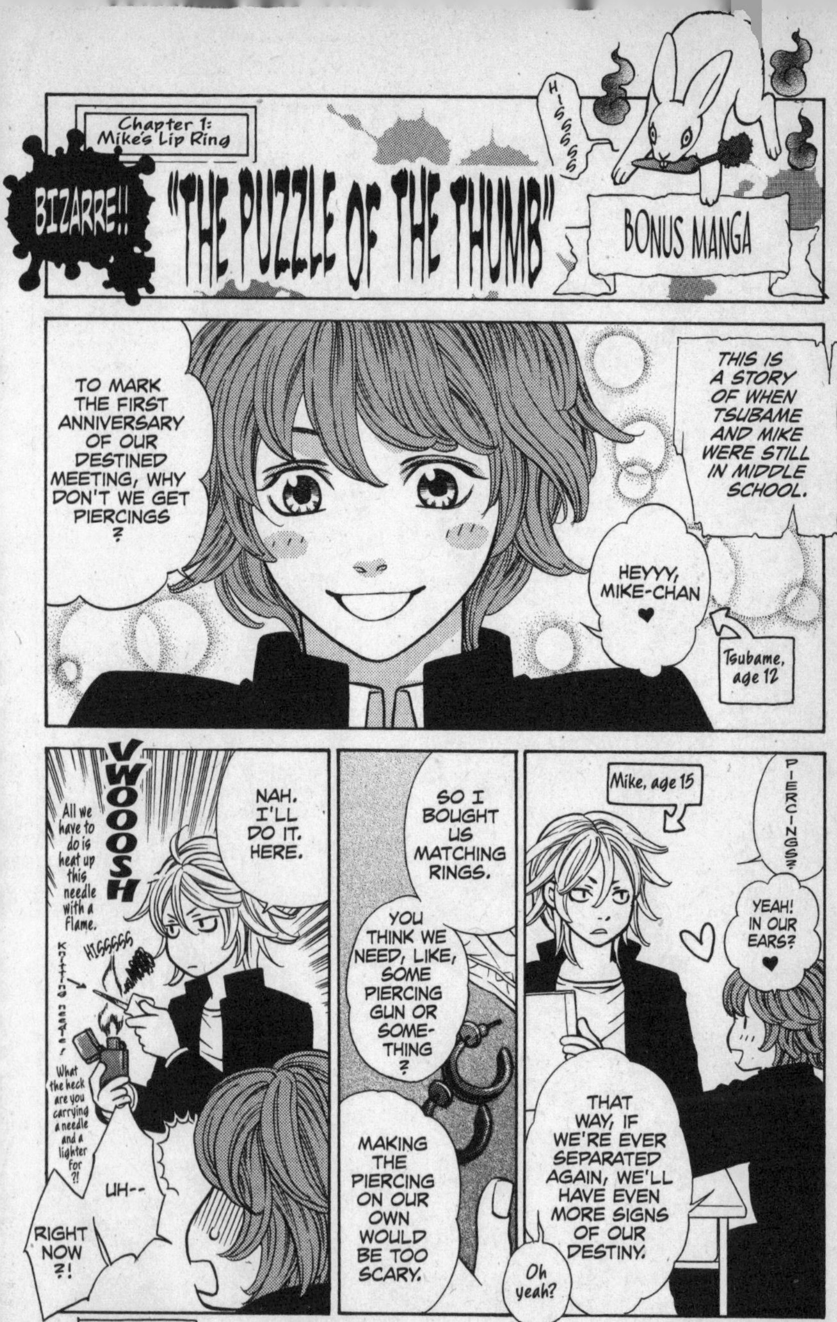
BONUS MANGA
HISSSSS
Chapter 1: Mike's Lip Ring
BIZARRE!! "THE PUZZLE OF THE THUMB"
THIS IS A STORY OF WHEN TSUBAME AND MIKE WERE STILL IN MIDDLE SCHOOL.
HEYYY, MIKE-CHAN ♥
Tsubame, age 12
TO MARK THE FIRST ANNIVERSARY OF OUR DESTINED MEETING, WHY DON'T WE GET PIERCINGS?
Mike, age 15
PIERCINGS?
YEAH! IN OUR EARS? ♥
THAT WAY, IF WE'RE EVER SEPARATED AGAIN, WE'LL HAVE EVEN MORE SIGNS OF OUR DESTINY.
Oh yeah?
SO I BOUGHT US MATCHING RINGS.
YOU THINK WE NEED, LIKE, SOME PIERCING GUN OR SOME-THING?
MAKING THE PIERCING ON OUR OWN WOULD BE TOO SCARY.
NAH. I'LL DO IT. HERE.
VWOOOOSH
All we have to do is heat up this needle with a flame.
HISSSSS
Knitting needle!
What the heck are you carrying a needle and a lighter for?!
UH--
RIGHT NOW?!

To be continued on page 191

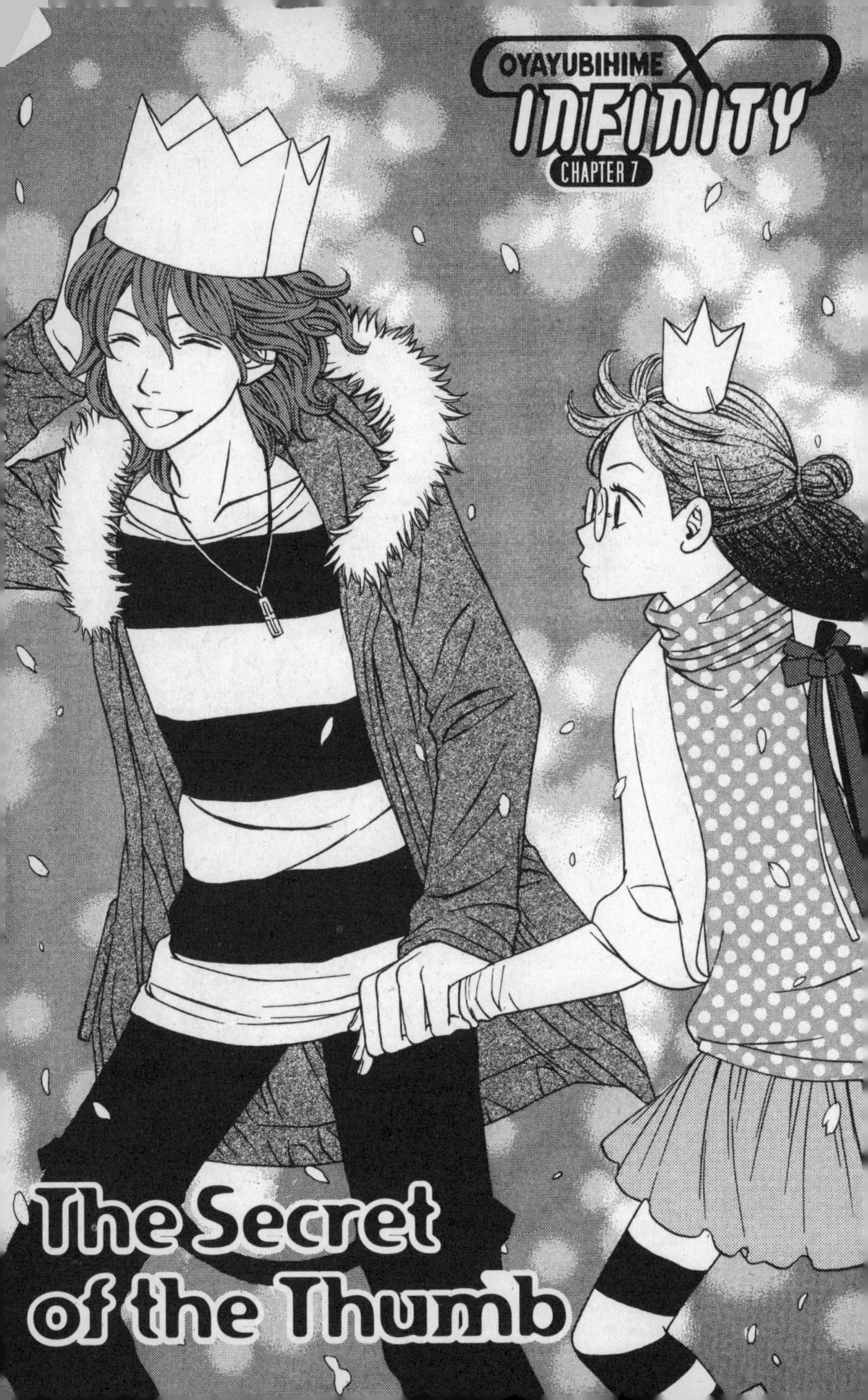
OYAYUBIHIME
INFINITY
CHAPTER 7
The Secret of the Thumb

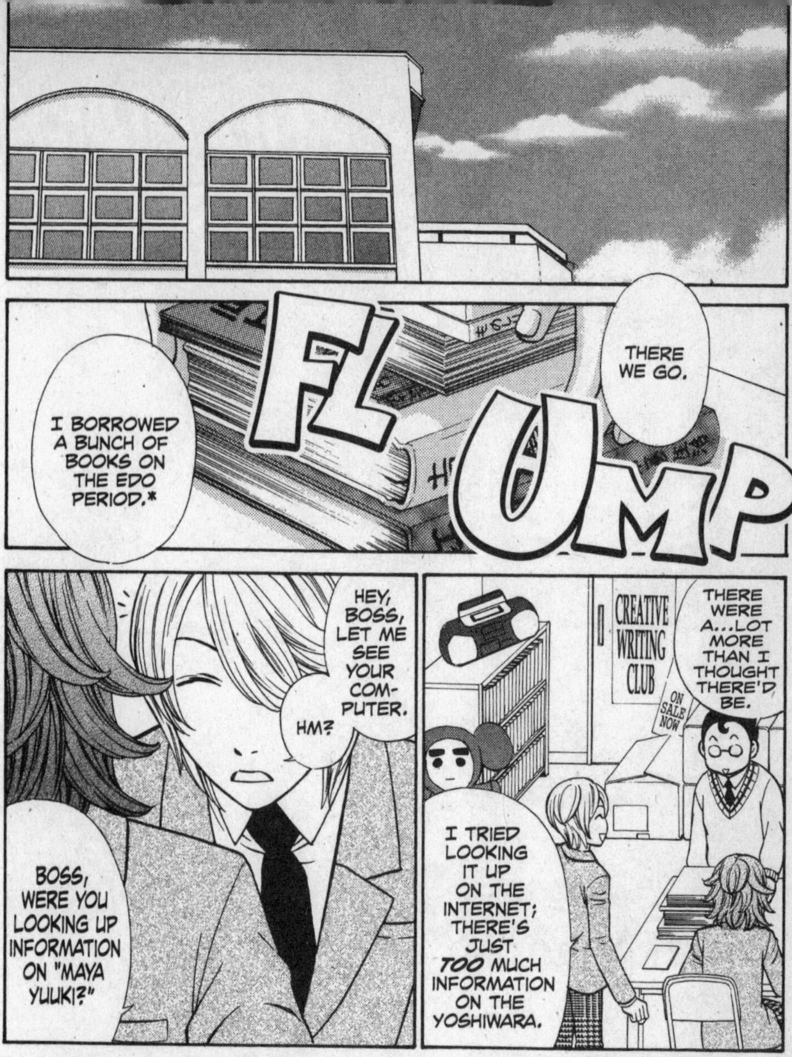
THERE WE GO.
FLUMP
I BORROWED A BUNCH OF BOOKS ON THE EDO PERIOD.*
CREATIVE WRITING CLUB
ON SALE NOW
THERE WERE A...LOT MORE THAN I THOUGHT THERE'D BE.
I TRIED LOOKING IT UP ON THE INTERNET; THERE'S JUST *TOO* MUCH INFORMATION ON THE YOSHIWARA.
HEY, BOSS, LET ME SEE YOUR COM-PUTER.
HM?
BOSS, WERE YOU LOOKING UP INFORMATION ON "MAYA YUUKI?"

Character Guide: 4

Mayu Himemiya

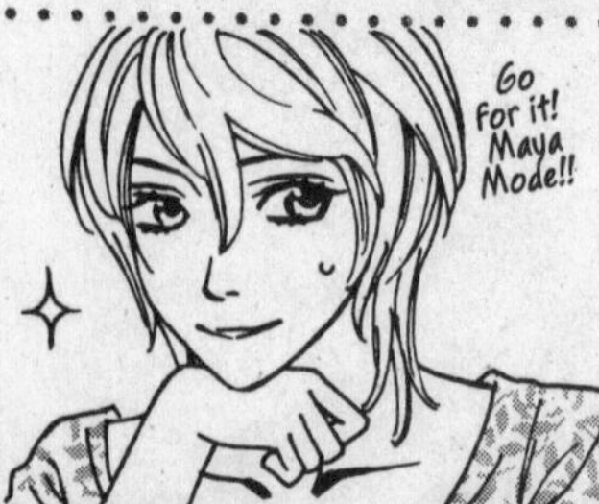
Go for it! Maya Mode!!

Birthday: 5/4

Blood Type: B

She has two faces:
"Mayu," and "Maya Mode."
Both are gorgeous in their own unique ways.
Some readers prefer her in Maya mode,
some readers prefer the regular Mayu.

(*Edo Period: in Japanese history, lasting from app. 1603 to 1867.)

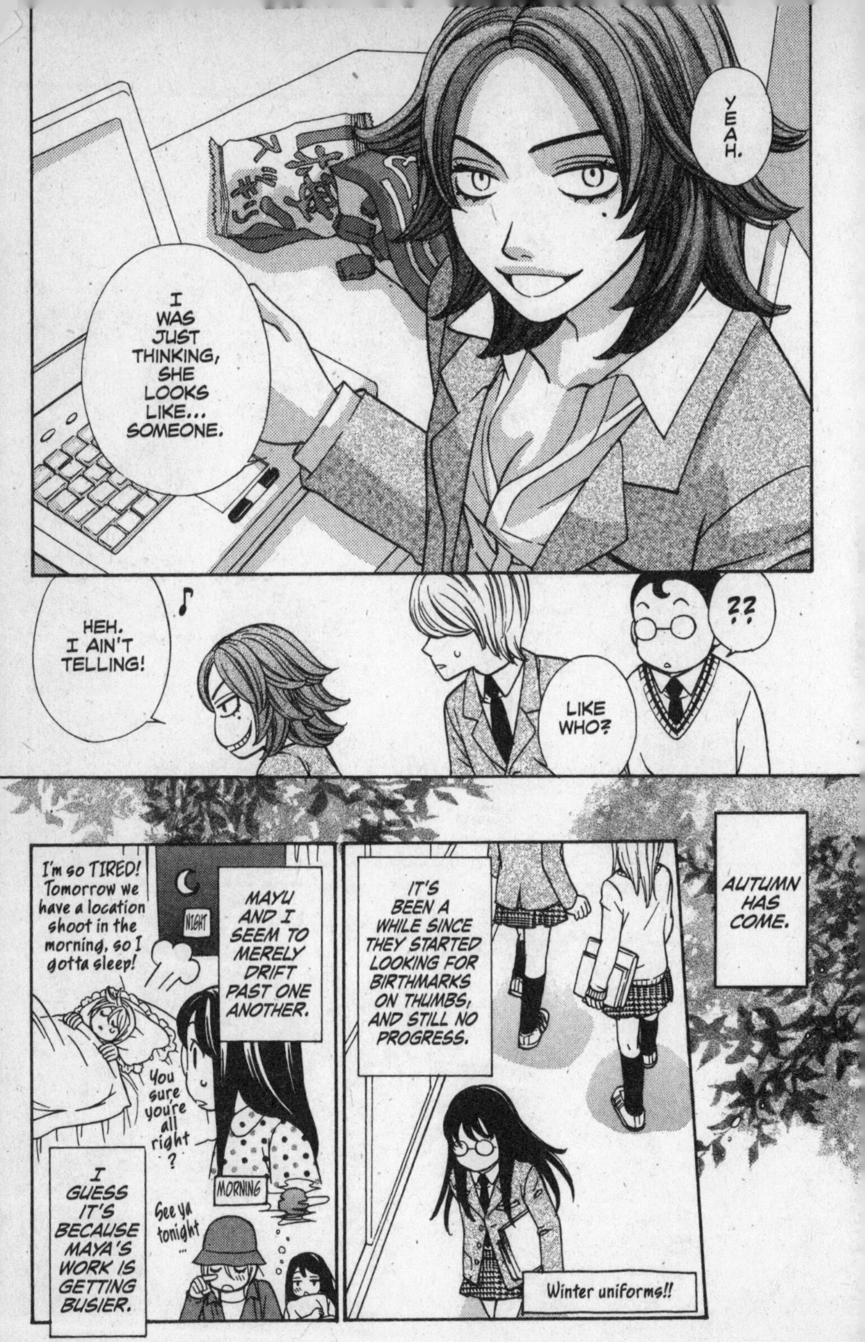
YEAH.
I WAS JUST THINKING, SHE LOOKS LIKE... SOMEONE.
??
LIKE WHO?
HEH. I AIN'T TELLING!
AUTUMN HAS COME.
IT'S BEEN A WHILE SINCE THEY STARTED LOOKING FOR BIRTHMARKS ON THUMBS, AND STILL NO PROGRESS.
Winter uniforms!!
MAYU AND I SEEM TO MERELY DRIFT PAST ONE ANOTHER.
NIGHT
I'm so TIRED! Tomorrow we have a location shoot in the morning, so I gotta sleep!
You sure you're all right?
MORNING
See ya tonight...
I GUESS IT'S BECAUSE MAYA'S WORK IS GETTING BUSIER.

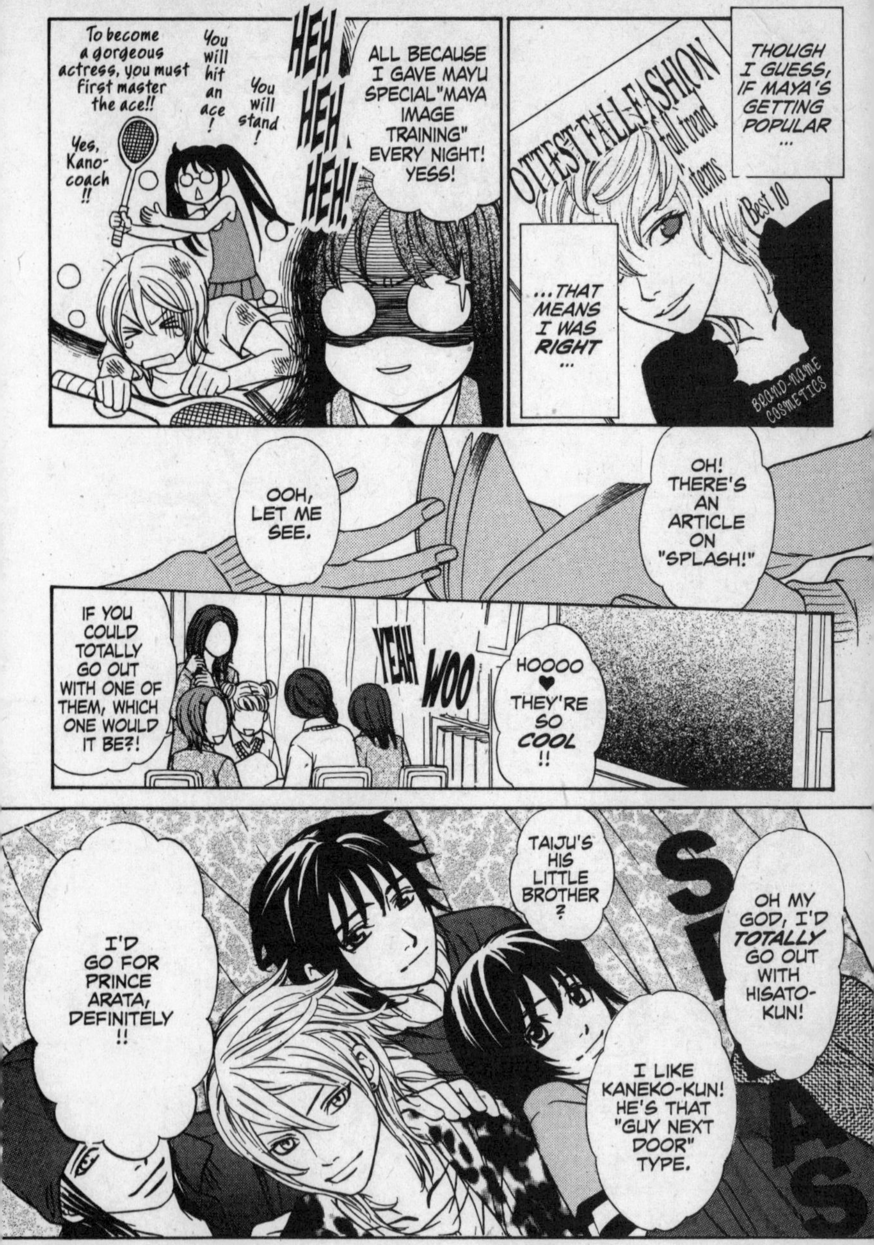
THOUGH I GUESS, IF MAYA'S GETTING POPULAR ...
OTTEST FALL FASHION
fall trend items
Best 10
...THAT MEANS I WAS RIGHT ...
BRAND-NAME COSMETICS
ALL BECAUSE I GAVE MAYU SPECIAL "MAYA IMAGE TRAINING" EVERY NIGHT! YESS!
HEH HEH HEH!
You will stand!
You will hit an ace!
To become a gorgeous actress, you must first master the ace!!
Yes, Kano-coach!!
OH! THERE'S AN ARTICLE ON "SPLASH!"
OOH, LET ME SEE.
HOOOO ♥ THEY'RE SO COOL!!
YEAH
WOO
IF YOU COULD TOTALLY GO OUT WITH ONE OF THEM, WHICH ONE WOULD IT BE?!
OH MY GOD, I'D TOTALLY GO OUT WITH HISATO-KUN!
TAIJU'S HIS LITTLE BROTHER?
I LIKE KANEKO-KUN! HE'S THAT "GUY NEXT DOOR" TYPE.
I'D GO FOR PRINCE ARATA, DEFINITELY!!

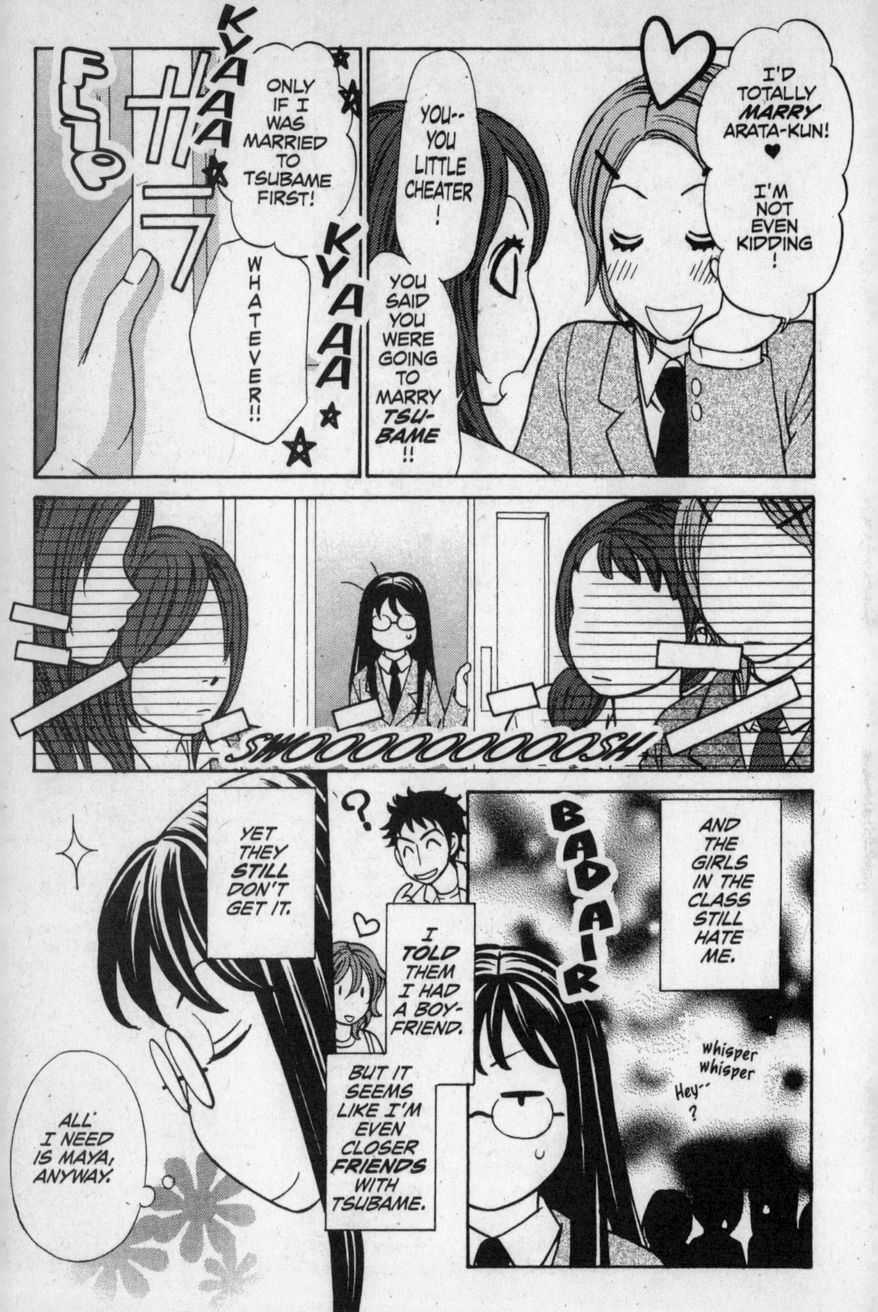
I'D TOTALLY MARRY ARATA-KUN! ♥
I'M NOT EVEN KIDDING!
YOU-- YOU LITTLE CHEATER!
YOU SAID YOU WERE GOING TO MARRY TSUBAME!!
KYAAAA
ONLY IF I WAS MARRIED TO TSUBAME FIRST!
KYAAAA
WHATEVER!!
FLIP
SWOOOOOOOOOOSH
AND THE GIRLS IN THE CLASS STILL HATE ME.
BADAIR
whisper whisper
Hey--?
I TOLD THEM I HAD A BOY-FRIEND.
BUT IT SEEMS LIKE I'M EVEN CLOSER FRIENDS WITH TSUBAME.
YET THEY STILL DON'T GET IT.
ALL I NEED IS MAYA, ANYWAY.

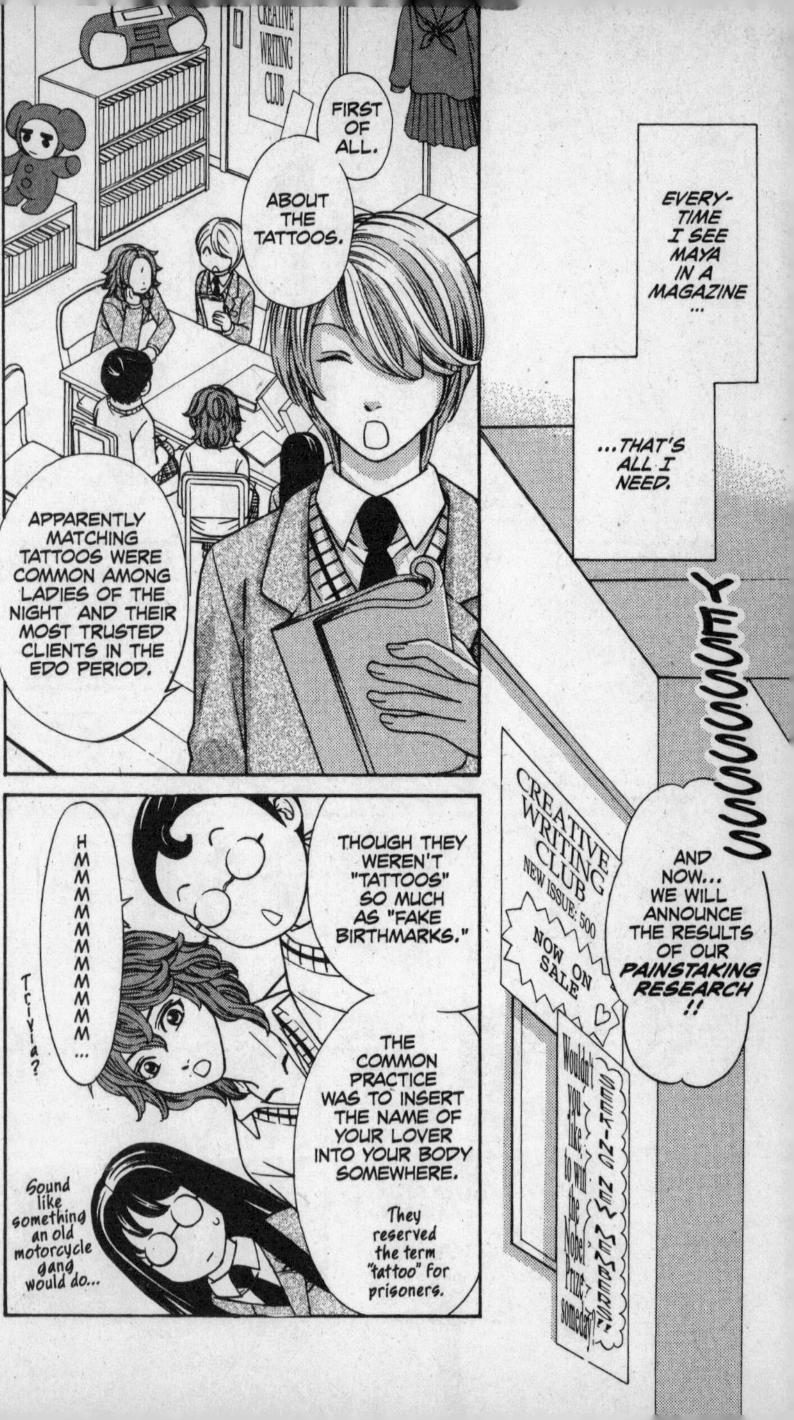
EVERY-TIME I SEE MAYA IN A MAGAZINE...
...THAT'S ALL I NEED.
YESSSSSSS
AND NOW... WE WILL ANNOUNCE THE RESULTS OF OUR PAINSTAKING RESEARCH!!
CREATIVE WRITING CLUB NEW ISSUE: 500 NOW ON SALE
SEEKING NEW MEMBERS!!
Wouldn't you like to win the Nobel Prize someday?
CREATIVE WRITING CLUB
FIRST OF ALL.
ABOUT THE TATTOOS.
APPARENTLY MATCHING TATTOOS WERE COMMON AMONG LADIES OF THE NIGHT AND THEIR MOST TRUSTED CLIENTS IN THE EDO PERIOD.
THOUGH THEY WEREN'T "TATTOOS" SO MUCH AS "FAKE BIRTHMARKS."
HMMMMMMMMMMMMM...
Trivia?
THE COMMON PRACTICE WAS TO INSERT THE NAME OF YOUR LOVER INTO YOUR BODY SOMEWHERE.
They reserved the term "tattoo" for prisoners.
Sound like something an old motorcycle gang would do...

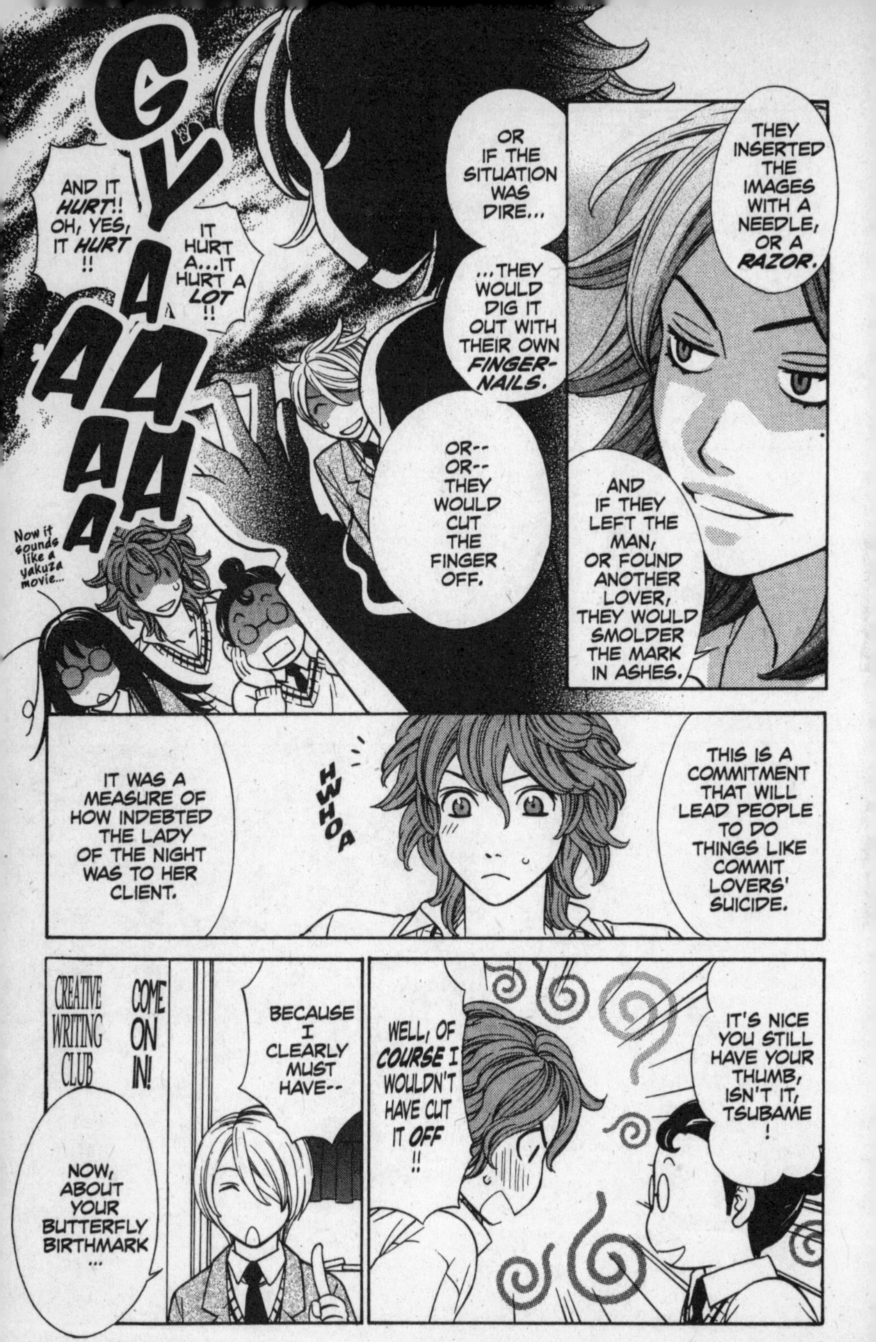
THEY INSERTED THE IMAGES WITH A NEEDLE, OR A *RAZOR*.
AND IF THEY LEFT THE MAN, OR FOUND ANOTHER LOVER, THEY WOULD SMOLDER THE MARK IN ASHES.
OR IF THE SITUATION WAS DIRE...
...THEY WOULD DIG IT OUT WITH THEIR OWN *FINGER-NAILS*.
OR-- OR-- THEY WOULD CUT THE FINGER OFF.
IT HURT A...IT HURT A *LOT*!!
AND IT *HURT*!! OH, YES, IT *HURT*!!
GYAAAAAA
Now it sounds like a yakuza movie...
THIS IS A COMMITMENT THAT WILL LEAD PEOPLE TO DO THINGS LIKE COMMIT LOVERS' SUICIDE.
HWHOA
IT WAS A MEASURE OF HOW INDEBTED THE LADY OF THE NIGHT WAS TO HER CLIENT.
IT'S NICE YOU STILL HAVE YOUR THUMB, ISN'T IT, TSUBAME!
WELL, OF *COURSE* I WOULDN'T HAVE CUT IT *OFF*!!
BECAUSE I CLEARLY MUST HAVE--
COME ON IN!
CREATIVE WRITING CLUB
NOW, ABOUT YOUR BUTTERFLY BIRTHMARK...

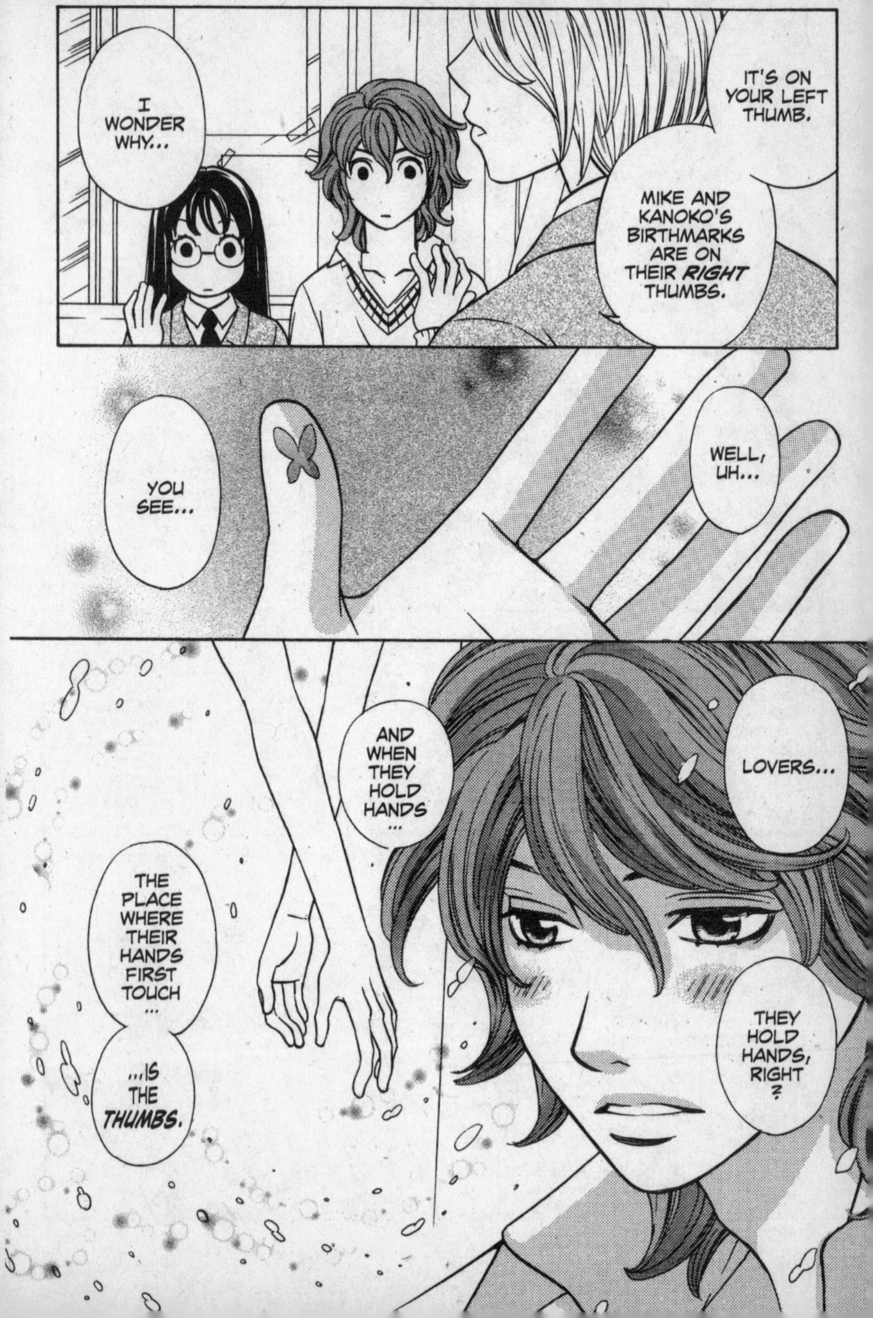
IT'S ON YOUR LEFT THUMB.
MIKE AND KANOKO'S BIRTHMARKS ARE ON THEIR *RIGHT* THUMBS.
I WONDER WHY...
WELL, UH...
YOU SEE...
LOVERS...
THEY HOLD HANDS, RIGHT?
AND WHEN THEY HOLD HANDS...
THE PLACE WHERE THEIR HANDS FIRST TOUCH...
...IS THE *THUMBS*.

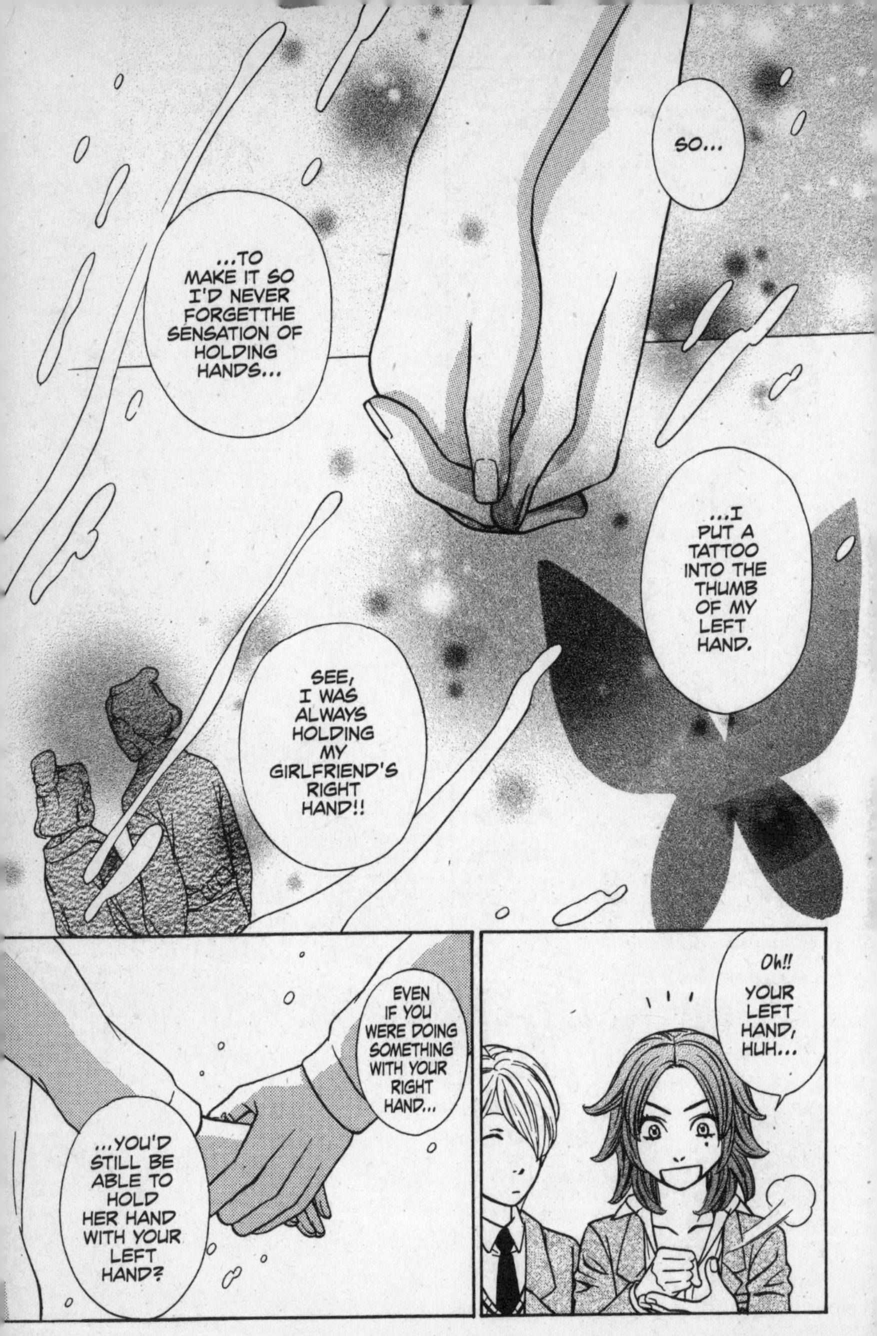
SO...
...TO MAKE IT SO I'D NEVER FORGETTHE SENSATION OF HOLDING HANDS...
...I PUT A TATTOO INTO THE THUMB OF MY LEFT HAND.
SEE, I WAS ALWAYS HOLDING MY GIRLFRIEND'S RIGHT HAND!!
Oh!! YOUR LEFT HAND, HUH...
EVEN IF YOU WERE DOING SOMETHING WITH YOUR RIGHT HAND...
...YOU'D STILL BE ABLE TO HOLD HER HAND WITH YOUR LEFT HAND?

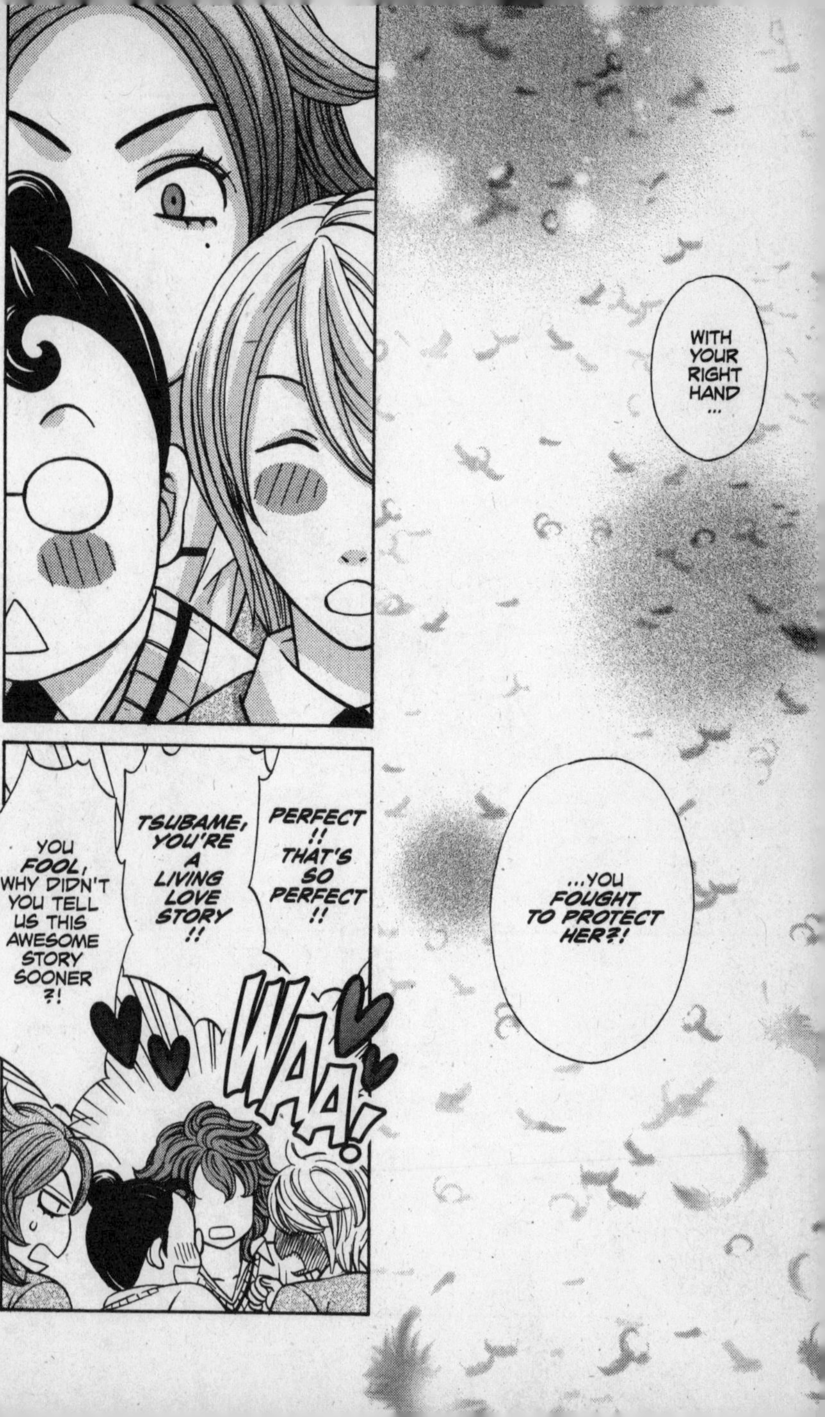
WITH YOUR RIGHT HAND ...
...YOU FOUGHT TO PROTECT HER?!
PERFECT!! THAT'S SO PERFECT!!
TSUBAME, YOU'RE A LIVING LOVE STORY!!
YOU FOOL, WHY DIDN'T YOU TELL US THIS AWESOME STORY SOONER?!
WAA!

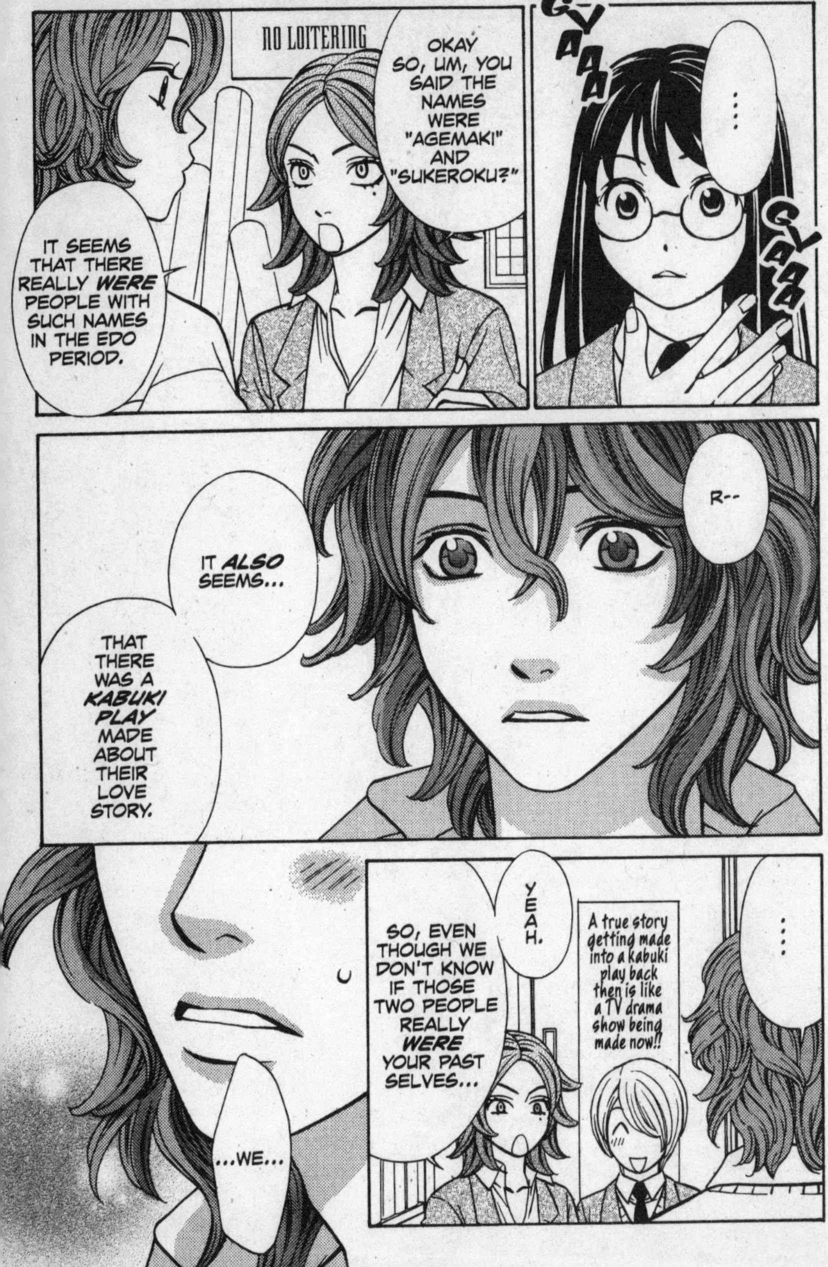
GYAAA
....
GYAAA
NO LOITERING
OKAY SO, UM, YOU SAID THE NAMES WERE "AGEMAKI" AND "SUKEROKU?"
IT SEEMS THAT THERE REALLY WERE PEOPLE WITH SUCH NAMES IN THE EDO PERIOD.
R--
IT ALSO SEEMS...
THAT THERE WAS A KABUKI PLAY MADE ABOUT THEIR LOVE STORY.
....
A true story getting made into a kabuki play back then is like a TV drama show being made now!!
YEAH.
SO, EVEN THOUGH WE DON'T KNOW IF THOSE TWO PEOPLE REALLY WERE YOUR PAST SELVES...
...WE...

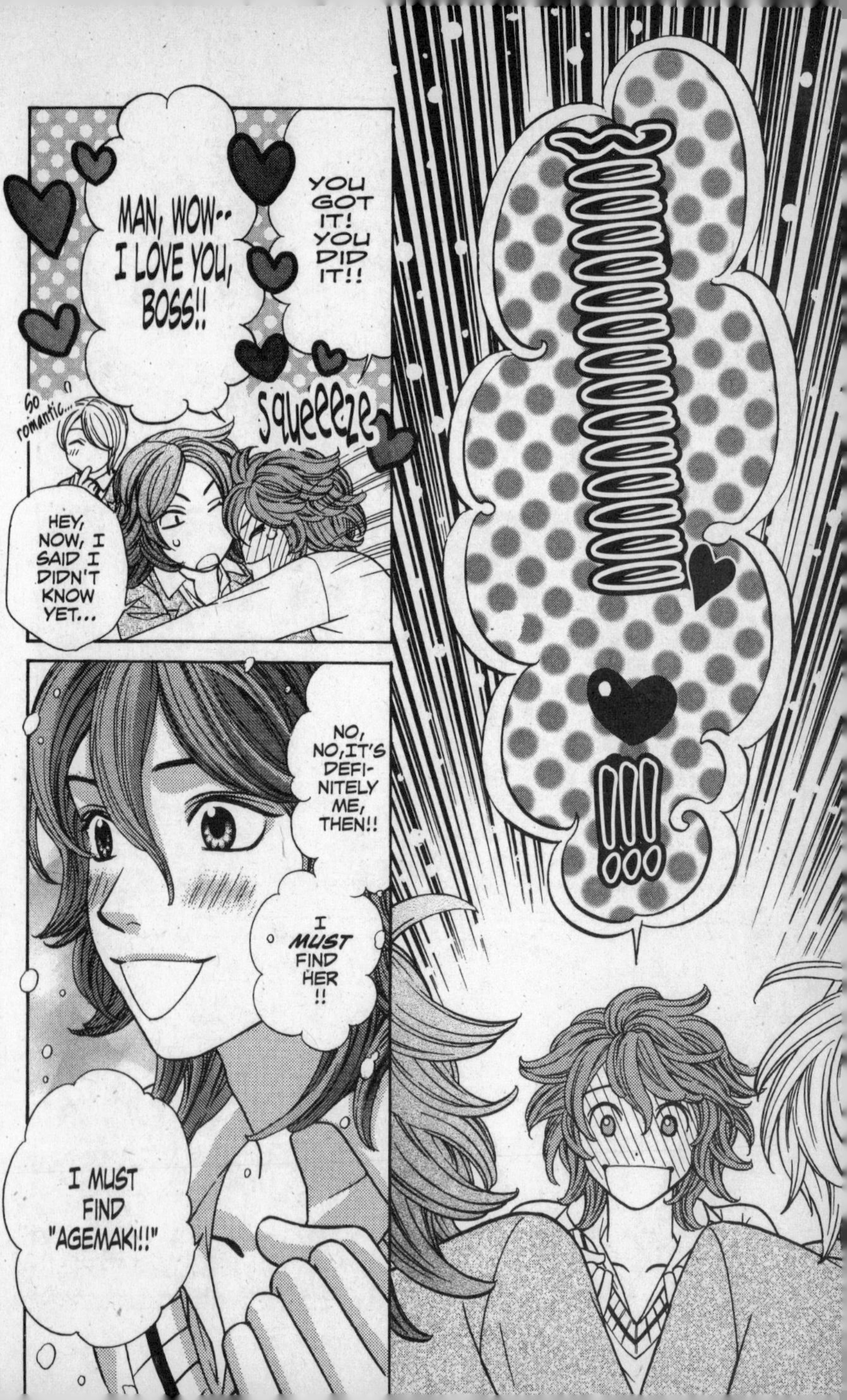

WOOOOOOOOOOOOOOO♥♥!!!
MAN, WOW.. I LOVE YOU, BOSS!!
YOU GOT IT! YOU DID IT!!
SQUEEEZE
So romantic...
HEY, NOW, I SAID I DIDN'T KNOW YET...
NO, NO, IT'S DEFINITELY ME, THEN!!
I *MUST* FIND HER!!
I MUST FIND "AGEMAKI!!"

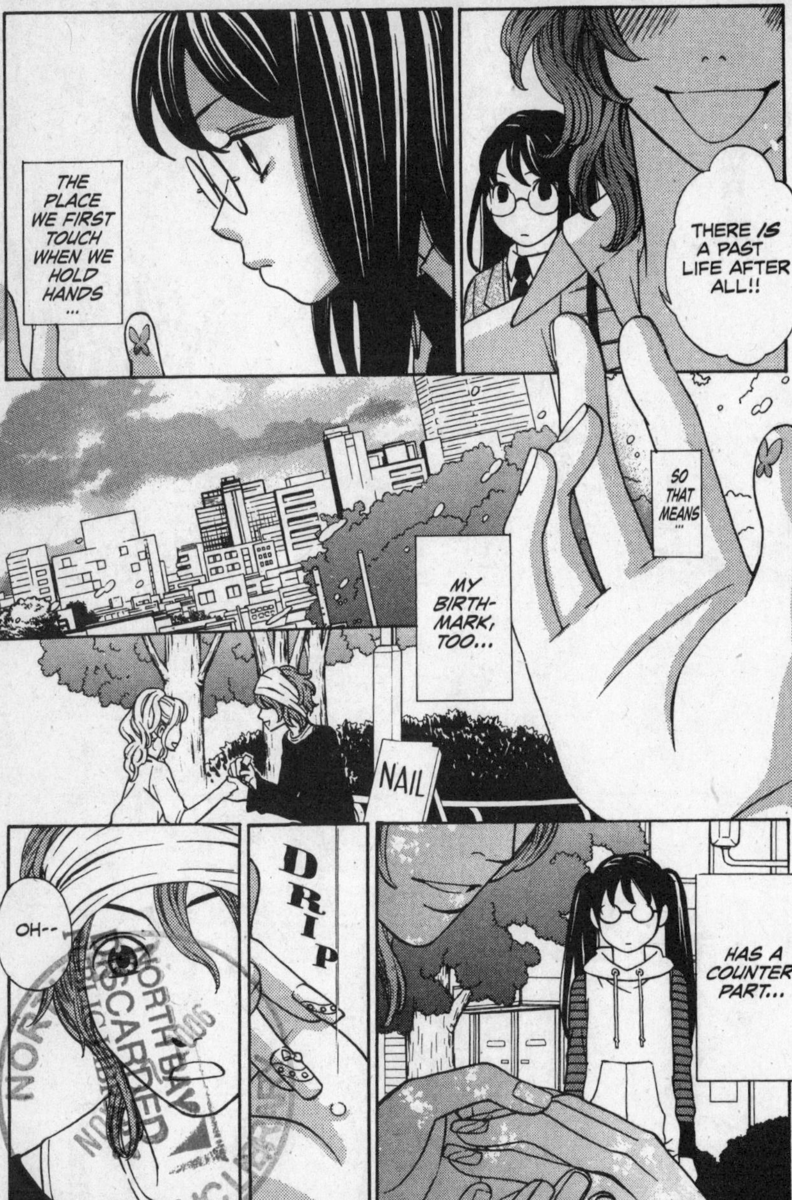
THERE IS A PAST LIFE AFTER ALL!!
THE PLACE WE FIRST TOUCH WHEN WE HOLD HANDS ...
SO THAT MEANS ...
MY BIRTH-MARK, TOO...
NAIL
HAS A COUNTER-PART...
DRIP
OH--

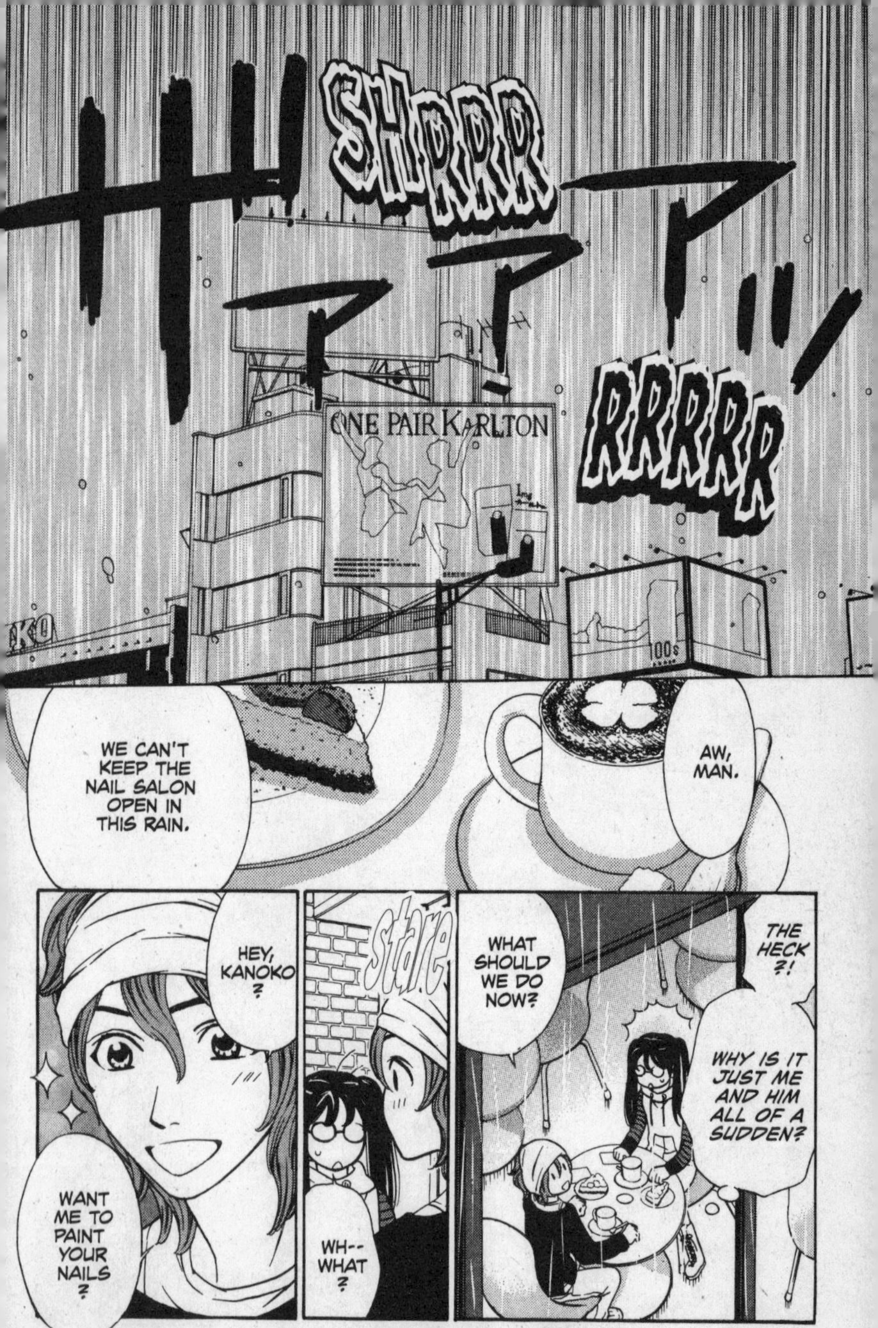
SHRRR
RRRRR
ONE PAIR KARLTON
AW, MAN.
WE CAN'T KEEP THE NAIL SALON OPEN IN THIS RAIN.
THE HECK?!
WHY IS IT JUST ME AND HIM ALL OF A SUDDEN?
WHAT SHOULD WE DO NOW?
stare
WH-- WHAT?
HEY, KANOKO?
WANT ME TO PAINT YOUR NAILS?

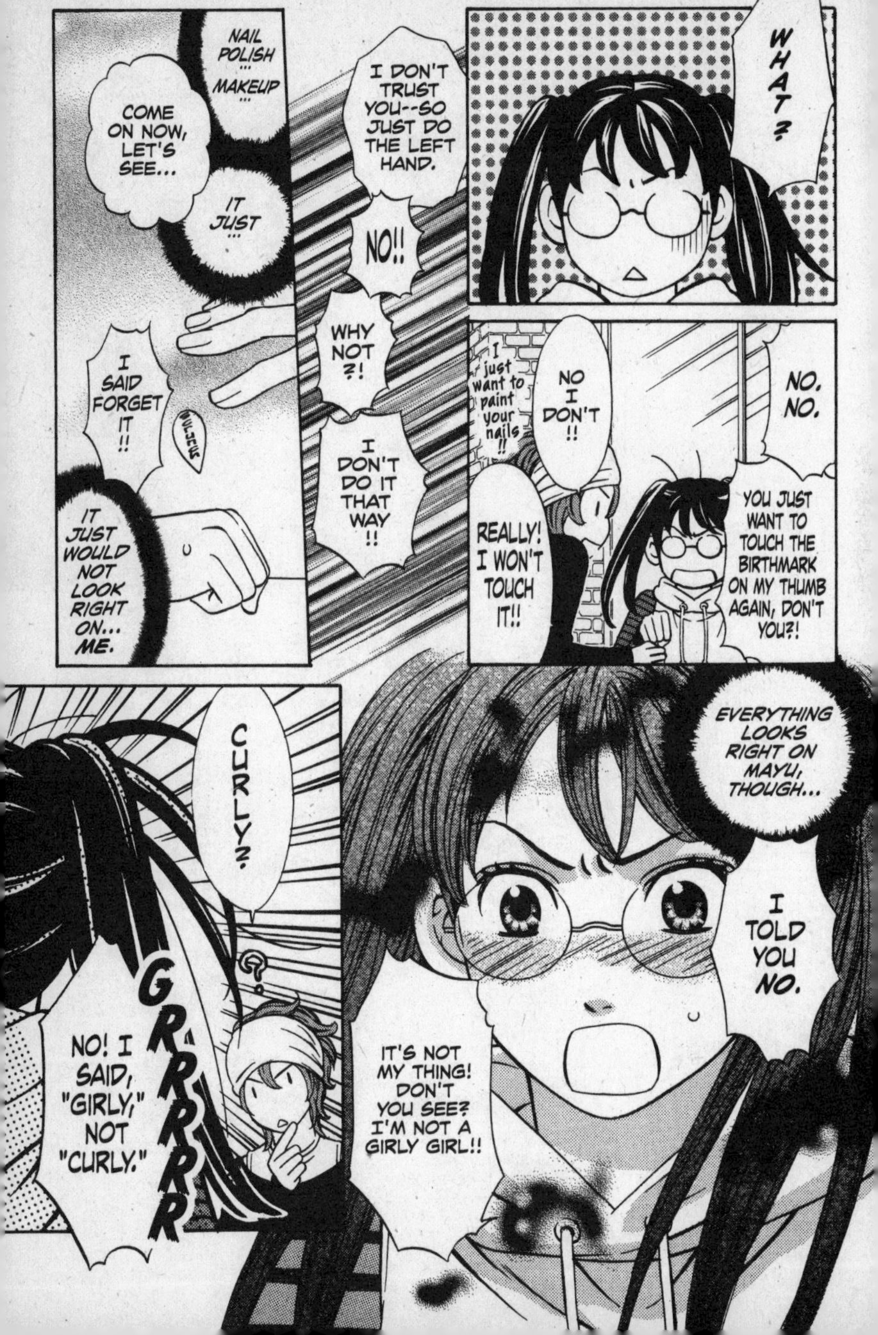
WHAT?!
NO. NO.
YOU JUST WANT TO TOUCH THE BIRTHMARK ON MY THUMB AGAIN, DON'T YOU?!
NO I DON'T!!
I just want to paint your nails!!
REALLY! I WON'T TOUCH IT!!
I DON'T TRUST YOU--SO JUST DO THE LEFT HAND.
NO!!
WHY NOT?!
I DON'T DO IT THAT WAY!!
NAIL POLISH... MAKEUP...
COME ON NOW, LET'S SEE...
IT JUST...
I SAID FORGET IT!!
IT JUST WOULD NOT LOOK RIGHT ON... ME.
EVERYTHING LOOKS RIGHT ON MAYU, THOUGH...
I TOLD YOU NO.
IT'S NOT MY THING! DON'T YOU SEE? I'M NOT A GIRLY GIRL!!
CURLY?
GRRRRR
NO! I SAID, "GIRLY," NOT "CURLY."

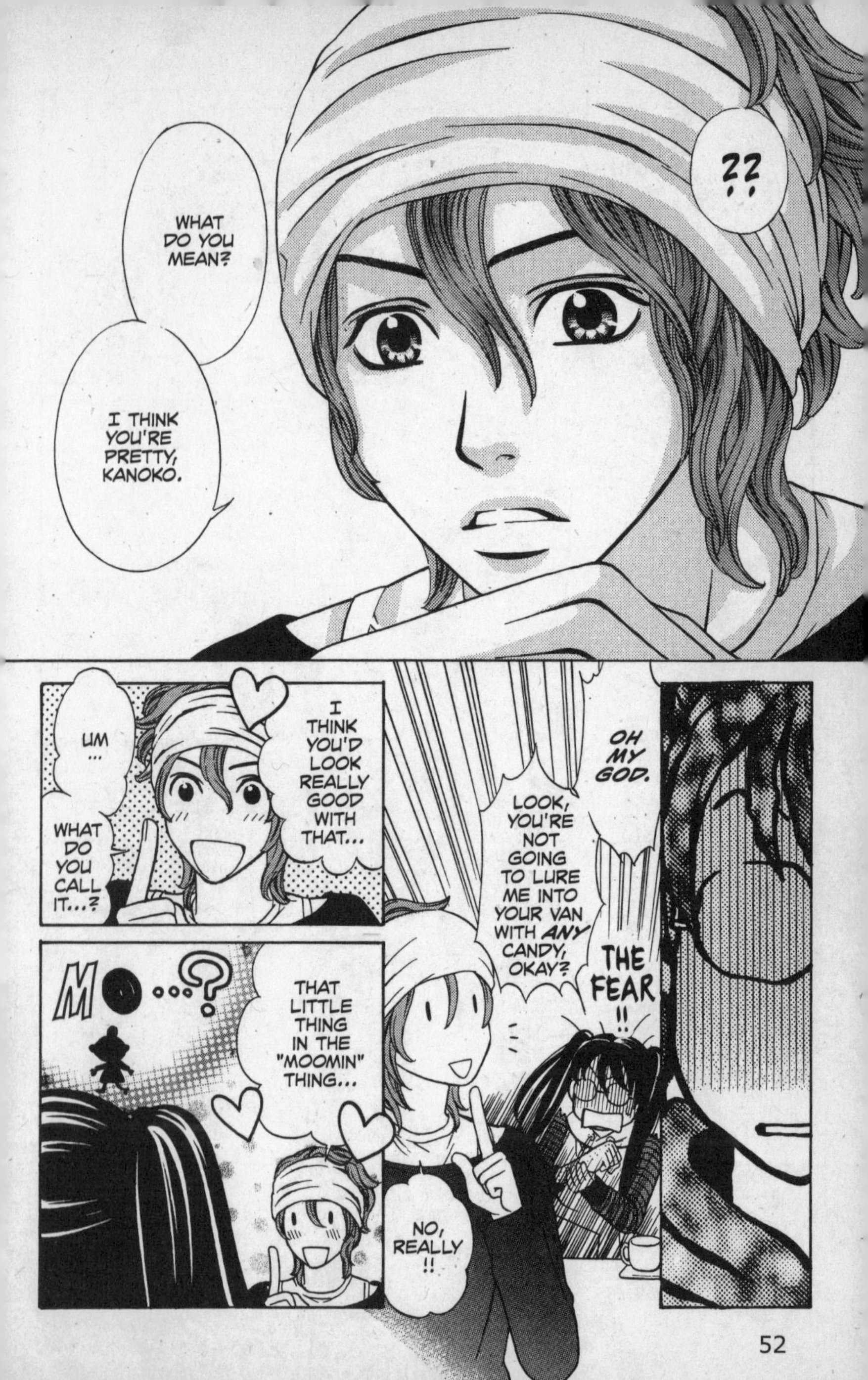
??
WHAT DO YOU MEAN?
I THINK YOU'RE PRETTY, KANOKO.
OH MY GOD.
LOOK, YOU'RE NOT GOING TO LURE ME INTO YOUR VAN WITH *ANY* CANDY, OKAY?
THE FEAR!!
I THINK YOU'D LOOK REALLY GOOD WITH THAT...
UM ... WHAT DO YOU CALL IT...?
THAT LITTLE THING IN THE "MOOMIN" THING...
M●...?
NO, REALLY!!

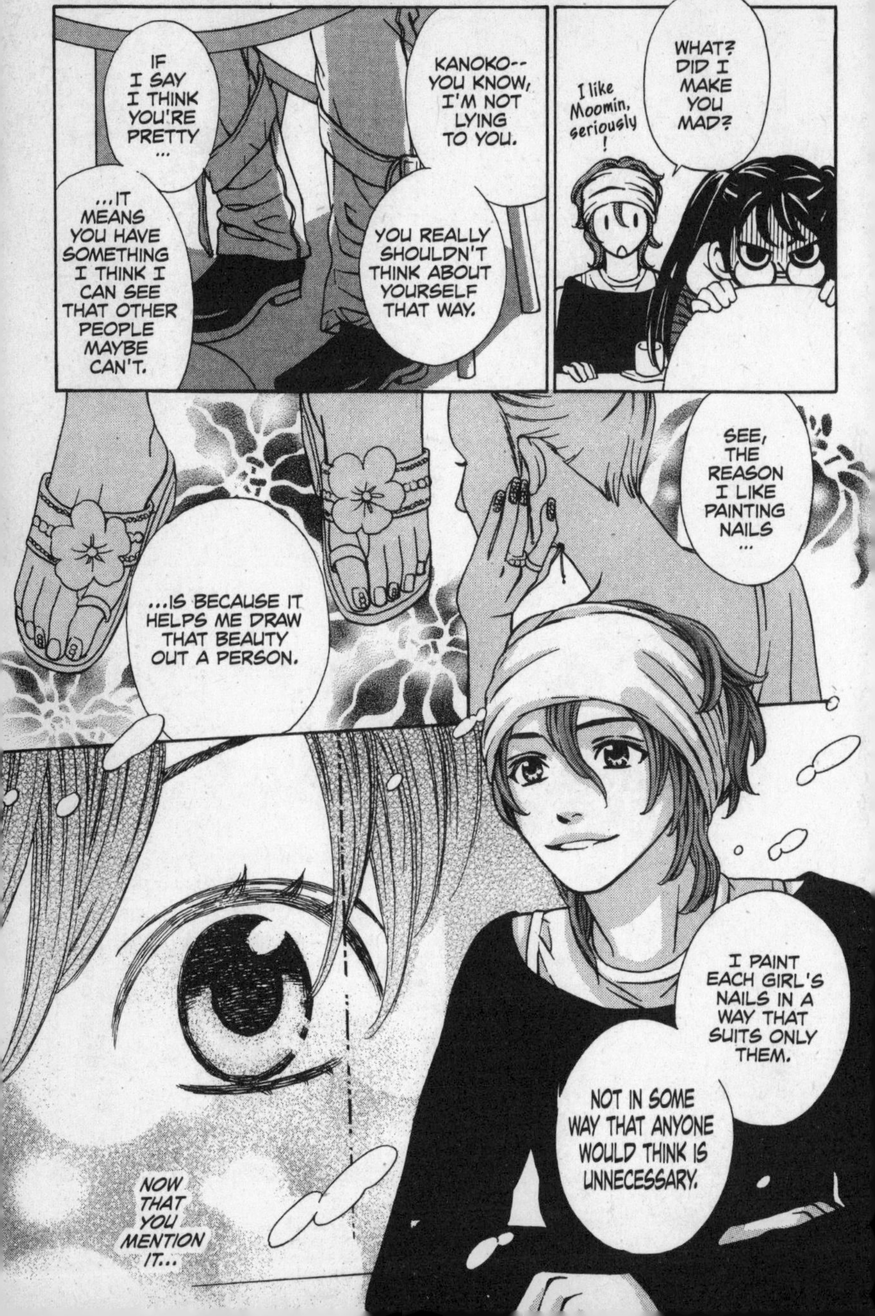
WHAT? DID I MAKE YOU MAD?
I like Moomin, seriously!
KANOKO-- YOU KNOW, I'M NOT LYING TO YOU.
YOU REALLY SHOULDN'T THINK ABOUT YOURSELF THAT WAY.
IF I SAY I THINK YOU'RE PRETTY ...
...IT MEANS YOU HAVE SOMETHING I THINK I CAN SEE THAT OTHER PEOPLE MAYBE CAN'T.
SEE, THE REASON I LIKE PAINTING NAILS ...
...IS BECAUSE IT HELPS ME DRAW THAT BEAUTY OUT A PERSON.
I PAINT EACH GIRL'S NAILS IN A WAY THAT SUITS ONLY THEM.
NOT IN SOME WAY THAT ANYONE WOULD THINK IS UNNECESSARY.
NOW THAT YOU MENTION IT...

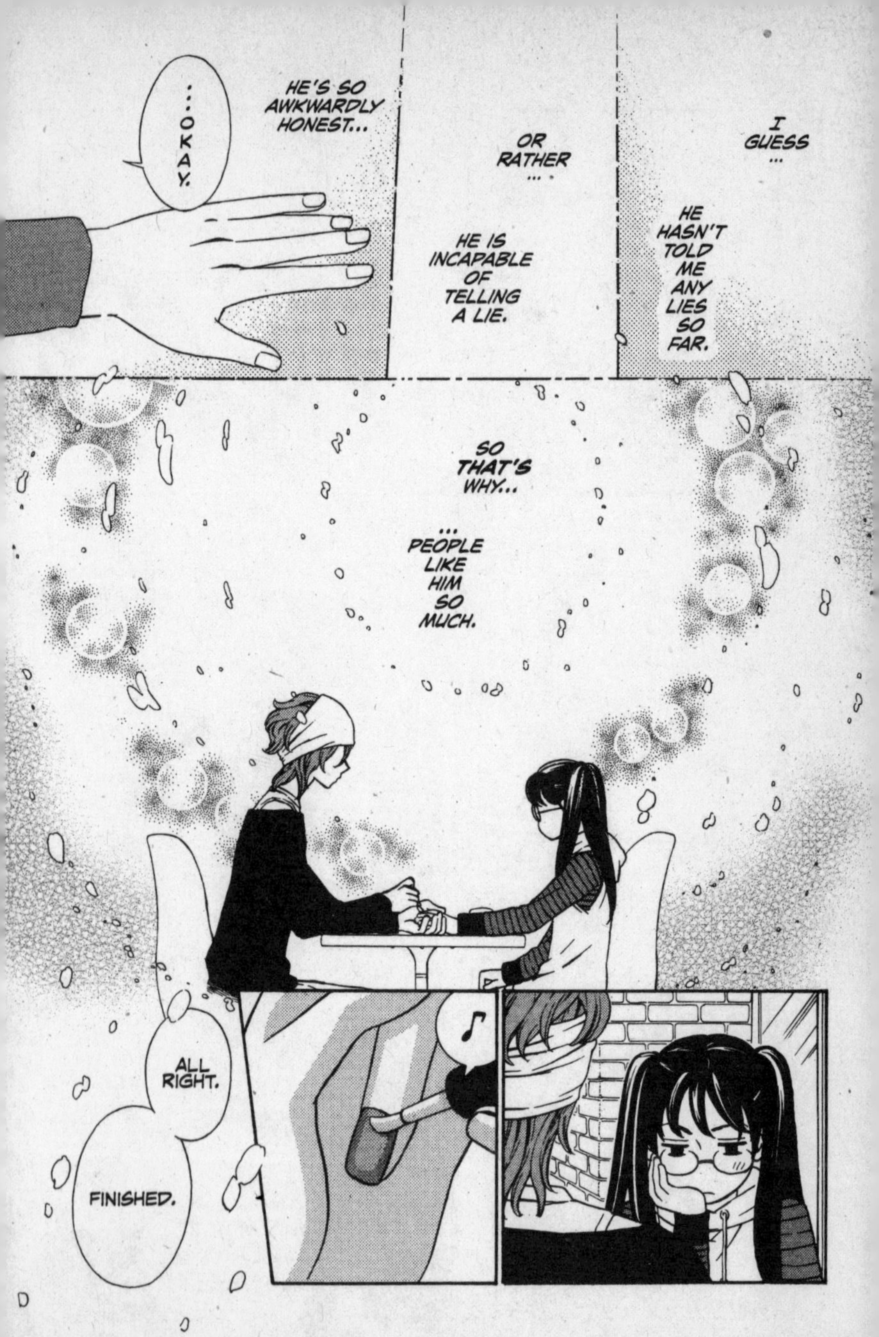
I GUESS...
HE HASN'T TOLD ME ANY LIES SO FAR.
OR RATHER...
HE IS INCAPABLE OF TELLING A LIE.
HE'S SO AWKWARDLY HONEST...
...OKAY.
SO THAT'S WHY...
...PEOPLE LIKE HIM SO MUCH.
♪
ALL RIGHT.
FINISHED.

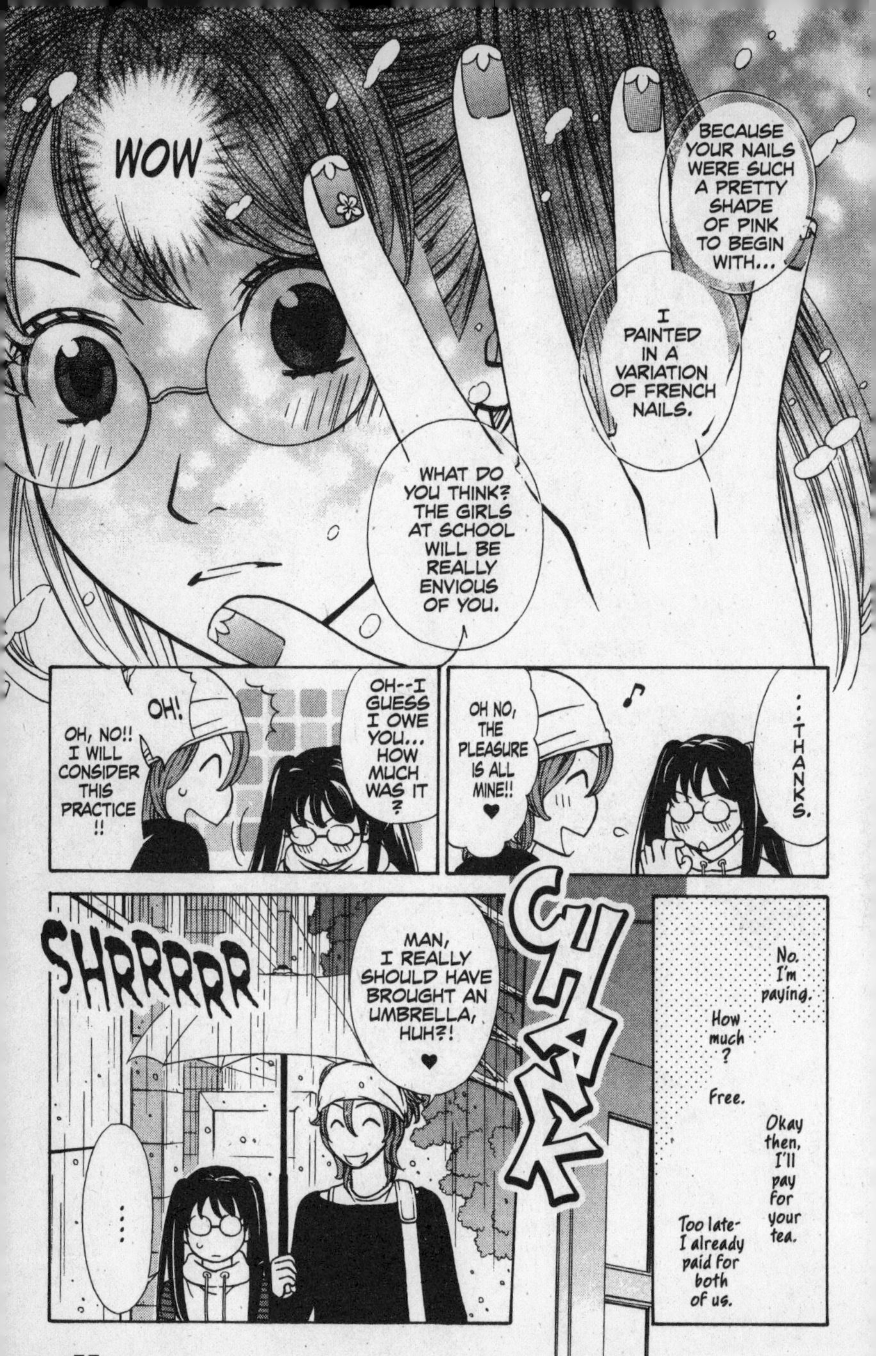
BECAUSE YOUR NAILS WERE SUCH A PRETTY SHADE OF PINK TO BEGIN WITH...
I PAINTED IN A VARIATION OF FRENCH NAILS.
WOW
WHAT DO YOU THINK? THE GIRLS AT SCHOOL WILL BE REALLY ENVIOUS OF YOU.
...THANKS.
OH NO, THE PLEASURE IS ALL MINE!! ♥
OH--I GUESS I OWE YOU... HOW MUCH WAS IT?
OH!
OH, NO!! I WILL CONSIDER THIS PRACTICE!!
No. I'm paying.
How much?
Free.
Okay then, I'll pay for your tea.
Too late- I already paid for both of us.
CHANK
MAN, I REALLY SHOULD HAVE BROUGHT AN UMBRELLA, HUH?! ♥
SHRRRRR
....

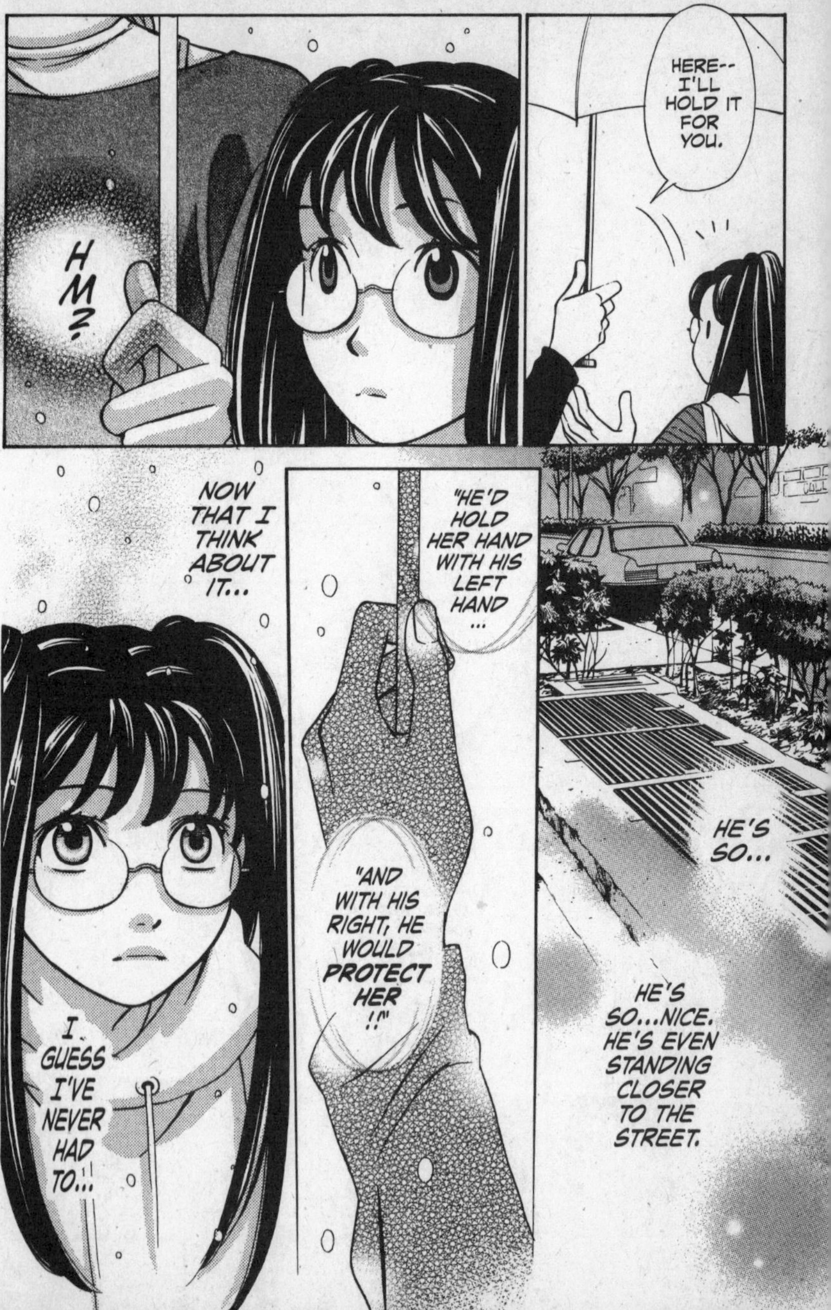
HERE-- I'LL HOLD IT FOR YOU.
HM?
HE'S SO...
HE'S SO...NICE. HE'S EVEN STANDING CLOSER TO THE STREET.
"HE'D HOLD HER HAND WITH HIS LEFT HAND...
"AND WITH HIS RIGHT, HE WOULD PROTECT HER!!"
NOW THAT I THINK ABOUT IT...
I GUESS I'VE NEVER HAD TO...!!

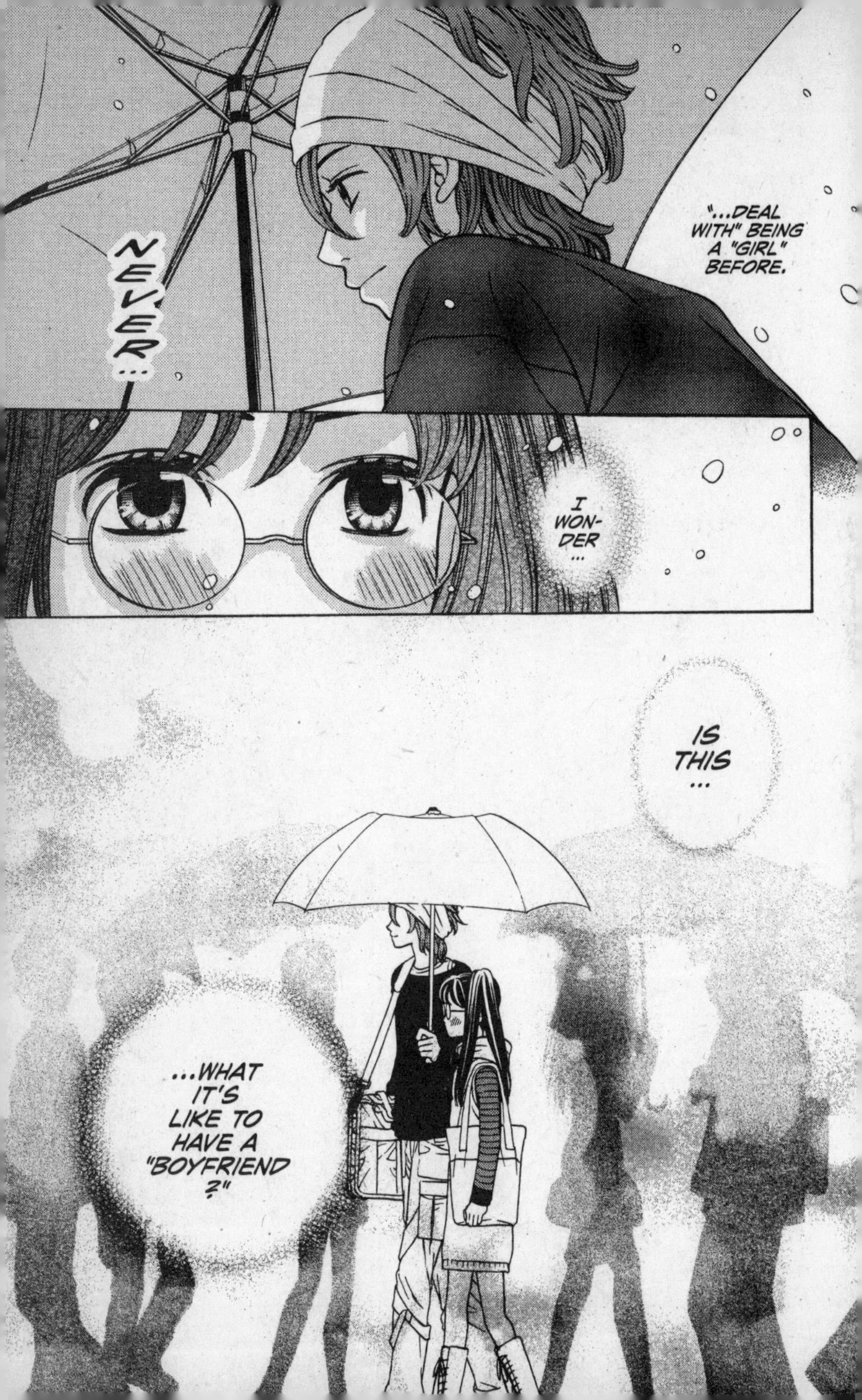
"...DEAL WITH" BEING A "GIRL" BEFORE.
NEVER...
I WONDER...
IS THIS...
...WHAT IT'S LIKE TO HAVE A "BOYFRIEND?"

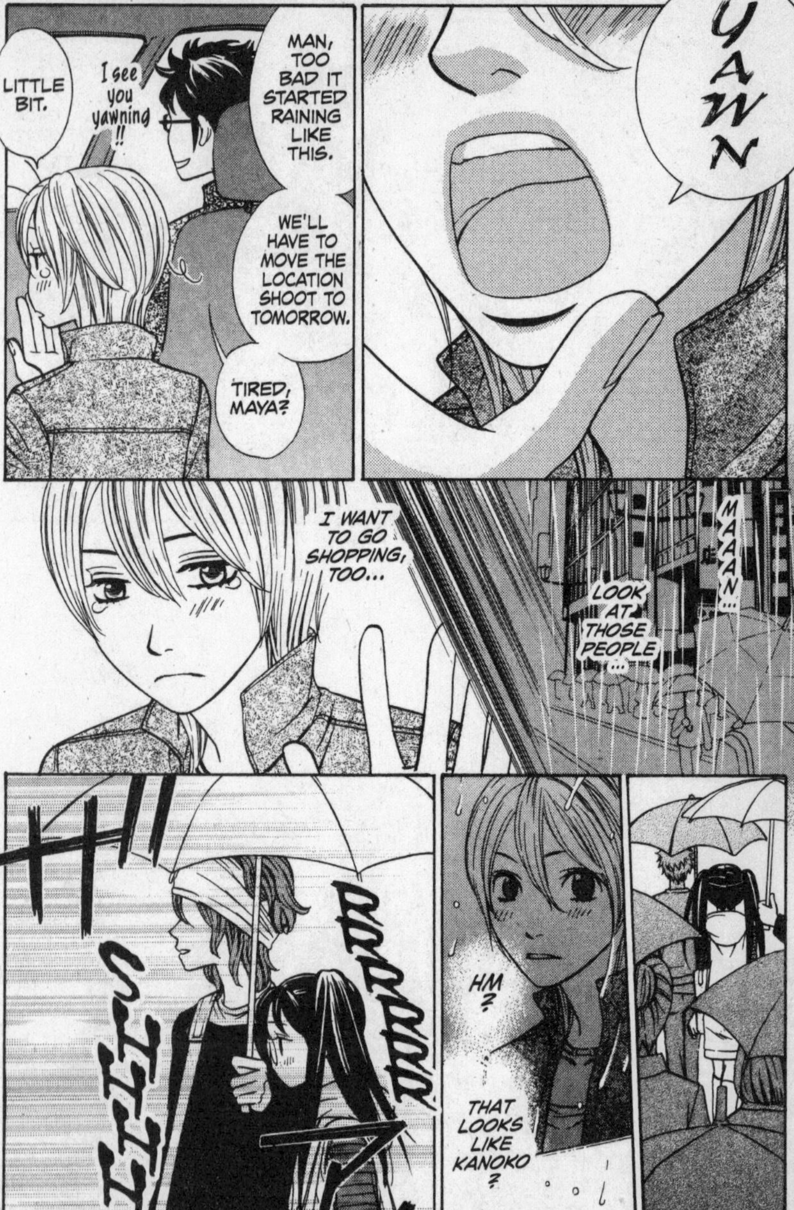
YAWN
MAN, TOO BAD IT STARTED RAINING LIKE THIS.
WE'LL HAVE TO MOVE THE LOCATION SHOOT TO TOMORROW.
TIRED, MAYA?
I see you yawning!!
LITTLE BIT.
MAAAAN...
LOOK AT THOSE PEOPLE...
I WANT TO GO SHOPPING, TOO...
HM?
THAT LOOKS LIKE KANOKO?

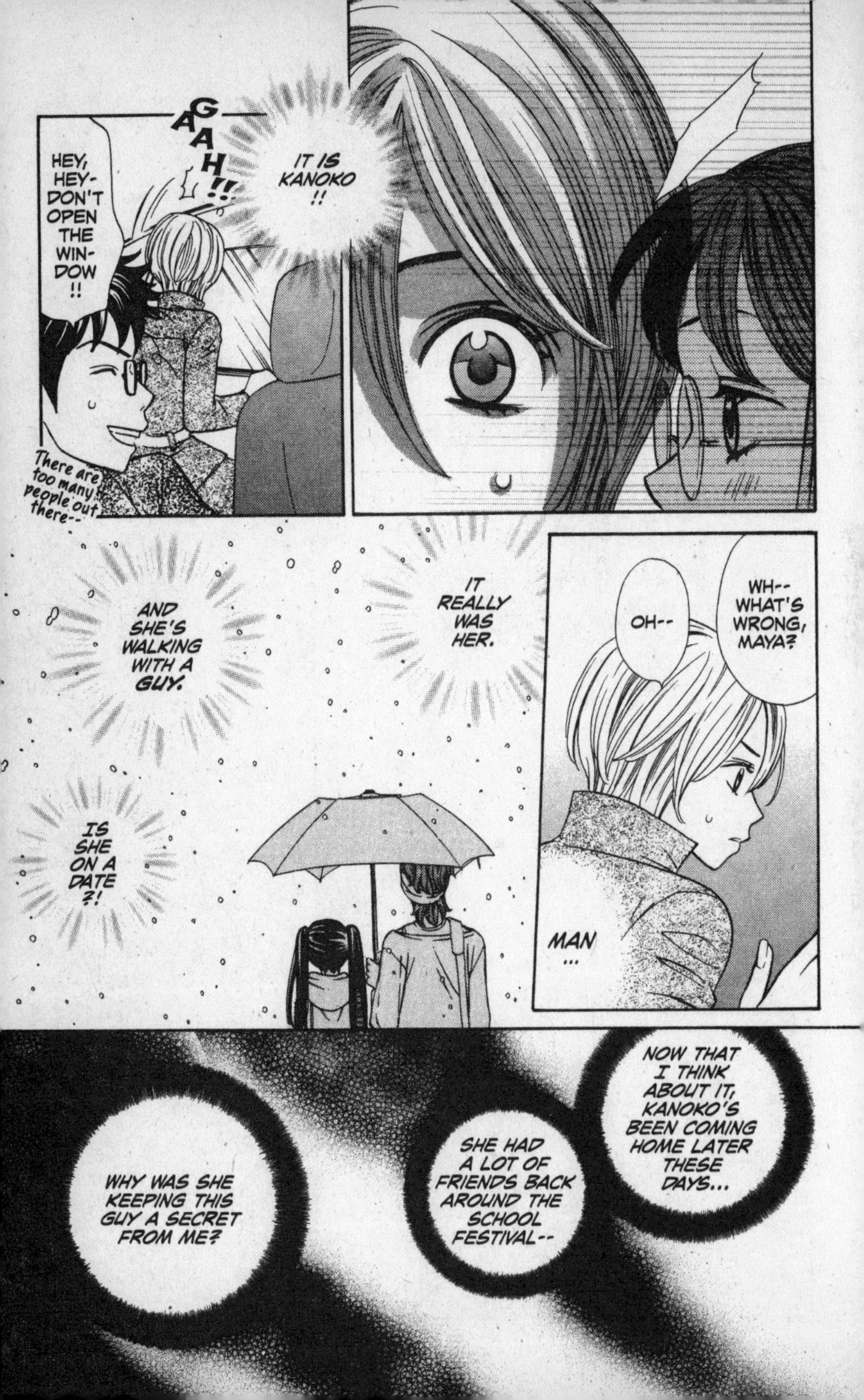
IT IS KANOKO!!
GAAH!!
HEY, HEY- DON'T OPEN THE WIN-DOW!!
There are too many people out there--
WH-- WHAT'S WRONG, MAYA?
OH--
MAN...
IT REALLY WAS HER.
AND SHE'S WALKING WITH A GUY.
IS SHE ON A DATE?!
NOW THAT I THINK ABOUT IT, KANOKO'S BEEN COMING HOME LATER THESE DAYS...
SHE HAD A LOT OF FRIENDS BACK AROUND THE SCHOOL FESTIVAL--
WHY WAS SHE KEEPING THIS GUY A SECRET FROM ME?

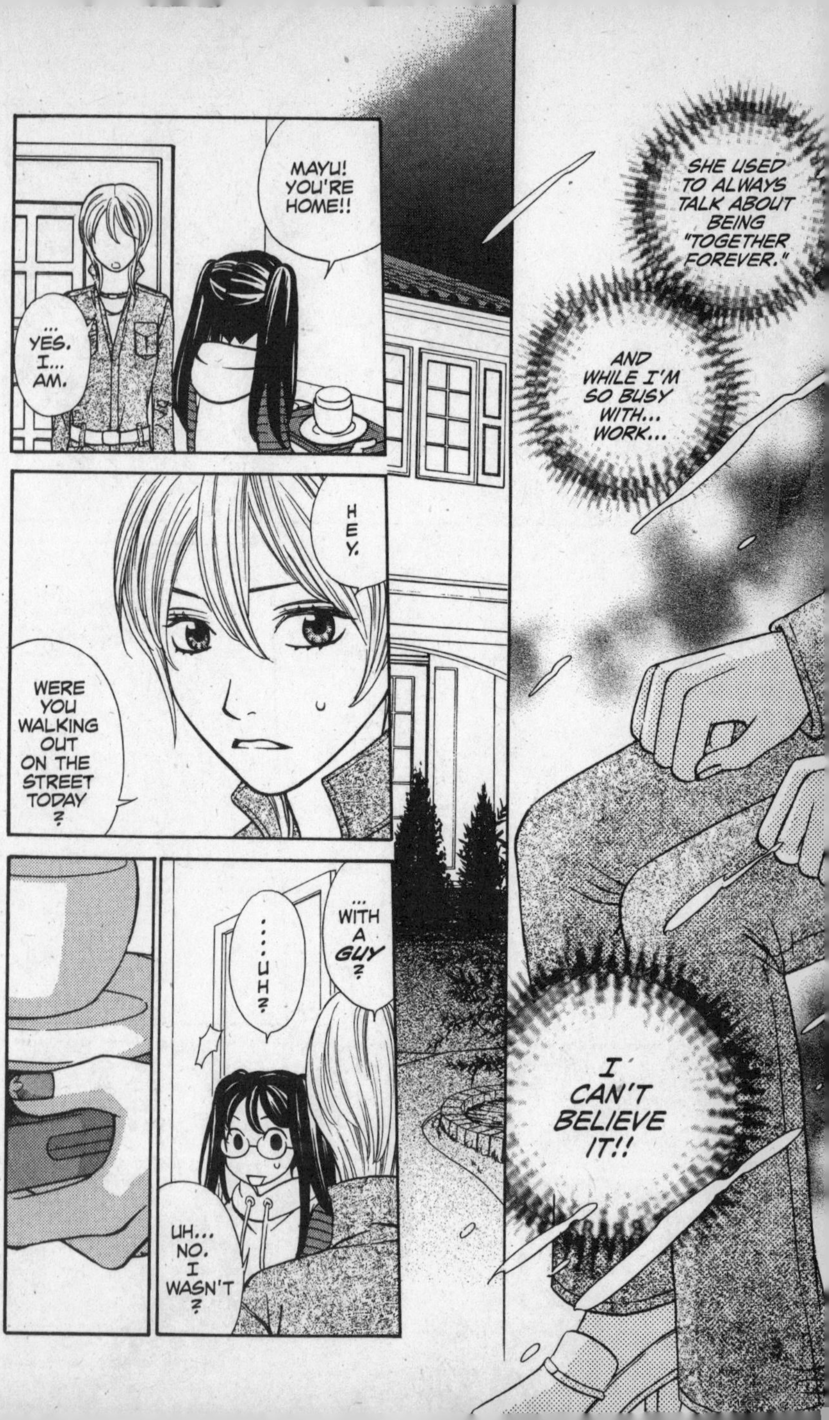
SHE USED TO ALWAYS TALK ABOUT BEING "TOGETHER FOREVER."
AND WHILE I'M SO BUSY WITH... WORK...
I CAN'T BELIEVE IT!!
MAYU! YOU'RE HOME!!
... YES. I... AM.
HEY.
WERE YOU WALKING OUT ON THE STREET TODAY?
... WITH A GUY?
...UH?
UH... NO. I WASN'T?

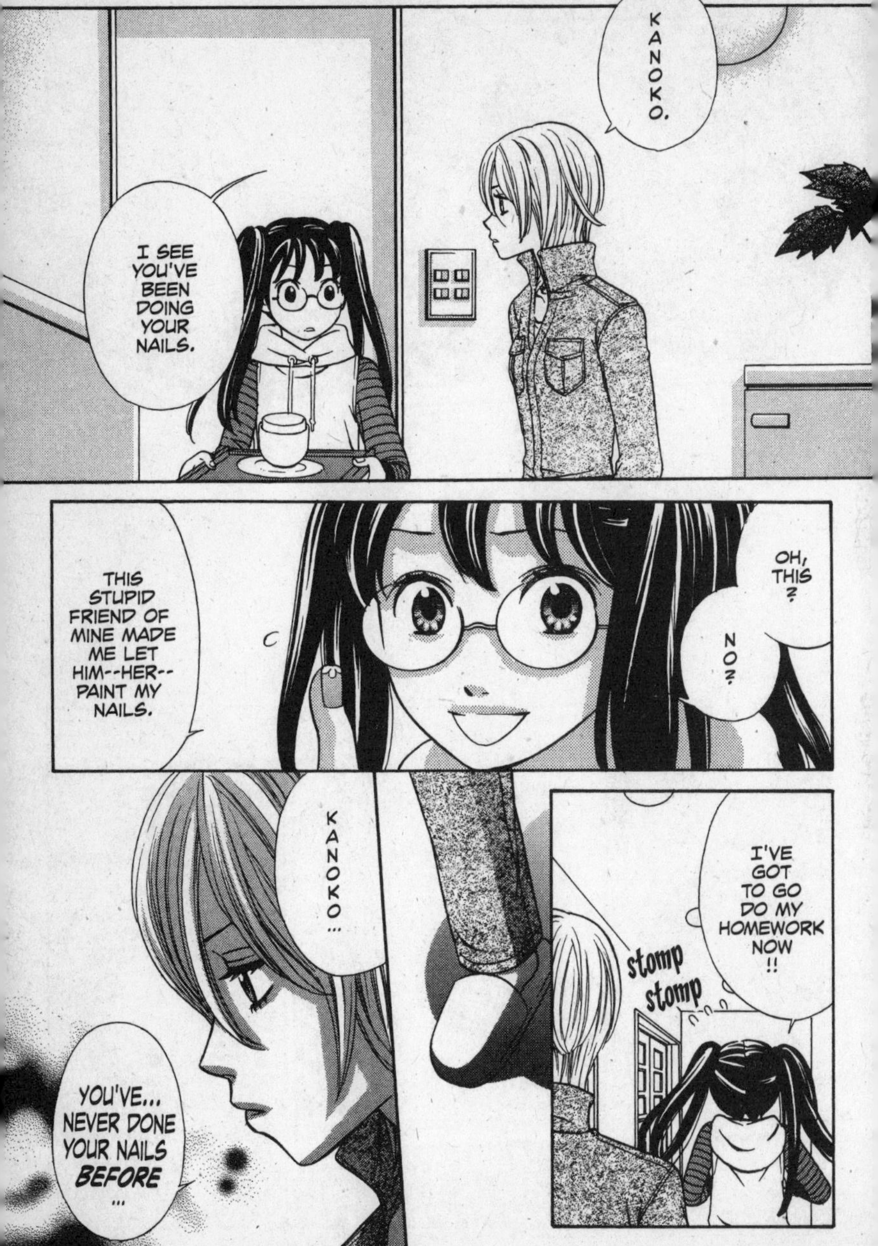
KANOKO.
I SEE YOU'VE BEEN DOING YOUR NAILS.
OH, THIS?
NO?
THIS STUPID FRIEND OF MINE MADE ME LET HIM--HER--PAINT MY NAILS.
I'VE GOT TO GO DO MY HOMEWORK NOW!!
stomp stomp
KANOKO...
YOU'VE... NEVER DONE YOUR NAILS *BEFORE*...

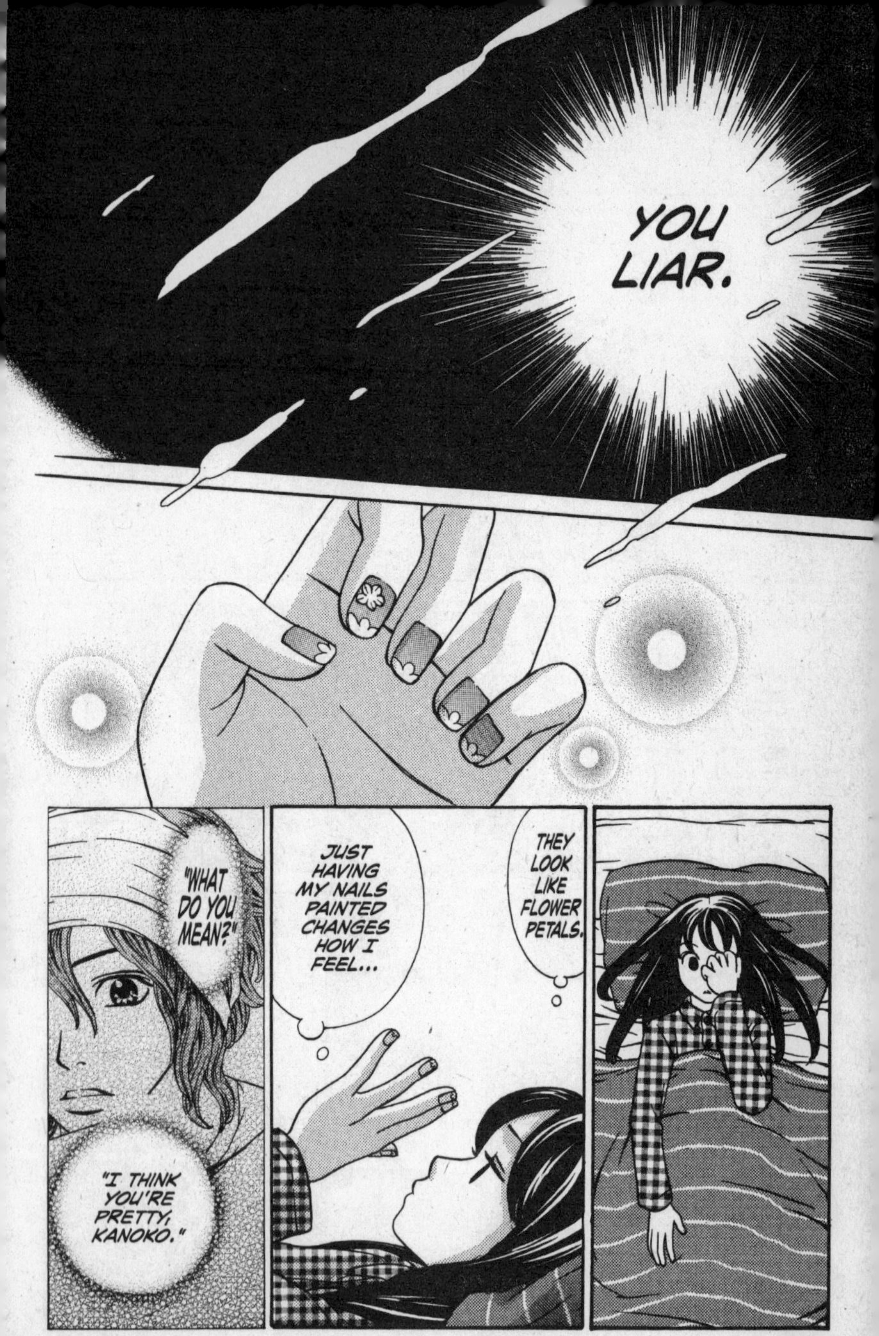
YOU LIAR.
THEY LOOK LIKE FLOWER PETALS.
JUST HAVING MY NAILS PAINTED CHANGES HOW I FEEL...
"WHAT DO YOU MEAN?"
"I THINK YOU'RE PRETTY, KANOKO."

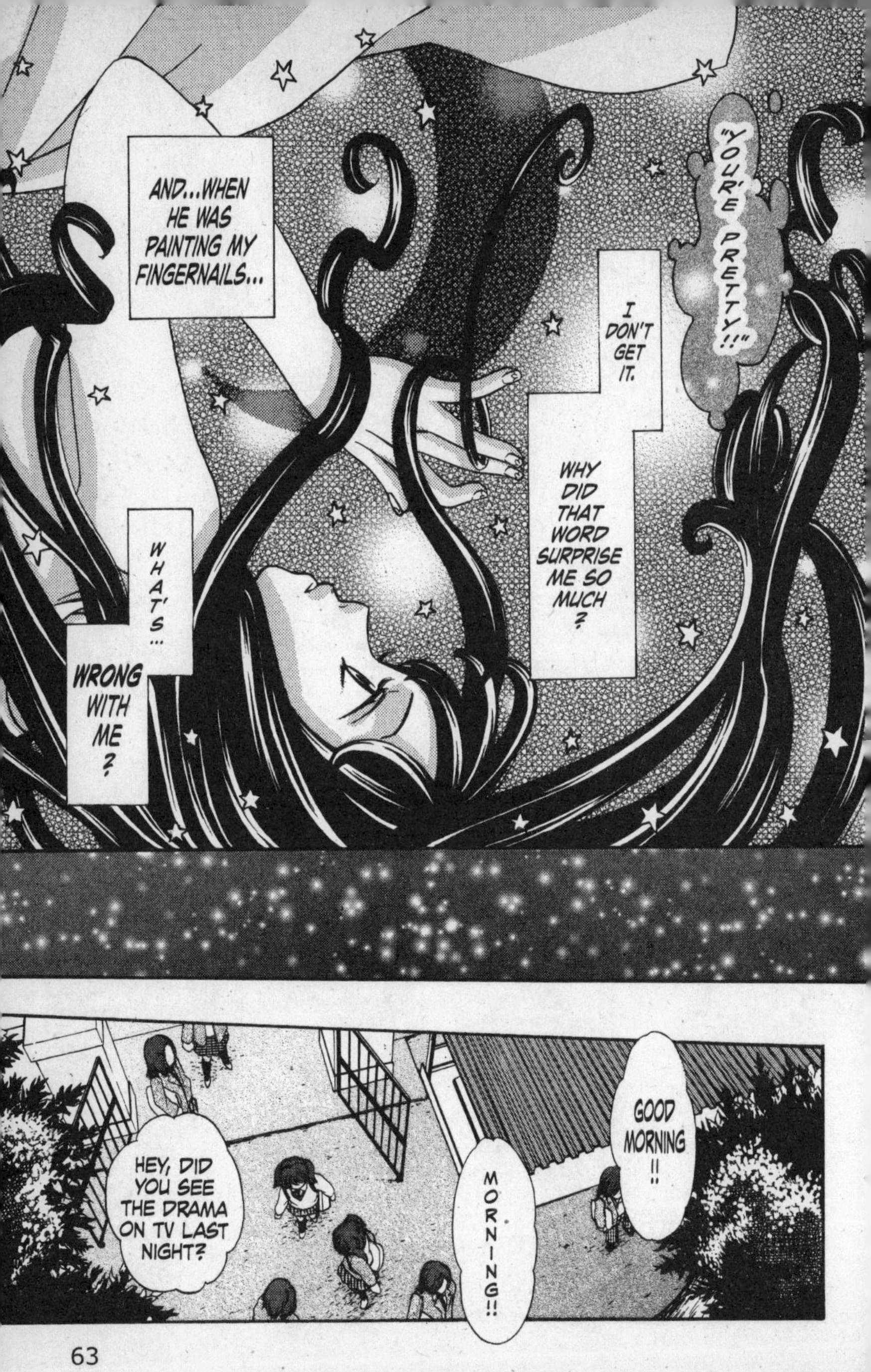
AND...WHEN HE WAS PAINTING MY FINGERNAILS...
"YOU'RE PRETTY!!"
I DON'T GET IT.
WHY DID THAT WORD SURPRISE ME SO MUCH?
WHAT'S...
WRONG WITH ME?
GOOD MORNING!!
MORNING!!
HEY, DID YOU SEE THE DRAMA ON TV LAST NIGHT?

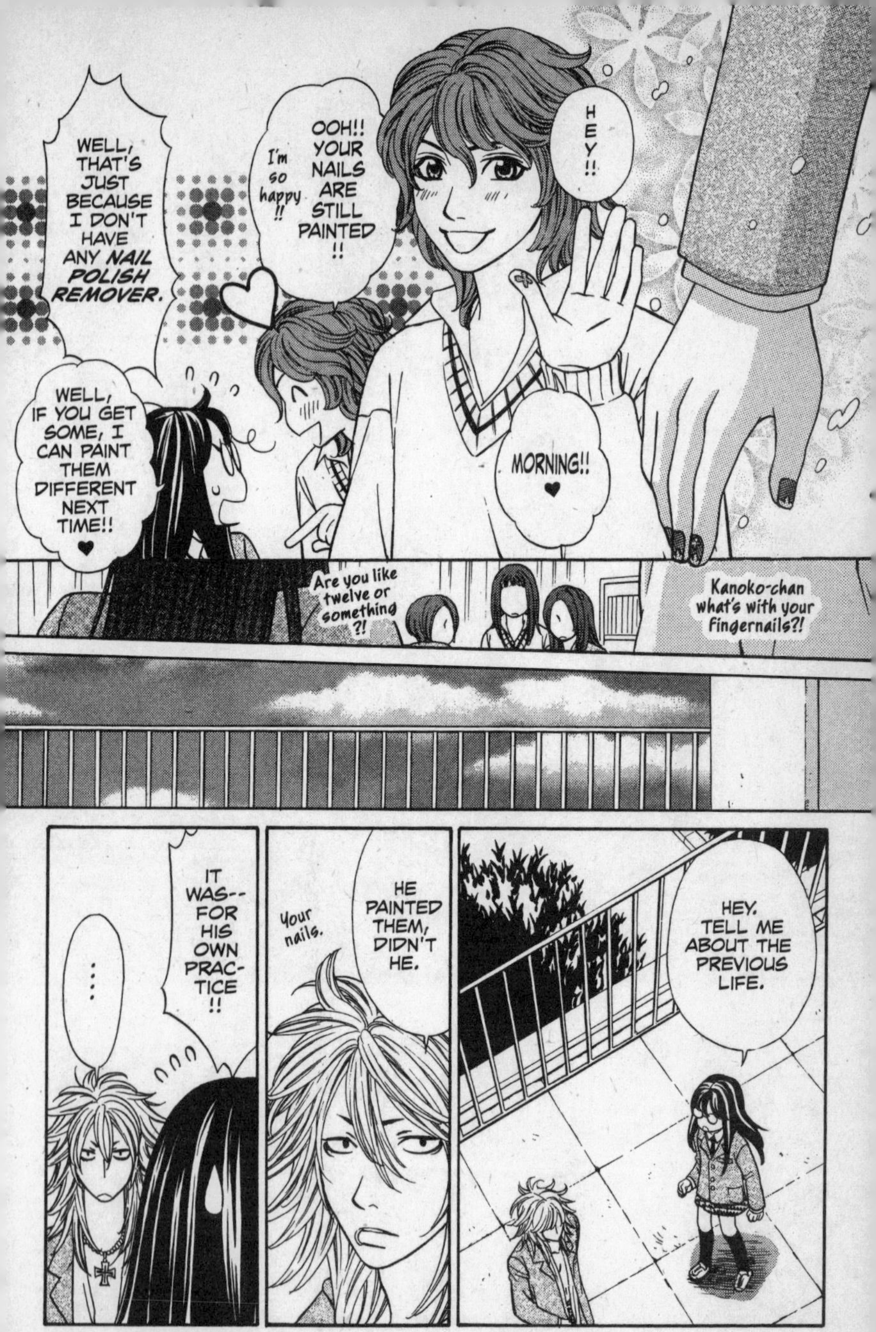
HEY!!
OOH!! YOUR NAILS ARE STILL PAINTED!!
I'm so happy!!
WELL, THAT'S JUST BECAUSE I DON'T HAVE ANY NAIL POLISH REMOVER.
MORNING!! ♥
WELL, IF YOU GET SOME, I CAN PAINT THEM DIFFERENT NEXT TIME!! ♥
Kanoko-chan what's with your fingernails?!
Are you like twelve or something?!
HEY. TELL ME ABOUT THE PREVIOUS LIFE.
HE PAINTED THEM, DIDN'T HE.
Your nails.
IT WAS-- FOR HIS OWN PRACTICE!!
....

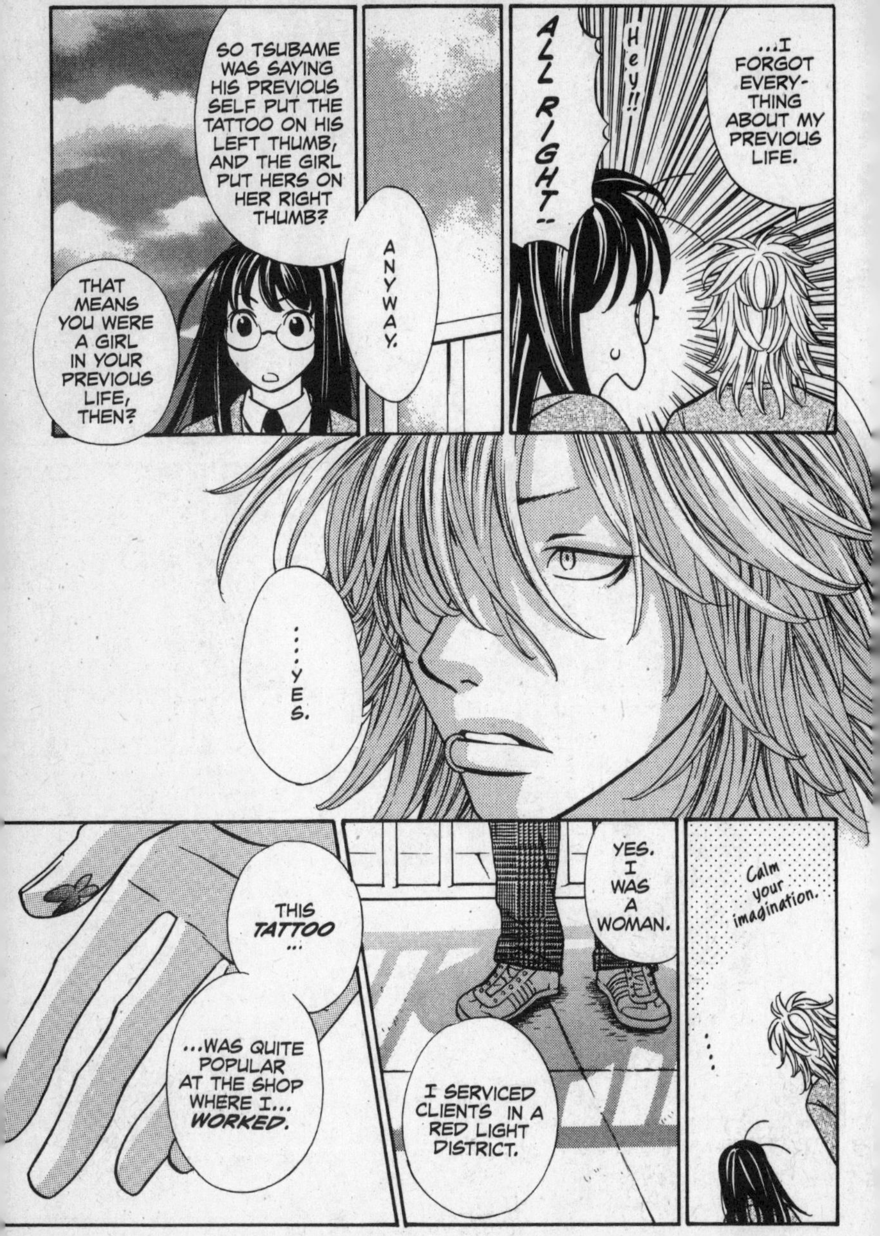
...I FORGOT EVERYTHING ABOUT MY PREVIOUS LIFE.
Hey!!
ALL RIGHT--
ANYWAY.
SO TSUBAME WAS SAYING HIS PREVIOUS SELF PUT THE TATTOO ON HIS LEFT THUMB, AND THE GIRL PUT HERS ON HER RIGHT THUMB?
THAT MEANS YOU WERE A GIRL IN YOUR PREVIOUS LIFE, THEN?
.....YES.
Calm your imagination.
...
YES. I WAS A WOMAN.
I SERVICED CLIENTS IN A RED LIGHT DISTRICT.
THIS *TATTOO*...
...WAS QUITE POPULAR AT THE SHOP WHERE I... *WORKED*.

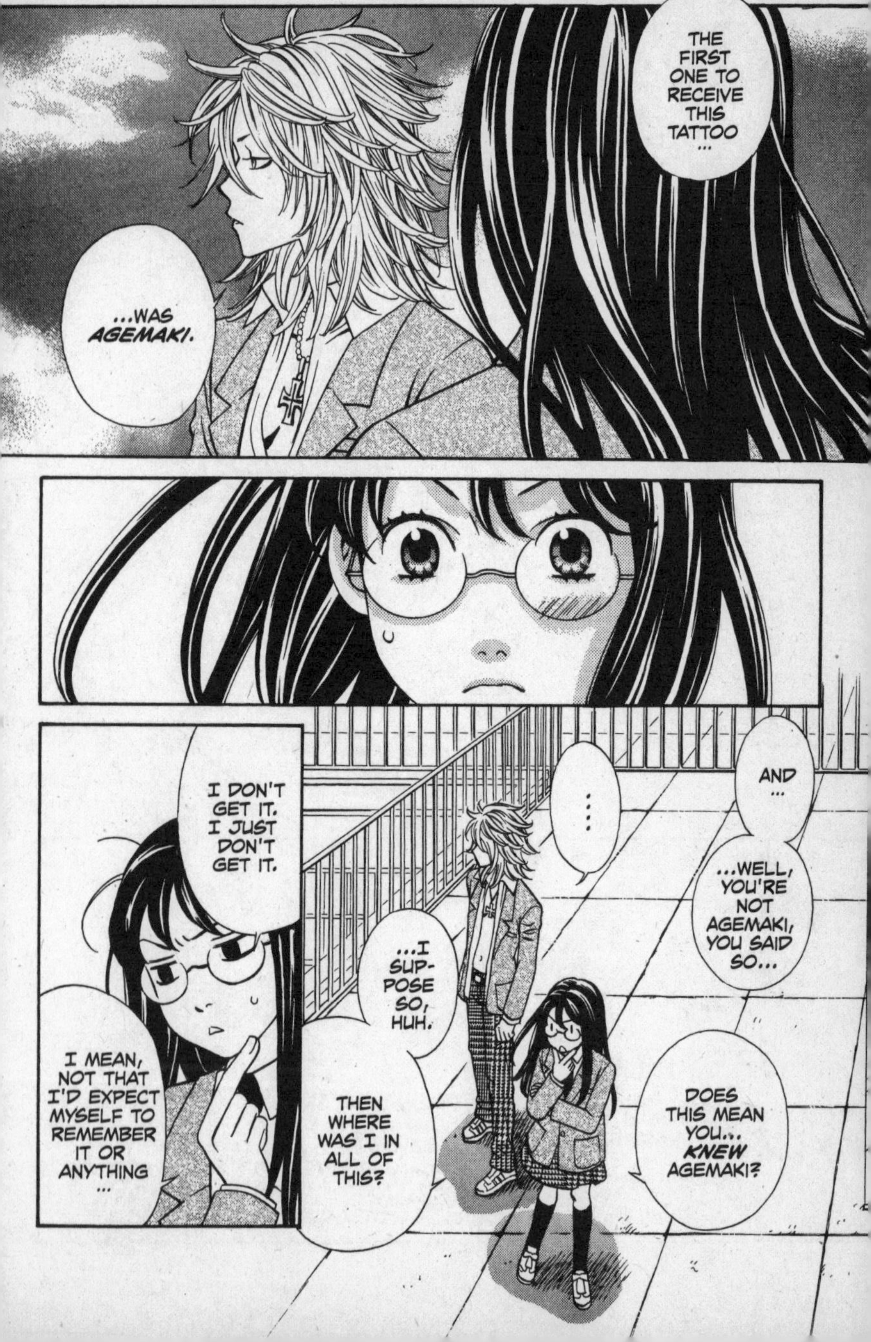
THE FIRST ONE TO RECEIVE THIS TATTOO ...
...WAS *AGEMAKI.*
AND ...
...WELL, YOU'RE NOT AGEMAKI, YOU SAID SO...
....
DOES THIS MEAN YOU... *KNEW* AGEMAKI?
...I SUPPOSE SO, HUH.
THEN WHERE WAS I IN ALL OF THIS?
I DON'T GET IT. I JUST DON'T GET IT.
I MEAN, NOT THAT I'D EXPECT MYSELF TO REMEMBER IT OR ANYTHING ...

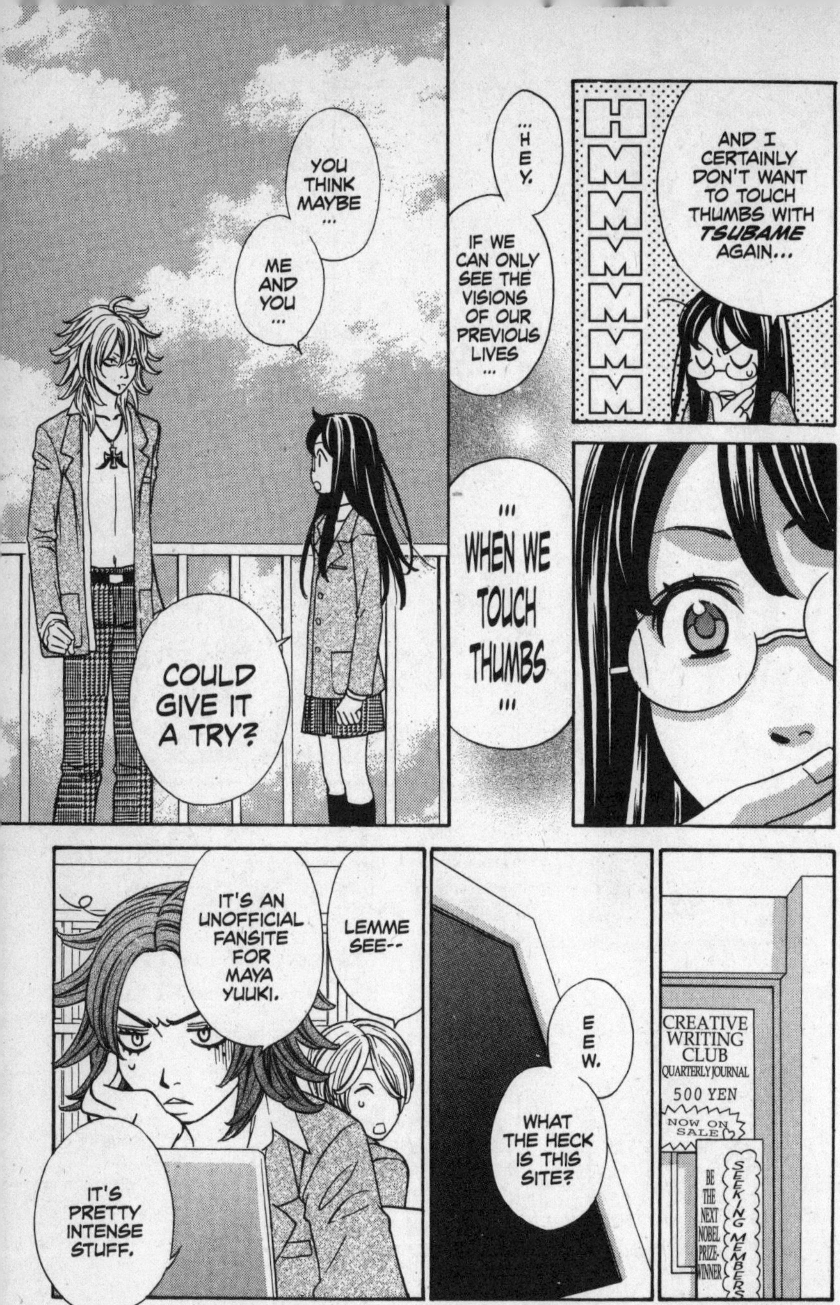

AND I CERTAINLY DON'T WANT TO TOUCH THUMBS WITH ***TSUBAME*** AGAIN...
HMMMMMM
...HEY.
IF WE CAN ONLY SEE THE VISIONS OF OUR PREVIOUS LIVES ...
...WHEN WE TOUCH THUMBS...
YOU THINK MAYBE ...
ME AND YOU ...
COULD GIVE IT A TRY?
CREATIVE WRITING CLUB
QUARTERLY JOURNAL
500 YEN
NOW ON SALE
BE THE NEXT NOBEL PRIZE-WINNER
SEEKING MEMBERS
EEW.
WHAT THE HECK IS THIS SITE?
LEMME SEE--
IT'S AN UNOFFICIAL FANSITE FOR MAYA YUUKI.
IT'S PRETTY INTENSE STUFF.

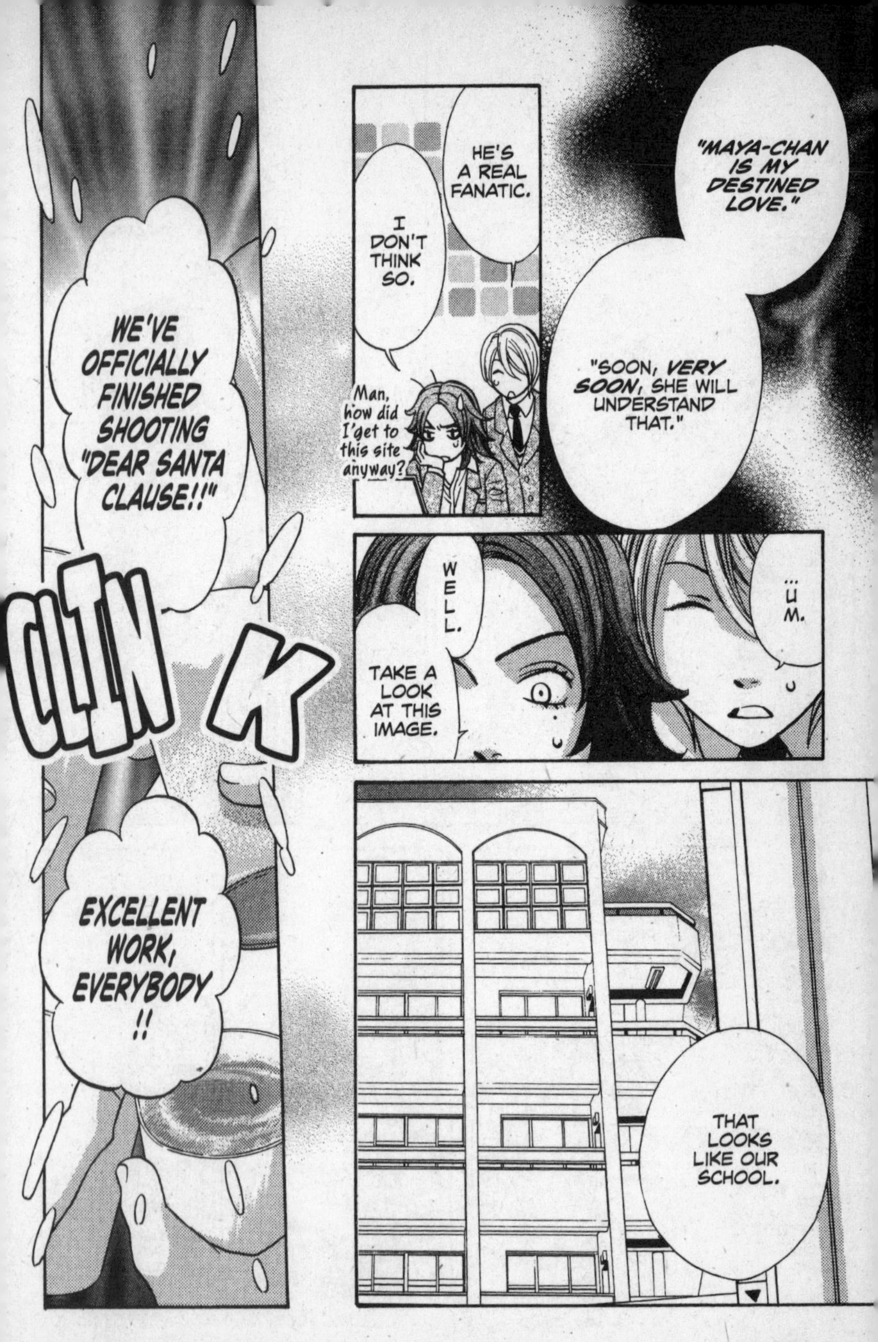
"MAYA-CHAN IS MY DESTINED LOVE."
"SOON, VERY SOON, SHE WILL UNDERSTAND THAT."
HE'S A REAL FANATIC.
I DON'T THINK SO.
Man, how did I get to this site anyway?
...UM.
WELL.
TAKE A LOOK AT THIS IMAGE.
THAT LOOKS LIKE OUR SCHOOL.
WE'VE OFFICIALLY FINISHED SHOOTING "DEAR SANTA CLAUSE!!"
CLINK
EXCELLENT WORK, EVERYBODY!!

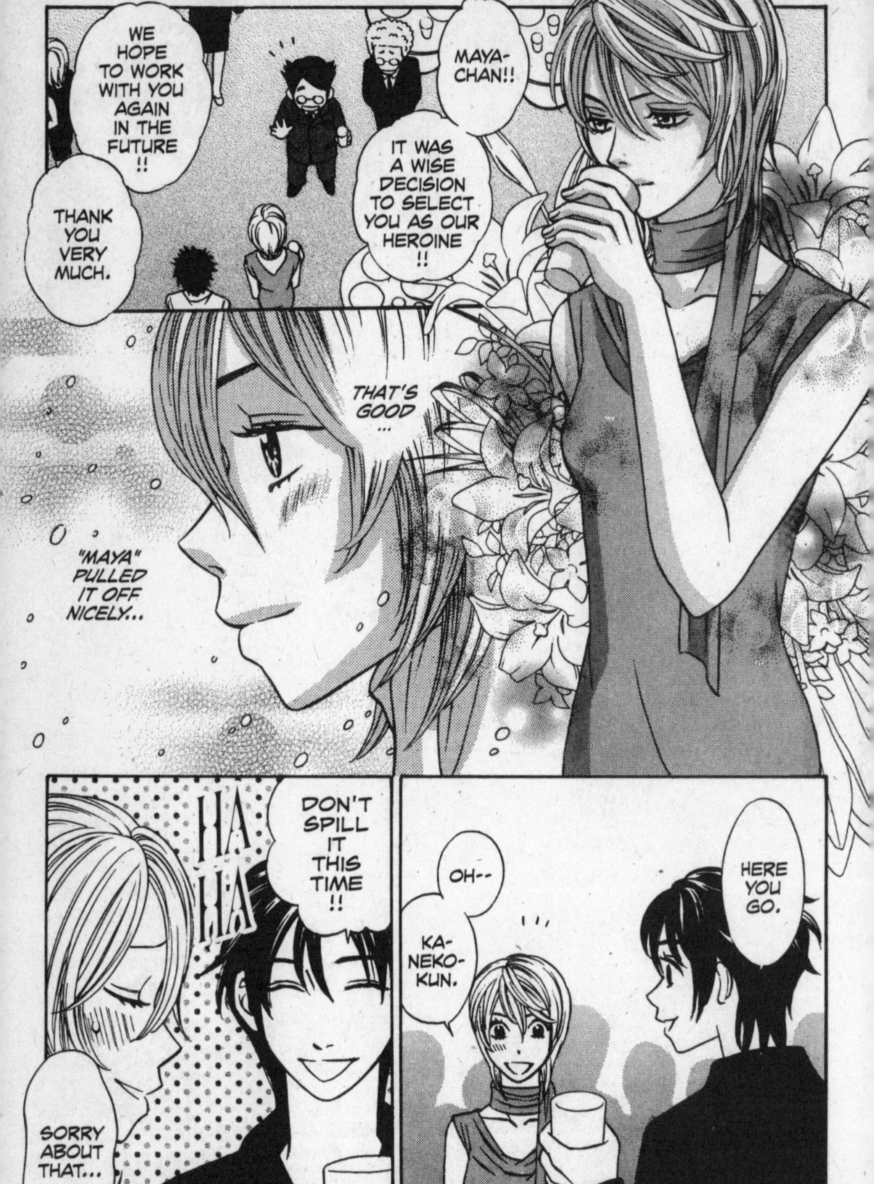
MAYA-CHAN!!
IT WAS A WISE DECISION TO SELECT YOU AS OUR HEROINE !!
WE HOPE TO WORK WITH YOU AGAIN IN THE FUTURE !!
THANK YOU VERY MUCH.
THAT'S GOOD ...
"MAYA" PULLED IT OFF NICELY...
HERE YOU GO.
OH--
KA-NEKO-KUN.
DON'T SPILL IT THIS TIME !!
HA HA
SORRY ABOUT THAT...

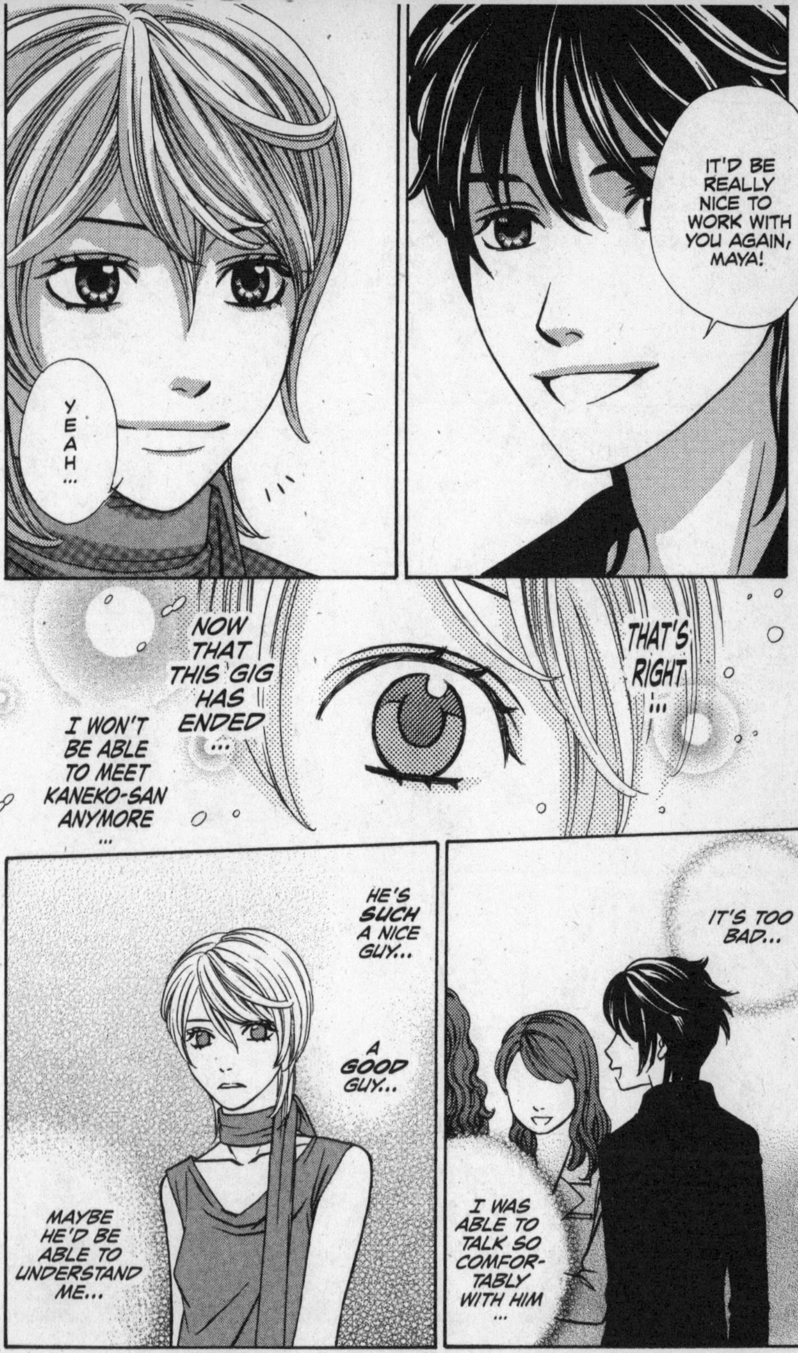
IT'D BE REALLY NICE TO WORK WITH YOU AGAIN, MAYA!
YEAH...
THAT'S RIGHT...
NOW THAT THIS GIG HAS ENDED...
I WON'T BE ABLE TO MEET KANEKO-SAN ANYMORE...
IT'S TOO BAD...
I WAS ABLE TO TALK SO COMFORTABLY WITH HIM...
HE'S SUCH A NICE GUY...
A GOOD GUY...
MAYBE HE'D BE ABLE TO UNDERSTAND ME...

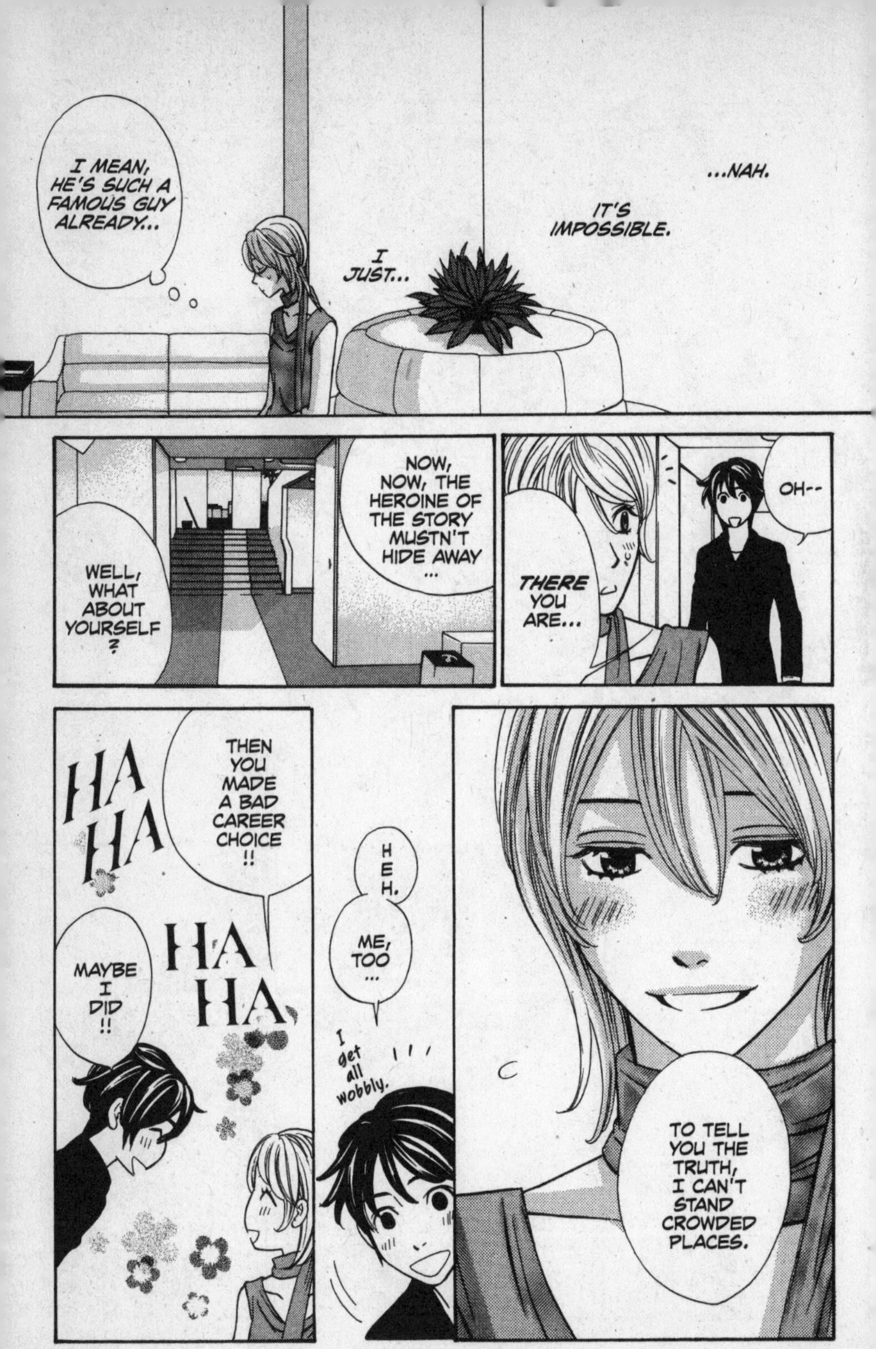
...NAH.
IT'S IMPOSSIBLE.
I JUST...
I MEAN, HE'S SUCH A FAMOUS GUY ALREADY...
OH--
THERE YOU ARE...
NOW, NOW, THE HEROINE OF THE STORY MUSTN'T HIDE AWAY...
WELL, WHAT ABOUT YOURSELF?
TO TELL YOU THE TRUTH, I CAN'T STAND CROWDED PLACES.
HEH.
ME, TOO...
I get all wobbly.
THEN YOU MADE A BAD CAREER CHOICE!!
HA HA
HA HA
MAYBE I DID!!

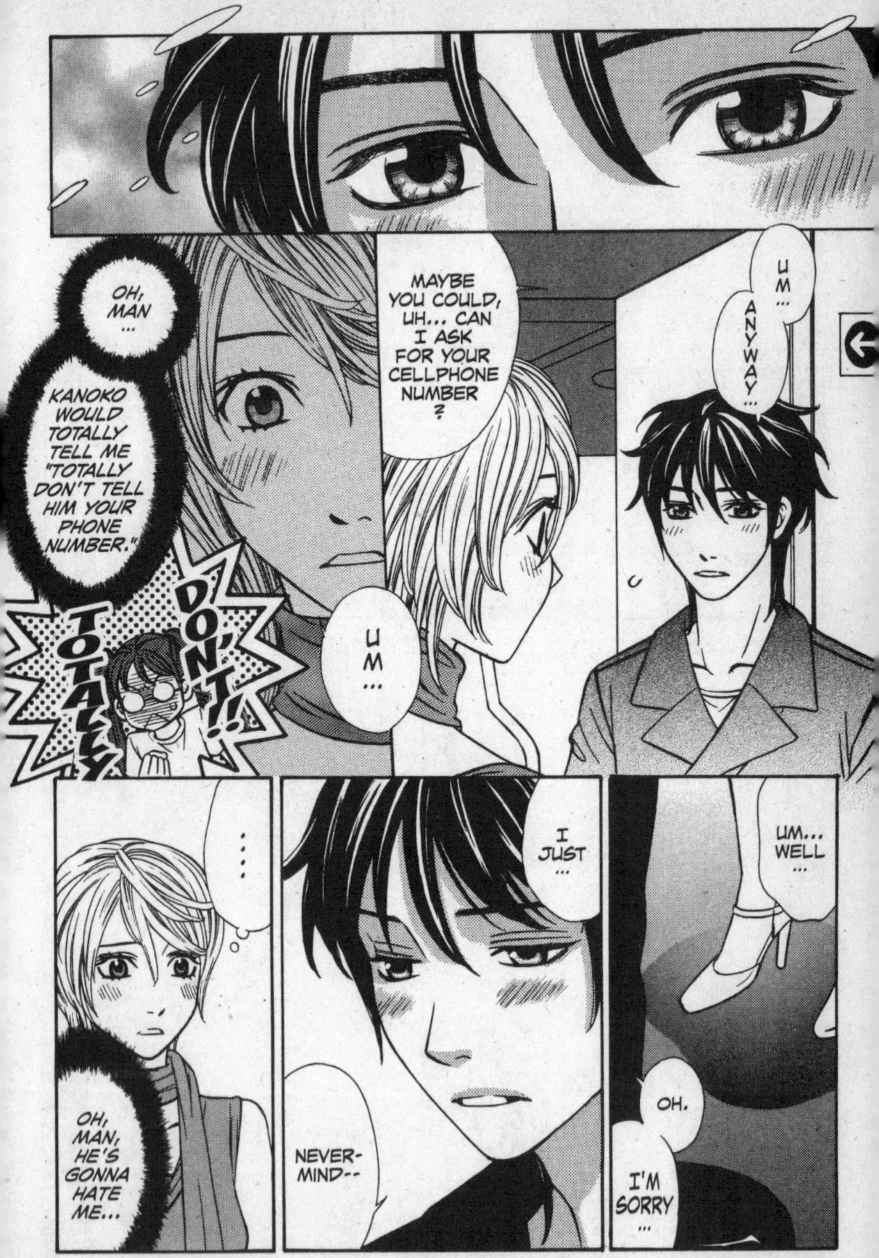
UM...
ANYWAY...
MAYBE YOU COULD, UH... CAN I ASK FOR YOUR CELLPHONE NUMBER?
UM...
OH, MAN...
KANOKO WOULD TOTALLY TELL ME "TOTALLY DON'T TELL HIM YOUR PHONE NUMBER."
TOTALLY DON'T!!
UM... WELL...
OH.
I'M SORRY...
I JUST...
NEVER-MIND--
....
OH, MAN, HE'S GONNA HATE ME...

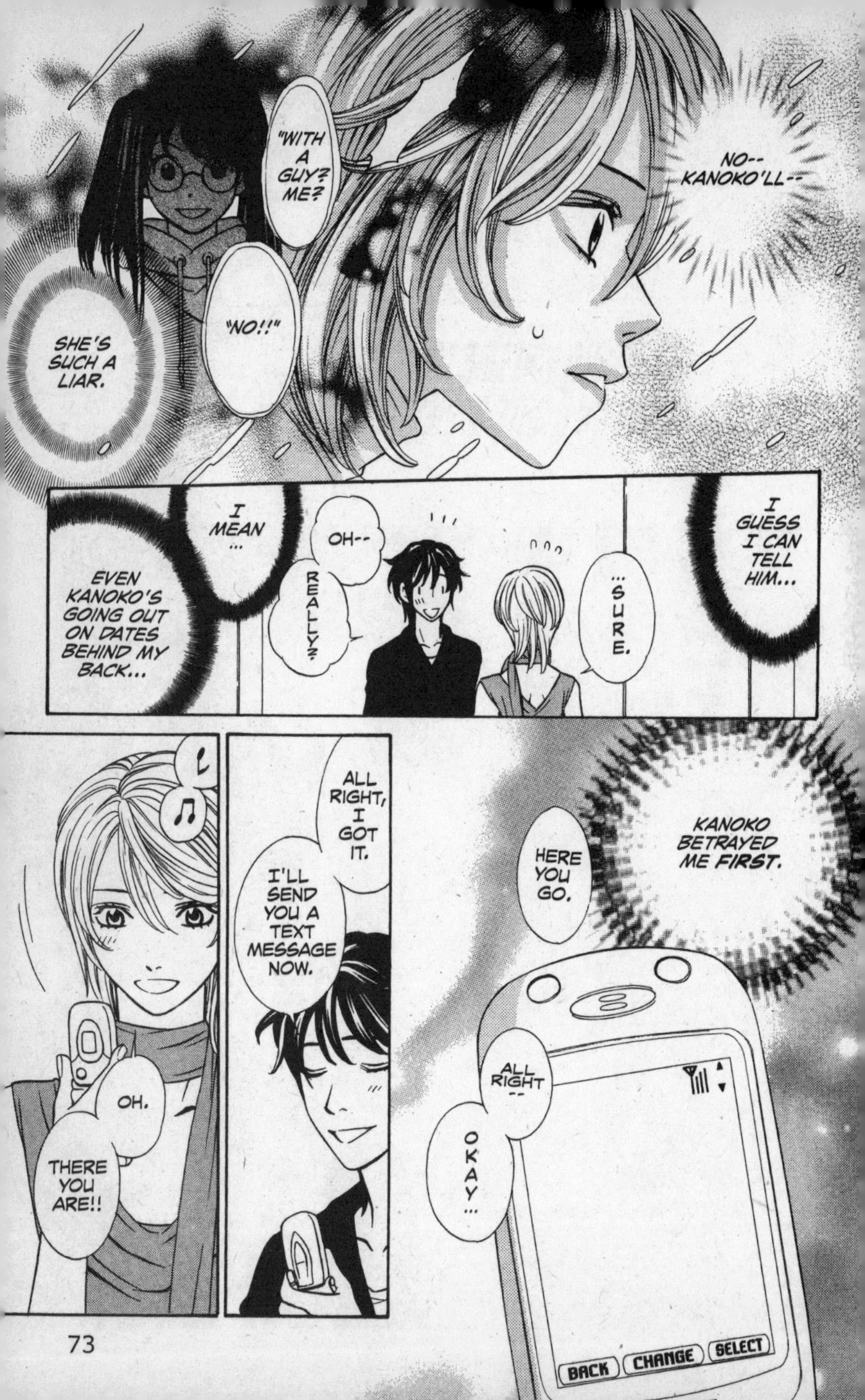
NO-- KANOKO'LL--
"WITH A GUY? ME?
"NO!!"
SHE'S SUCH A LIAR.
I GUESS I CAN TELL HIM...
...SURE.
OH--
REALLY?
I MEAN...
EVEN KANOKO'S GOING OUT ON DATES BEHIND MY BACK...
KANOKO BETRAYED ME FIRST.
HERE YOU GO.
ALL RIGHT--
OKAY...
BACK
CHANGE
SELECT
ALL RIGHT, I GOT IT.
I'LL SEND YOU A TEXT MESSAGE NOW.
OH.
THERE YOU ARE!!

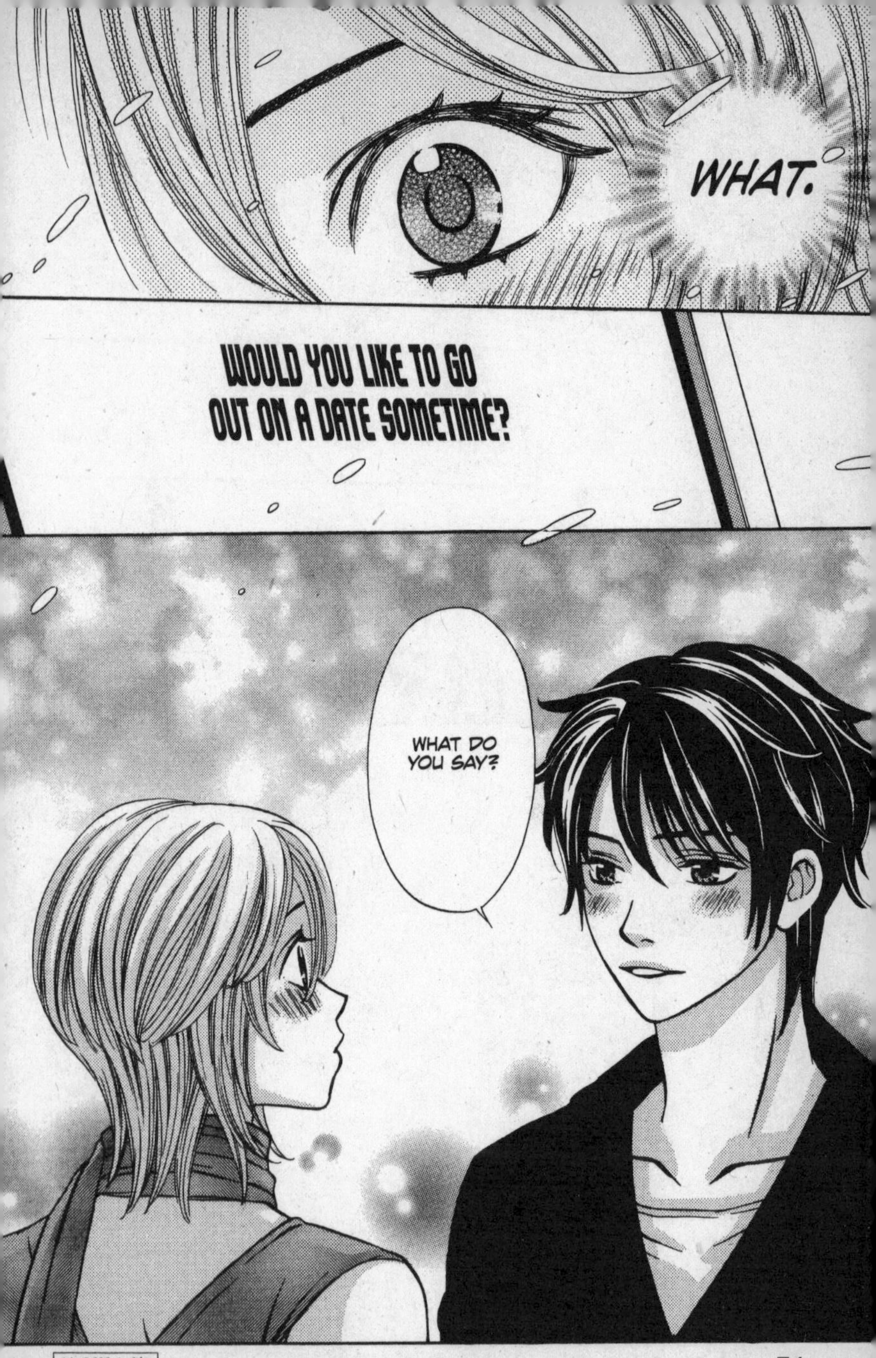
WHAT.
WOULD YOU LIKE TO GO OUT ON A DATE SOMETIME?
WHAT DO YOU SAY?

CHAPTER 1/END.

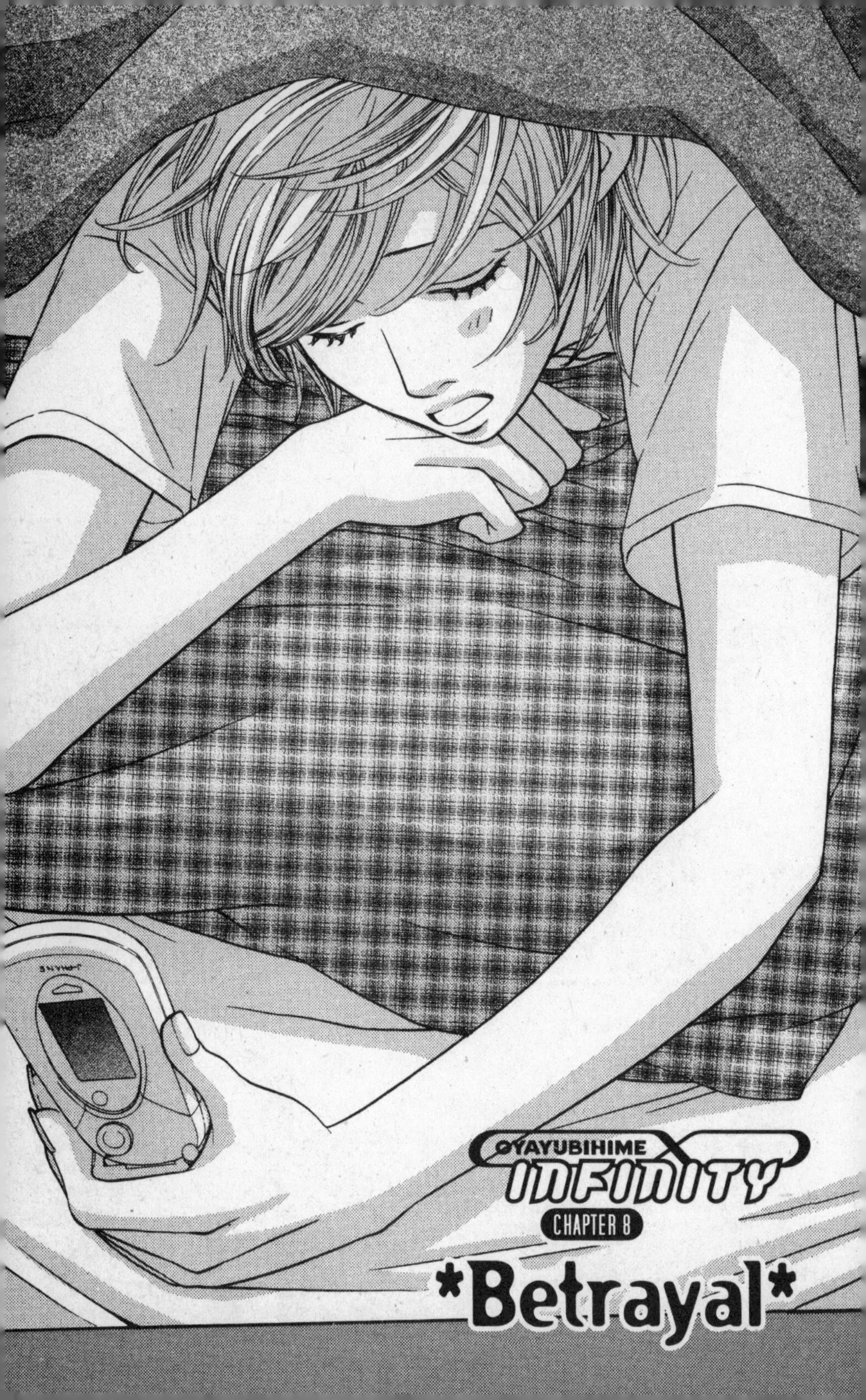
OYAYUBIHIME
INFINITY
CHAPTER 8
Betrayal

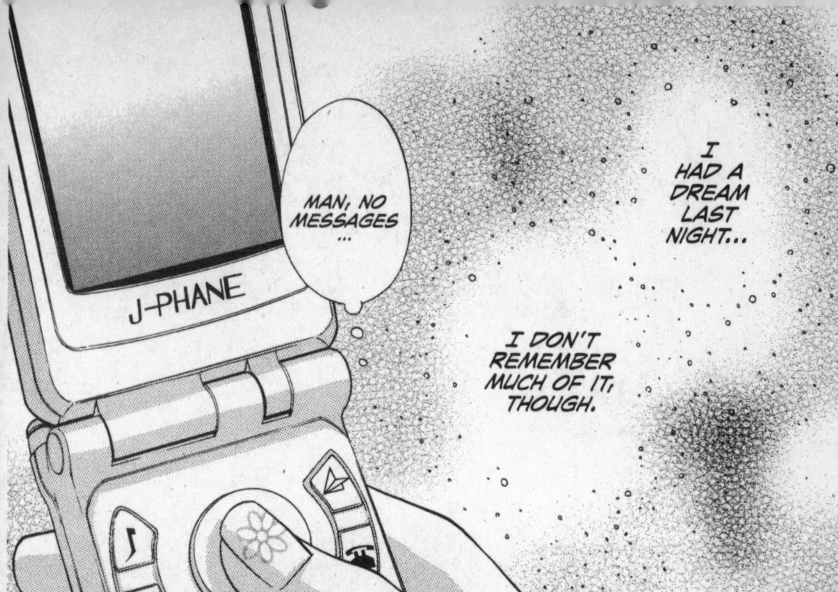
I HAD A DREAM LAST NIGHT...
I DON'T REMEMBER MUCH OF IT, THOUGH.
MAN, NO MESSAGES...
J-PHANE
MAYU ISN'T TEXTING SO MUCH LATELY.
I DON'T EVEN GET TO TALK TO HER AT HOME ANYMORE.
DID I DO SOMETHING TO OFFEND HER?
YOU'RE ALWAYS SENDING TEXTS, HUH, KANOKO?

Character Guide: 5

Kiki Nomura

Birthday: 8/2

Blood Type: O

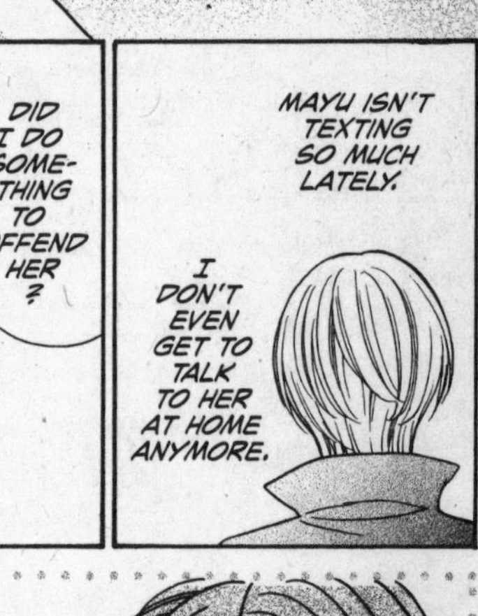
Hi. I'm seventeen.

Kiki is the school literary magazine editor and an aspiring novelist. Since appearing on the scene, the story's progress has sped up nicely! She seems to be kind of weirdly like a father to the characters, spurring them on when they get lazy. Either way, the author really likes her, so give her a hand!!

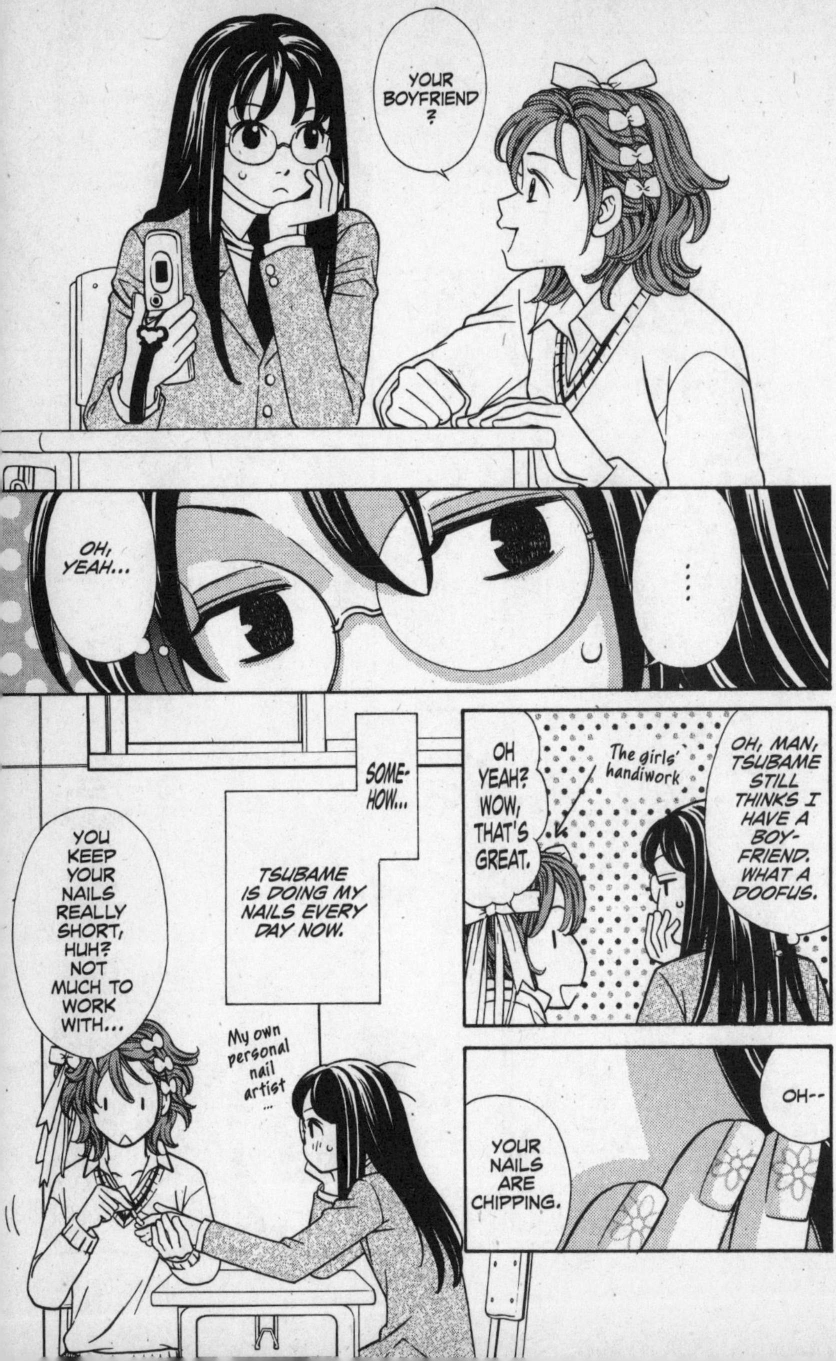
YOUR BOYFRIEND?
....
OH, YEAH...
OH, MAN, TSUBAME STILL THINKS I HAVE A BOY-FRIEND. WHAT A DOOFUS.
The girls' handiwork
OH YEAH? WOW, THAT'S GREAT.
OH--
YOUR NAILS ARE CHIPPING.
SOME-HOW...
TSUBAME IS DOING MY NAILS EVERY DAY NOW.
YOU KEEP YOUR NAILS REALLY SHORT, HUH? NOT MUCH TO WORK WITH...
My own personal nail artist...

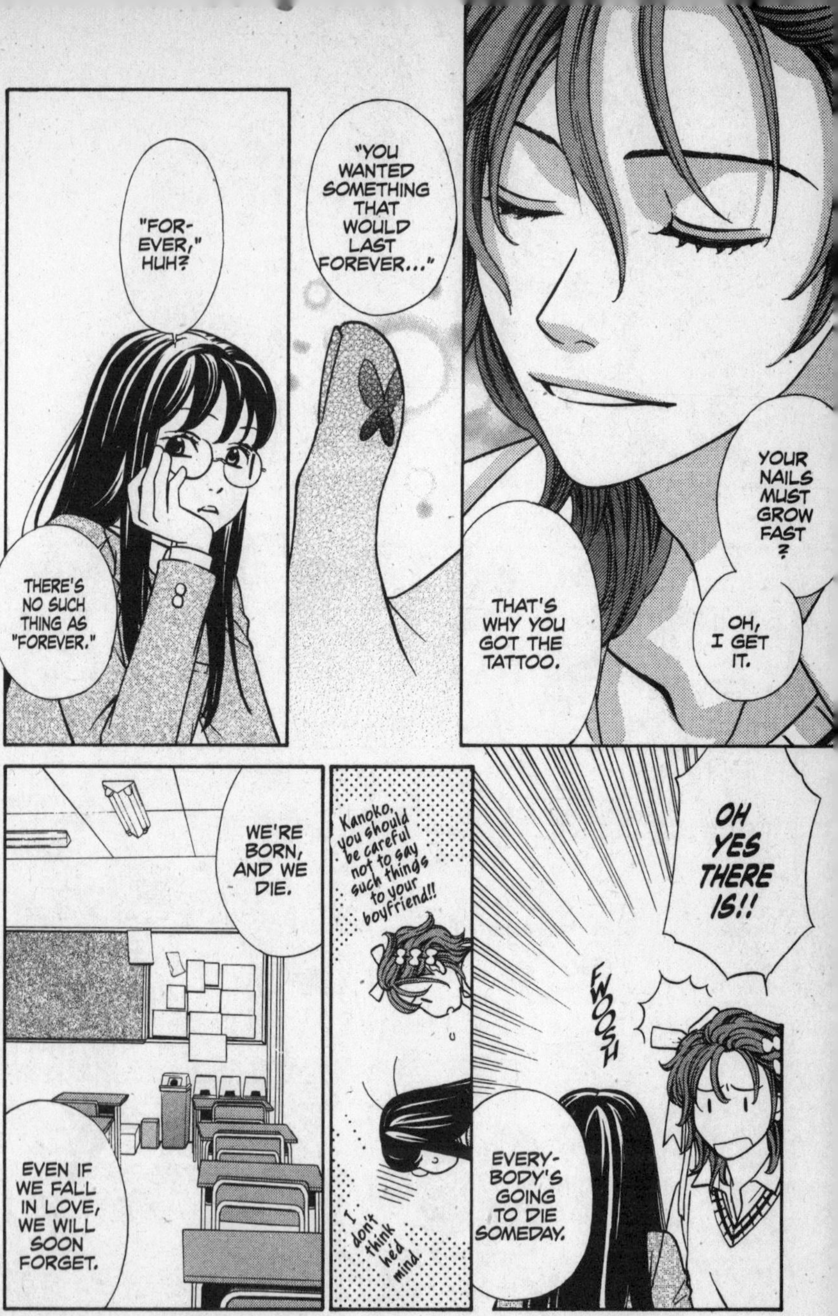
YOUR NAILS MUST GROW FAST?
OH, I GET IT.
THAT'S WHY YOU GOT THE TATTOO.
"YOU WANTED SOMETHING THAT WOULD LAST FOREVER..."
"FOR-EVER," HUH?
THERE'S NO SUCH THING AS "FOREVER."
OH YES THERE IS!!
FWOOSH
EVERY-BODY'S GOING TO DIE SOMEDAY.
Kanoko, you should be careful not to say such things to your boyfriend!!
I don't think he'd mind.
WE'RE BORN, AND WE DIE.
EVEN IF WE FALL IN LOVE, WE WILL SOON FORGET.

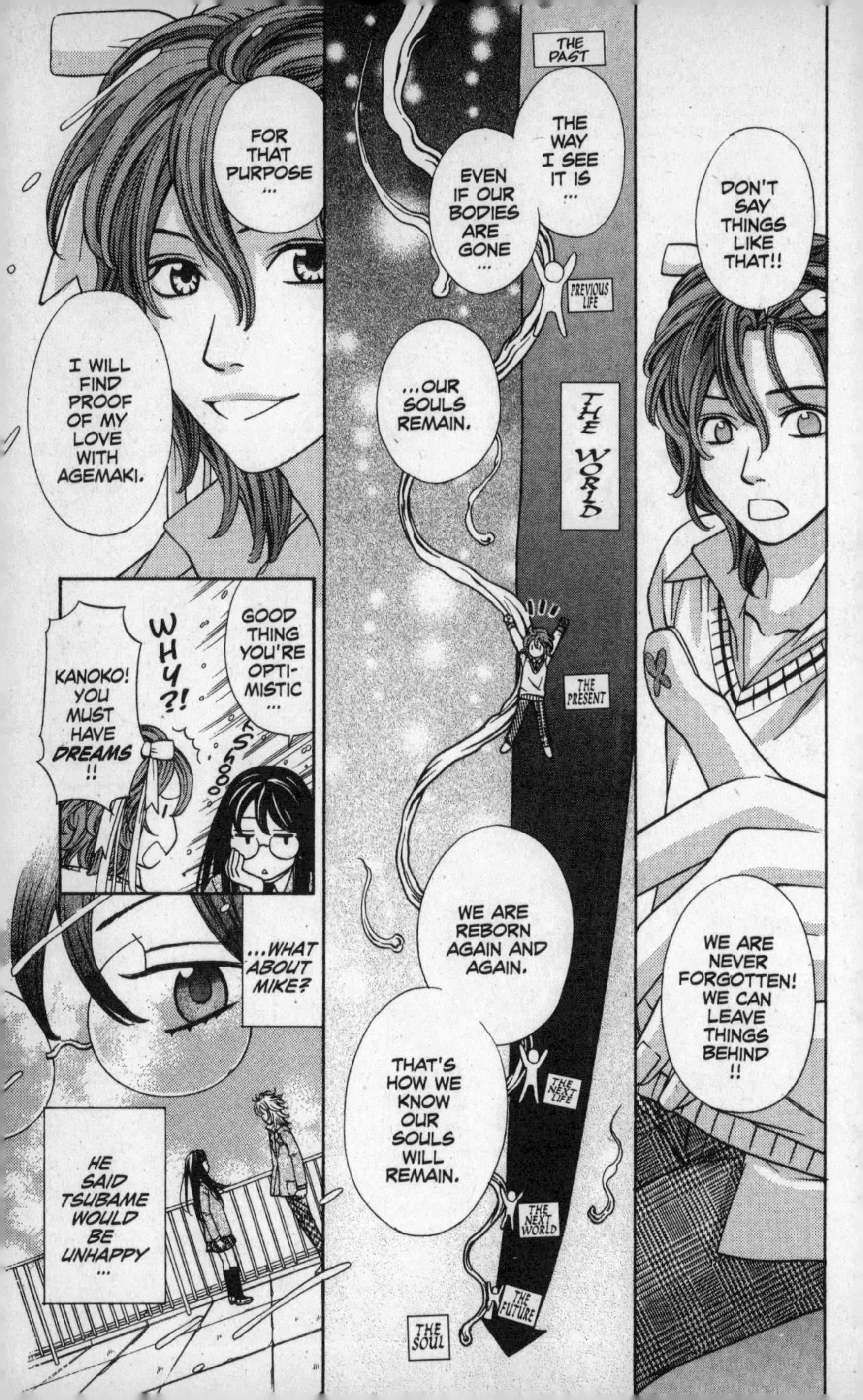
DON'T SAY THINGS LIKE THAT!!
WE ARE NEVER FORGOTTEN! WE CAN LEAVE THINGS BEHIND!!
THE PAST
THE WAY I SEE IT IS...
EVEN IF OUR BODIES ARE GONE...
PREVIOUS LIFE
...OUR SOULS REMAIN.
THE WORLD
THE PRESENT
WE ARE REBORN AGAIN AND AGAIN.
THAT'S HOW WE KNOW OUR SOULS WILL REMAIN.
THE NEXT LIFE
THE NEXT WORLD
THE FUTURE
THE SOUL
FOR THAT PURPOSE...
I WILL FIND PROOF OF MY LOVE WITH AGEMAKI.
GOOD THING YOU'RE OPTIMISTIC...
WHY?!
KANOKO! YOU MUST HAVE *DREAMS*!!
FSHOOO
...WHAT ABOUT MIKE?
HE SAID TSUBAME WOULD BE UNHAPPY...

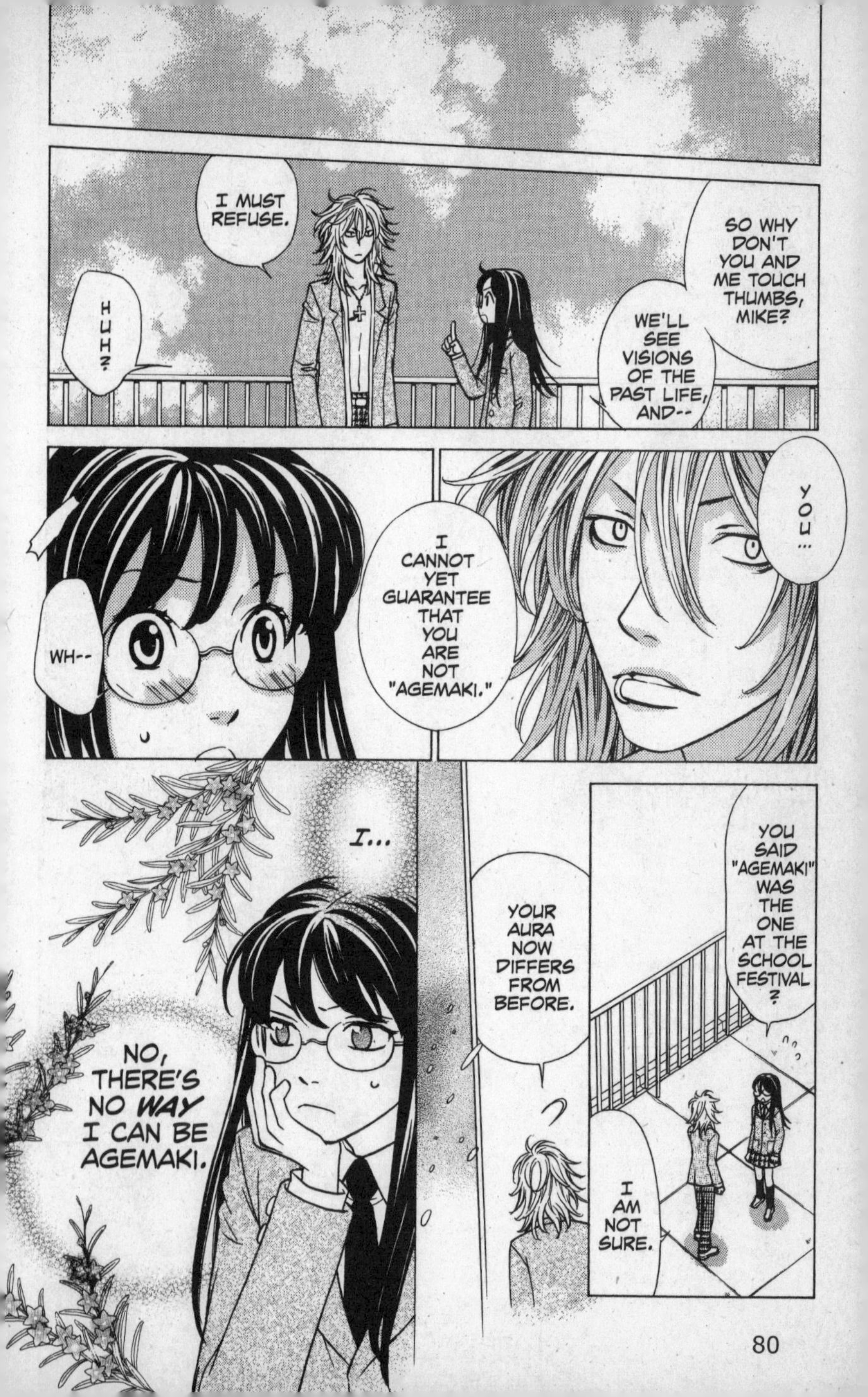
SO WHY DON'T YOU AND ME TOUCH THUMBS, MIKE?
WE'LL SEE VISIONS OF THE PAST LIFE, AND--
I MUST REFUSE.
HUH?
YOU...
I CANNOT YET GUARANTEE THAT YOU ARE NOT "AGEMAKI."
WH--
YOU SAID "AGEMAKI" WAS THE ONE AT THE SCHOOL FESTIVAL?
YOUR AURA NOW DIFFERS FROM BEFORE.
I AM NOT SURE.
I...
NO, THERE'S NO *WAY* I CAN BE AGEMAKI.

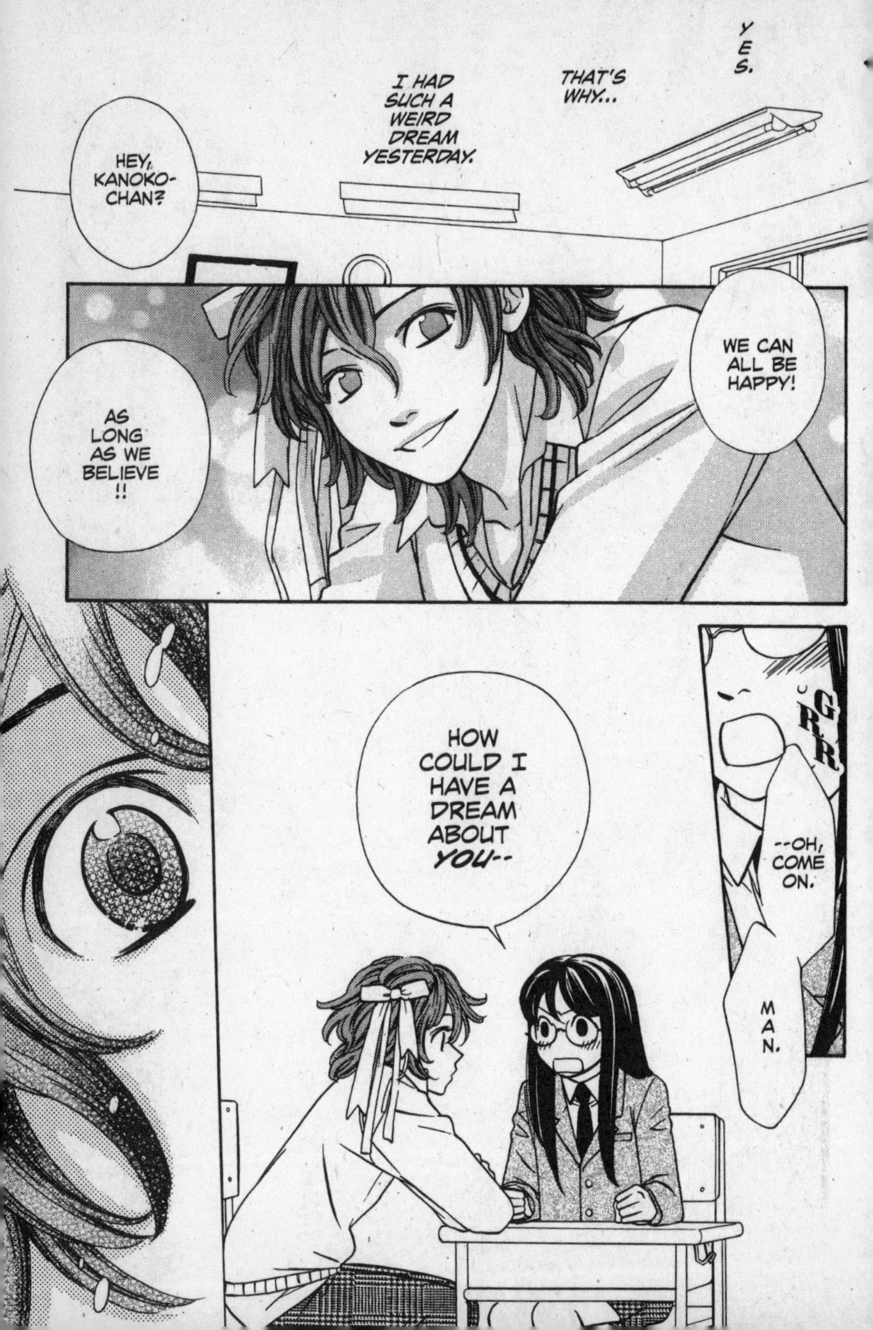

YES.
THAT'S WHY...
I HAD SUCH A WEIRD DREAM YESTERDAY.
HEY, KANOKO-CHAN?
WE CAN ALL BE HAPPY!
AS LONG AS WE BELIEVE!!
HOW COULD I HAVE A DREAM ABOUT *YOU*--
GRRR
--OH, COME ON.
MAN.

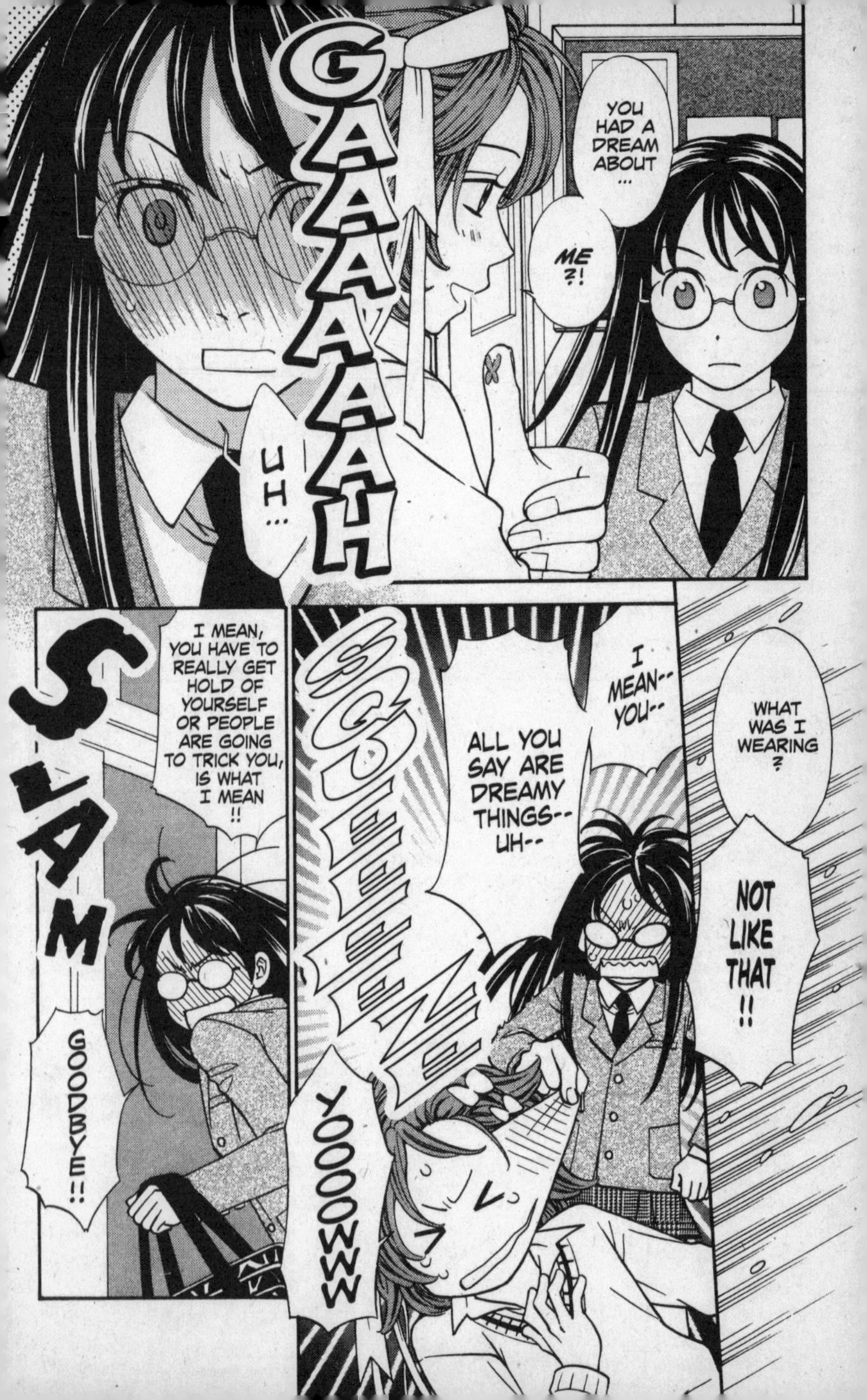
YOU HAD A DREAM ABOUT ...
ME?!
GAAAAAAH
UH...
WHAT WAS I WEARING?
NOT LIKE THAT!!
I MEAN-- YOU--
ALL YOU SAY ARE DREAMY THINGS-- UH--
SQUEEEEZE
YOOOOWWW
I MEAN, YOU HAVE TO REALLY GET HOLD OF YOURSELF OR PEOPLE ARE GOING TO TRICK YOU, IS WHAT I MEAN!!
SLAM
GOODBYE!!

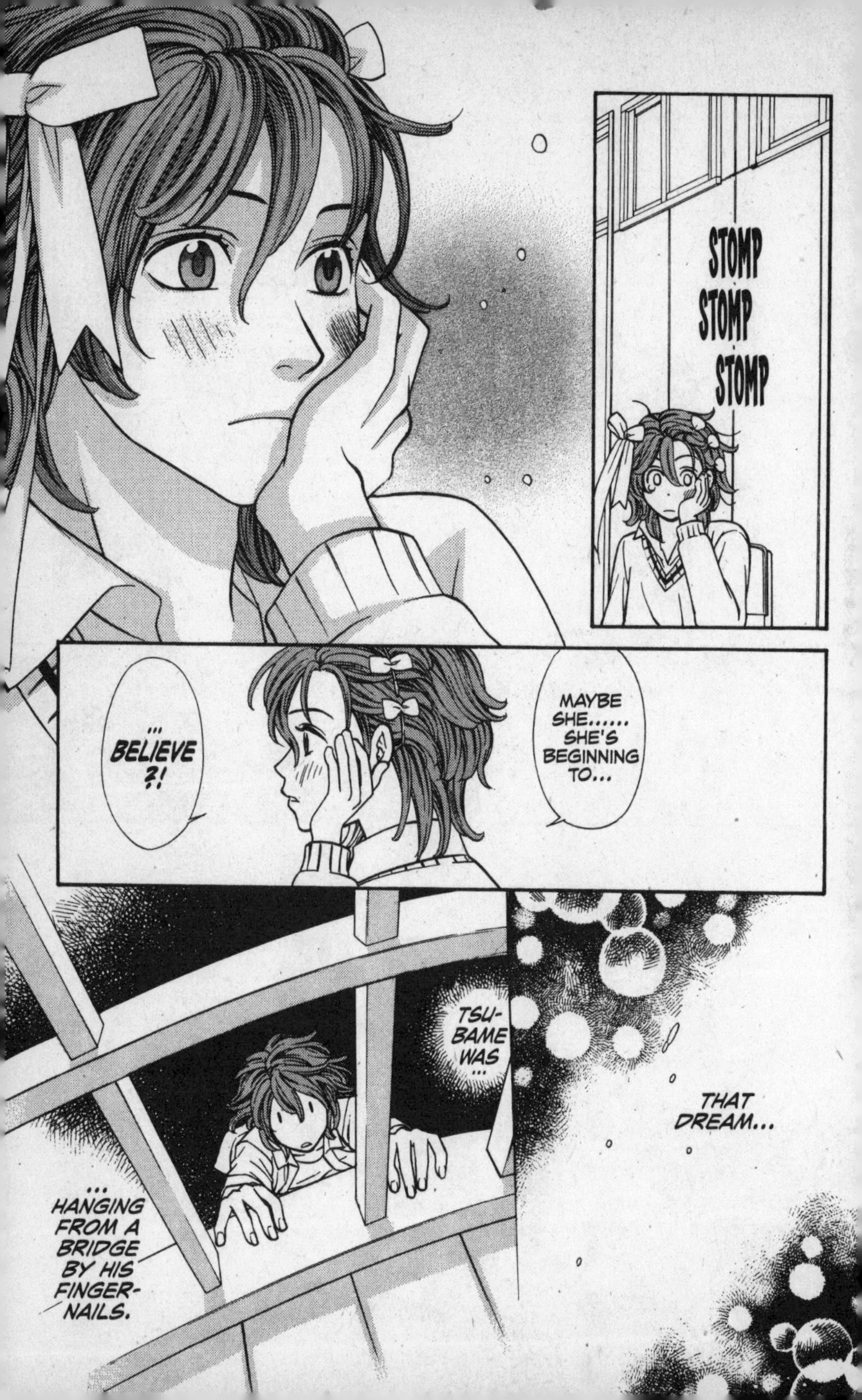
STOMP STOMP STOMP
MAYBE SHE...... SHE'S BEGINNING TO...
... BELIEVE ?!
THAT DREAM...
TSU-BAME WAS ...
... HANGING FROM A BRIDGE BY HIS FINGER-NAILS.

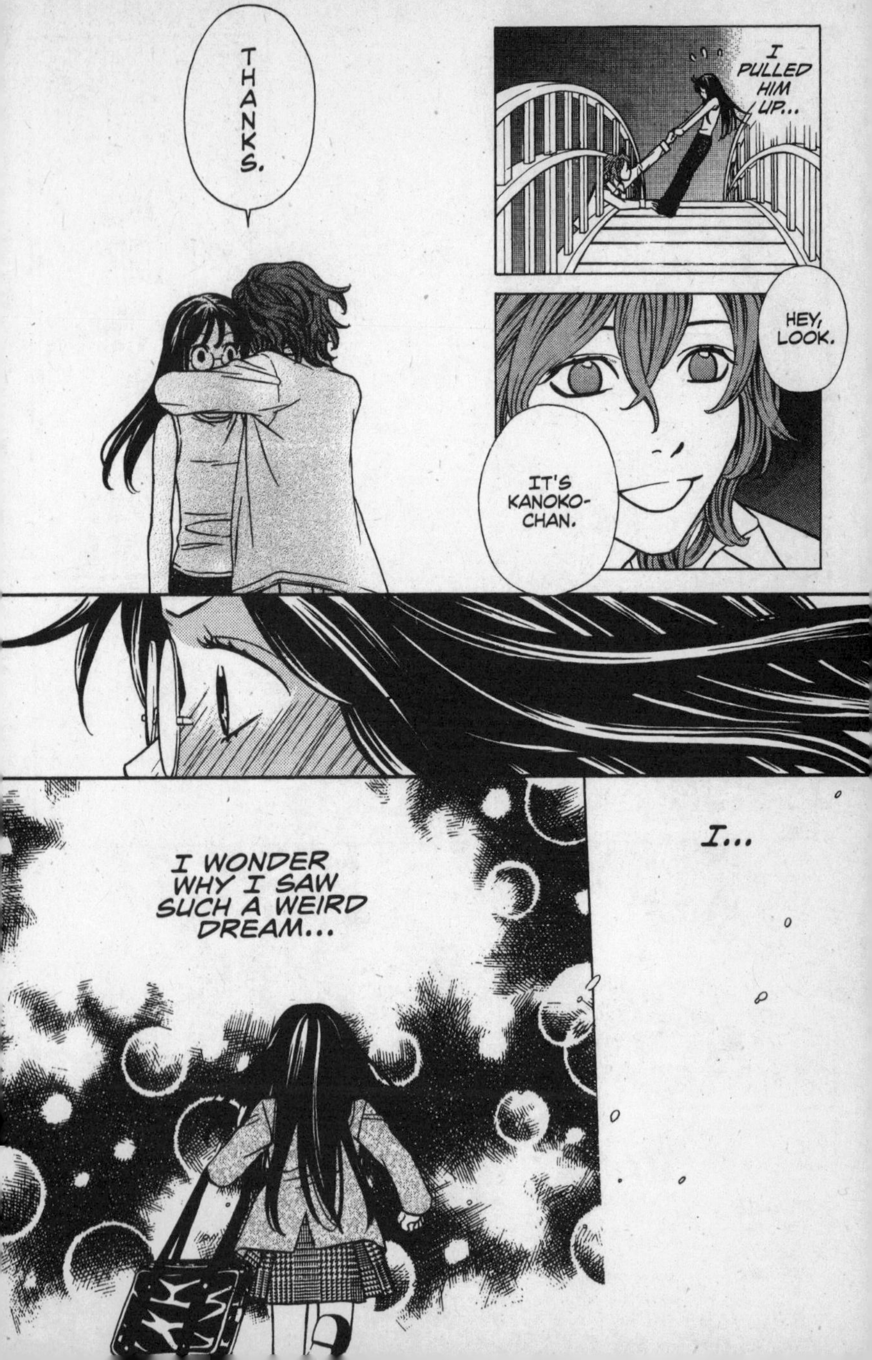
I PULLED HIM UP...
HEY, LOOK.
IT'S KANOKO-CHAN.
THANKS.
I...
I WONDER WHY I SAW SUCH A WEIRD DREAM...

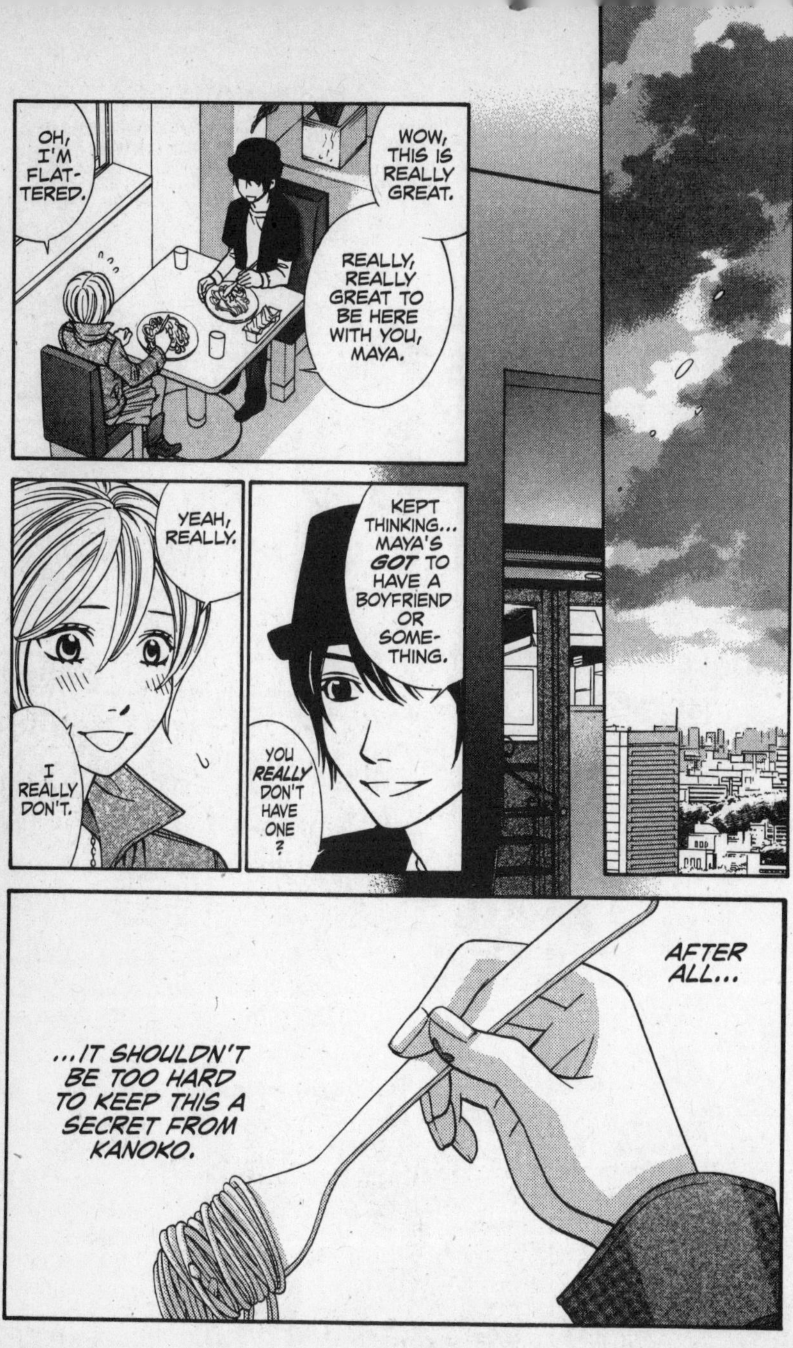
WOW, THIS IS REALLY GREAT.
REALLY, REALLY GREAT TO BE HERE WITH YOU, MAYA.
OH, I'M FLAT-TERED.
KEPT THINKING... MAYA'S *GOT* TO HAVE A BOYFRIEND OR SOME-THING.
YOU *REALLY* DON'T HAVE ONE?
YEAH, REALLY.
I REALLY DON'T.
AFTER ALL...
...IT SHOULDN'T BE TOO HARD TO KEEP THIS A SECRET FROM KANOKO.

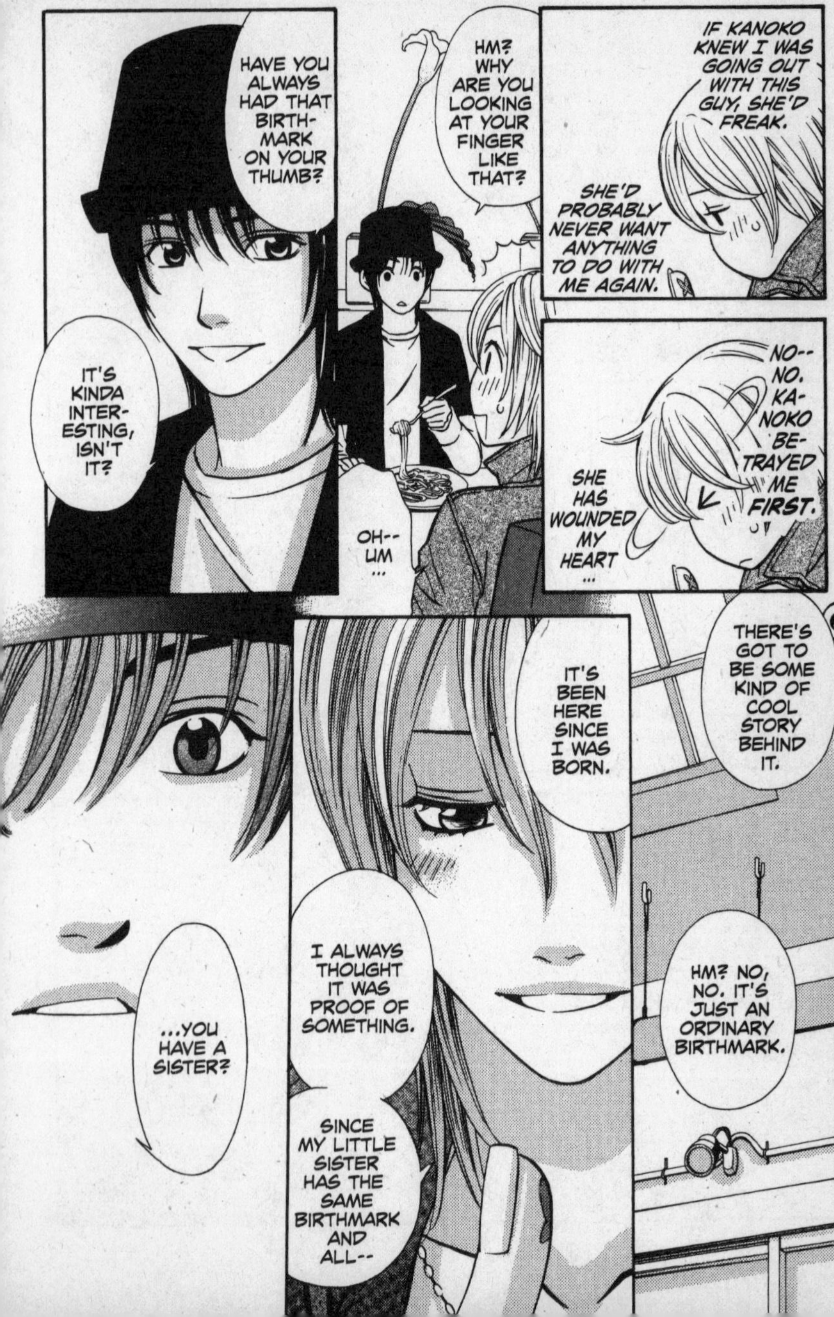
IF KANOKO KNEW I WAS GOING OUT WITH THIS GUY, SHE'D FREAK.
SHE'D PROBABLY NEVER WANT ANYTHING TO DO WITH ME AGAIN.
NO-- NO. KANOKO BETRAYED ME FIRST.
SHE HAS WOUNDED MY HEART...
HM? WHY ARE YOU LOOKING AT YOUR FINGER LIKE THAT?
OH-- UM...
HAVE YOU ALWAYS HAD THAT BIRTHMARK ON YOUR THUMB?
IT'S KINDA INTERESTING, ISN'T IT?
THERE'S GOT TO BE SOME KIND OF COOL STORY BEHIND IT.
HM? NO, NO. IT'S JUST AN ORDINARY BIRTHMARK.
IT'S BEEN HERE SINCE I WAS BORN.
I ALWAYS THOUGHT IT WAS PROOF OF SOMETHING.
SINCE MY LITTLE SISTER HAS THE SAME BIRTHMARK AND ALL--
...YOU HAVE A SISTER?

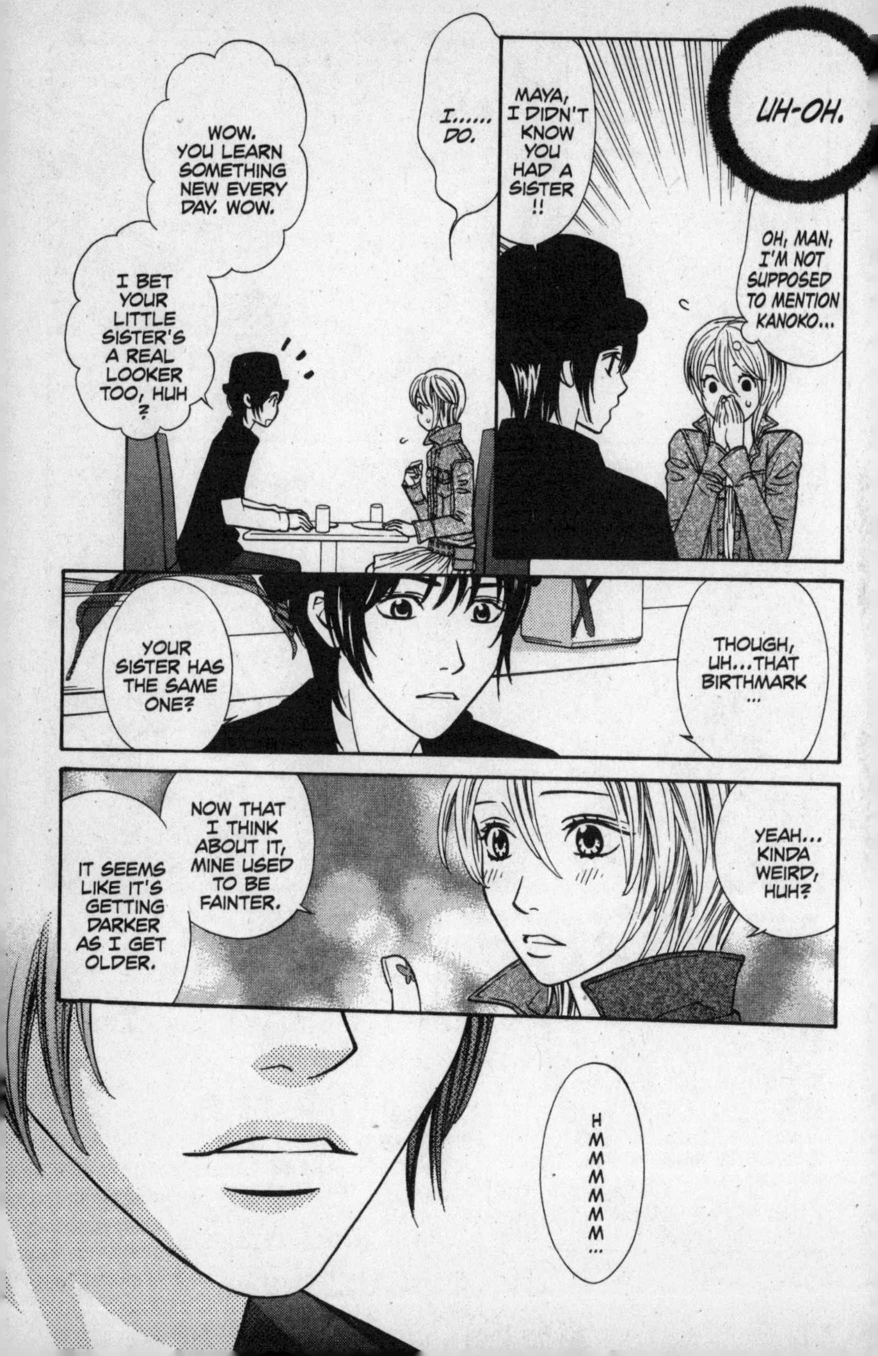
UH-OH.
MAYA, I DIDN'T KNOW YOU HAD A SISTER !!
OH, MAN, I'M NOT SUPPOSED TO MENTION KANOKO...
I...... DO.
WOW. YOU LEARN SOMETHING NEW EVERY DAY. WOW.
I BET YOUR LITTLE SISTER'S A REAL LOOKER TOO, HUH?
THOUGH, UH...THAT BIRTHMARK...
YOUR SISTER HAS THE SAME ONE?
YEAH... KINDA WEIRD, HUH?
NOW THAT I THINK ABOUT IT, MINE USED TO BE FAINTER.
IT SEEMS LIKE IT'S GETTING DARKER AS I GET OLDER.
HMMMMMM...

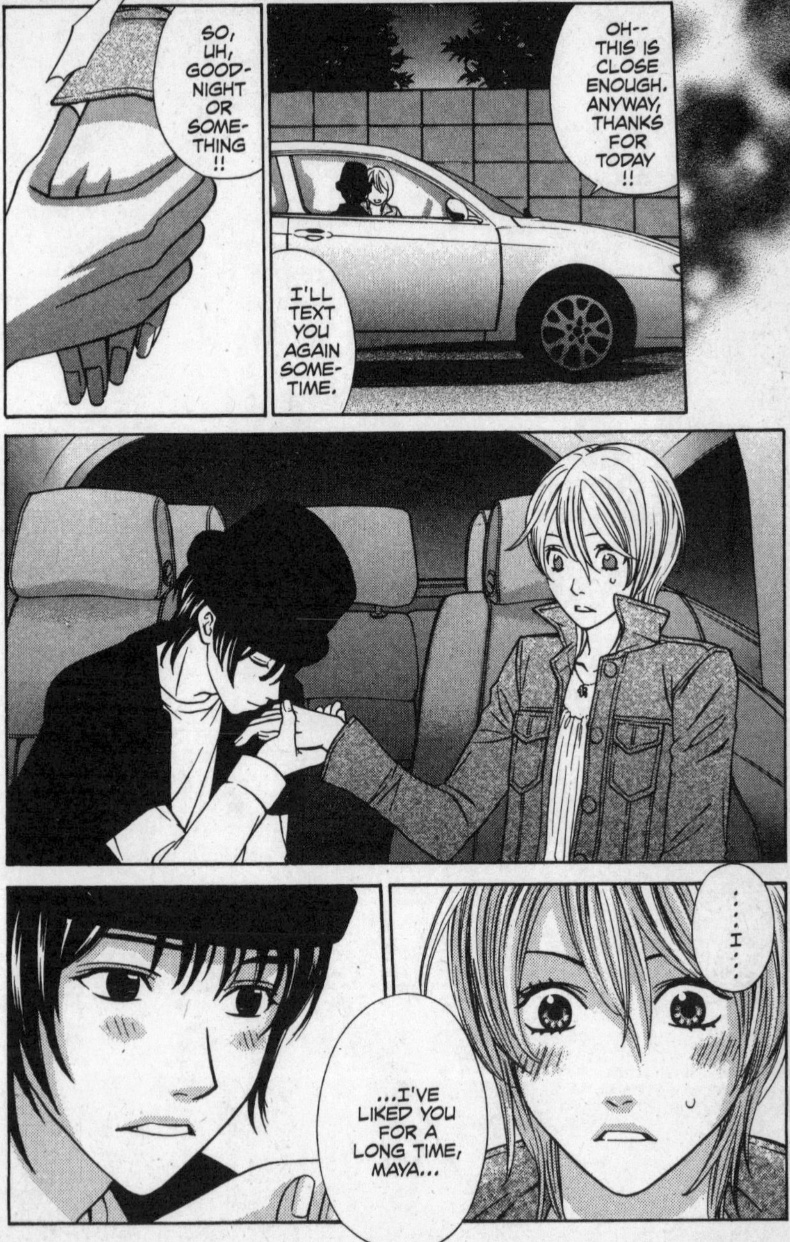
OH-- THIS IS CLOSE ENOUGH. ANYWAY, THANKS FOR TODAY !!
I'LL TEXT YOU AGAIN SOMETIME.
SO, UH, GOOD-NIGHT OR SOMETHING !!
...I...
...I'VE LIKED YOU FOR A LONG TIME, MAYA...

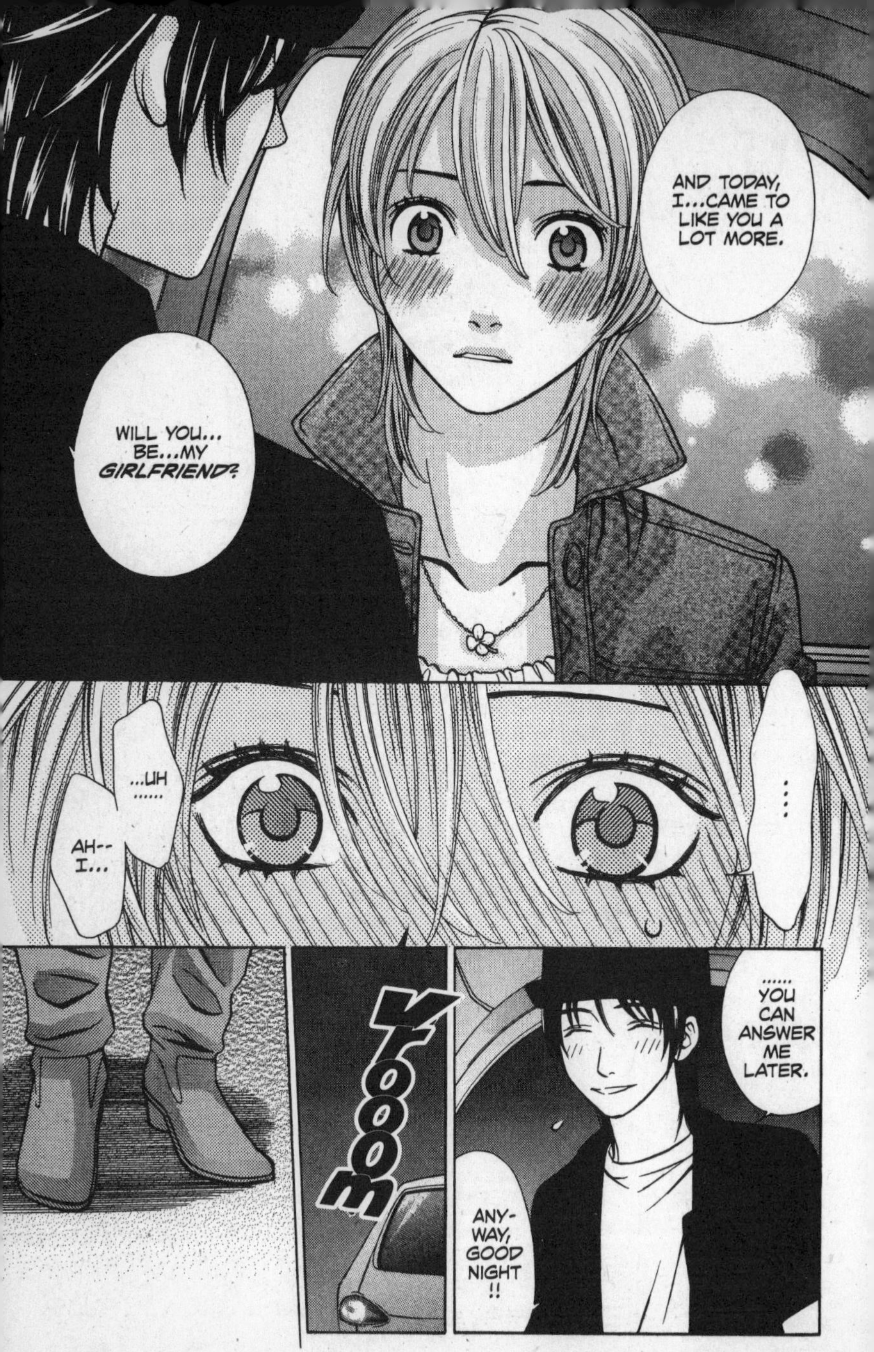
AND TODAY, I...CAME TO LIKE YOU A LOT MORE.
WILL YOU... BE...MY GIRLFRIEND?
....
...UH ......
AH-- I...
...... YOU CAN ANSWER ME LATER.
ANY-WAY, GOOD NIGHT !!
VROOOM

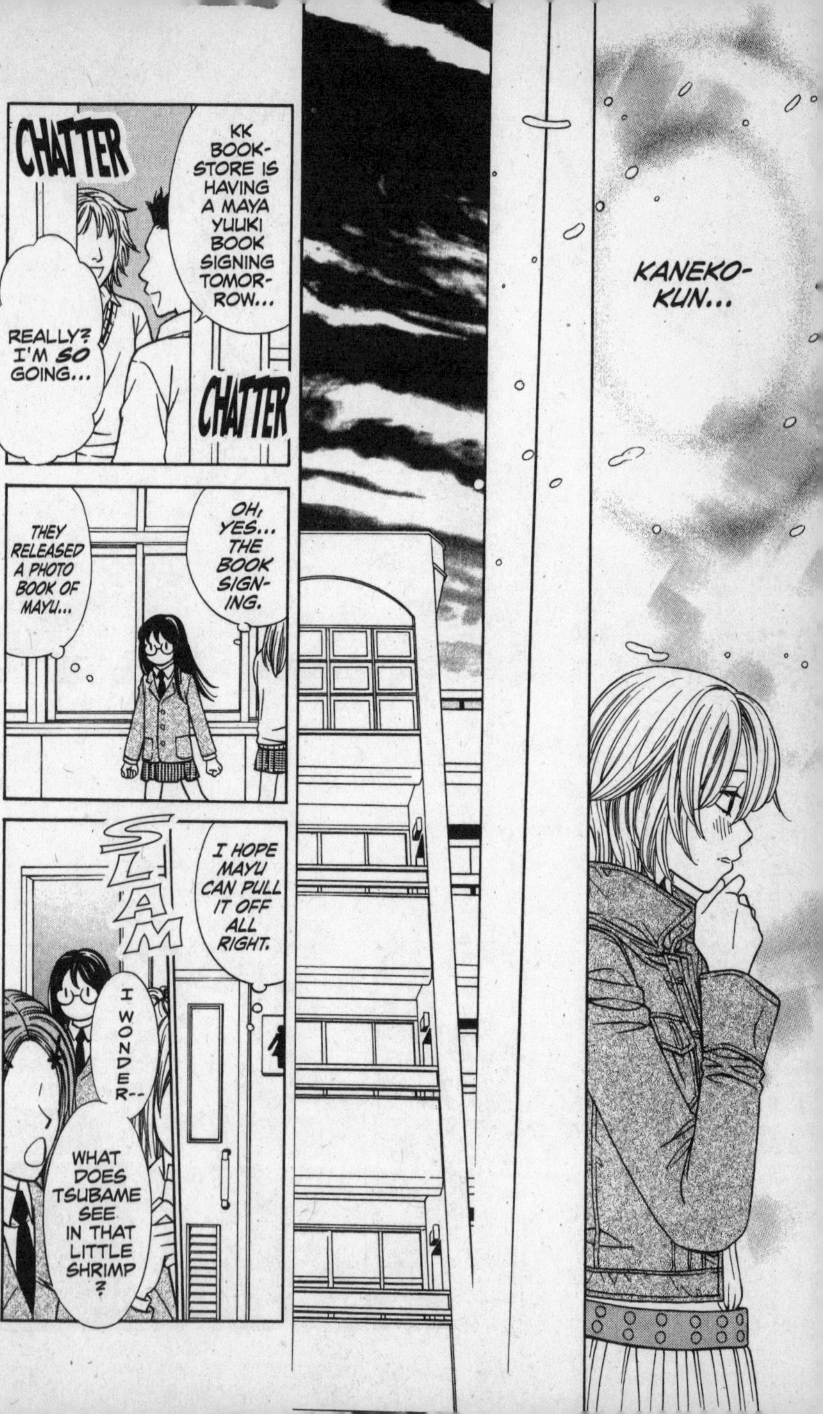
KANEKO-KUN...
KK BOOKSTORE IS HAVING A MAYA YUUKI BOOK SIGNING TOMORROW...
CHATTER
REALLY? I'M SO GOING...
CHATTER
OH, YES... THE BOOK SIGNING.
THEY RELEASED A PHOTO BOOK OF MAYU...
I HOPE MAYU CAN PULL IT OFF ALL RIGHT.
SLAM
I WONDER--
WHAT DOES TSUBAME SEE IN THAT LITTLE SHRIMP?

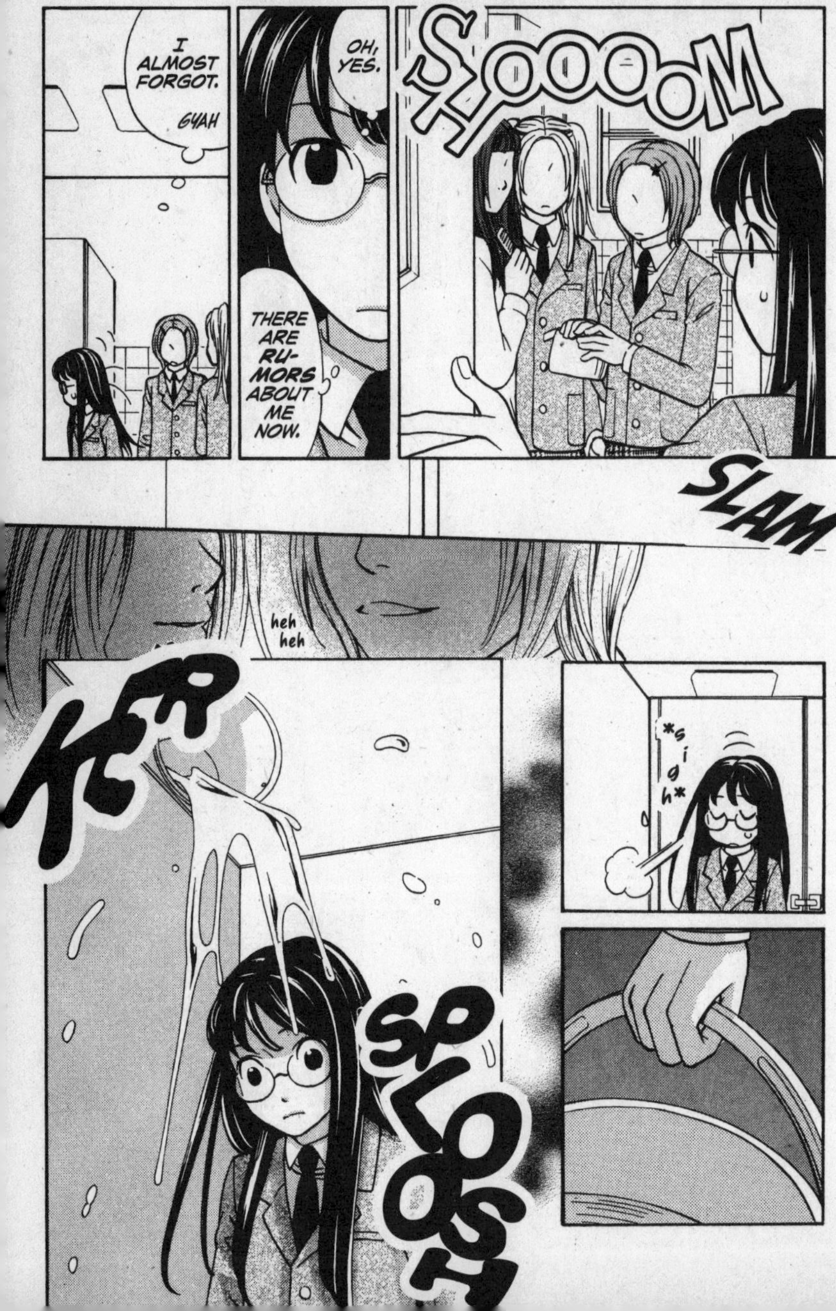
SHOOOOM
OH, YES.
THERE ARE RU-MORS ABOUT ME NOW.
I ALMOST FORGOT.
GYAH
SLAM
heh heh
sigh
KER
SPLOOSH

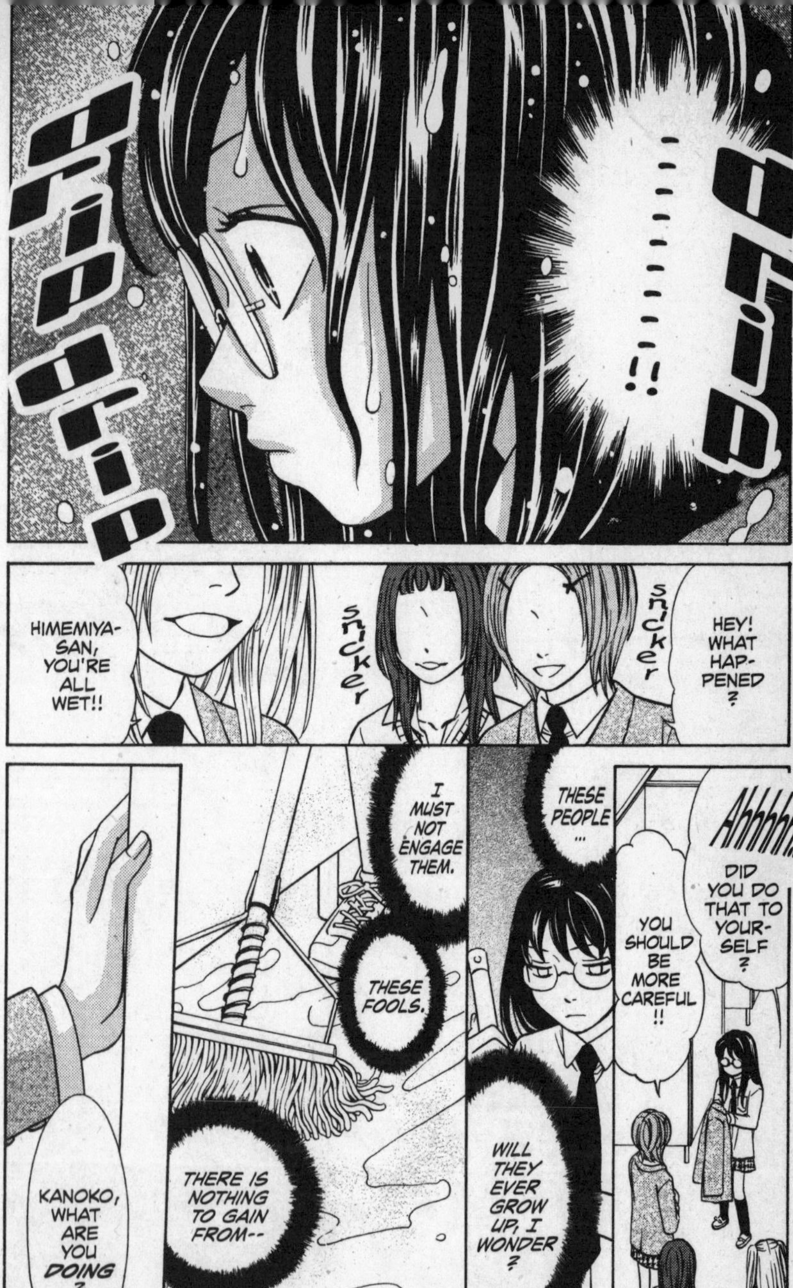
Drip
......!!
Drip drip
HEY! WHAT HAPPENED?
snicker
snicker
HIMEMIYA-SAN, YOU'RE ALL WET!!
Ahhhhh...
DID YOU DO THAT TO YOURSELF?
YOU SHOULD BE MORE CAREFUL!!
THESE PEOPLE...
WILL THEY EVER GROW UP, I WONDER?
I MUST NOT ENGAGE THEM.
THESE FOOLS.
THERE IS NOTHING TO GAIN FROM--
KANOKO, WHAT ARE YOU DOING?

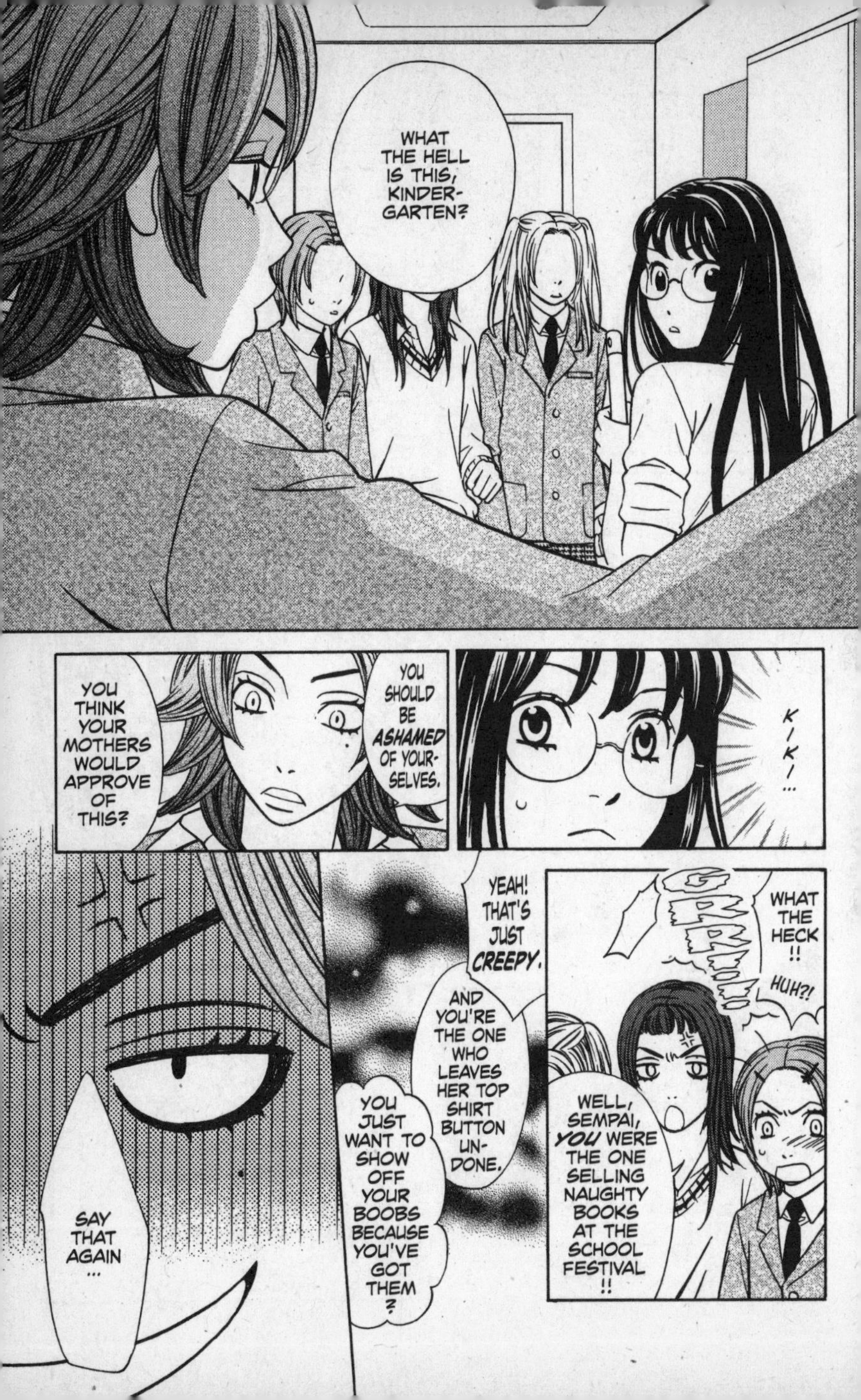
WHAT THE HELL IS THIS, KINDER-GARTEN?
KIKI...
YOU SHOULD BE ASHAMED OF YOUR-SELVES.
YOU THINK YOUR MOTHERS WOULD APPROVE OF THIS?
WHAT THE HECK !!
HUH?!
WELL, SEMPAI, YOU WERE THE ONE SELLING NAUGHTY BOOKS AT THE SCHOOL FESTIVAL !!
YEAH! THAT'S JUST CREEPY.
AND YOU'RE THE ONE WHO LEAVES HER TOP SHIRT BUTTON UN-DONE.
YOU JUST WANT TO SHOW OFF YOUR BOOBS BECAUSE YOU'VE GOT THEM?
SAY THAT AGAIN...

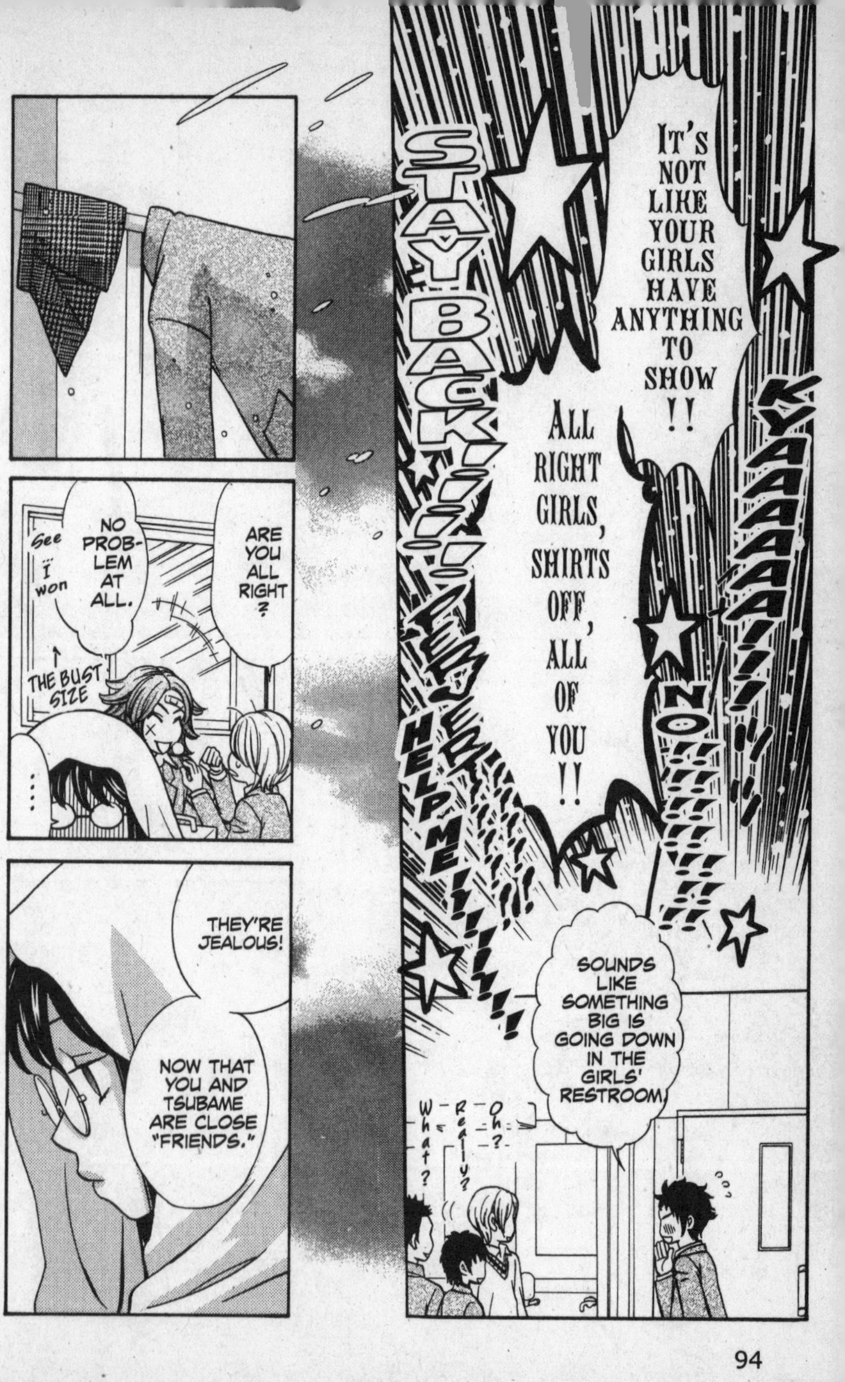
IT'S NOT LIKE YOUR GIRLS HAVE ANYTHING TO SHOW!!
KYAAAAAA!!!!
ALL RIGHT GIRLS, SHIRTS OFF, ALL OF YOU!!
STAY BACK!!!
NO!!!
HELP ME!!!
SOUNDS LIKE SOMETHING BIG IS GOING DOWN IN THE GIRLS' RESTROOM.
Oh?
Really?
What?
ARE YOU ALL RIGHT?
NO PROBLEM AT ALL.
See... I won
↑ THE BUST SIZE
....
THEY'RE JEALOUS!
NOW THAT YOU AND TSUBAME ARE CLOSE "FRIENDS."

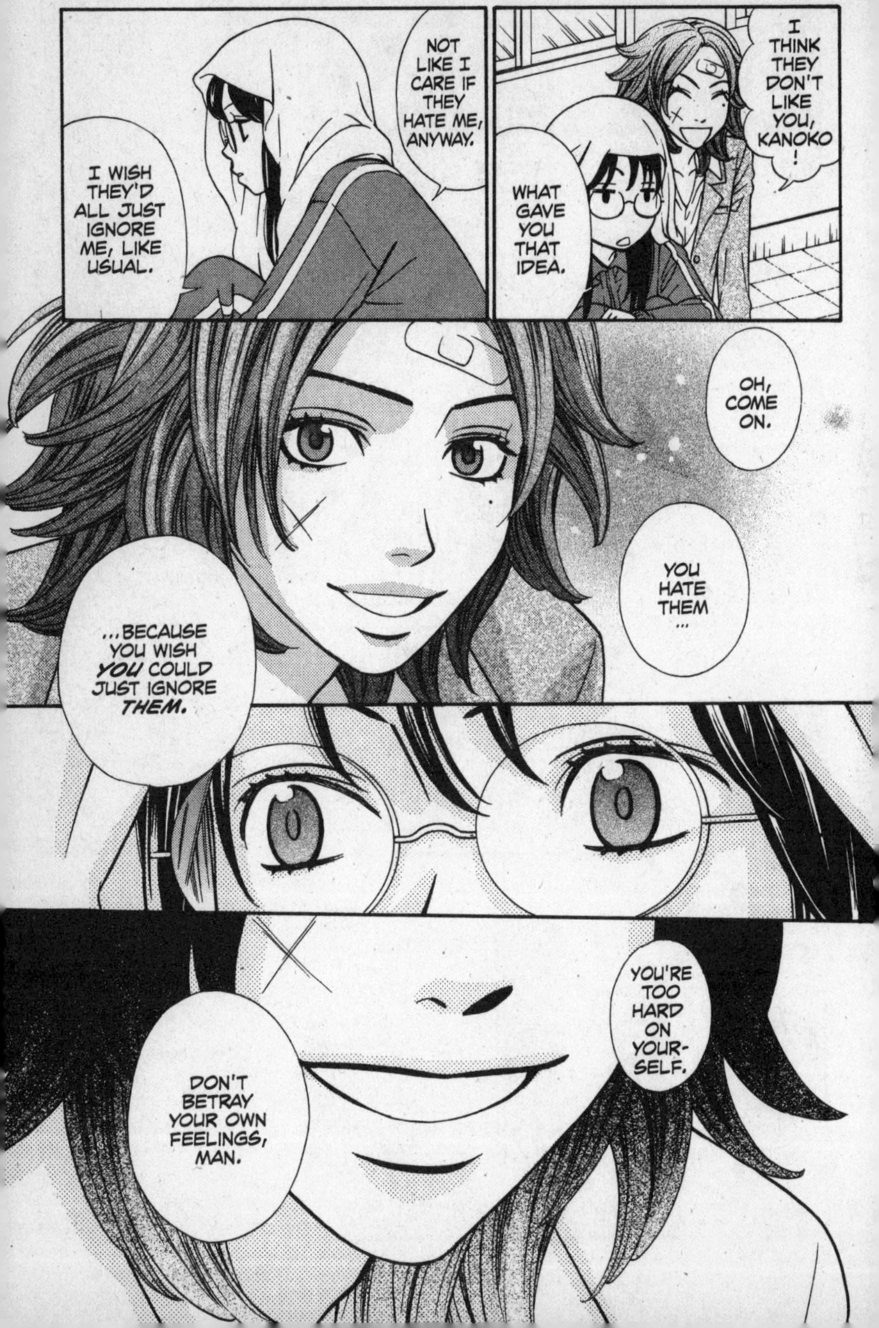
I THINK THEY DON'T LIKE YOU, KANOKO!
WHAT GAVE YOU THAT IDEA.
NOT LIKE I CARE IF THEY HATE ME, ANYWAY.
I WISH THEY'D ALL JUST IGNORE ME, LIKE USUAL.
OH, COME ON.
YOU HATE THEM...
...BECAUSE YOU WISH *YOU* COULD JUST IGNORE *THEM*.
YOU'RE TOO HARD ON YOUR-SELF.
DON'T BETRAY YOUR OWN FEELINGS, MAN.

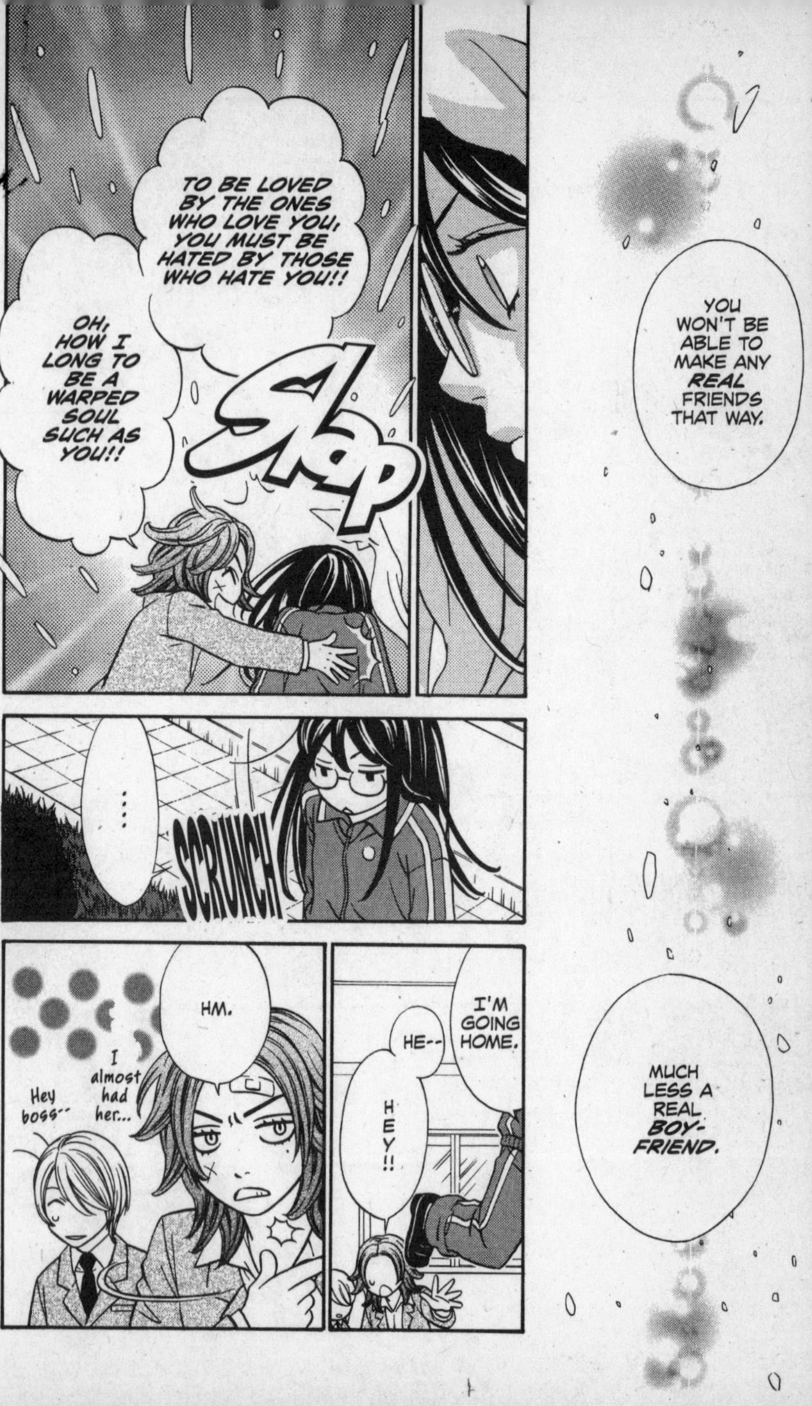
YOU WON'T BE ABLE TO MAKE ANY *REAL* FRIENDS THAT WAY.
MUCH LESS A REAL *BOY-FRIEND.*
TO BE LOVED BY THE ONES WHO LOVE YOU, YOU MUST BE HATED BY THOSE WHO HATE YOU!!
OH, HOW I LONG TO BE A WARPED SOUL SUCH AS YOU!!
Slap
....
SCRUNCH
I'M GOING HOME.
HE--
HEY!!
HM.
I almost had her...
Hey boss--

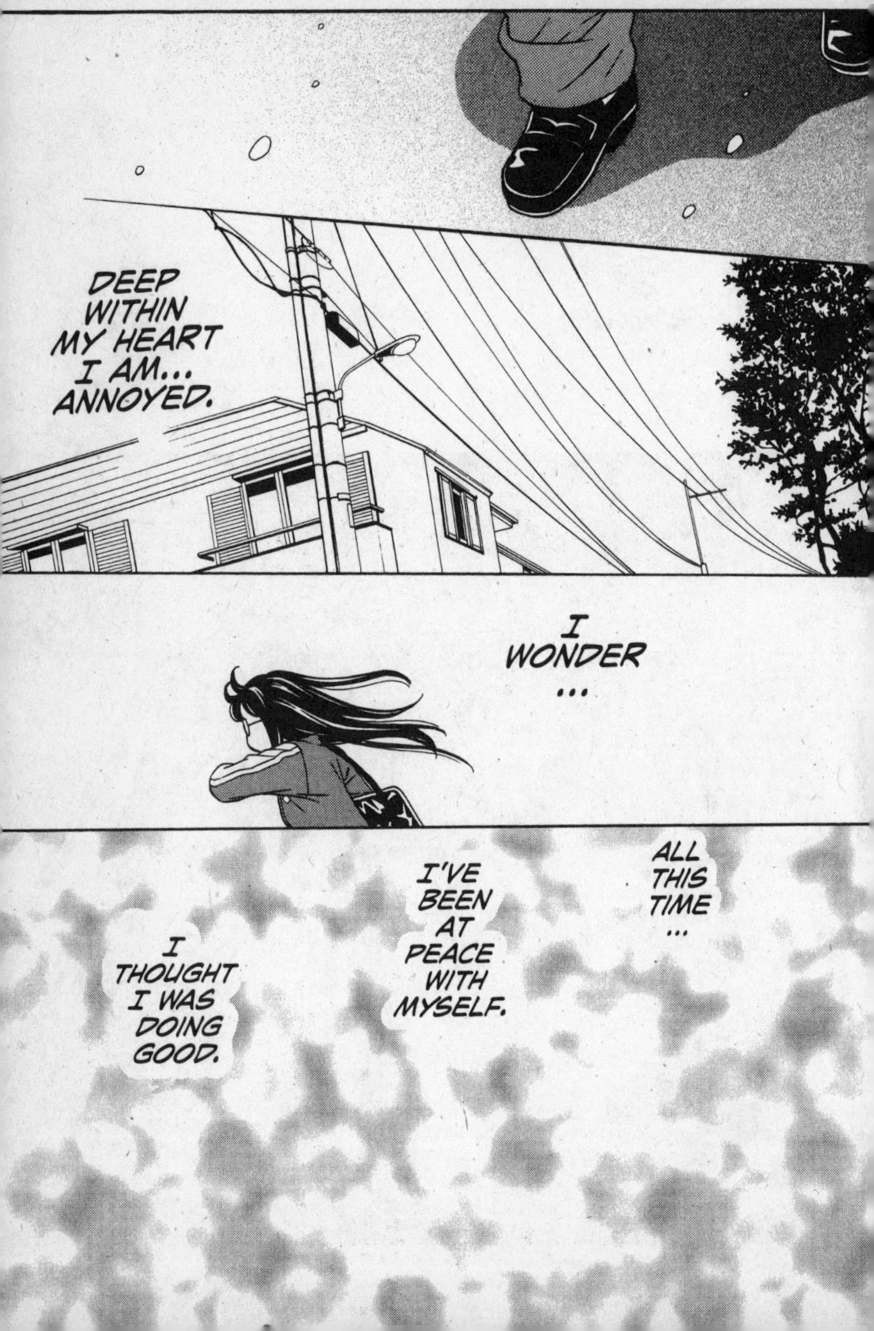
DEEP WITHIN MY HEART I AM... ANNOYED.
I WONDER ...
ALL THIS TIME ...
I'VE BEEN AT PEACE WITH MYSELF.
I THOUGHT I WAS DOING GOOD.

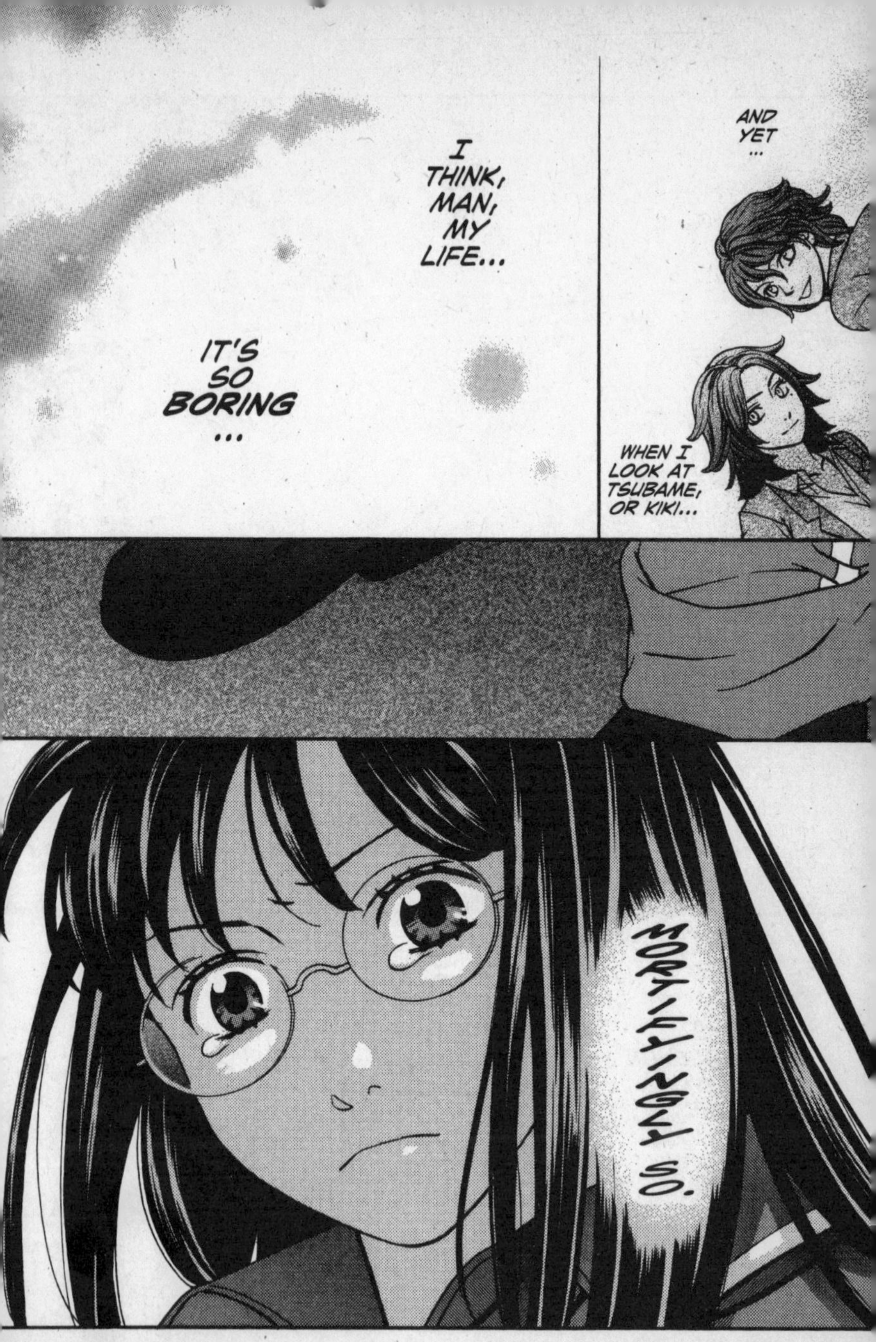
AND YET ...
WHEN I LOOK AT TSUBAME, OR KIKI...
I THINK, MAN, MY LIFE...
IT'S SO BORING ...
MORTIFYINGLY SO.

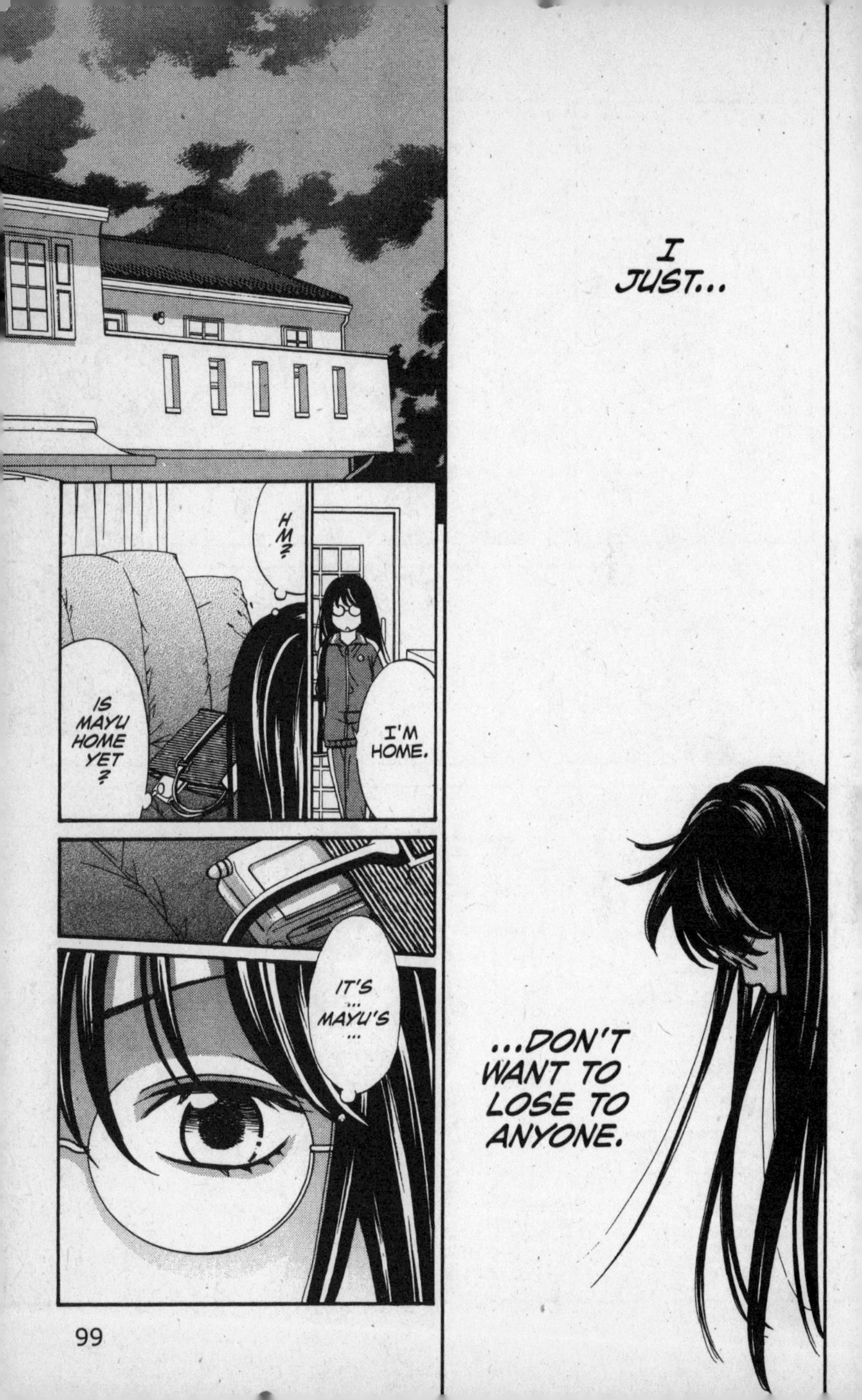
I JUST...
...DON'T WANT TO LOSE TO ANYONE.
HM?
I'M HOME.
IS MAYU HOME YET?
IT'S ... MAYU'S ...

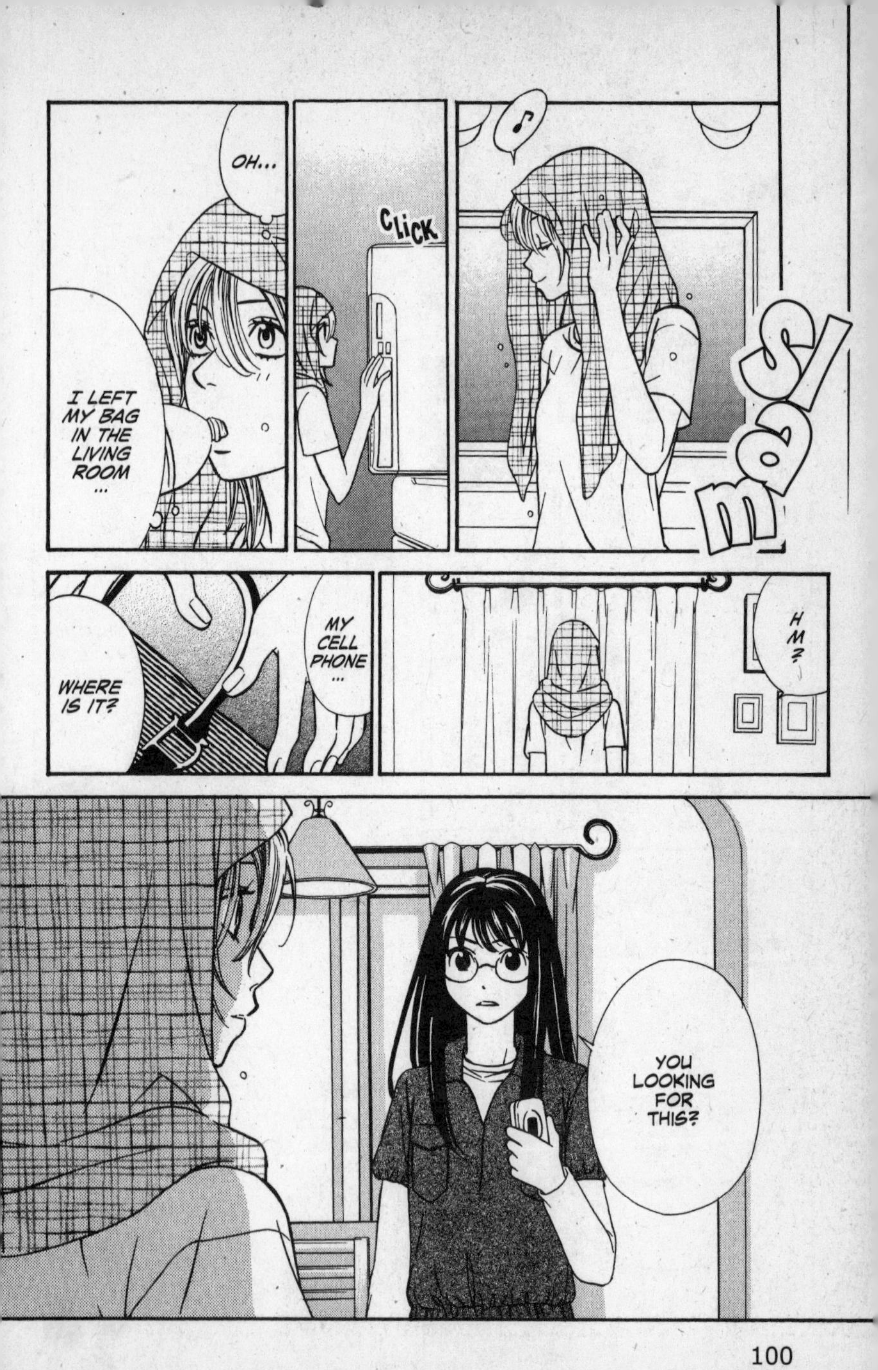
♪
wash
CLICK
OH...
I LEFT MY BAG IN THE LIVING ROOM ...
HM?
MY CELL PHONE ...
WHERE IS IT?
YOU LOOKING FOR THIS?

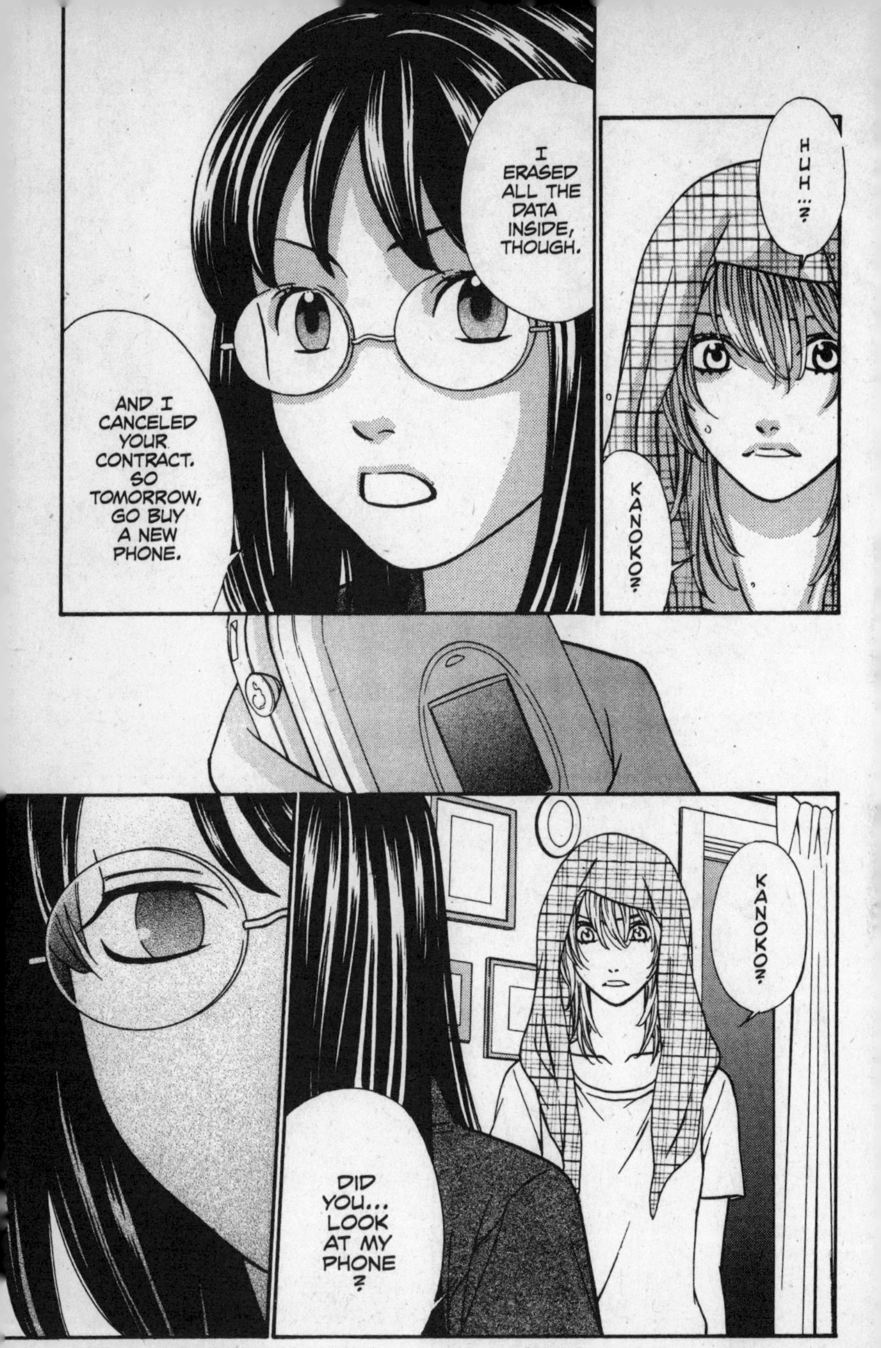
HUH...?
KANOKO?
I ERASED ALL THE DATA INSIDE, THOUGH.
AND I CANCELED YOUR CONTRACT. SO TOMORROW, GO BUY A NEW PHONE.
KANOKO?
DID YOU... LOOK AT MY PHONE?

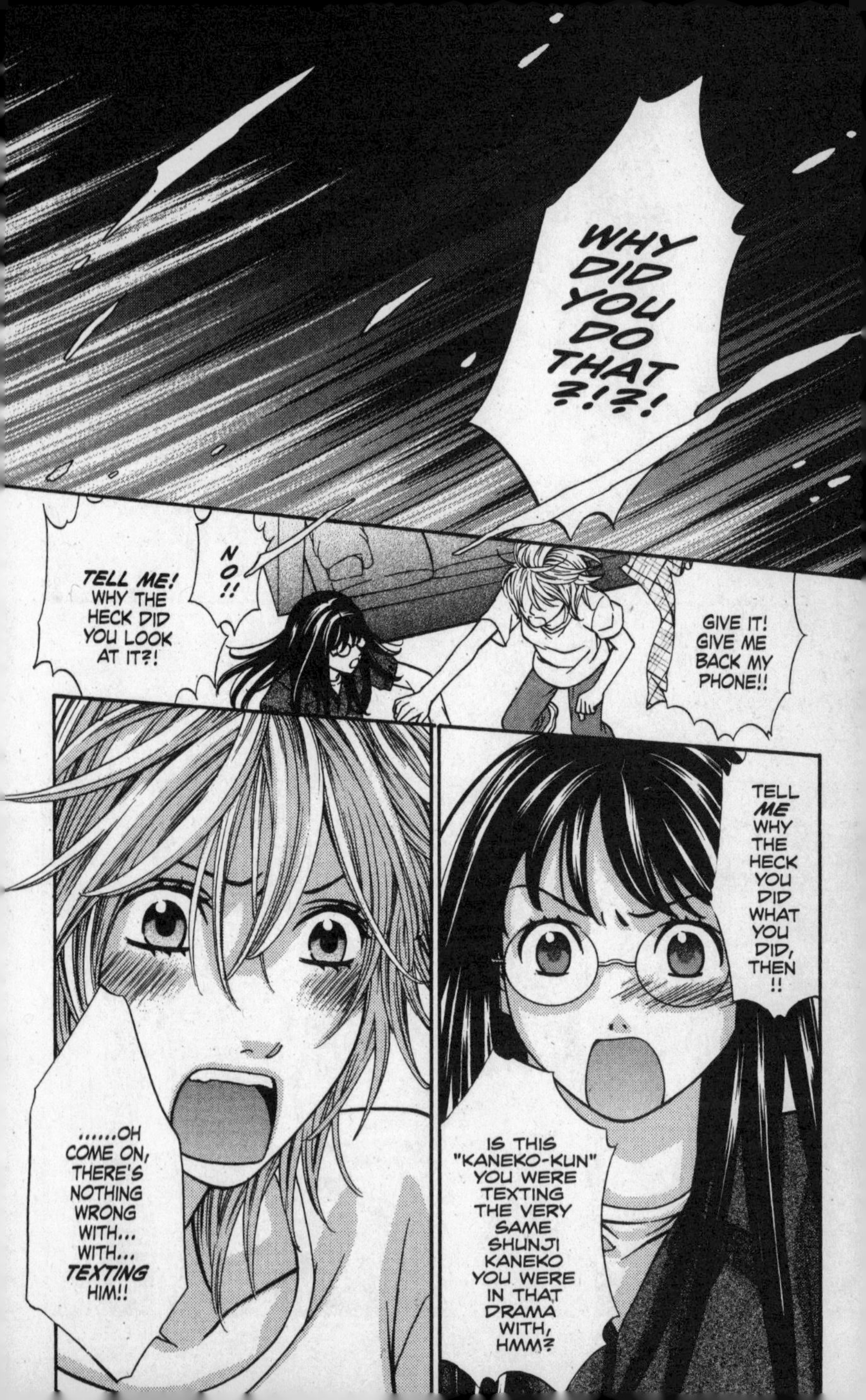
WHY DID YOU DO THAT ?!?!
GIVE IT! GIVE ME BACK MY PHONE!!
NO!!
TELL ME! WHY THE HECK DID YOU LOOK AT IT?!
TELL ME WHY THE HECK YOU DID WHAT YOU DID, THEN!!
IS THIS "KANEKO-KUN" YOU WERE TEXTING THE VERY SAME SHUNJI KANEKO YOU WERE IN THAT DRAMA WITH, HMM?
......OH COME ON, THERE'S NOTHING WRONG WITH... WITH... TEXTING HIM!!

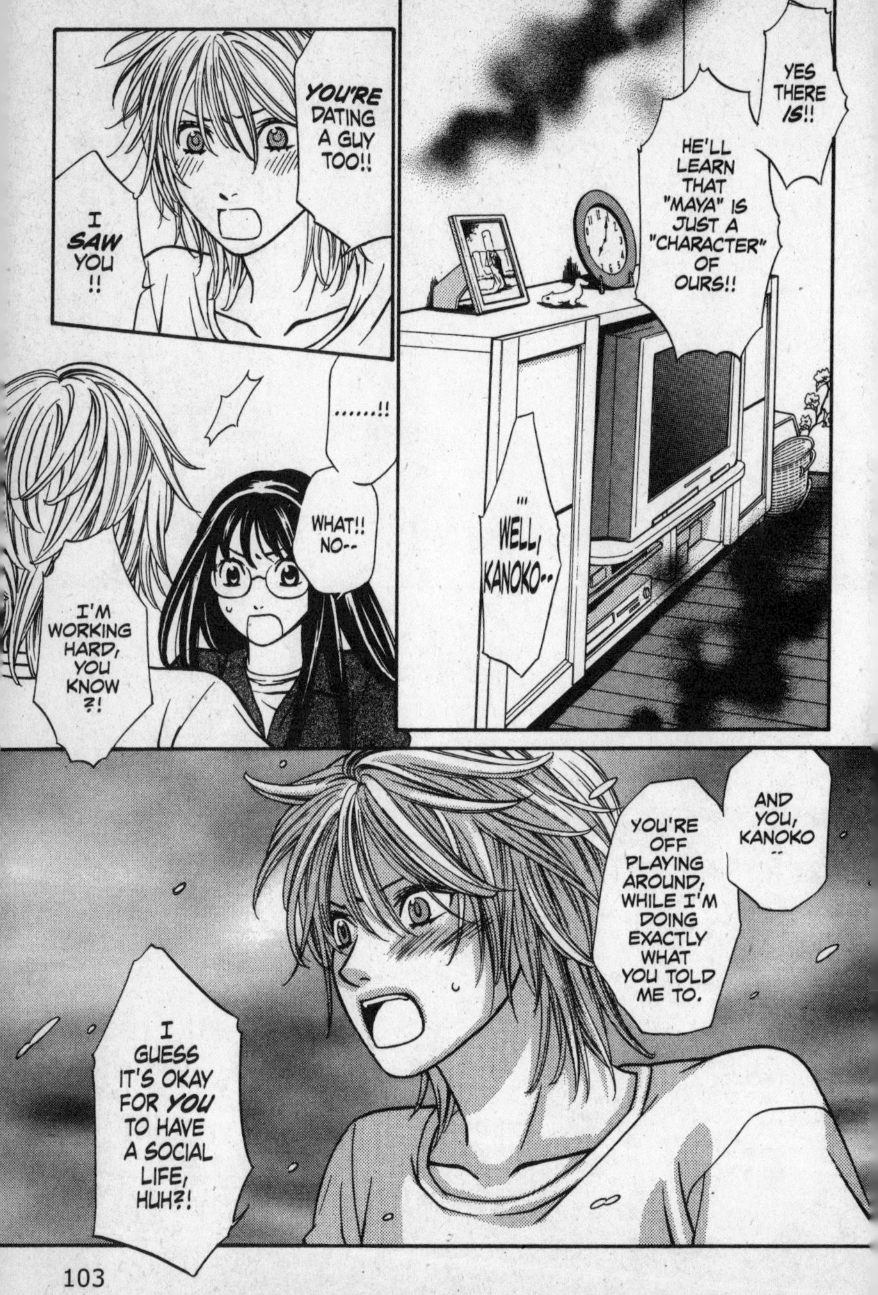
YES THERE IS!!
HE'LL LEARN THAT "MAYA" IS JUST A "CHARACTER" OF OURS!!
...WELL, KANOKO--
YOU'RE DATING A GUY TOO!!
I SAW YOU!!
......!!
WHAT!! NO--
I'M WORKING HARD, YOU KNOW?!
AND YOU, KANOKO--
YOU'RE OFF PLAYING AROUND, WHILE I'M DOING EXACTLY WHAT YOU TOLD ME TO.
I GUESS IT'S OKAY FOR YOU TO HAVE A SOCIAL LIFE, HUH?!

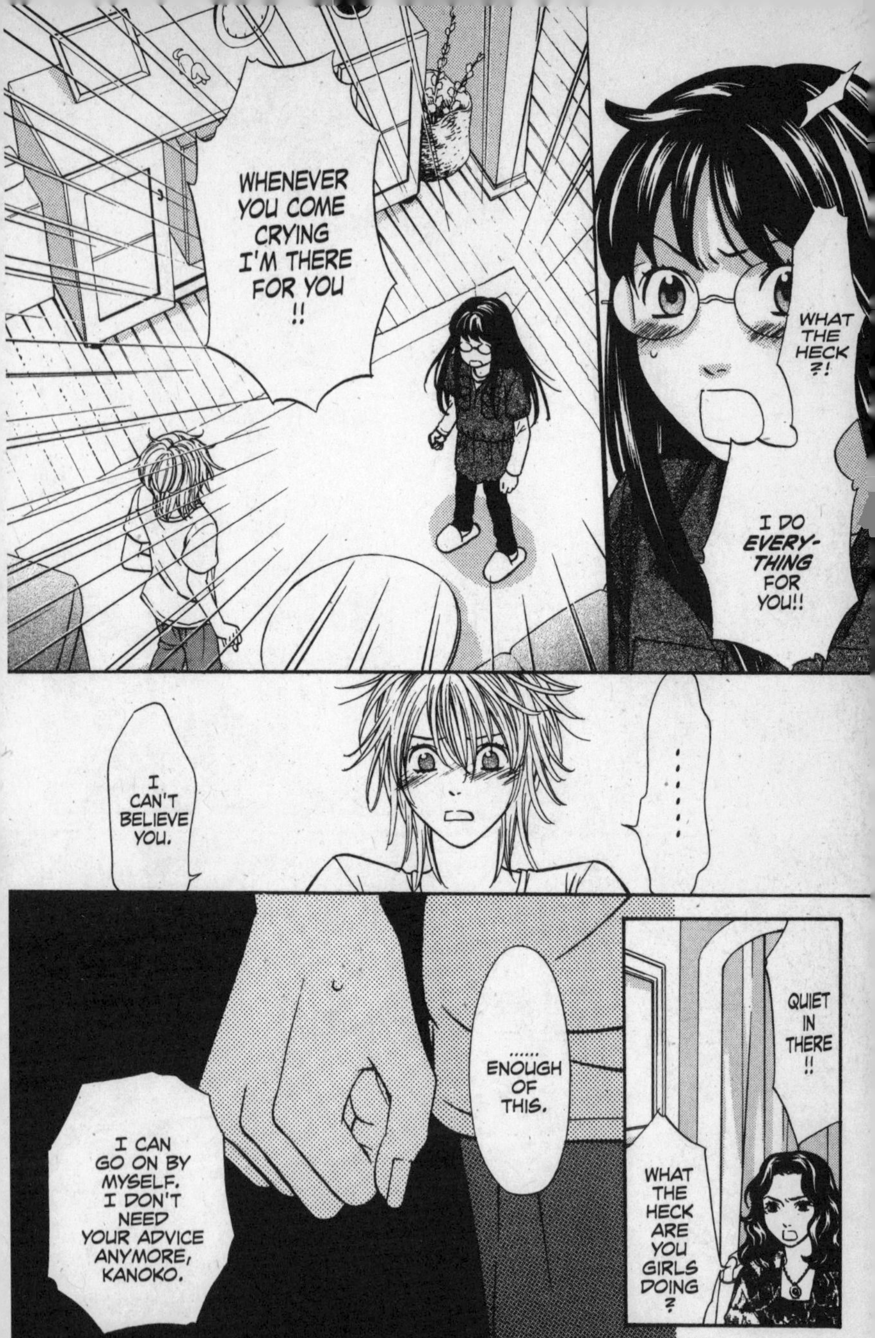
WHAT THE HECK ?!
I DO *EVERYTHING* FOR YOU!!
WHENEVER YOU COME CRYING I'M THERE FOR YOU !!
......
I CAN'T BELIEVE YOU.
QUIET IN THERE !!
WHAT THE HECK ARE YOU GIRLS DOING ?
...... ENOUGH OF THIS.
I CAN GO ON BY MYSELF. I DON'T NEED YOUR ADVICE ANYMORE, KANOKO.

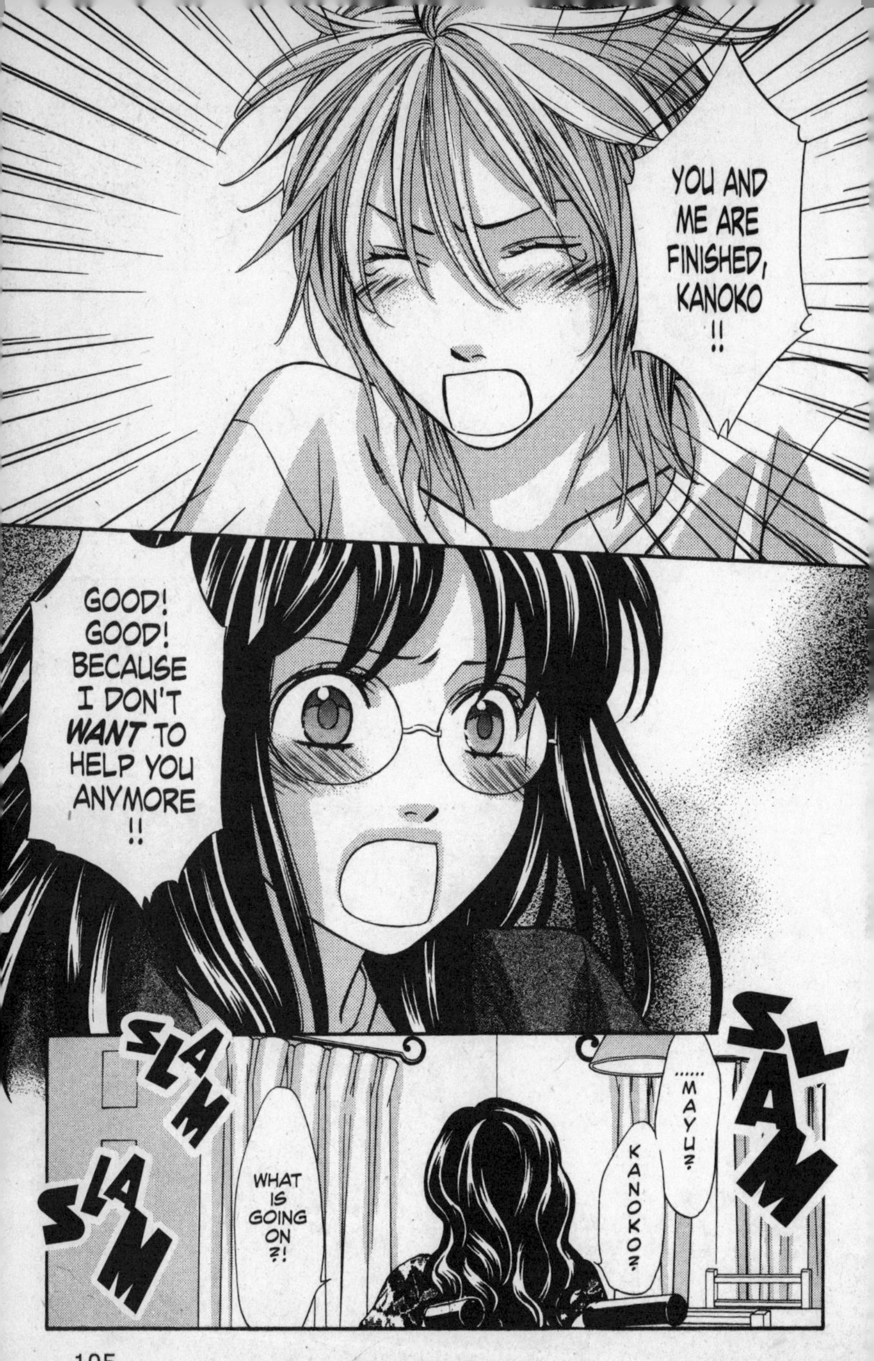
YOU AND ME ARE FINISHED, KANOKO !!
GOOD! GOOD! BECAUSE I DON'T *WANT* TO HELP YOU ANYMORE !!
SLAM
......MAYU?
KANOKO?
WHAT IS GOING ON ?!
SLAM
SLAM

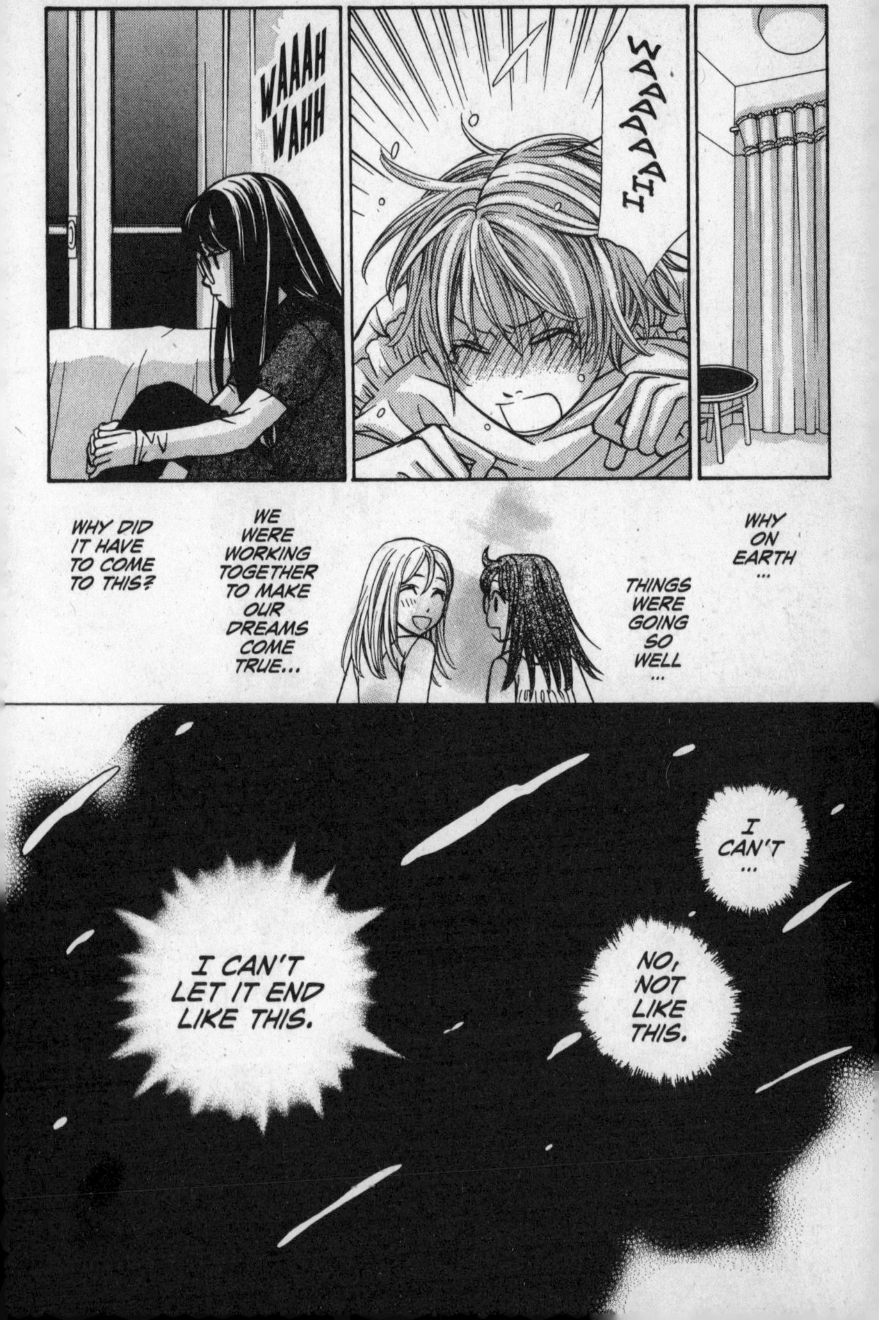
WAAAAAAH
WAAAH WAHH
WHY ON EARTH ...
THINGS WERE GOING SO WELL ...
WE WERE WORKING TOGETHER TO MAKE OUR DREAMS COME TRUE...
WHY DID IT HAVE TO COME TO THIS?
I CAN'T ...
NO, NOT LIKE THIS.
I CAN'T LET IT END LIKE THIS.

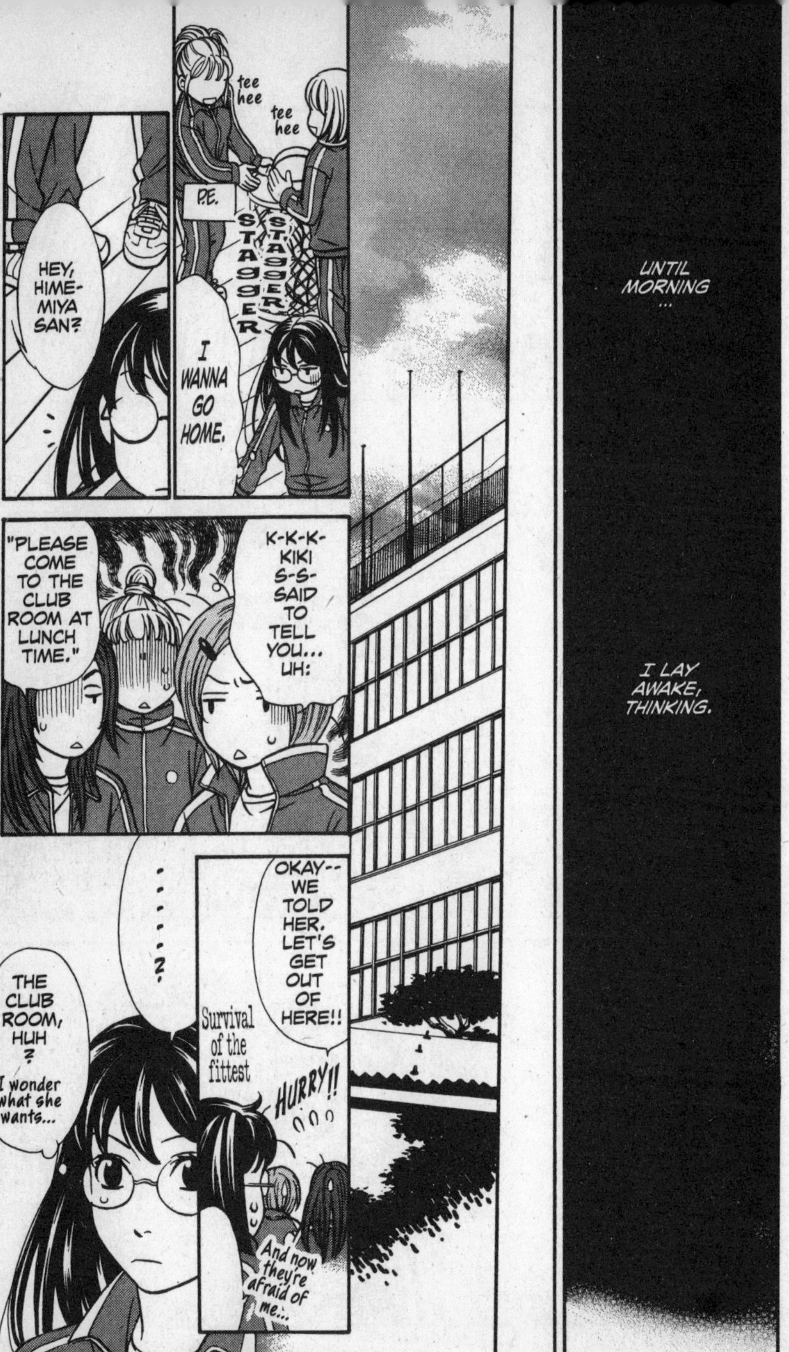
UNTIL MORNING ...
I LAY AWAKE, THINKING.
tee hee
tee hee
P.E.
STAGGER
STAGGER
I WANNA GO HOME.
HEY, HIME-MIYA SAN?
K-K-K-KIKI S-S-SAID TO TELL YOU... UH:
"PLEASE COME TO THE CLUB ROOM AT LUNCH TIME."
OKAY-- WE TOLD HER. LET'S GET OUT OF HERE!!
Survival of the fittest
HURRY!!
And now they're afraid of me...
......?
THE CLUB ROOM, HUH?
I wonder what she wants...

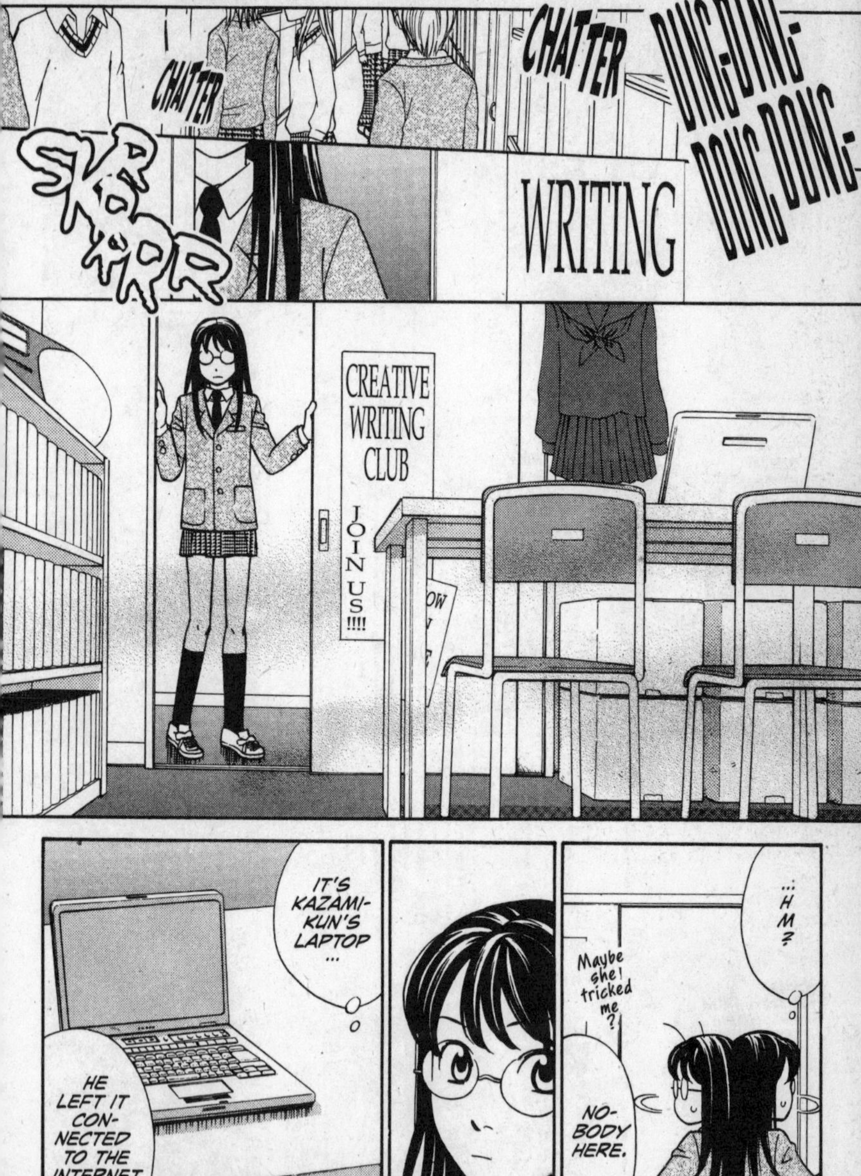
DING-DONG-
DONG-DONG-
CHATTER
CHATTER
WRITING
SKRRR
CREATIVE WRITING CLUB
JOIN US!!!!
...HM?
Maybe she tricked me?
NO-BODY HERE.
IT'S KAZAMI-KUN'S LAPTOP...
HE LEFT IT CON-NECTED TO THE INTERNET...

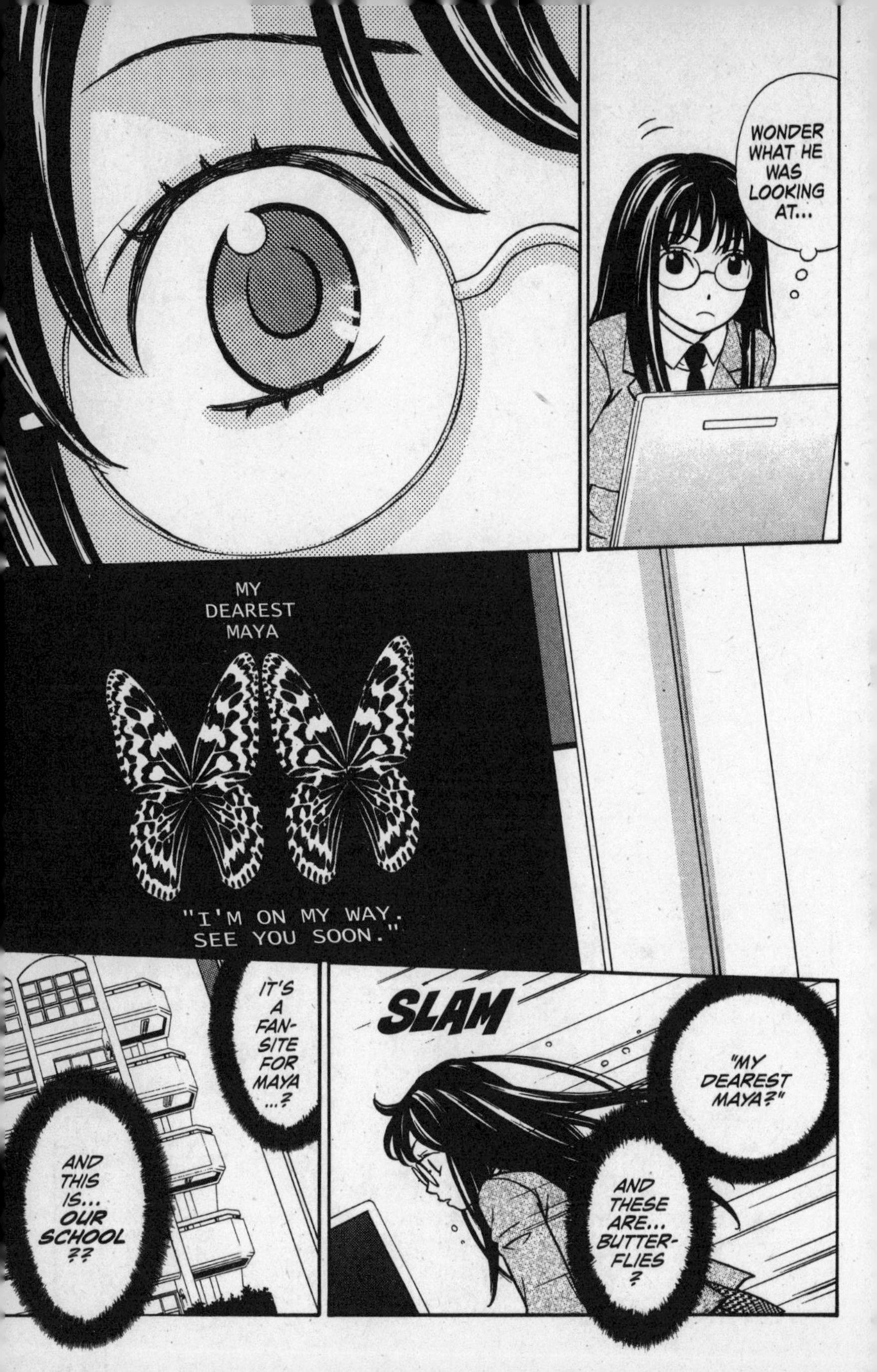
WONDER WHAT HE WAS LOOKING AT...
MY DEAREST MAYA
"I'M ON MY WAY. SEE YOU SOON."
SLAM
"MY DEAREST MAYA?"
AND THESE ARE... BUTTERFLIES?
IT'S A FAN-SITE FOR MAYA...?
AND THIS IS... OUR SCHOOL??

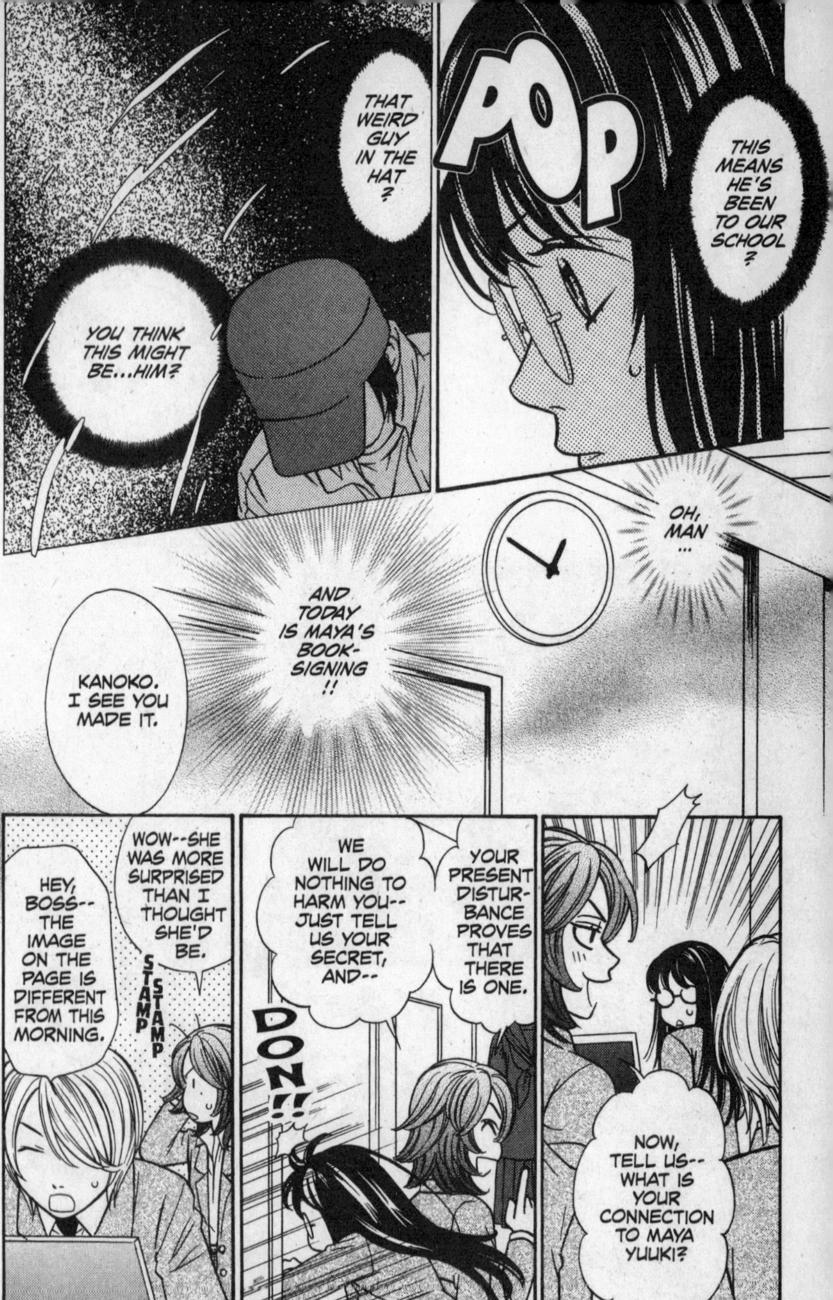
POP
THIS MEANS HE'S BEEN TO OUR SCHOOL?
THAT WEIRD GUY IN THE HAT?
YOU THINK THIS MIGHT BE...HIM?
OH, MAN...
AND TODAY IS MAYA'S BOOK-SIGNING!!
KANOKO. I SEE YOU MADE IT.
NOW, TELL US--WHAT IS YOUR CONNECTION TO MAYA YUUKI?
YOUR PRESENT DISTURBANCE PROVES THAT THERE IS ONE.
WE WILL DO NOTHING TO HARM YOU--JUST TELL US YOUR SECRET, AND--
DON!!
WOW--SHE WAS MORE SURPRISED THAN I THOUGHT SHE'D BE.
HEY, BOSS--THE IMAGE ON THE PAGE IS DIFFERENT FROM THIS MORNING.
STAMP STAMP

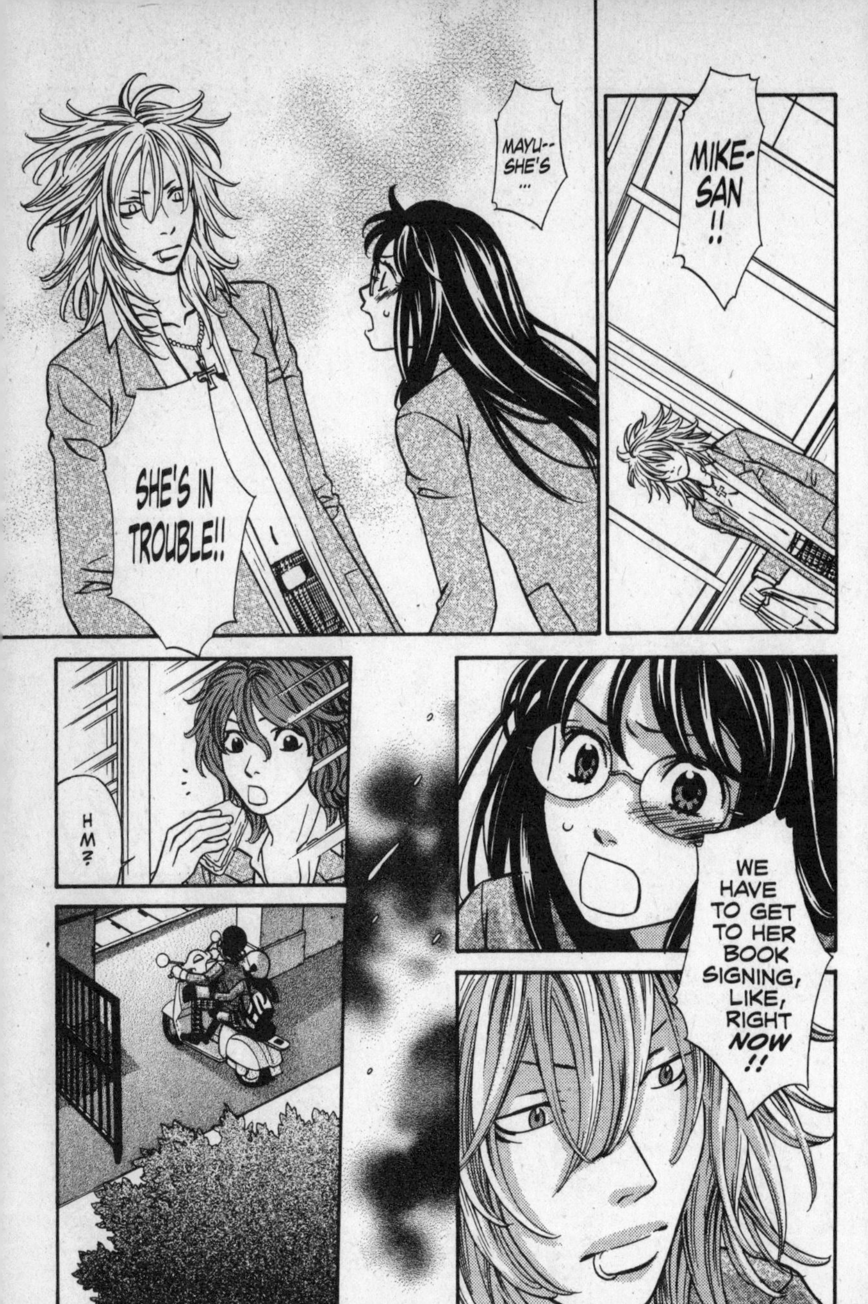
MIKE-SAN!!
MAYU--SHE'S...
SHE'S IN TROUBLE!!
WE HAVE TO GET TO HER BOOK SIGNING, LIKE, RIGHT *NOW*!!
HM?

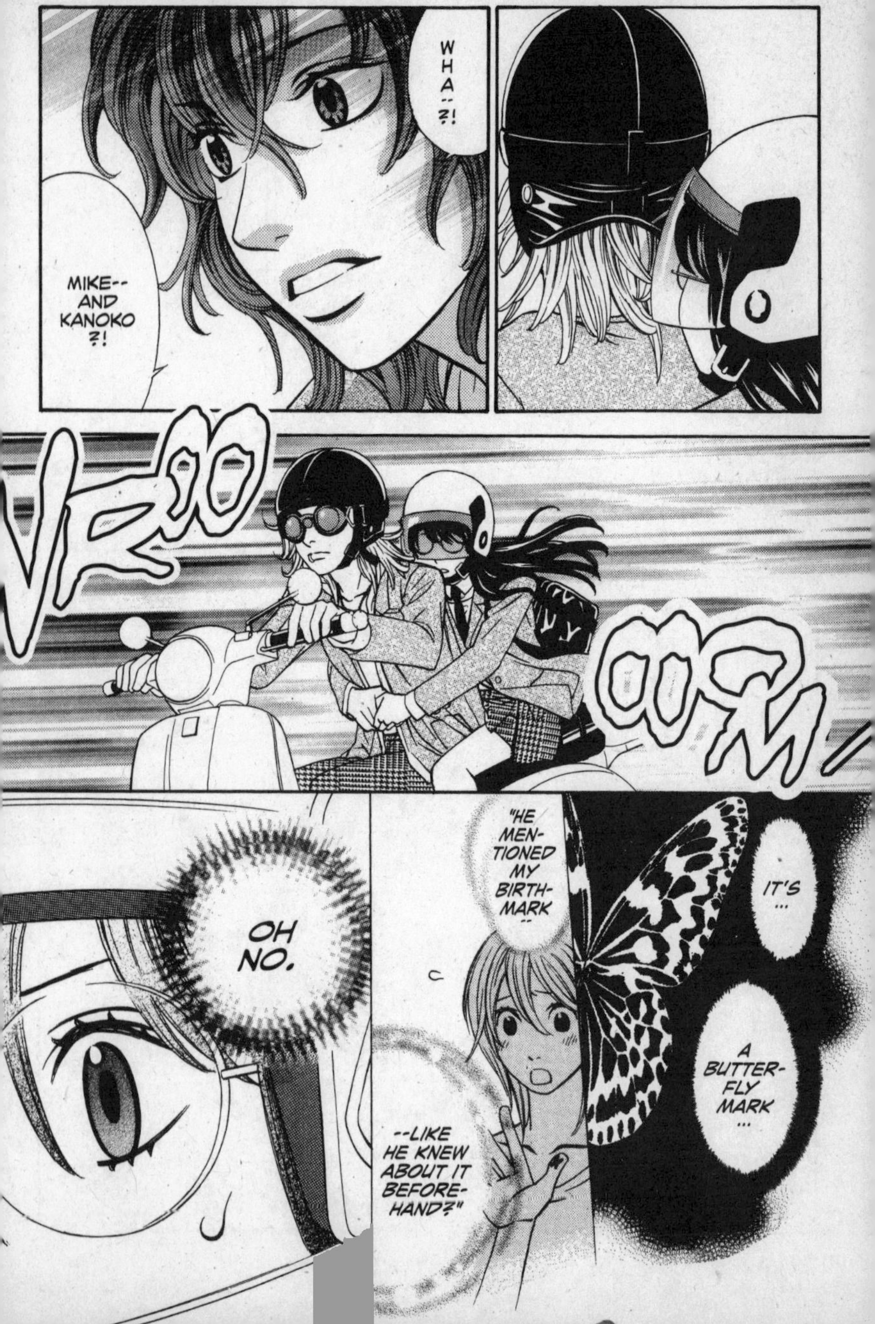
WHA--?!
MIKE-- AND KANOKO?!
VROO
OOM
"HE MENTIONED MY BIRTHMARK--
--LIKE HE KNEW ABOUT IT BEFOREHAND?"
IT'S...
A BUTTERFLY MARK...
OH NO.

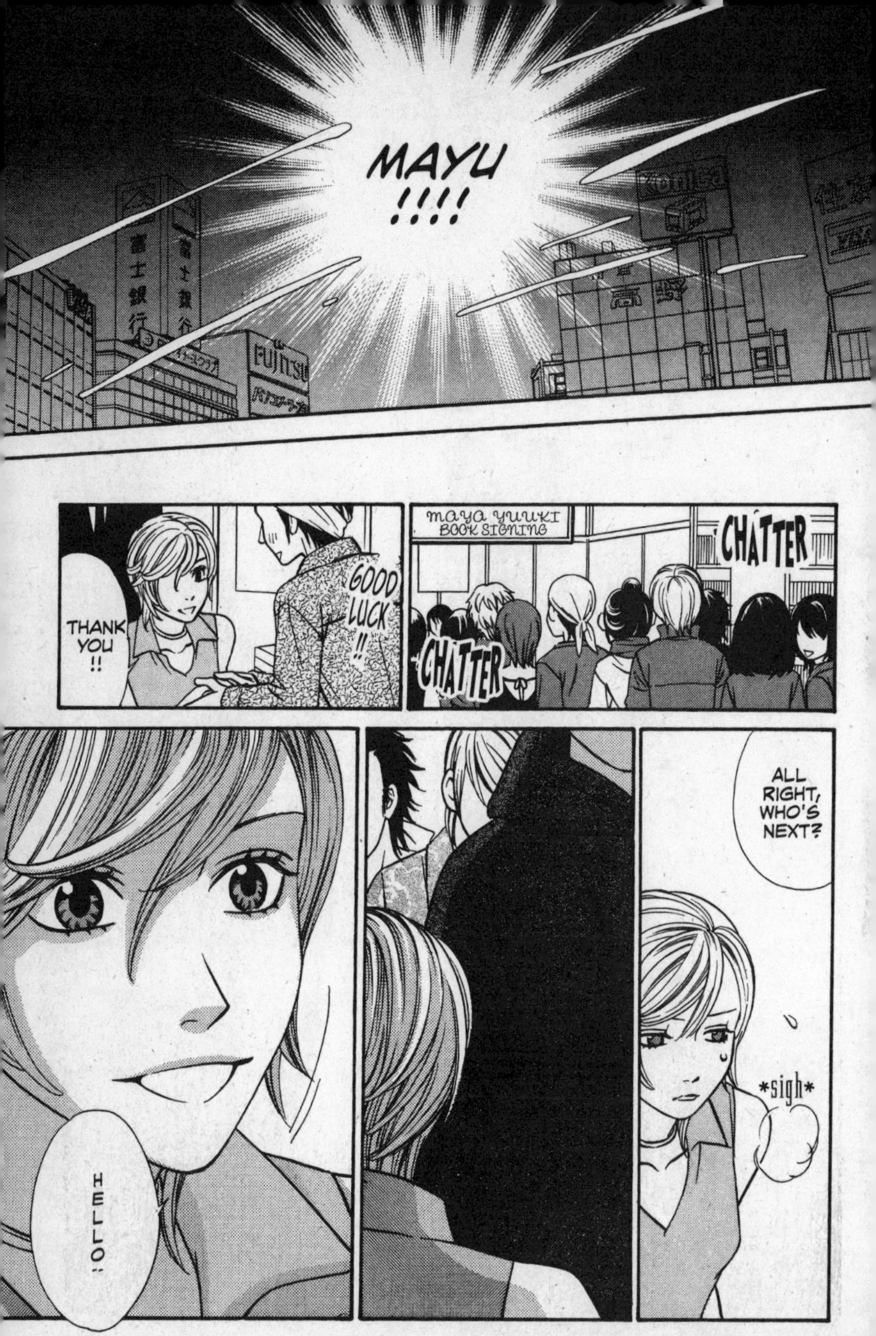
MAYU !!!!
FUJITSU
MAYA YUUKI BOOK SIGNING
CHATTER
CHATTER
GOOD LUCK !!
THANK YOU !!
ALL RIGHT, WHO'S NEXT?
sigh
HELLO..

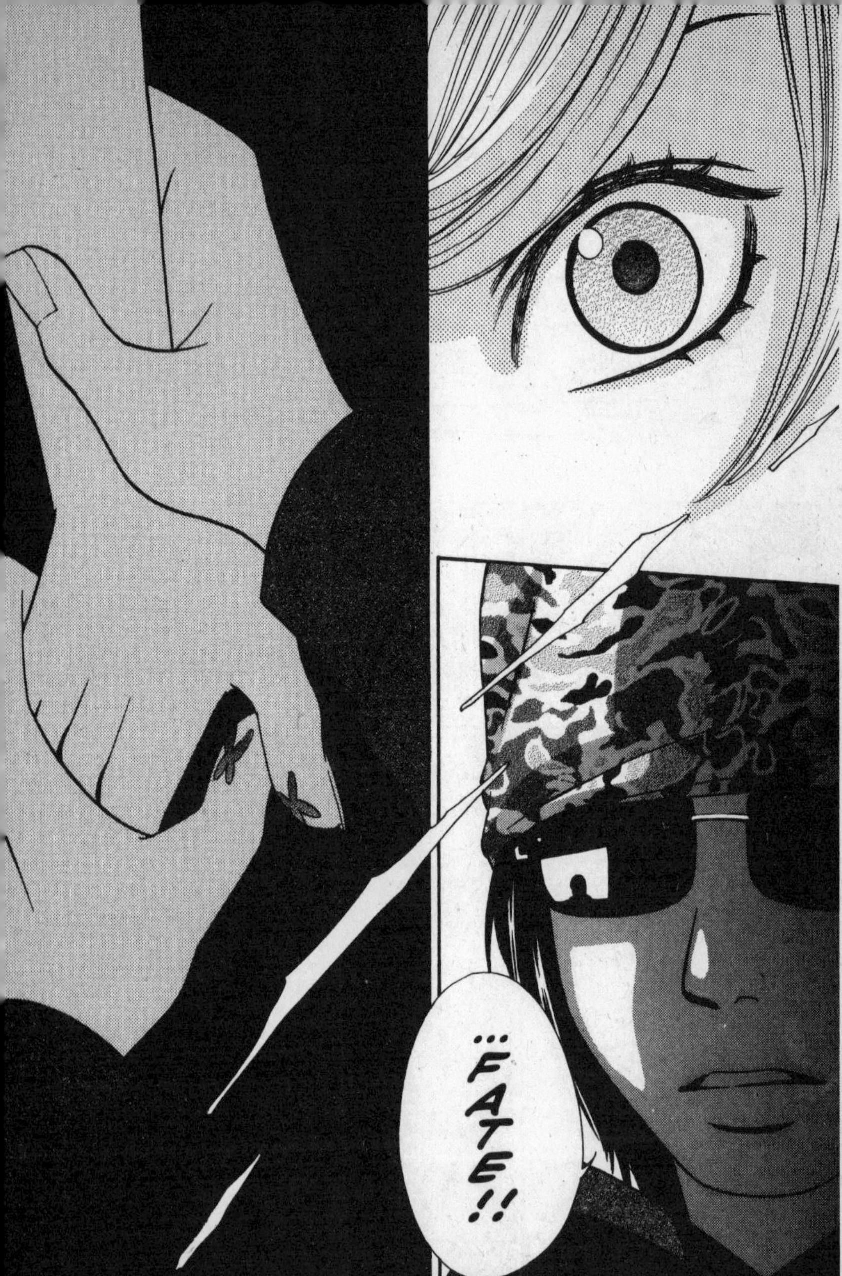
...FATE!!
CHAPTER 1/END.

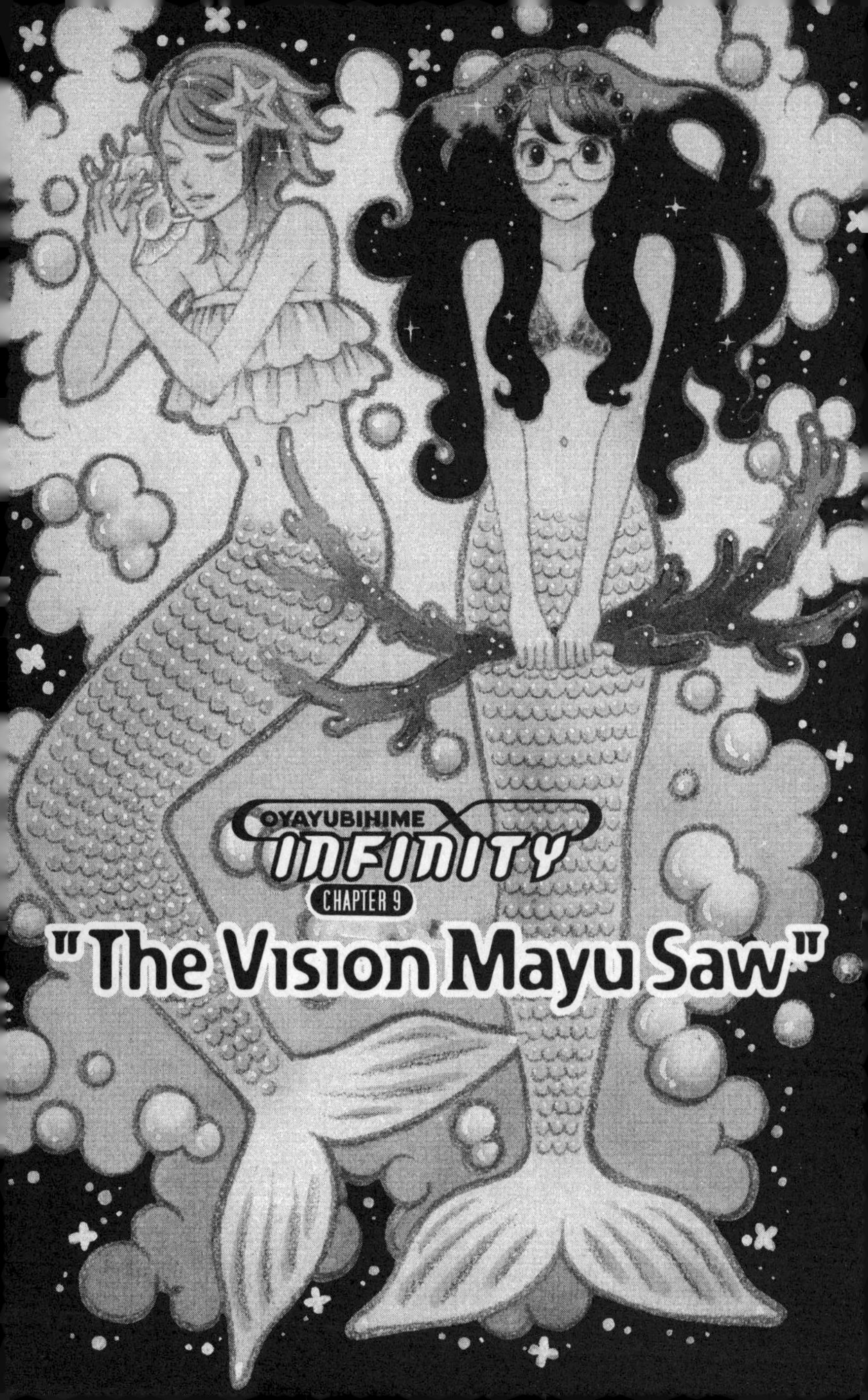
OYAYUBIHIME
INFINITY
CHAPTER 9
"The Vision Mayu Saw"

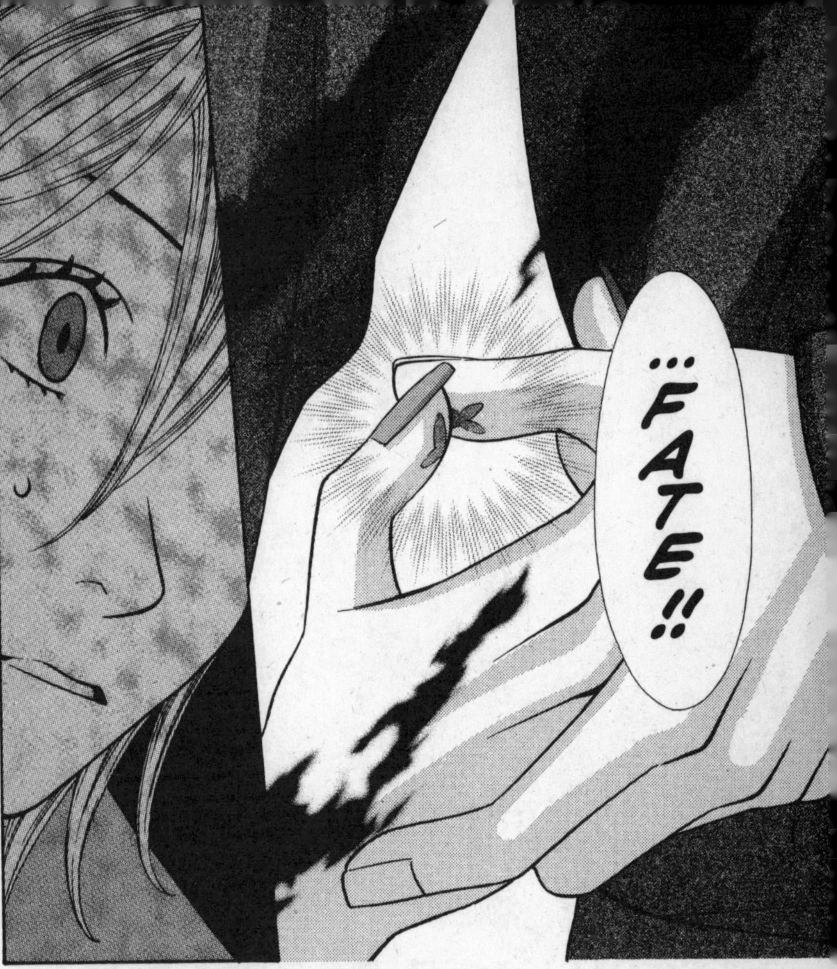
...FATE!!

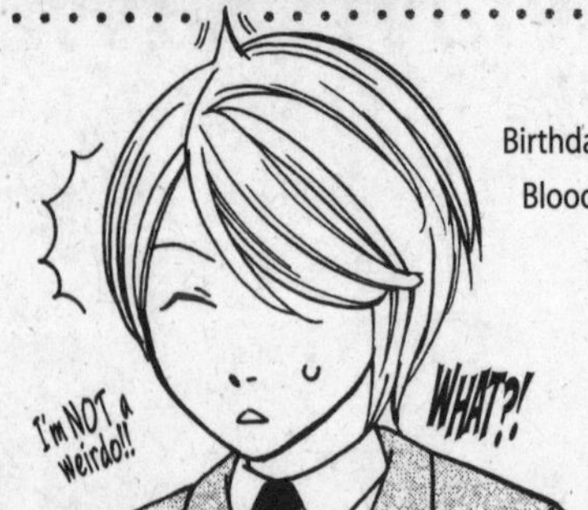
WHAT?!
I'm NOT a weirdo!!

Character Guide: 6

Chigusa Kazami

Birthday: 11/21

Blood Type: A

super unique

A freshman, he also seems to be the only one who actually gets anything done in the creative writing club. Though he seems like he has the most common sense at the moment, he's destined to become the most...unique person in the future. Of course, he doesn't know this yet. This kind of character appears often in my manga; this time, I'm going to make something of him...

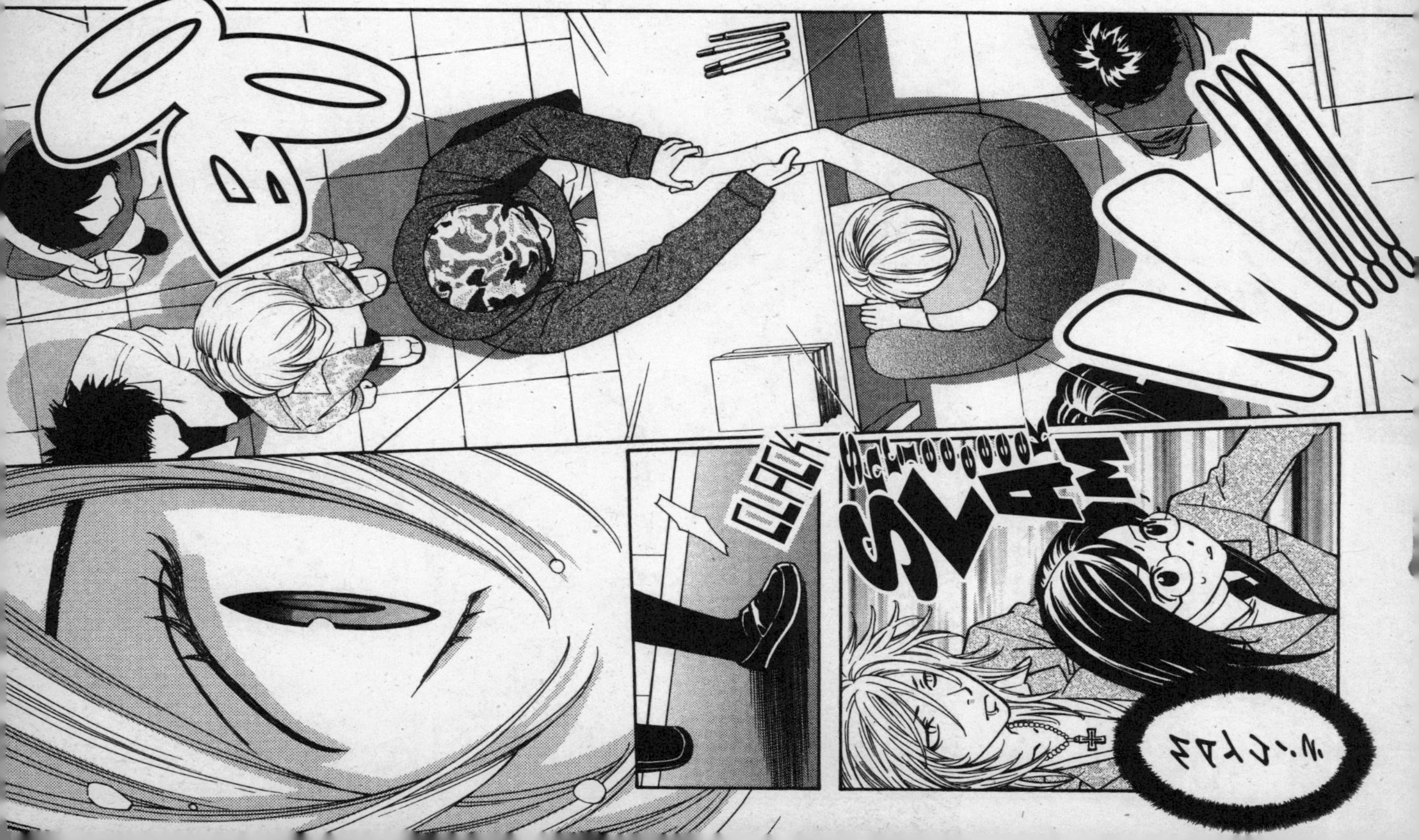
BOOM!!
Shrieeeeeek
SLAM
MAYU!?
CLACK

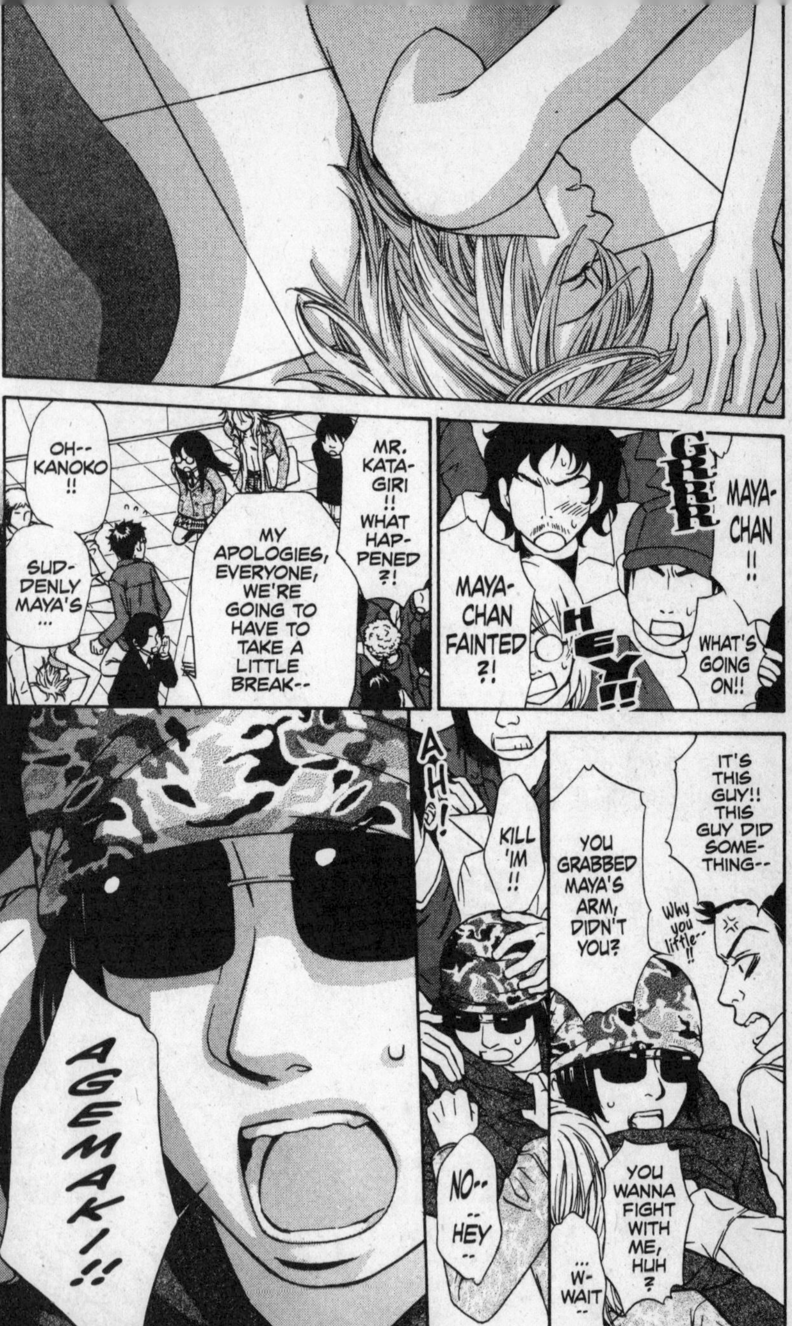
GRRR
MAYA-CHAN!!
HEY!!
MAYA-CHAN FAINTED?!
WHAT'S GOING ON!!
MR. KATA-GIRI!! WHAT HAP-PENED?!
MY APOLOGIES, EVERYONE, WE'RE GOING TO HAVE TO TAKE A LITTLE BREAK--
OH--KANOKO!!
SUD-DENLY MAYA'S...
IT'S THIS GUY!! THIS GUY DID SOME-THING--
Why you little--!!
YOU GRABBED MAYA'S ARM, DIDN'T YOU?
KILL 'IM!!
AH!
YOU WANNA FIGHT WITH ME, HUH?
...W-WAIT--
NO--..HEY--
AGEMAKI!!

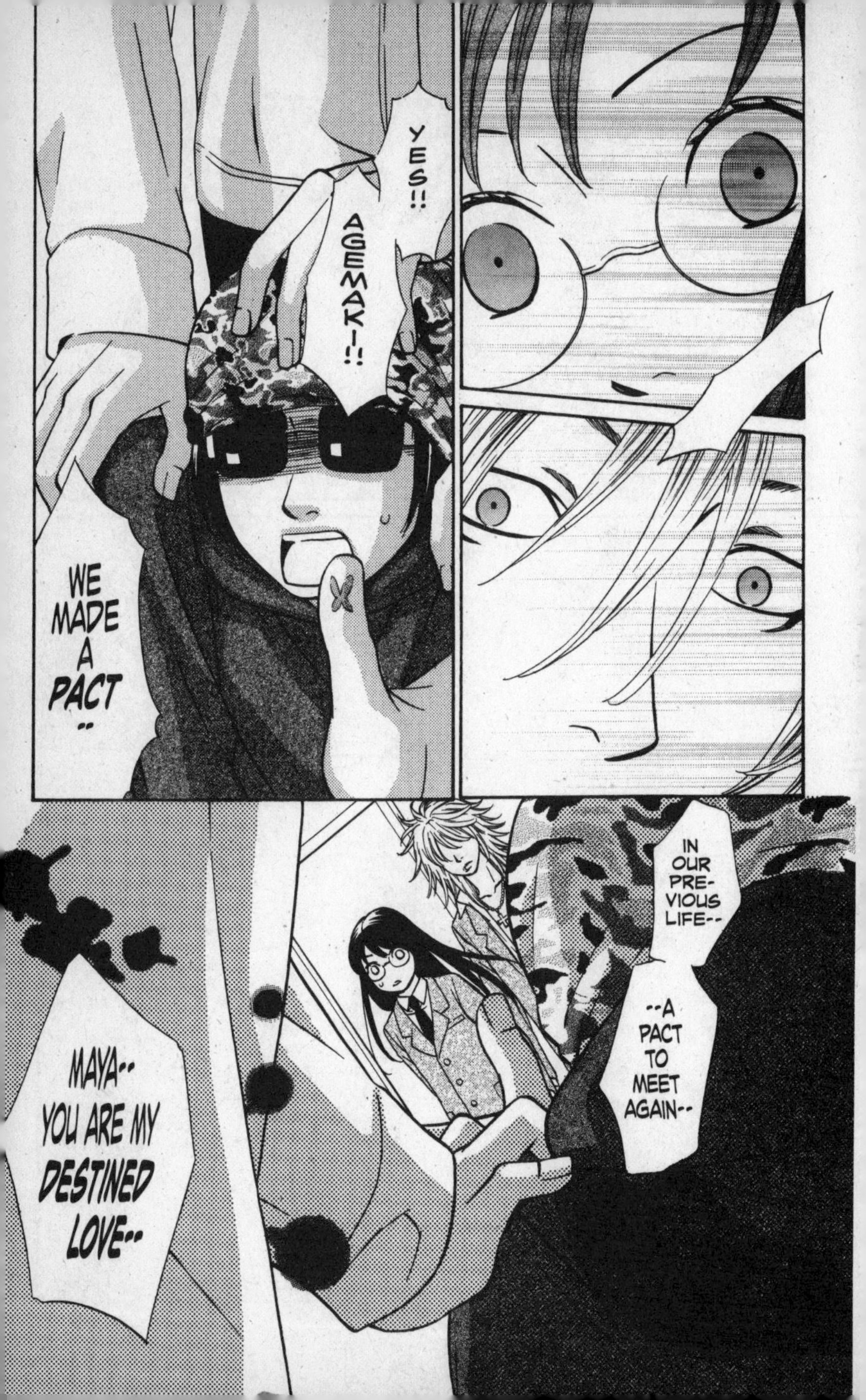
YES!! AGEMAKI!!
WE MADE A PACT--
IN OUR PREVIOUS LIFE--
--A PACT TO MEET AGAIN--
MAYA-- YOU ARE MY DESTINED LOVE--

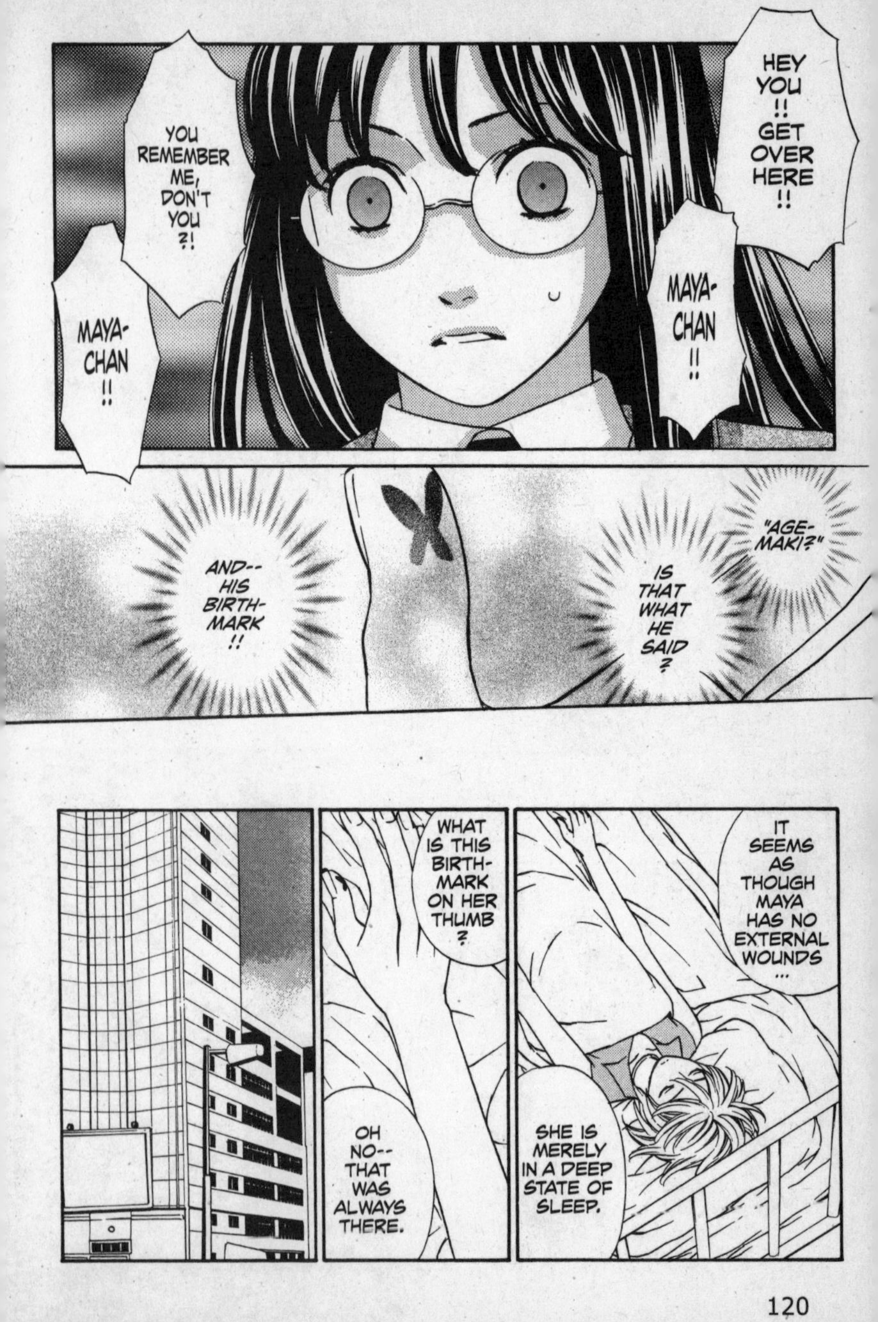
HEY YOU!! GET OVER HERE!!
MAYA-CHAN!!
YOU REMEMBER ME, DON'T YOU?!
MAYA-CHAN!!
"AGE-MAKI?"
IS THAT WHAT HE SAID?
AND--HIS BIRTH-MARK!!
IT SEEMS AS THOUGH MAYA HAS NO EXTERNAL WOUNDS...
SHE IS MERELY IN A DEEP STATE OF SLEEP.
WHAT IS THIS BIRTH-MARK ON HER THUMB?
OH NO--THAT WAS ALWAYS THERE.

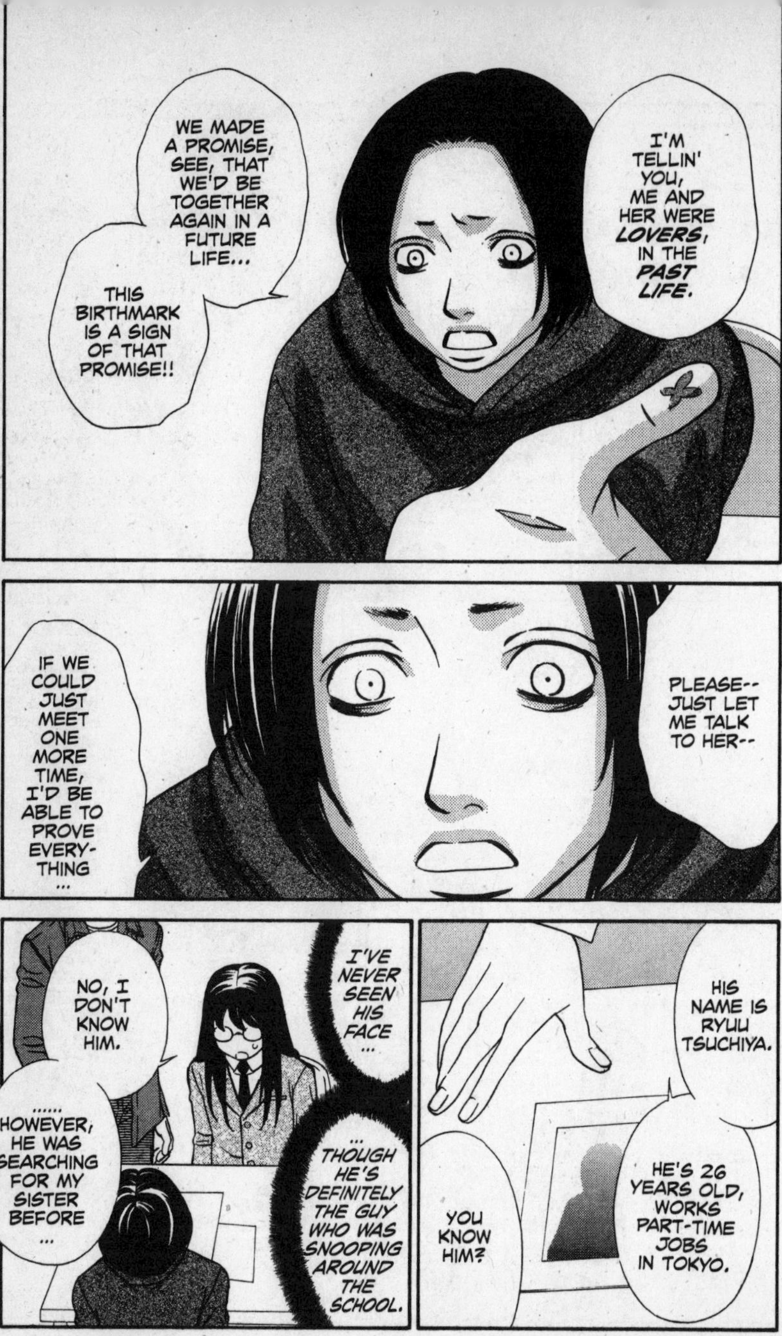
I'M TELLIN' YOU, ME AND HER WERE *LOVERS*, IN THE *PAST LIFE*.
WE MADE A PROMISE, SEE, THAT WE'D BE TOGETHER AGAIN IN A FUTURE LIFE...
THIS BIRTHMARK IS A SIGN OF THAT PROMISE!!
PLEASE-- JUST LET ME TALK TO HER--
IF WE COULD JUST MEET ONE MORE TIME, I'D BE ABLE TO PROVE EVERY-THING ...
HIS NAME IS RYUU TSUCHIYA.
HE'S 26 YEARS OLD, WORKS PART-TIME JOBS IN TOKYO.
YOU KNOW HIM?
I'VE NEVER SEEN HIS FACE ...
... THOUGH HE'S DEFINITELY THE GUY WHO WAS SNOOPING AROUND THE SCHOOL.
NO, I DON'T KNOW HIM.
...... HOWEVER, HE WAS SEARCHING FOR MY SISTER BEFORE ...

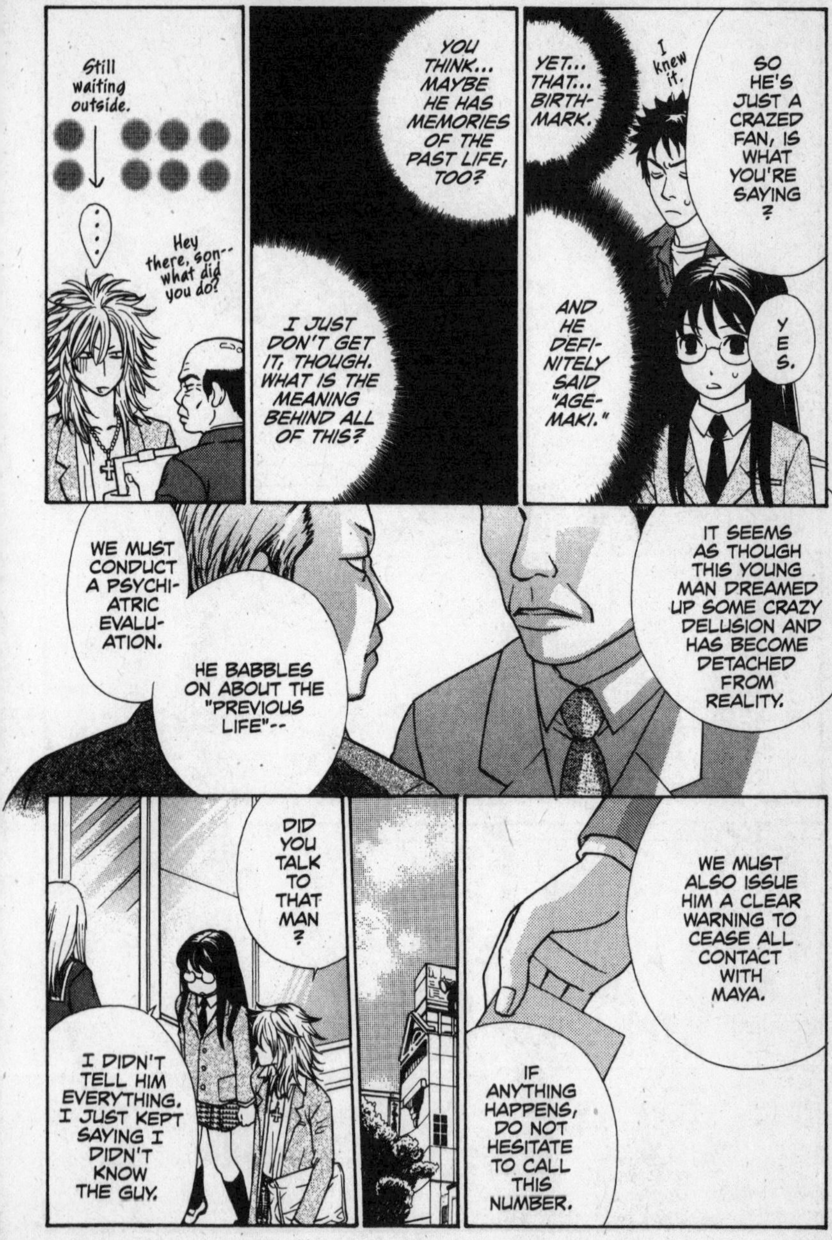
SO HE'S JUST A CRAZED FAN, IS WHAT YOU'RE SAYING?
I knew it.
YES.
YET... THAT... BIRTH-MARK.
AND HE DEFI-NITELY SAID "AGE-MAKI."
YOU THINK... MAYBE HE HAS MEMORIES OF THE PAST LIFE, TOO?
I JUST DON'T GET IT, THOUGH. WHAT IS THE MEANING BEHIND ALL OF THIS?
Still waiting outside.
...
Hey there, son--what did you do?
IT SEEMS AS THOUGH THIS YOUNG MAN DREAMED UP SOME CRAZY DELUSION AND HAS BECOME DETACHED FROM REALITY.
HE BABBLES ON ABOUT THE "PREVIOUS LIFE"--
WE MUST CONDUCT A PSYCHI-ATRIC EVALU-ATION.
WE MUST ALSO ISSUE HIM A CLEAR WARNING TO CEASE ALL CONTACT WITH MAYA.
IF ANYTHING HAPPENS, DO NOT HESITATE TO CALL THIS NUMBER.
DID YOU TALK TO THAT MAN?
I DIDN'T TELL HIM EVERYTHING. I JUST KEPT SAYING I DIDN'T KNOW THE GUY.

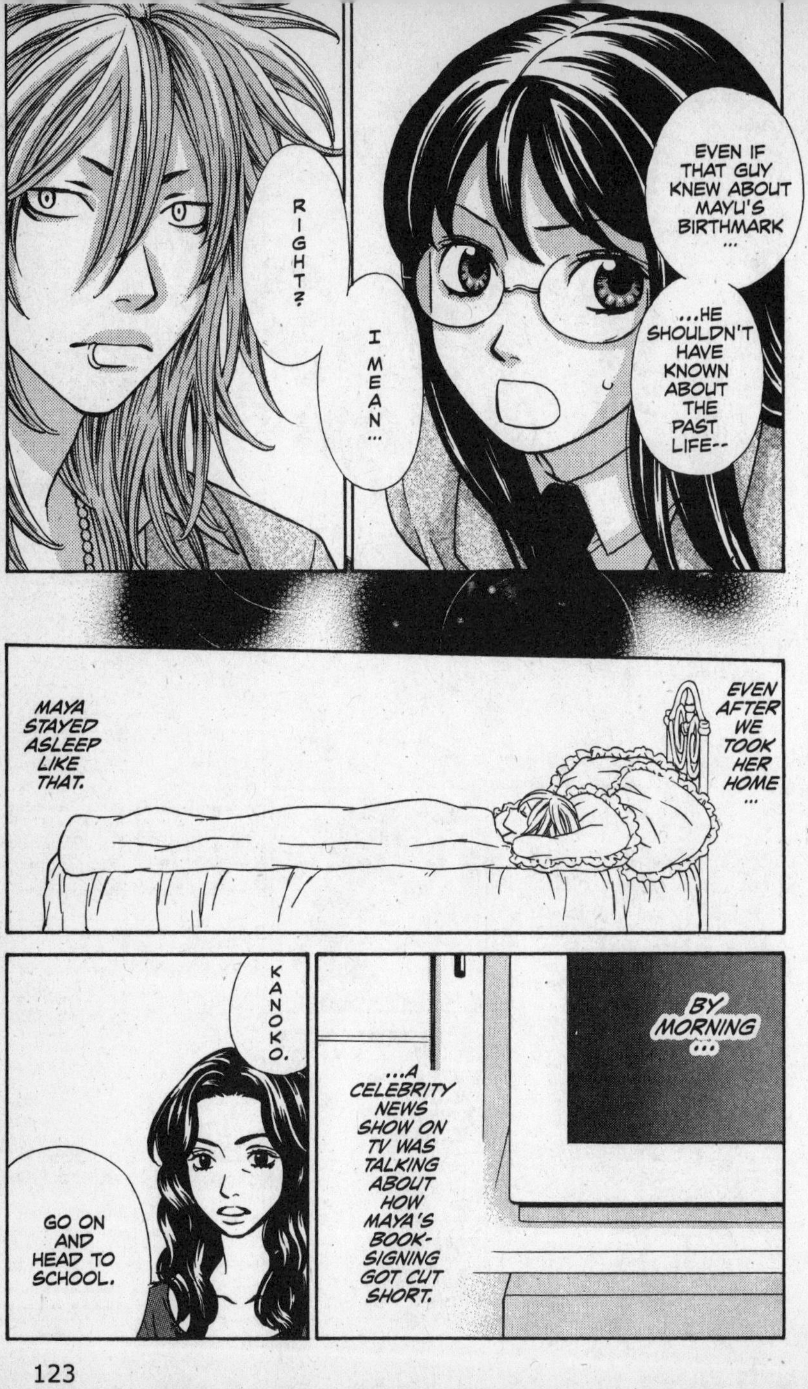
EVEN IF THAT GUY KNEW ABOUT MAYU'S BIRTHMARK...
...HE SHOULDN'T HAVE KNOWN ABOUT THE PAST LIFE--
I MEAN...
RIGHT?
EVEN AFTER WE TOOK HER HOME...
MAYA STAYED ASLEEP LIKE THAT.
BY MORNING...
...A CELEBRITY NEWS SHOW ON TV WAS TALKING ABOUT HOW MAYA'S BOOK-SIGNING GOT CUT SHORT.
KANOKO.
GO ON AND HEAD TO SCHOOL.

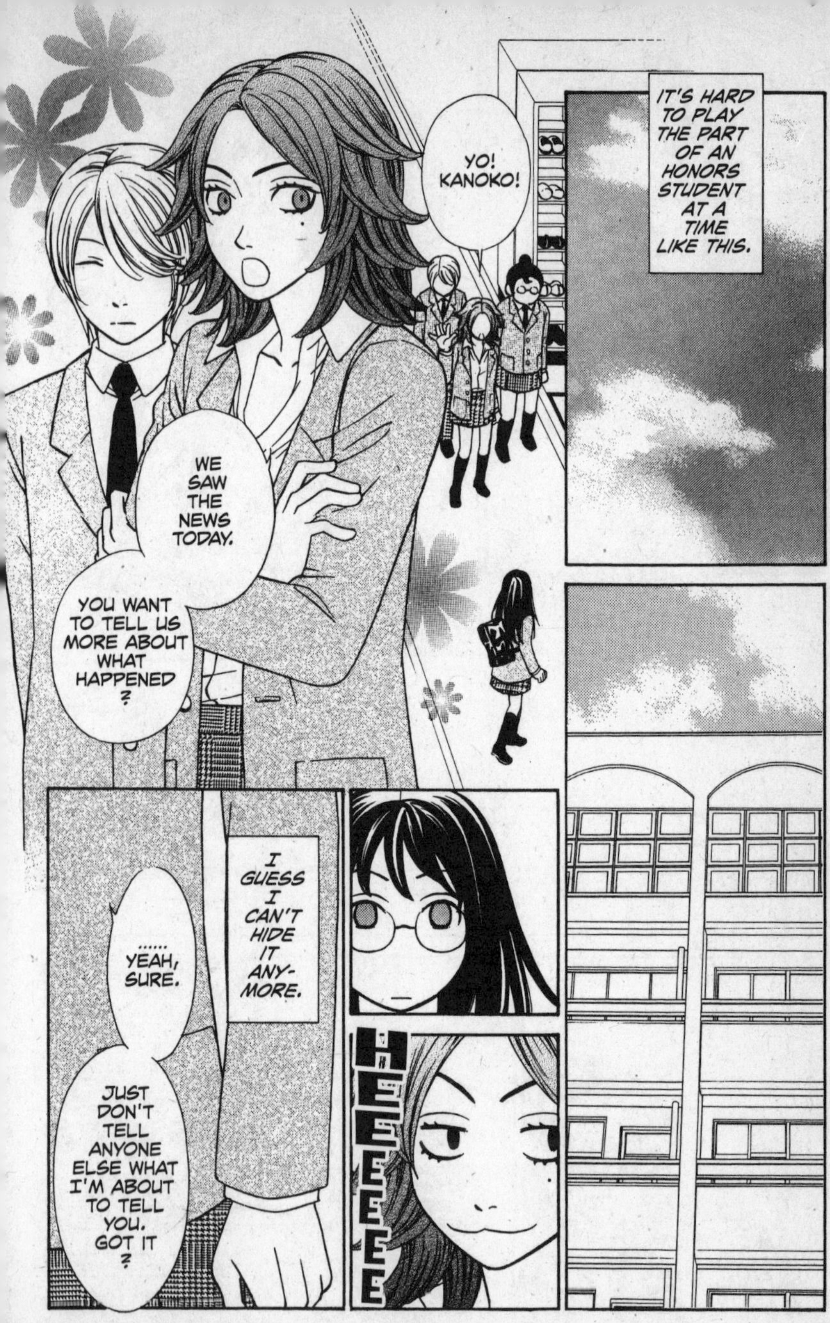
IT'S HARD TO PLAY THE PART OF AN HONORS STUDENT AT A TIME LIKE THIS.
YO! KANOKO!
WE SAW THE NEWS TODAY.
YOU WANT TO TELL US MORE ABOUT WHAT HAPPENED?
I GUESS I CAN'T HIDE IT ANY-MORE.
HEEEEEEE
...... YEAH, SURE.
JUST DON'T TELL ANYONE ELSE WHAT I'M ABOUT TO TELL YOU. GOT IT?

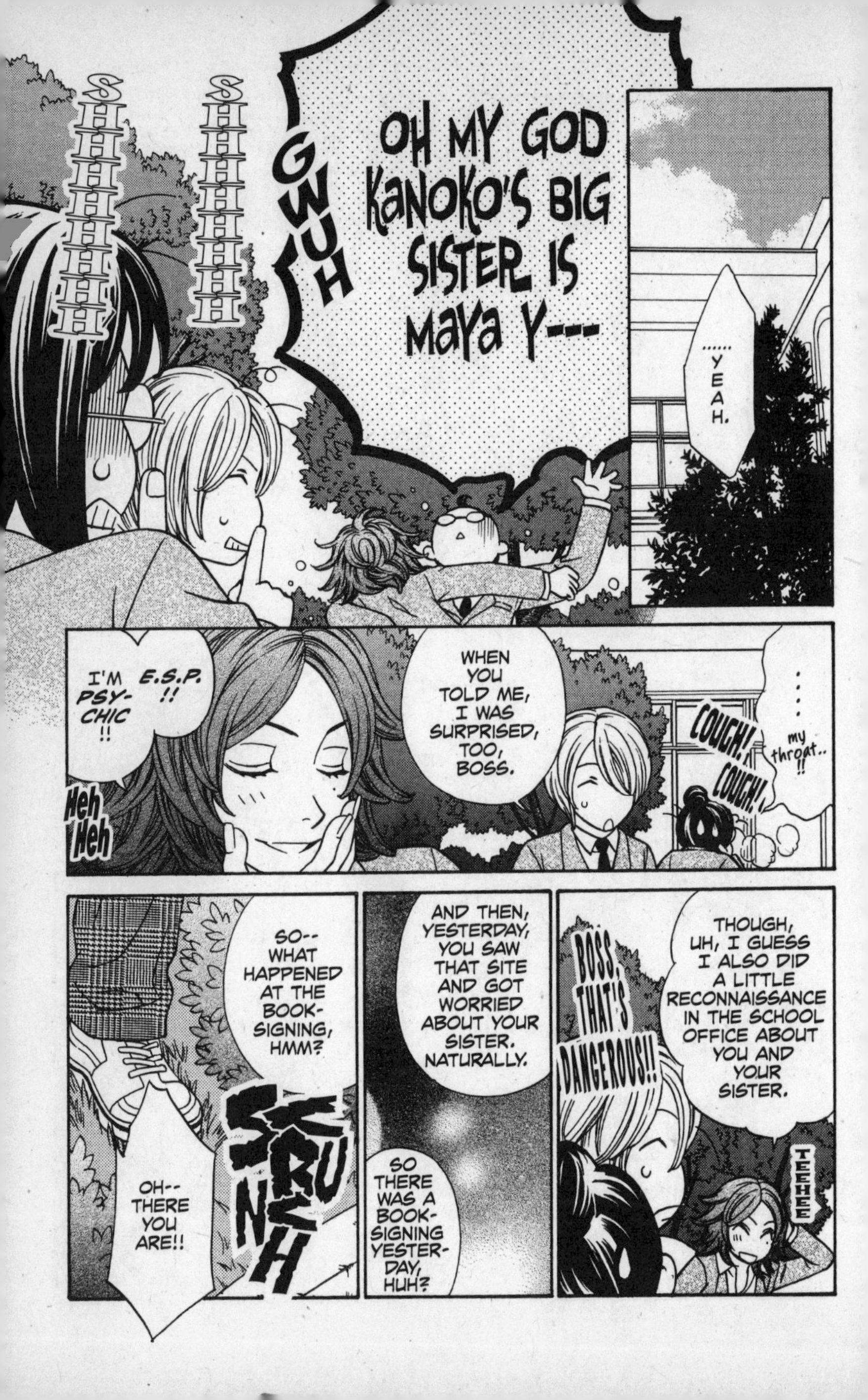
......YEAH.
OH MY GOD KANOKO'S BIG SISTER IS MAYA Y---
GWUH
SHHHHHHHH
SHHHHHHHHH
....
my throat..!!
COUGH! COUGH!
WHEN YOU TOLD ME, I WAS SURPRISED, TOO, BOSS.
E.S.P. !!
I'M PSY-CHIC !!
Heh Heh
THOUGH, UH, I GUESS I ALSO DID A LITTLE RECONNAISSANCE IN THE SCHOOL OFFICE ABOUT YOU AND YOUR SISTER.
BOSS, THAT'S DANGEROUS!!
TEEHEE
AND THEN, YESTERDAY, YOU SAW THAT SITE AND GOT WORRIED ABOUT YOUR SISTER. NATURALLY.
SO THERE WAS A BOOK-SIGNING YESTER-DAY, HUH?
SO-- WHAT HAPPENED AT THE BOOK-SIGNING, HMM?
SKRUNCH
OH-- THERE YOU ARE!!

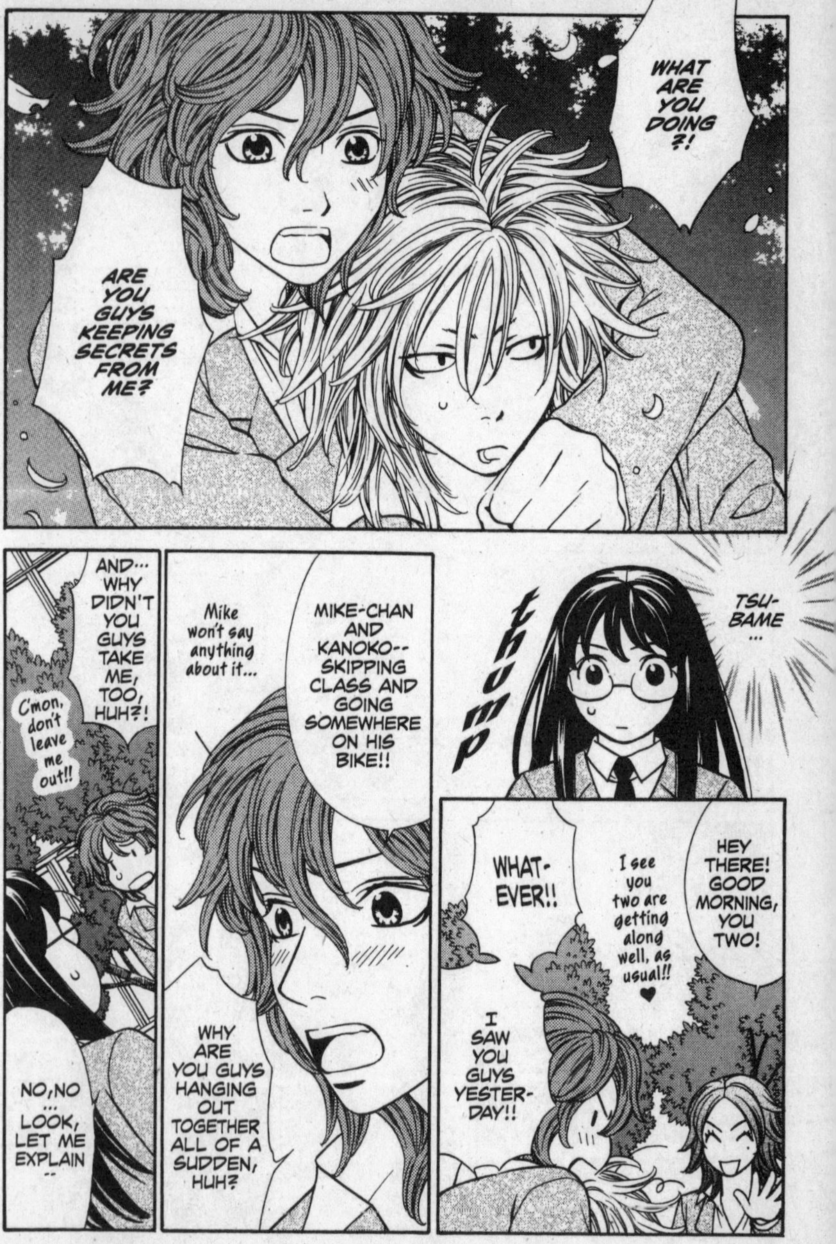
WHAT ARE YOU DOING?!
ARE YOU GUYS KEEPING SECRETS FROM ME?
TSU-BAME ...
thump
HEY THERE! GOOD MORNING, YOU TWO!
I see you two are getting along well, as usual!! ♥
WHAT-EVER!!
I SAW YOU GUYS YESTER-DAY!!
MIKE-CHAN AND KANOKO-- SKIPPING CLASS AND GOING SOMEWHERE ON HIS BIKE!!
Mike won't say anything about it...
WHY ARE YOU GUYS HANGING OUT TOGETHER ALL OF A SUDDEN, HUH?
AND... WHY DIDN'T YOU GUYS TAKE ME, TOO, HUH?!
C'mon, don't leave me out!!
NO, NO ... LOOK, LET ME EXPLAIN --

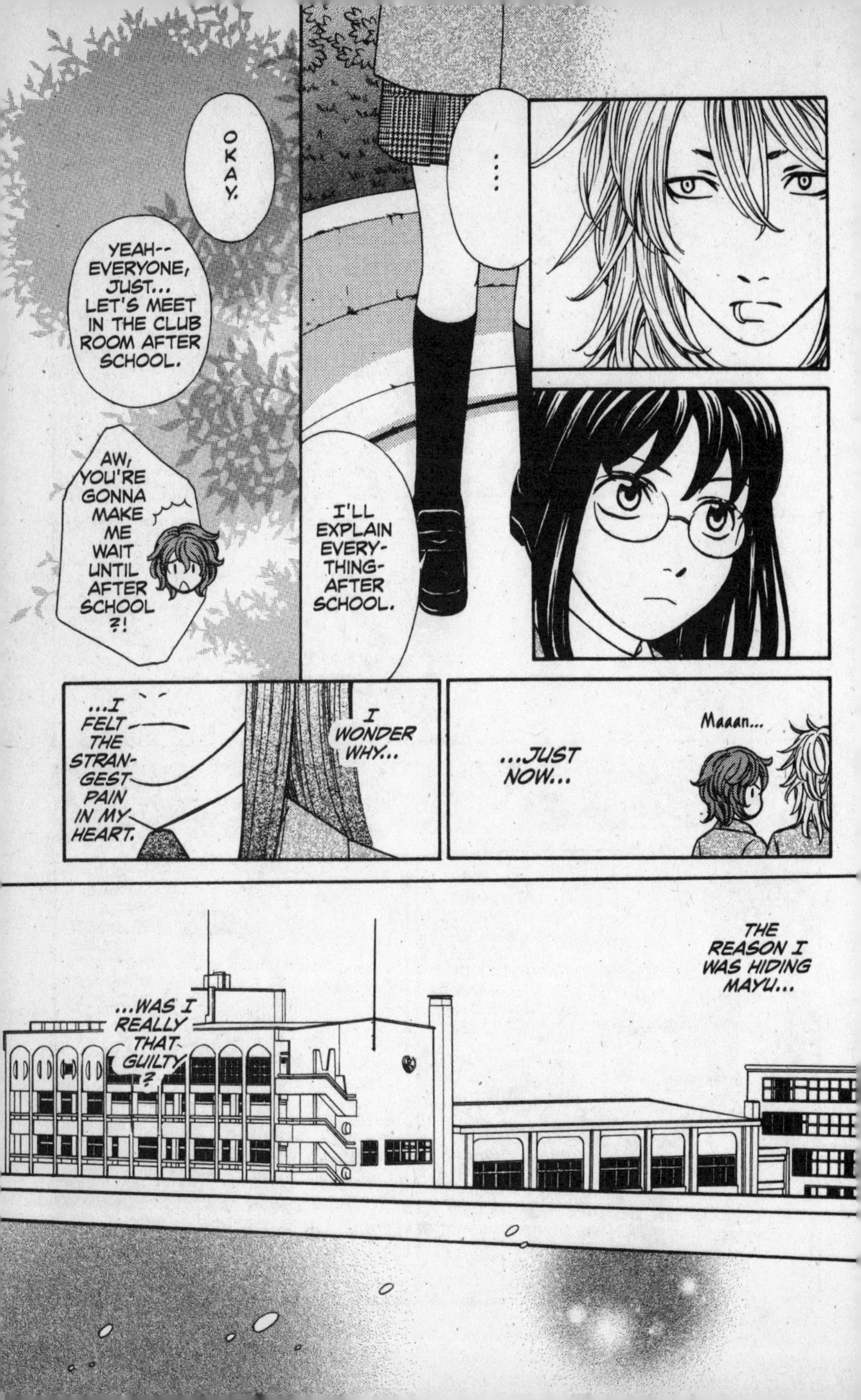
....
I'LL EXPLAIN EVERYTHING- AFTER SCHOOL.
OKAY.
YEAH--EVERYONE, JUST... LET'S MEET IN THE CLUB ROOM AFTER SCHOOL.
AW, YOU'RE GONNA MAKE ME WAIT UNTIL AFTER SCHOOL?!
Maaan...
...JUST NOW...
I WONDER WHY...
...I FELT THE STRANGEST PAIN IN MY HEART.
THE REASON I WAS HIDING MAYU...
...WAS I REALLY THAT GUILTY?

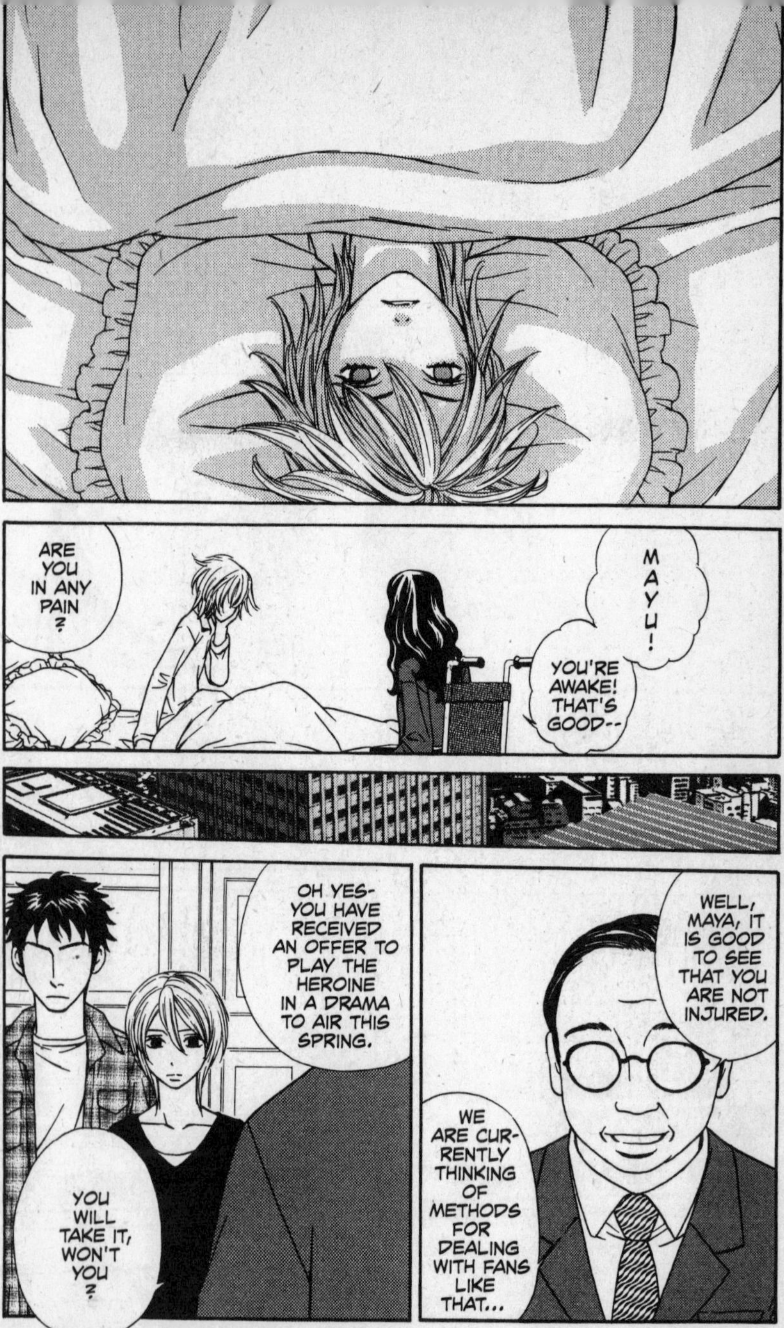
MAYU!
YOU'RE AWAKE! THAT'S GOOD--
ARE YOU IN ANY PAIN?
WELL, MAYA, IT IS GOOD TO SEE THAT YOU ARE NOT INJURED.
WE ARE CUR-RENTLY THINKING OF METHODS FOR DEALING WITH FANS LIKE THAT...
OH YES- YOU HAVE RECEIVED AN OFFER TO PLAY THE HEROINE IN A DRAMA TO AIR THIS SPRING.
YOU WILL TAKE IT, WON'T YOU?

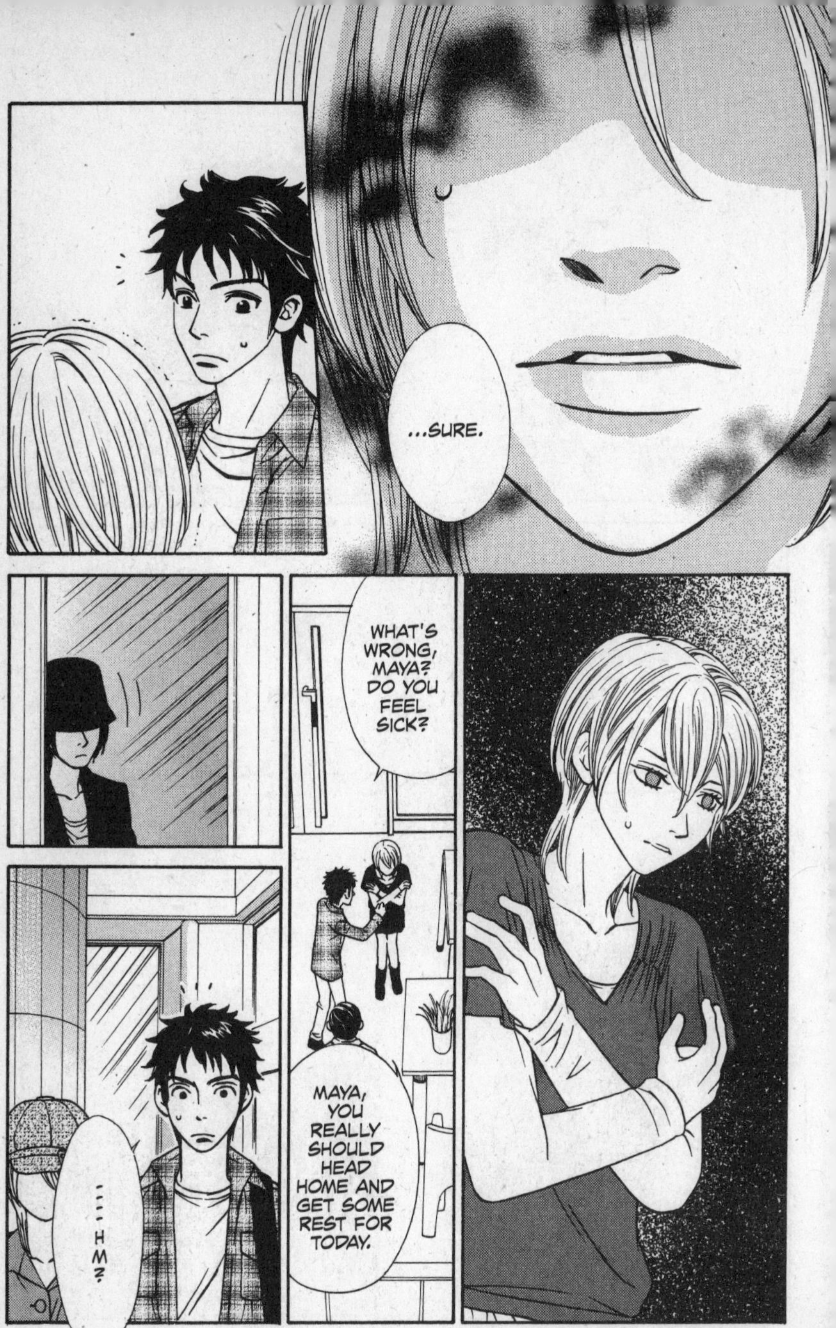
...SURE.
WHAT'S WRONG, MAYA? DO YOU FEEL SICK?
MAYA, YOU REALLY SHOULD HEAD HOME AND GET SOME REST FOR TODAY.
...HM?

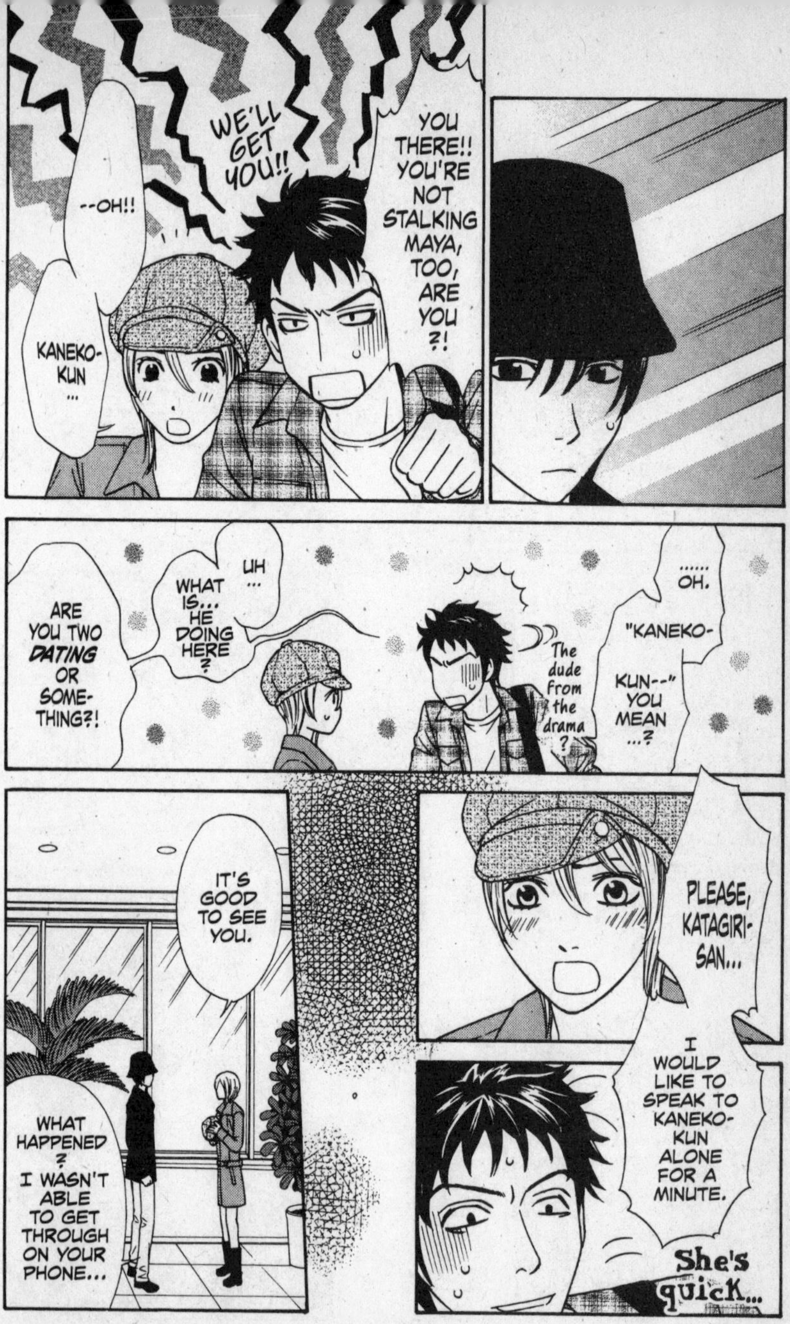
YOU THERE!! YOU'RE NOT STALKING MAYA, TOO, ARE YOU?!
WE'LL GET YOU!!
--OH!!
KANEKO-KUN ...
...... OH.
"KANEKO-KUN--" YOU MEAN ...?
The dude from the drama?
UH ...
WHAT IS... HE DOING HERE?
ARE YOU TWO DATING OR SOMETHING?!
PLEASE, KATAGIRI-SAN...
I WOULD LIKE TO SPEAK TO KANEKO-KUN ALONE FOR A MINUTE.
She's quick...
IT'S GOOD TO SEE YOU.
WHAT HAPPENED? I WASN'T ABLE TO GET THROUGH ON YOUR PHONE...

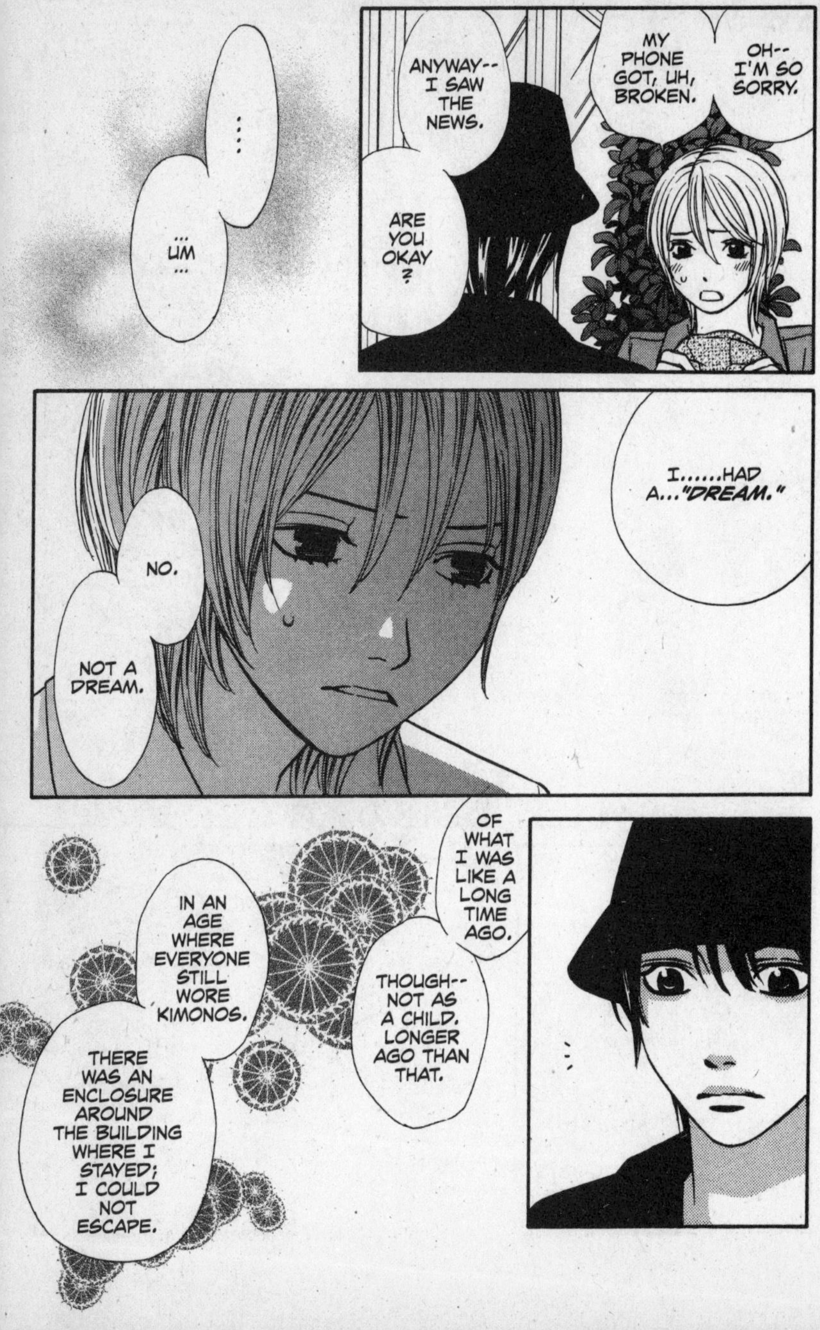

OH-- I'M SO SORRY.
MY PHONE GOT, UH, BROKEN.
ANYWAY-- I SAW THE NEWS.
ARE YOU OKAY?
....
...UM...
I......HAD A..."DREAM."
NO.
NOT A DREAM.
...
OF WHAT I WAS LIKE A LONG TIME AGO.
THOUGH-- NOT AS A CHILD. LONGER AGO THAN THAT.
IN AN AGE WHERE EVERYONE STILL WORE KIMONOS.
THERE WAS AN ENCLOSURE AROUND THE BUILDING WHERE I STAYED; I COULD NOT ESCAPE.

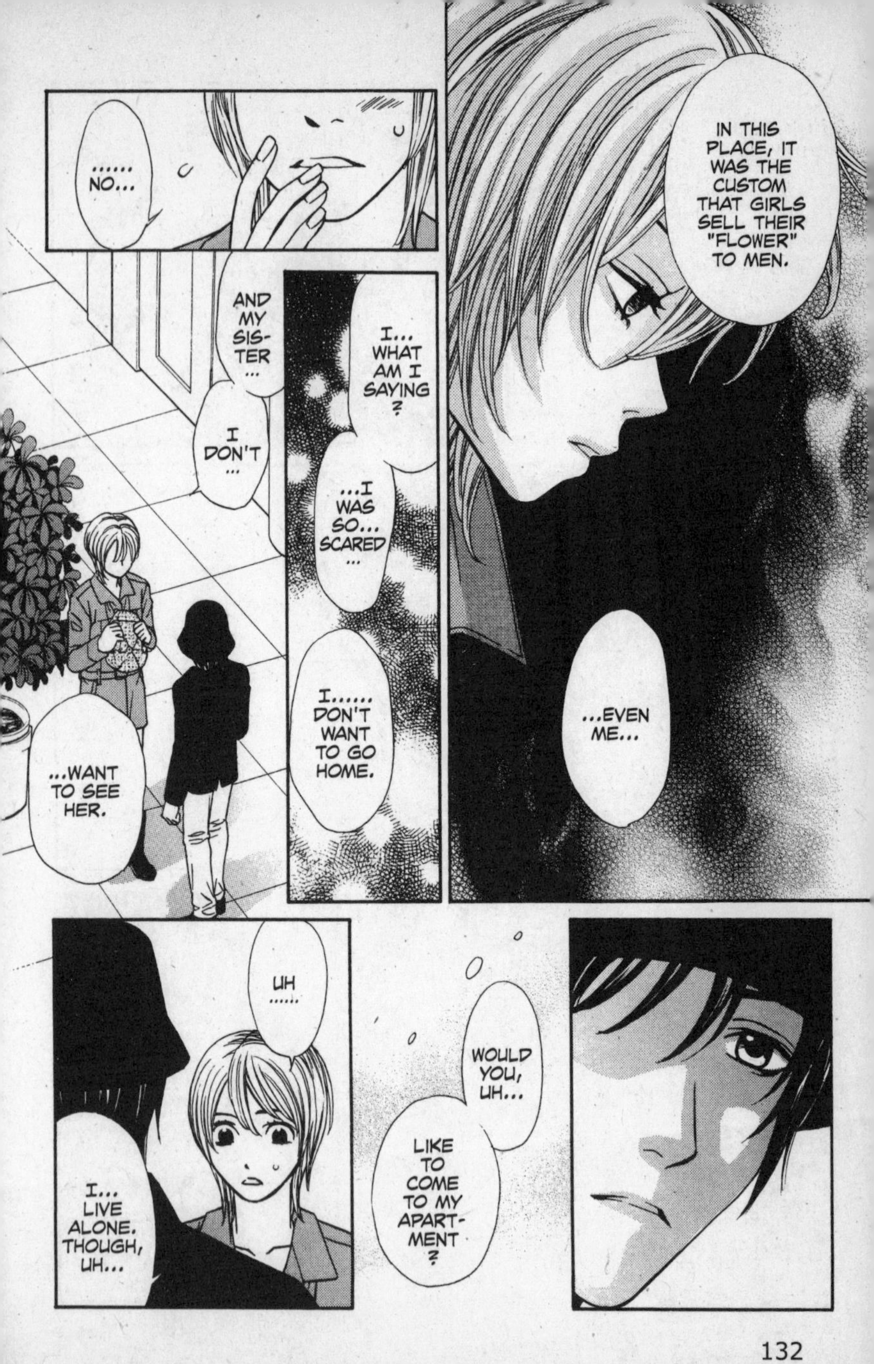
IN THIS PLACE, IT WAS THE CUSTOM THAT GIRLS SELL THEIR "FLOWER" TO MEN.
...EVEN ME...
......NO...
I... WHAT AM I SAYING?
...I WAS SO... SCARED...
I...... DON'T WANT TO GO HOME.
AND MY SISTER...
I DON'T...
...WANT TO SEE HER.
WOULD YOU, UH...
LIKE TO COME TO MY APARTMENT?
UH......
I... LIVE ALONE. THOUGH, UH...

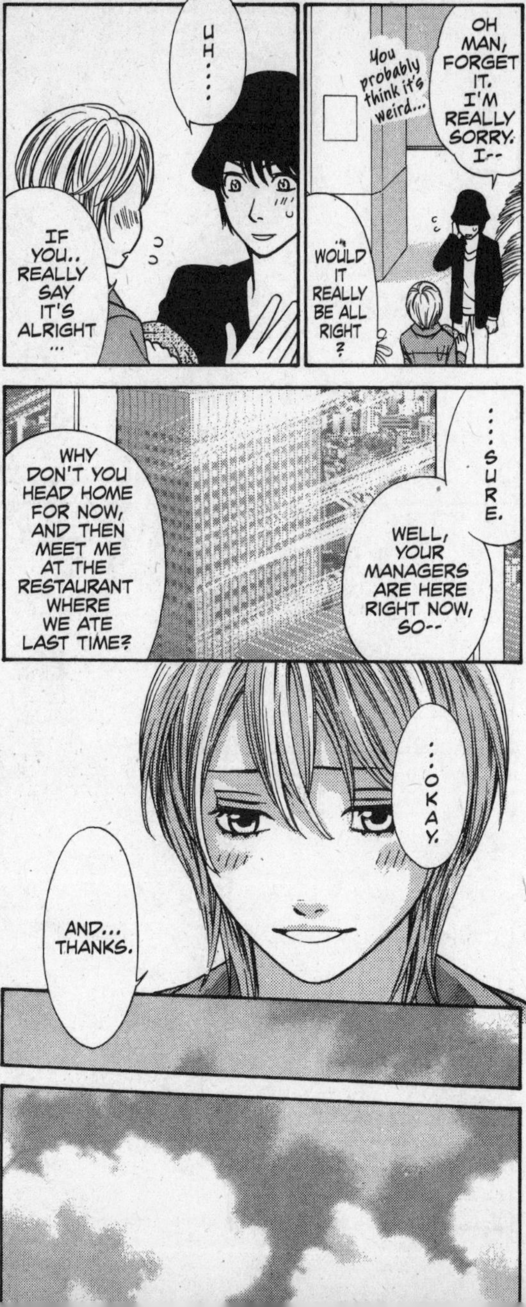
OH MAN, FORGET IT. I'M REALLY SORRY. I--
You probably think it's weird...
WOULD IT REALLY BE ALL RIGHT?
UH....
IF YOU.. REALLY SAY IT'S ALRIGHT ...
...SURE.
WELL, YOUR MANAGERS ARE HERE RIGHT NOW, SO--
WHY DON'T YOU HEAD HOME FOR NOW, AND THEN MEET ME AT THE RESTAURANT WHERE WE ATE LAST TIME?
...OKAY.
AND... THANKS.

THANK YOU VERY MUCH FOR READING

★

Thank you very much for picking up OYAYUBIHIME INFNITY Volume 2!! It's been a whole year since I first started work on this story. It went by really fast. There was a lot of planning stuff to get out of the way even before I could begin working. There are a lot of ups and downs and moments of crazy panic, though in the end, I got it finished, and here it is!!

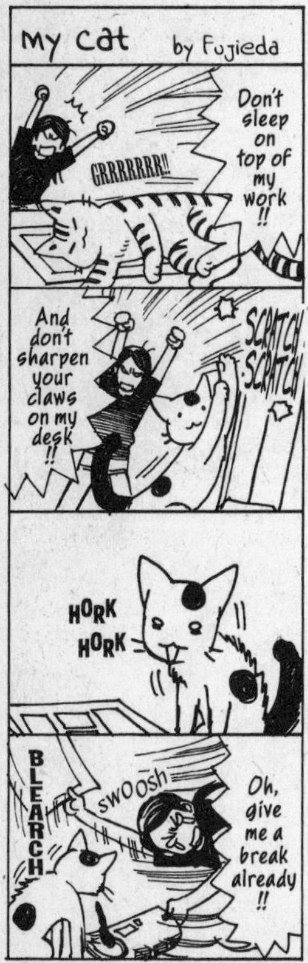
My Cat by Fujieda
Don't sleep on top of my work!!
GRRRRRRR!!
And don't sharpen your claws on my desk!!
SCRATCH SCRATCH
HORK HORK
BLEARCH
SWOOSH
Oh, give me a break already!!

Yes, that's a hairball.

FIN.

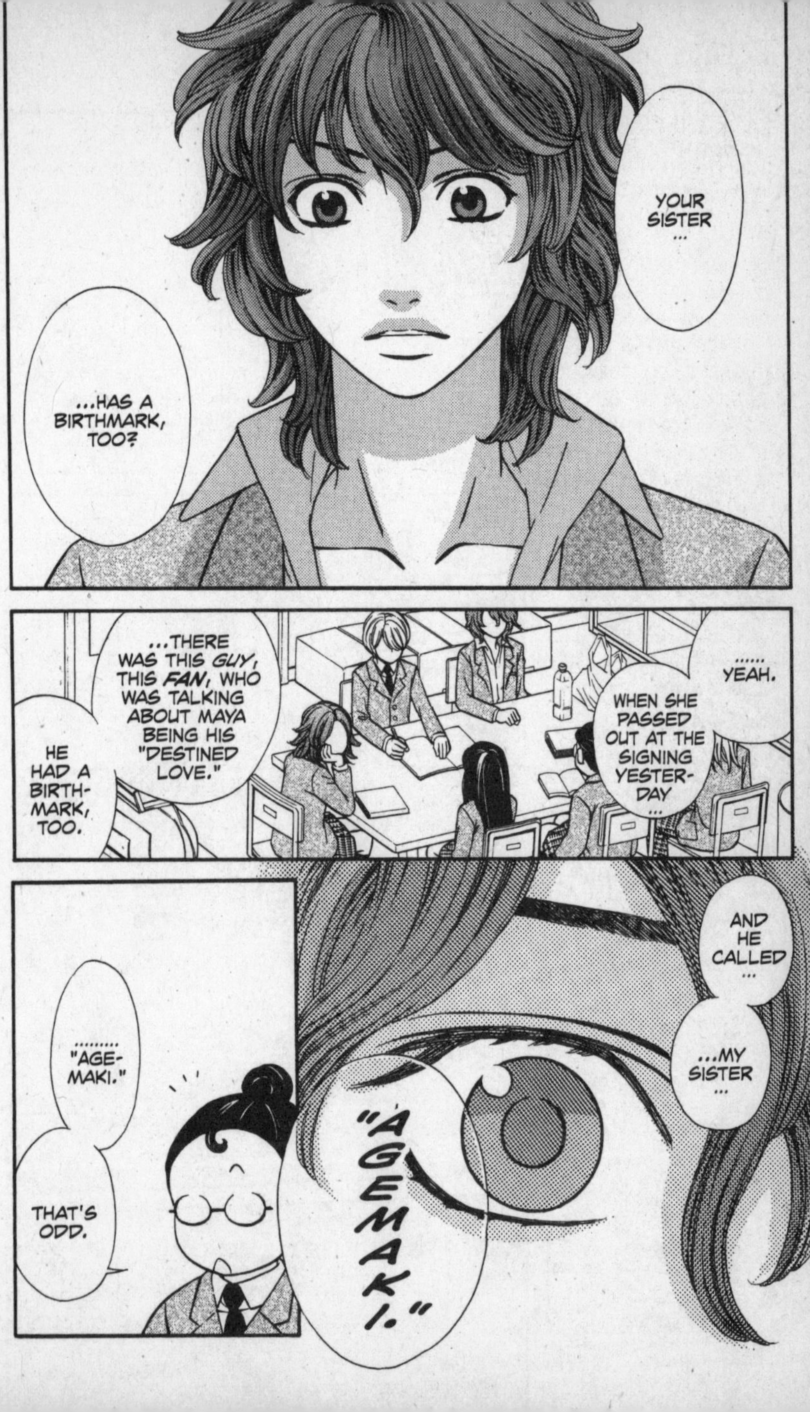

YOUR SISTER ...
...HAS A BIRTHMARK, TOO?
...... YEAH.
WHEN SHE PASSED OUT AT THE SIGNING YESTER-DAY ...
...THERE WAS THIS GUY, THIS FAN, WHO WAS TALKING ABOUT MAYA BEING HIS "DESTINED LOVE."
HE HAD A BIRTH-MARK, TOO.
AND HE CALLED ...
...MY SISTER ...
"AGEMAKI."
.... "AGE-MAKI."
THAT'S ODD.

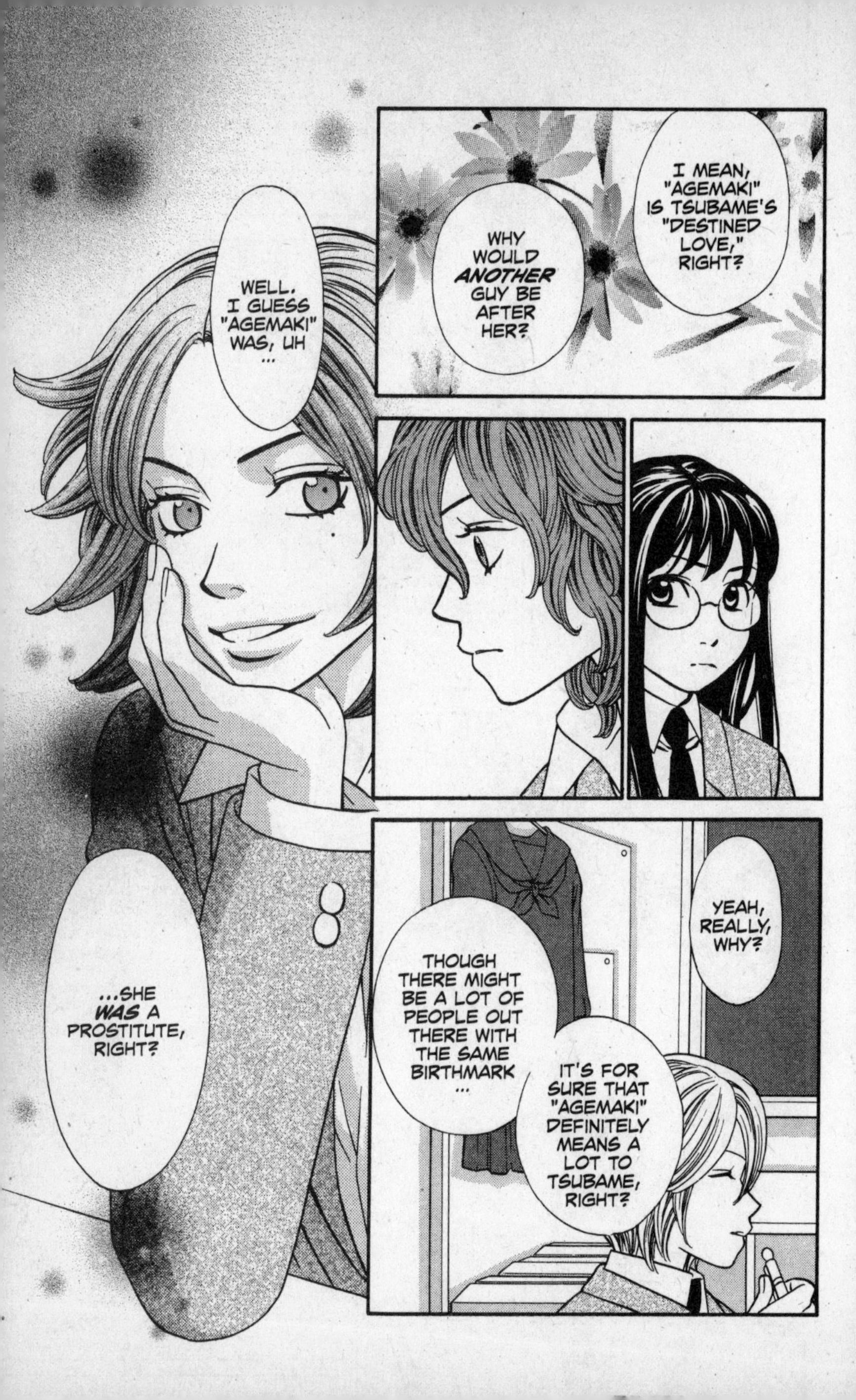
I MEAN, "AGEMAKI" IS TSUBAME'S "DESTINED LOVE," RIGHT?
WHY WOULD *ANOTHER* GUY BE AFTER HER?
YEAH, REALLY, WHY?
THOUGH THERE MIGHT BE A LOT OF PEOPLE OUT THERE WITH THE SAME BIRTHMARK ...
IT'S FOR SURE THAT "AGEMAKI" DEFINITELY MEANS A LOT TO TSUBAME, RIGHT?
WELL. I GUESS "AGEMAKI" WAS, UH ...
...SHE *WAS* A PROSTITUTE, RIGHT?

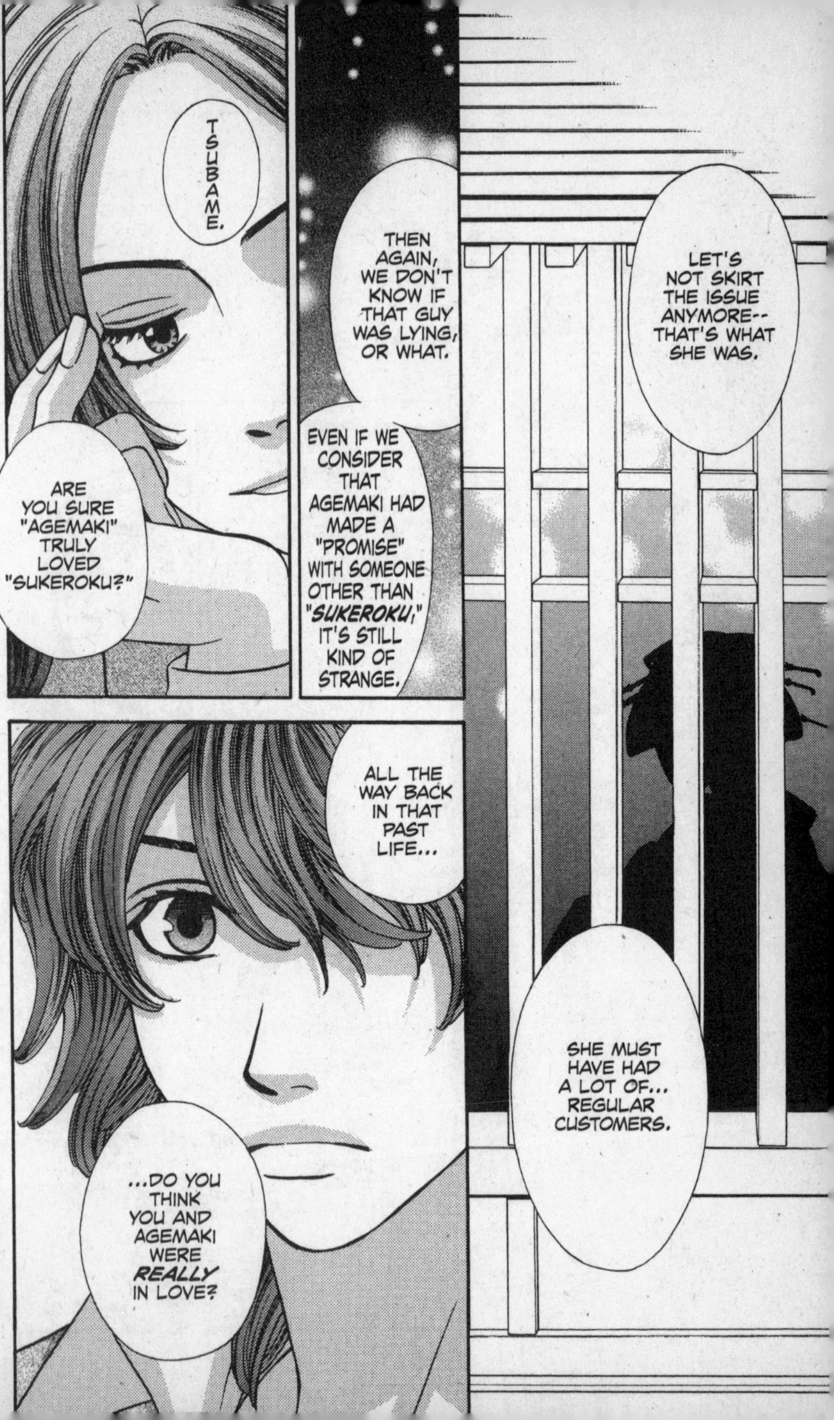
LET'S NOT SKIRT THE ISSUE ANYMORE-- THAT'S WHAT SHE WAS.
SHE MUST HAVE HAD A LOT OF... REGULAR CUSTOMERS.
THEN AGAIN, WE DON'T KNOW IF THAT GUY WAS LYING, OR WHAT.
EVEN IF WE CONSIDER THAT AGEMAKI HAD MADE A "PROMISE" WITH SOMEONE OTHER THAN "*SUKEROKU*," IT'S STILL KIND OF STRANGE.
TSUBAME.
ARE YOU SURE "AGEMAKI" TRULY LOVED "SUKEROKU?"
ALL THE WAY BACK IN THAT PAST LIFE...
...DO YOU THINK YOU AND AGEMAKI WERE *REALLY* IN LOVE?

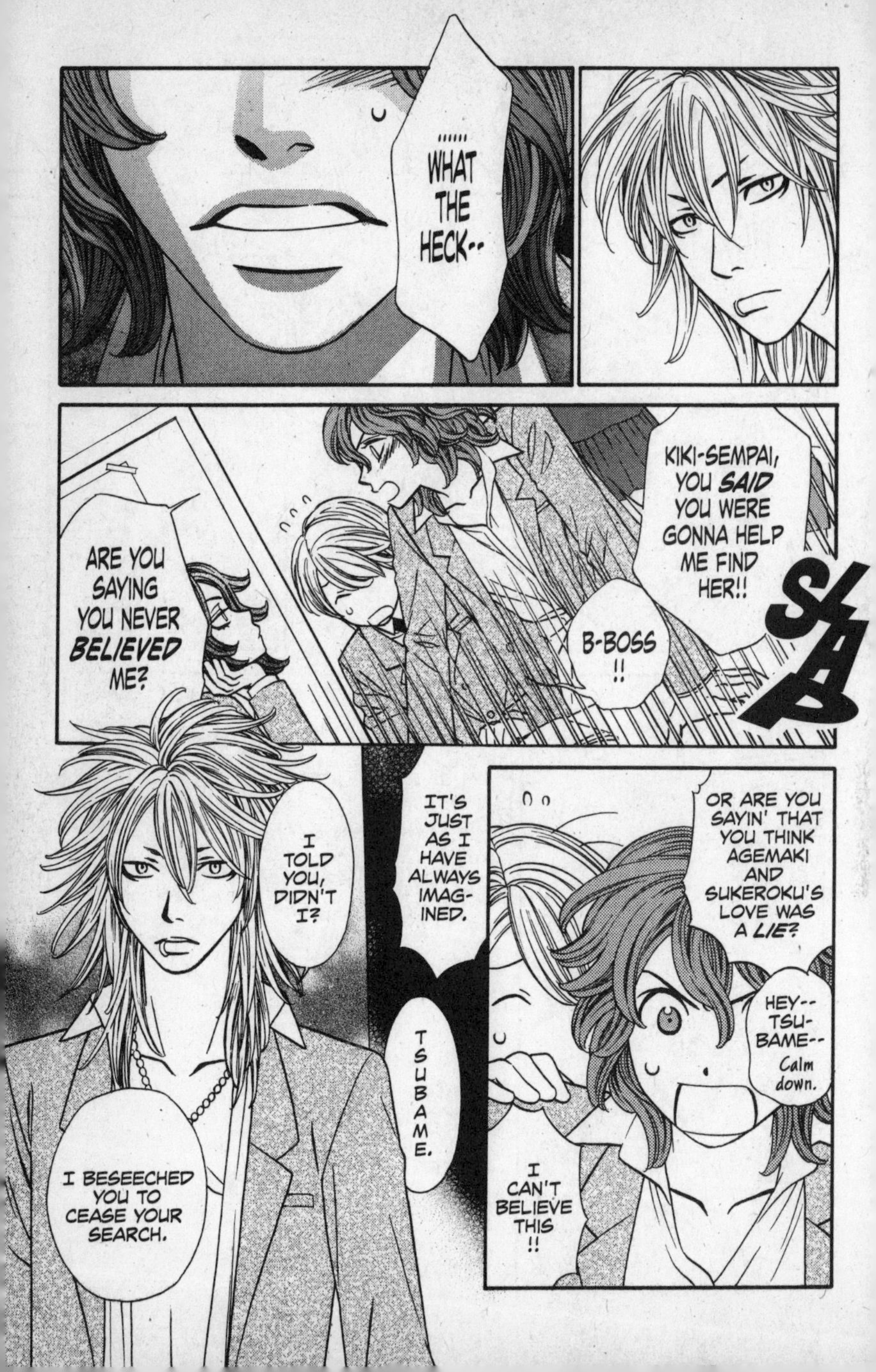
......WHAT THE HECK--
KIKI-SEMPAI, YOU SAID YOU WERE GONNA HELP ME FIND HER!!
SLAP
B-BOSS!!
ARE YOU SAYING YOU NEVER BELIEVED ME?
OR ARE YOU SAYIN' THAT YOU THINK AGEMAKI AND SUKEROKU'S LOVE WAS A LIE?
HEY--TSUBAME--
Calm down.
I CAN'T BELIEVE THIS!!
IT'S JUST AS I HAVE ALWAYS IMAGINED.
TSUBAME.
I TOLD YOU, DIDN'T I?
I BESEECHED YOU TO CEASE YOUR SEARCH.

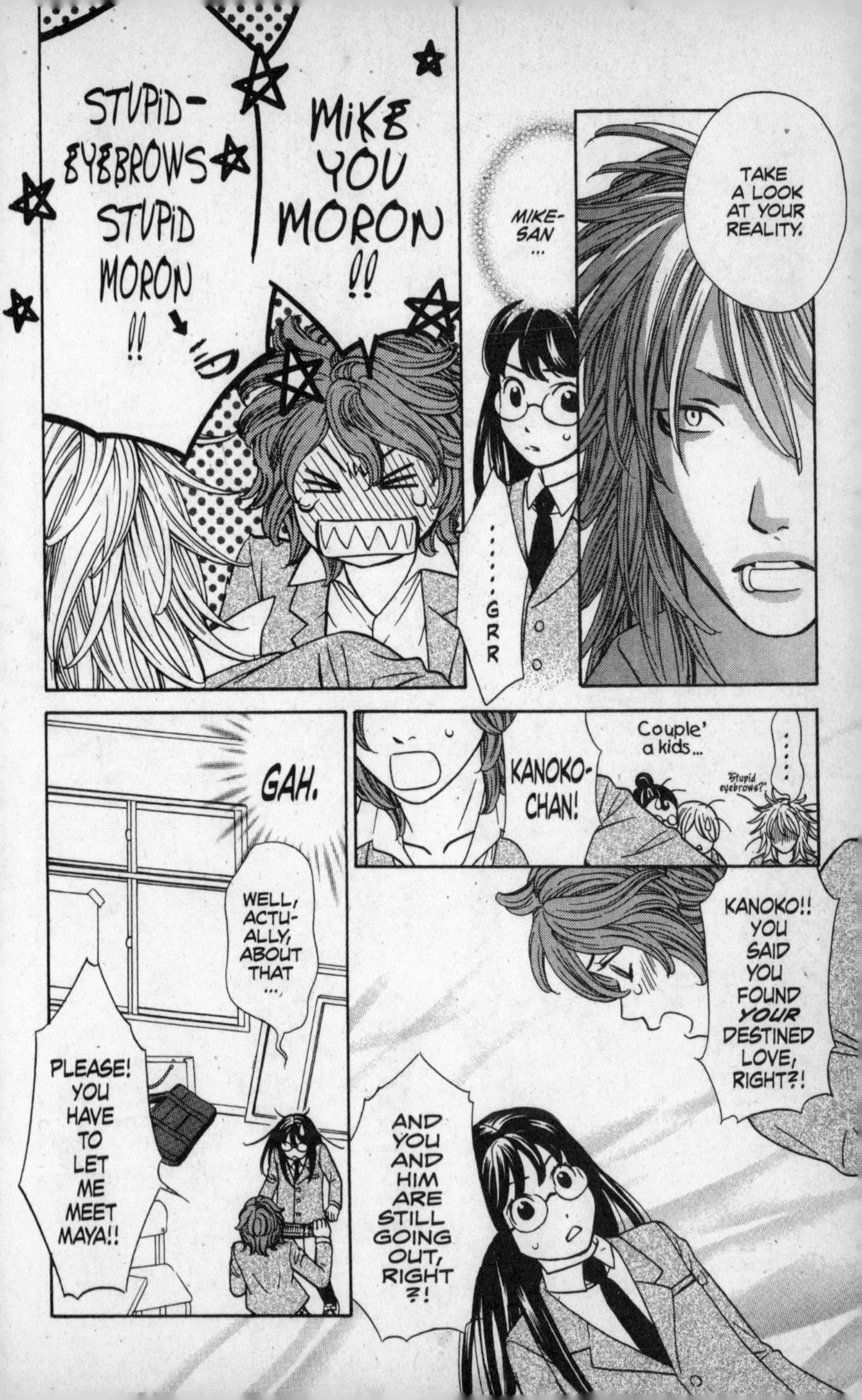
TAKE A LOOK AT YOUR REALITY.
MIKE-SAN...
.....GRR
MIKE YOU MORON!!
STUPID-EYEBROWS STUPID MORON!!
.....
"Stupid eyebrows?"
Couple' a kids...
KANOKO-CHAN!
KANOKO!! YOU SAID YOU FOUND YOUR DESTINED LOVE, RIGHT?!
AND YOU AND HIM ARE STILL GOING OUT, RIGHT?!
GAH.
WELL, ACTU-ALLY, ABOUT THAT...,
PLEASE! YOU HAVE TO LET ME MEET MAYA!!

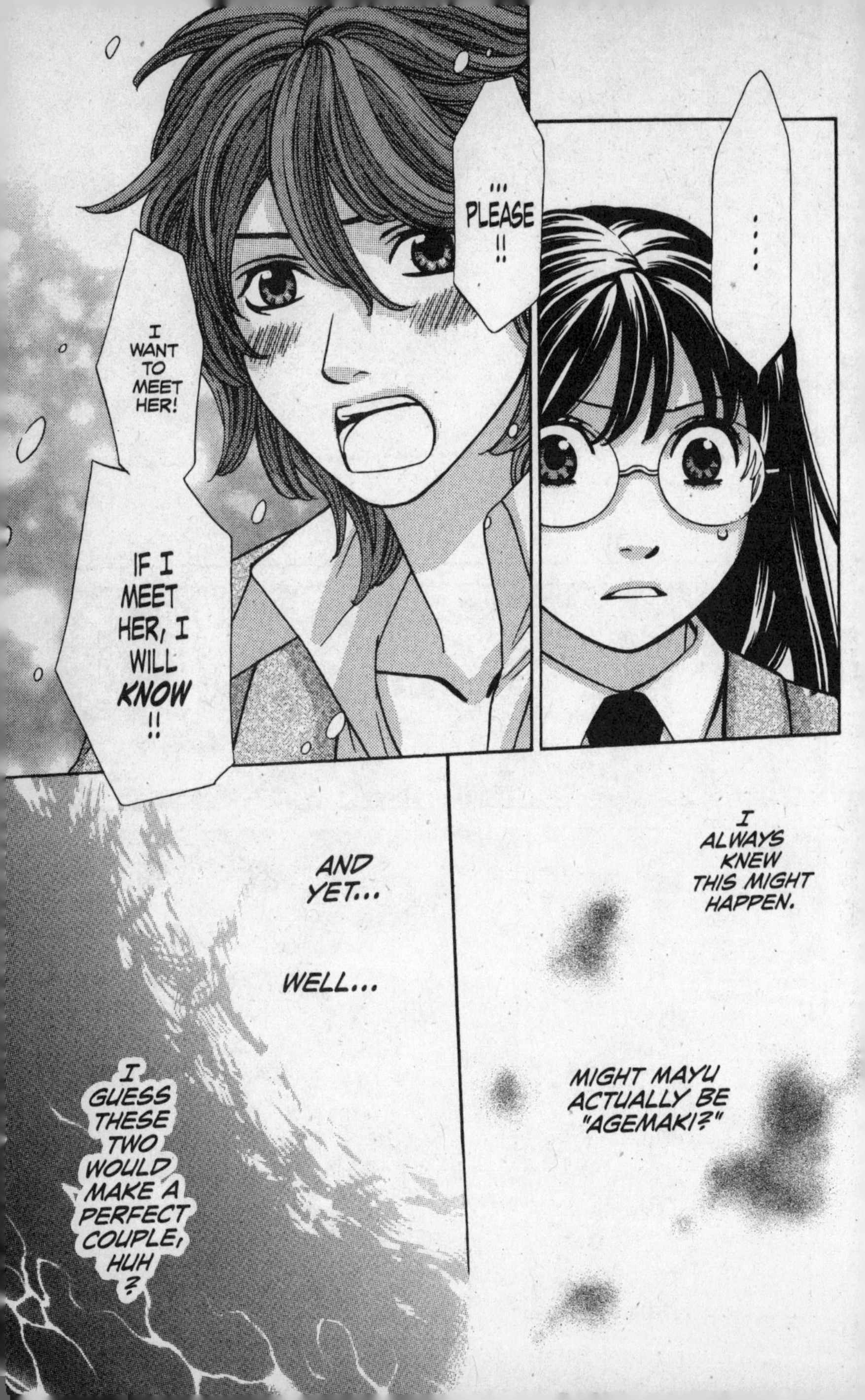
....
...PLEASE!!
I WANT TO MEET HER!
IF I MEET HER, I WILL *KNOW*!!
I ALWAYS KNEW THIS MIGHT HAPPEN.
MIGHT MAYU ACTUALLY BE "AGEMAKI?"
AND YET...
WELL...
I GUESS THESE TWO WOULD MAKE A PERFECT COUPLE, HUH?

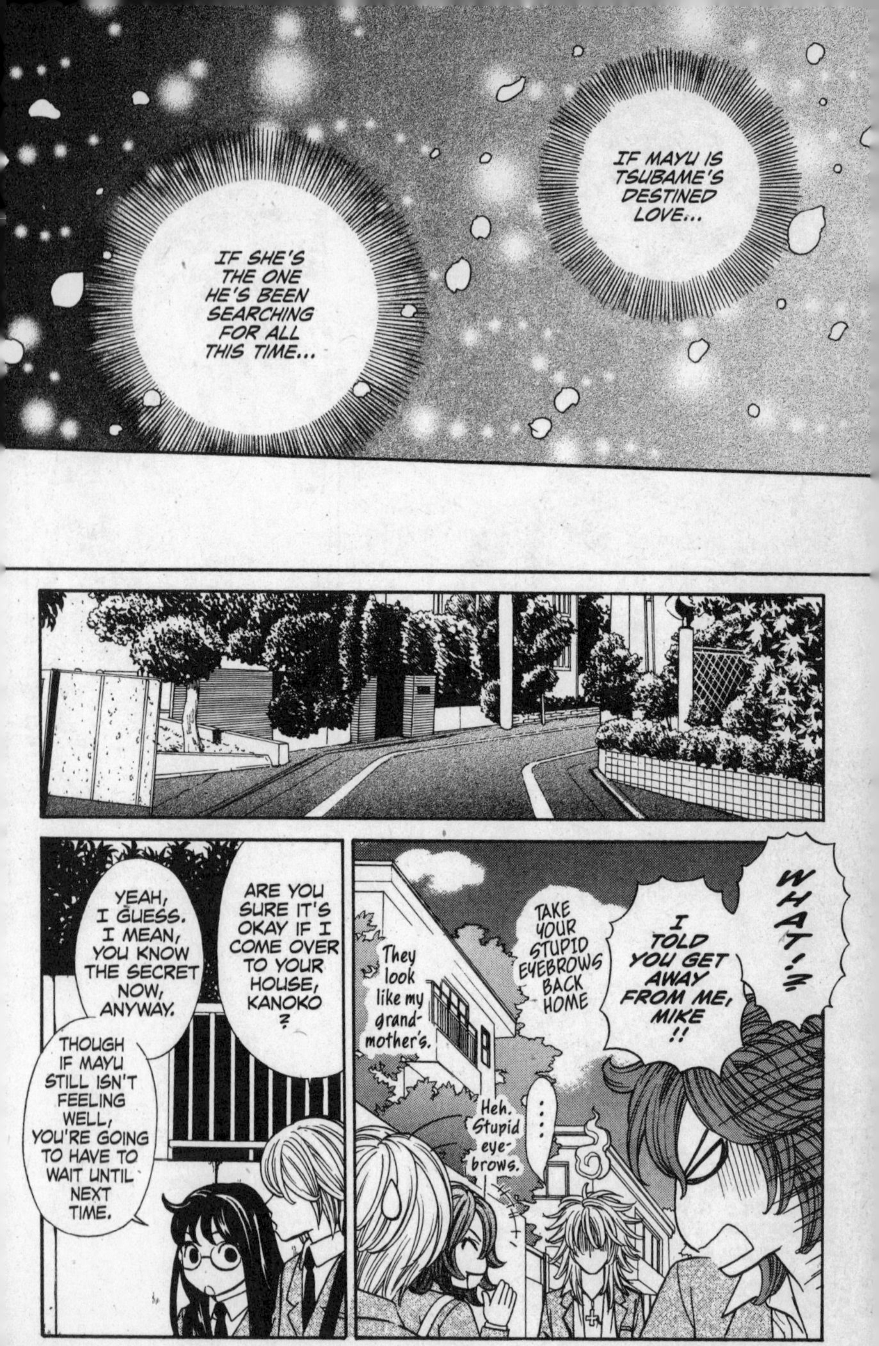
IF MAYU IS TSUBAME'S DESTINED LOVE...
IF SHE'S THE ONE HE'S BEEN SEARCHING FOR ALL THIS TIME...
WHAT!?!?
I TOLD YOU GET AWAY FROM ME, MIKE!!
TAKE YOUR STUPID EYEBROWS BACK HOME
They look like my grandmother's.
....
Heh. Stupid eye-brows.
ARE YOU SURE IT'S OKAY IF I COME OVER TO YOUR HOUSE, KANOKO?
YEAH, I GUESS. I MEAN, YOU KNOW THE SECRET NOW, ANYWAY.
THOUGH IF MAYU STILL ISN'T FEELING WELL, YOU'RE GOING TO HAVE TO WAIT UNTIL NEXT TIME.

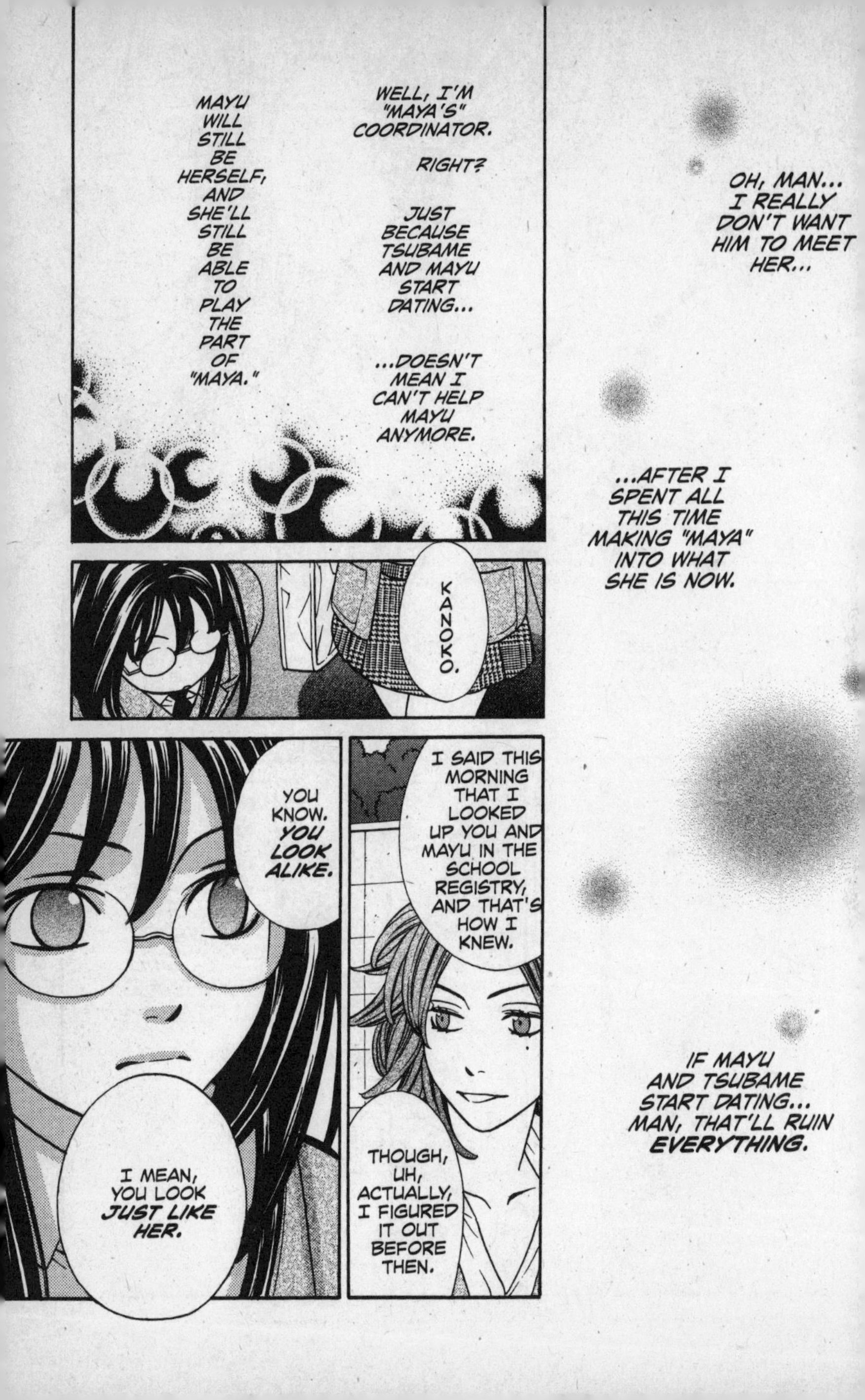
OH, MAN... I REALLY DON'T WANT HIM TO MEET HER...
...AFTER I SPENT ALL THIS TIME MAKING "MAYA" INTO WHAT SHE IS NOW.
IF MAYU AND TSUBAME START DATING... MAN, THAT'LL RUIN **EVERYTHING.**
WELL, I'M "MAYA'S" COORDINATOR.
RIGHT?
JUST BECAUSE TSUBAME AND MAYU START DATING...
...DOESN'T MEAN I CAN'T HELP MAYU ANYMORE.
MAYU WILL STILL BE HERSELF, AND SHE'LL STILL BE ABLE TO PLAY THE PART OF "MAYA."
KANOKO.
I SAID THIS MORNING THAT I LOOKED UP YOU AND MAYU IN THE SCHOOL REGISTRY, AND THAT'S HOW I KNEW.
THOUGH, UH, ACTUALLY, I FIGURED IT OUT BEFORE THEN.
YOU KNOW. ***YOU LOOK ALIKE.***
I MEAN, YOU LOOK ***JUST LIKE HER.***

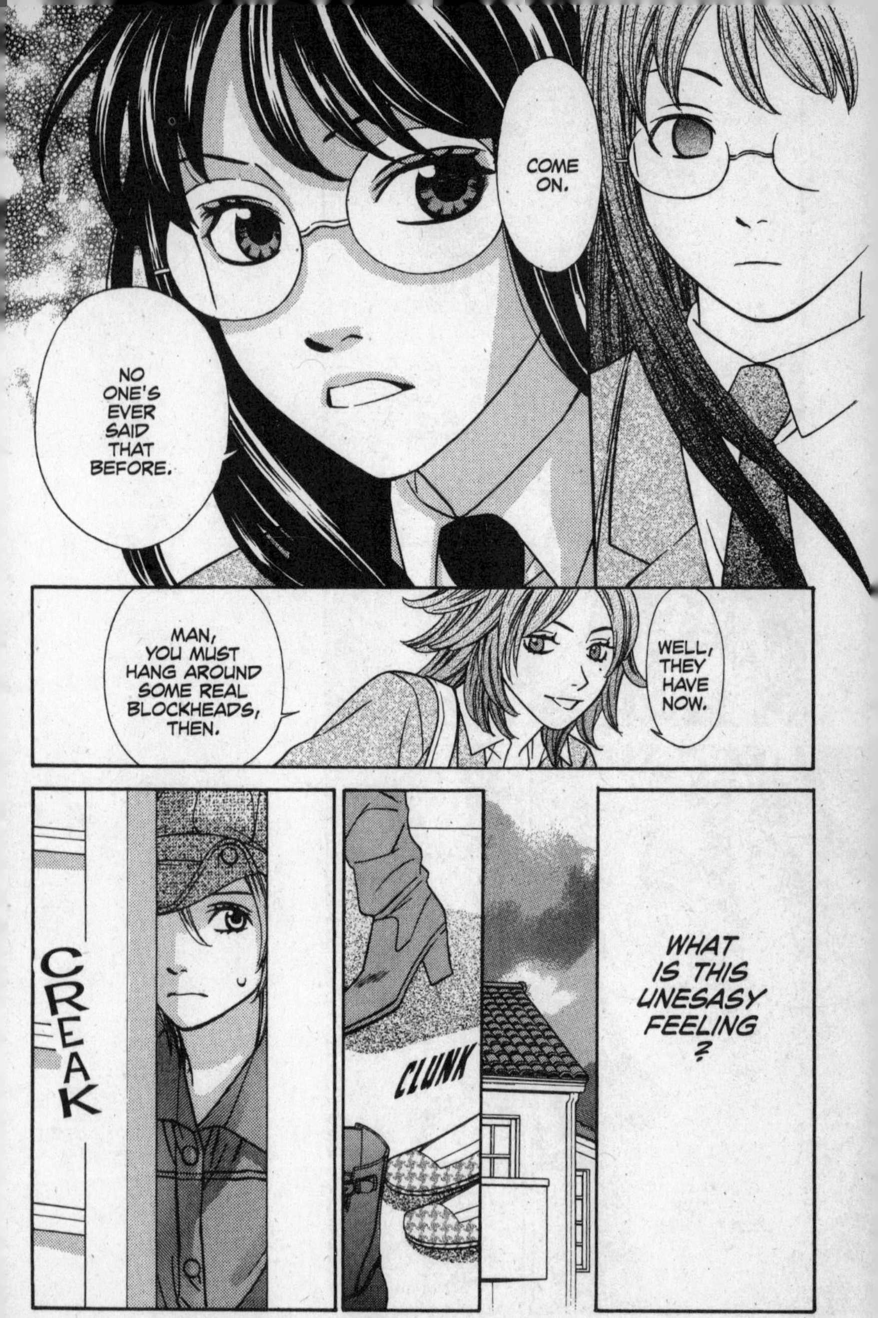
COME ON.
NO ONE'S EVER SAID THAT BEFORE.
WELL, THEY HAVE NOW.
MAN, YOU MUST HANG AROUND SOME REAL BLOCKHEADS, THEN.
WHAT IS THIS UNESASY FEELING?
CLUNK
CREAK

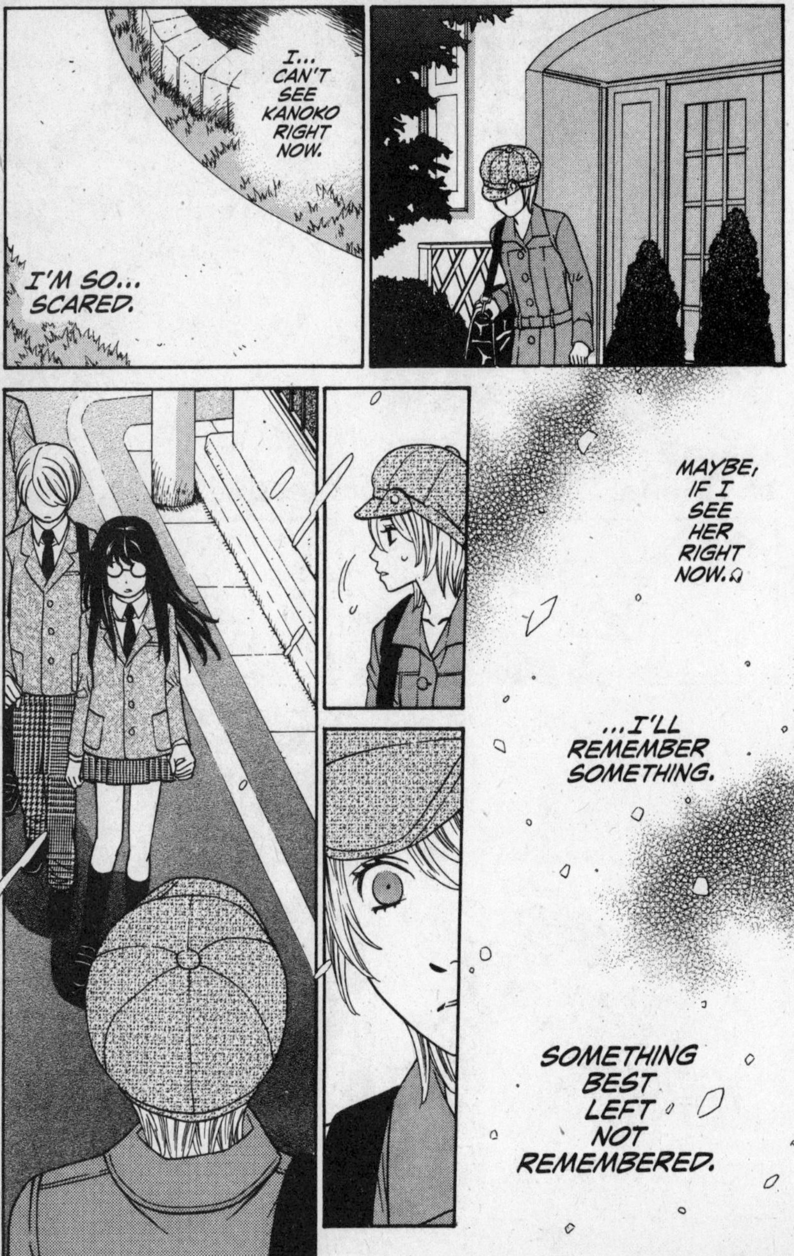
I... CAN'T SEE KANOKO RIGHT NOW.
I'M SO... SCARED.
MAYBE, IF I SEE HER RIGHT NOW...
...I'LL REMEMBER SOMETHING.
SOMETHING BEST LEFT NOT REMEMBERED.

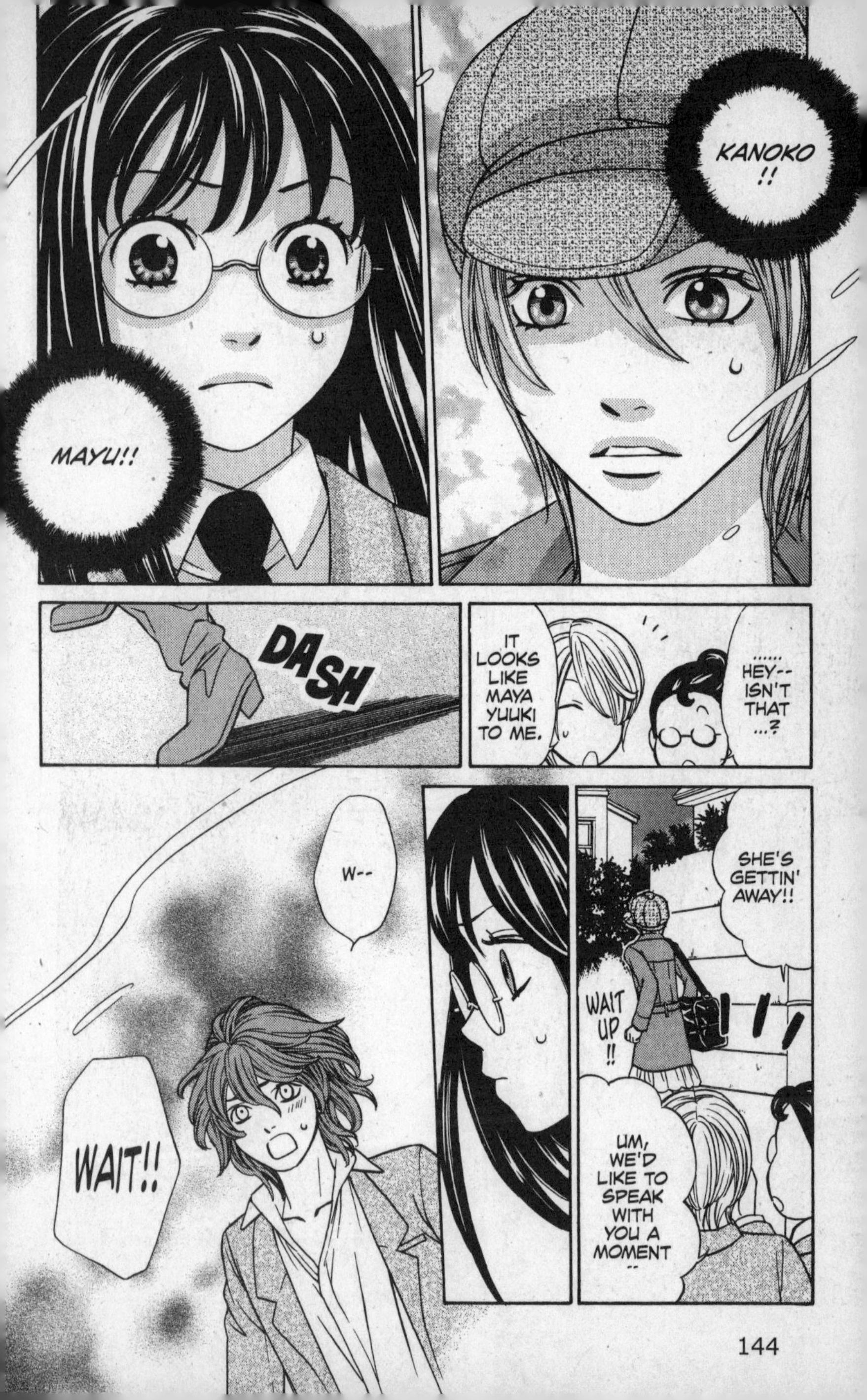
KANOKO !!
MAYU!!
...... HEY-- ISN'T THAT ...?
IT LOOKS LIKE MAYA YUUKI TO ME.
DASH
SHE'S GETTIN' AWAY!!
WAIT UP !!
UM, WE'D LIKE TO SPEAK WITH YOU A MOMENT --
W--
WAIT!!

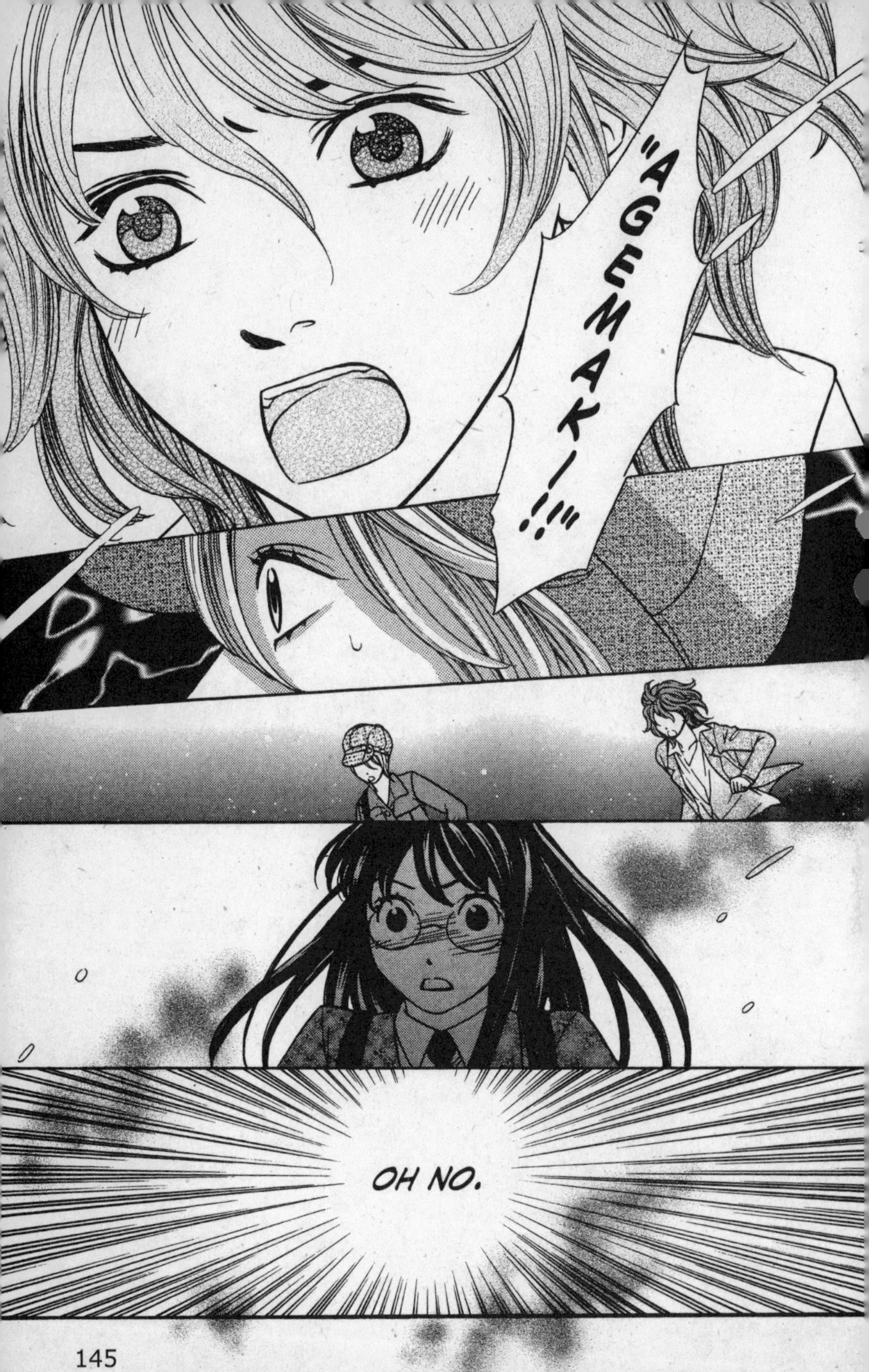
"AGEMAKI!!"
OH NO.

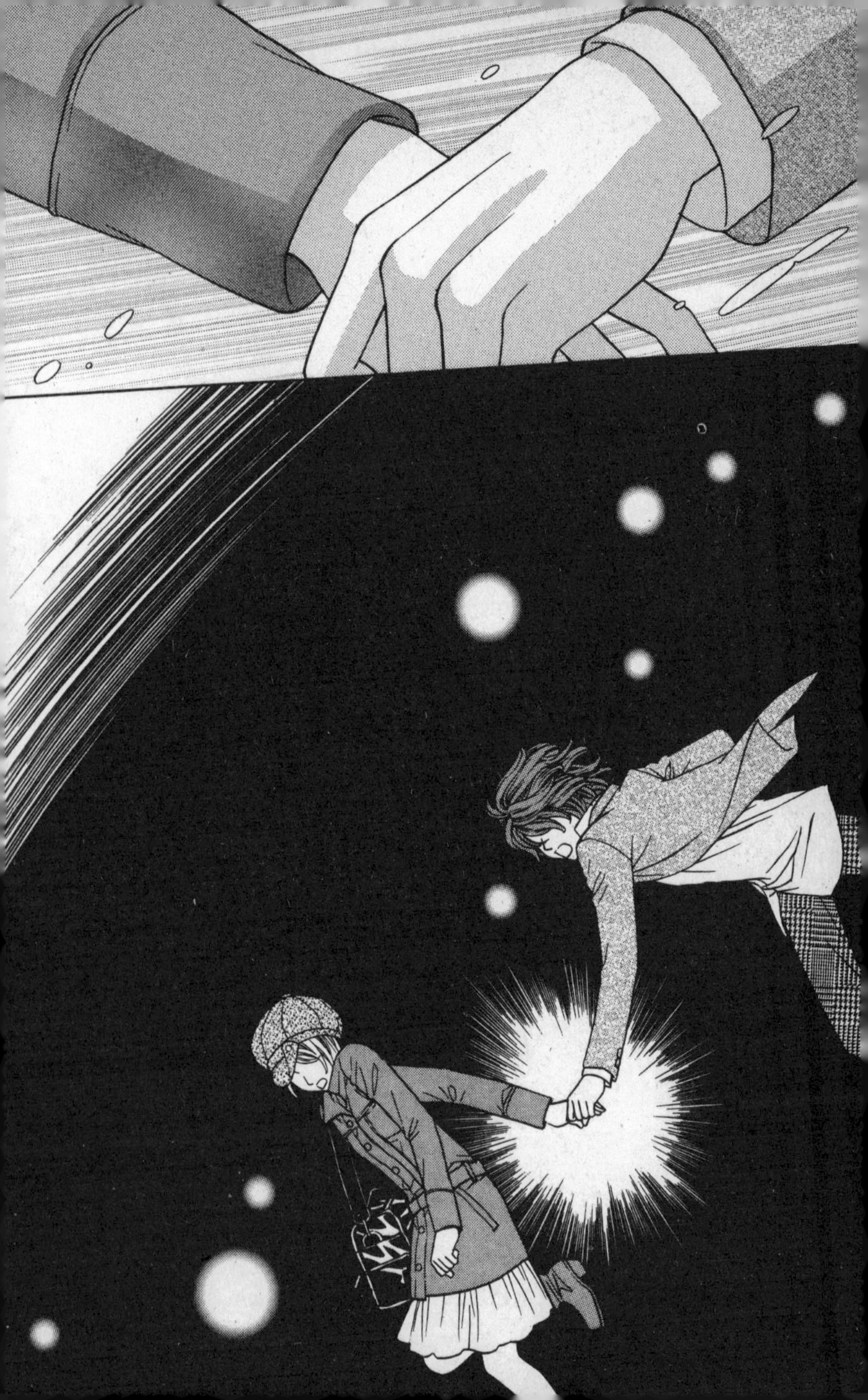

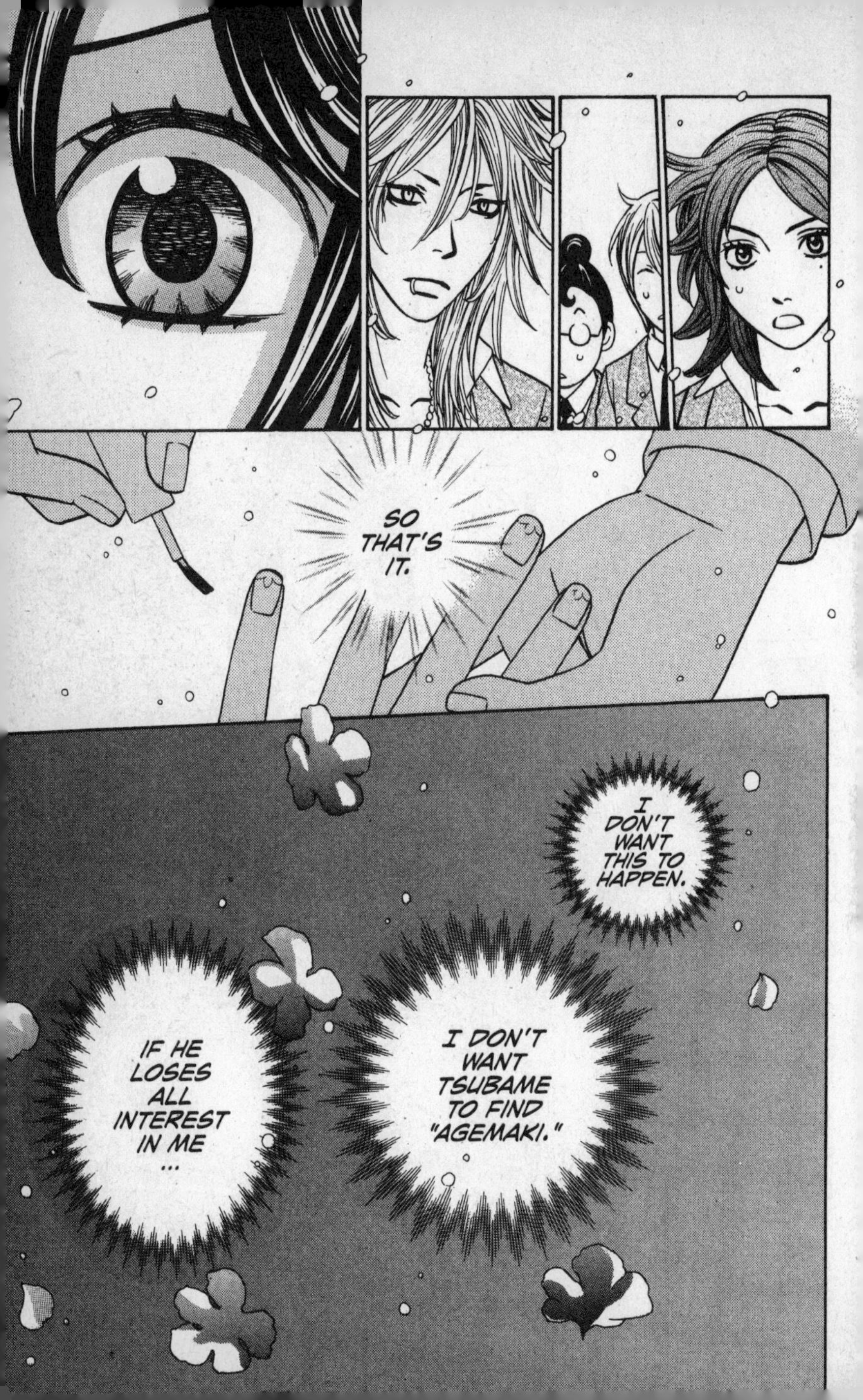
SO THAT'S IT.
I DON'T WANT THIS TO HAPPEN.
I DON'T WANT TSUBAME TO FIND "AGEMAKI."
IF HE LOSES ALL INTEREST IN ME ...

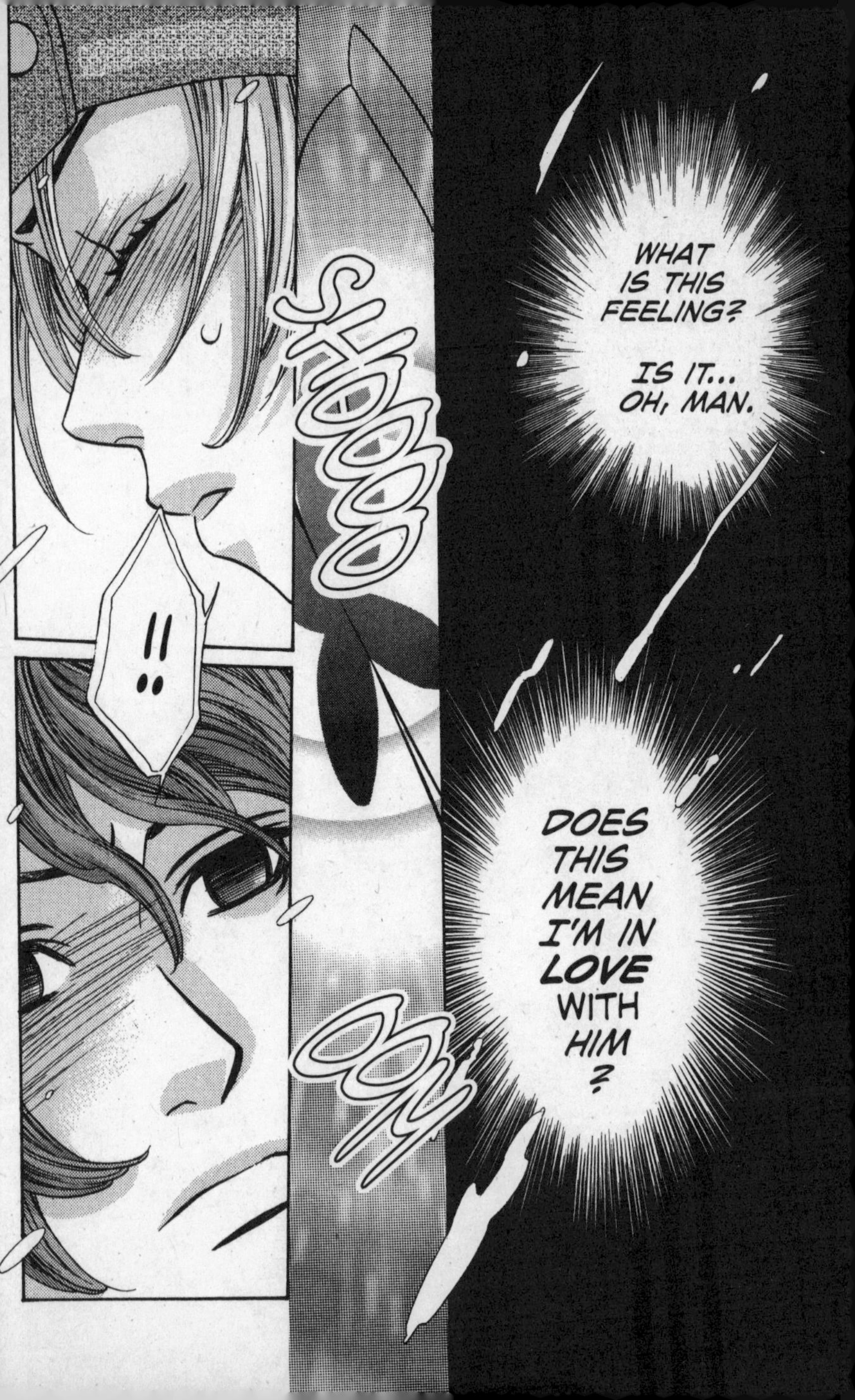
WHAT IS THIS FEELING?
IS IT... OH, MAN.
DOES THIS MEAN I'M IN LOVE WITH HIM?
SHOOOOOOOM
!!

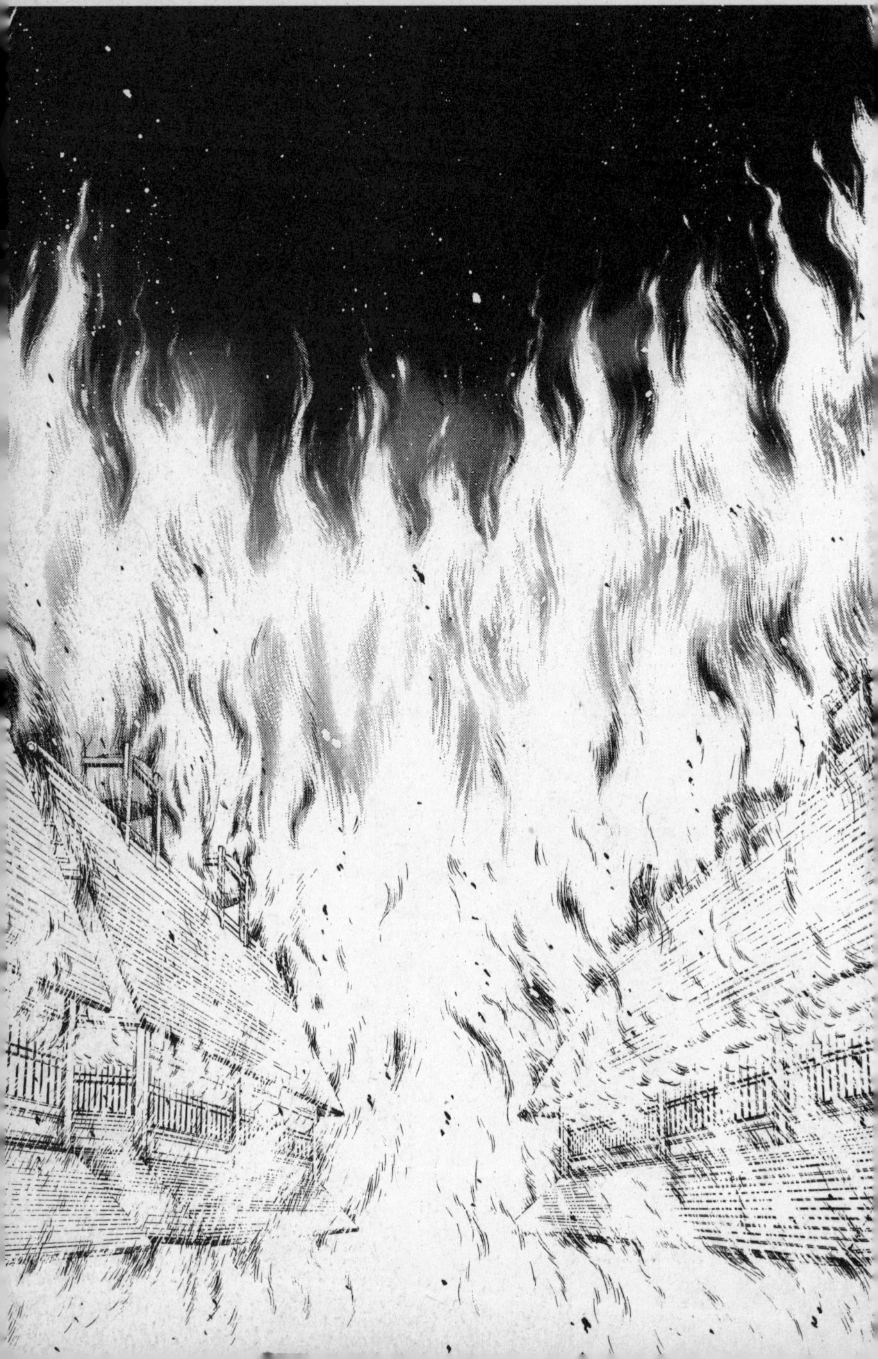

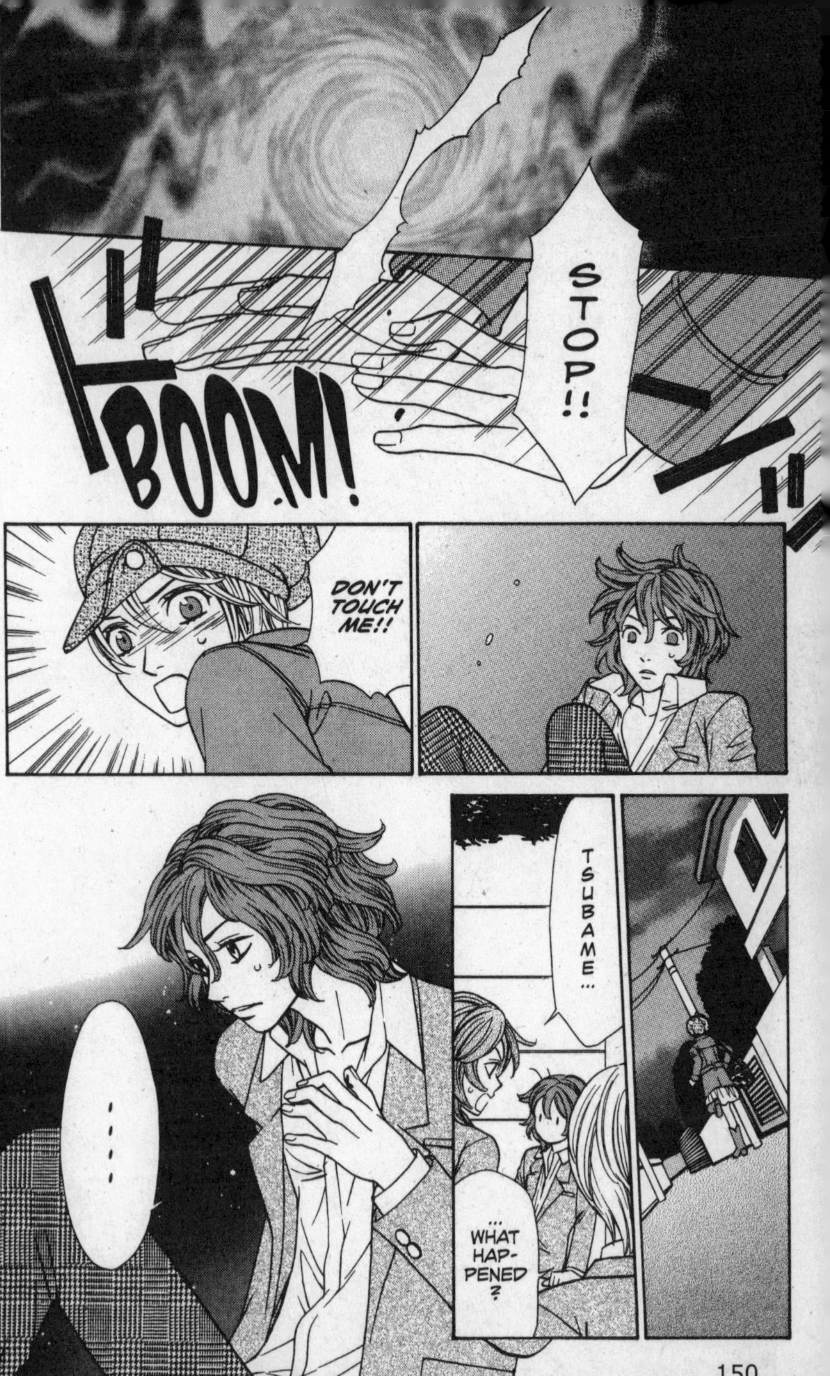
STOP!!
BOOM!
DON'T TOUCH ME!!
TSUBAME...
...WHAT HAP-PENED?
......

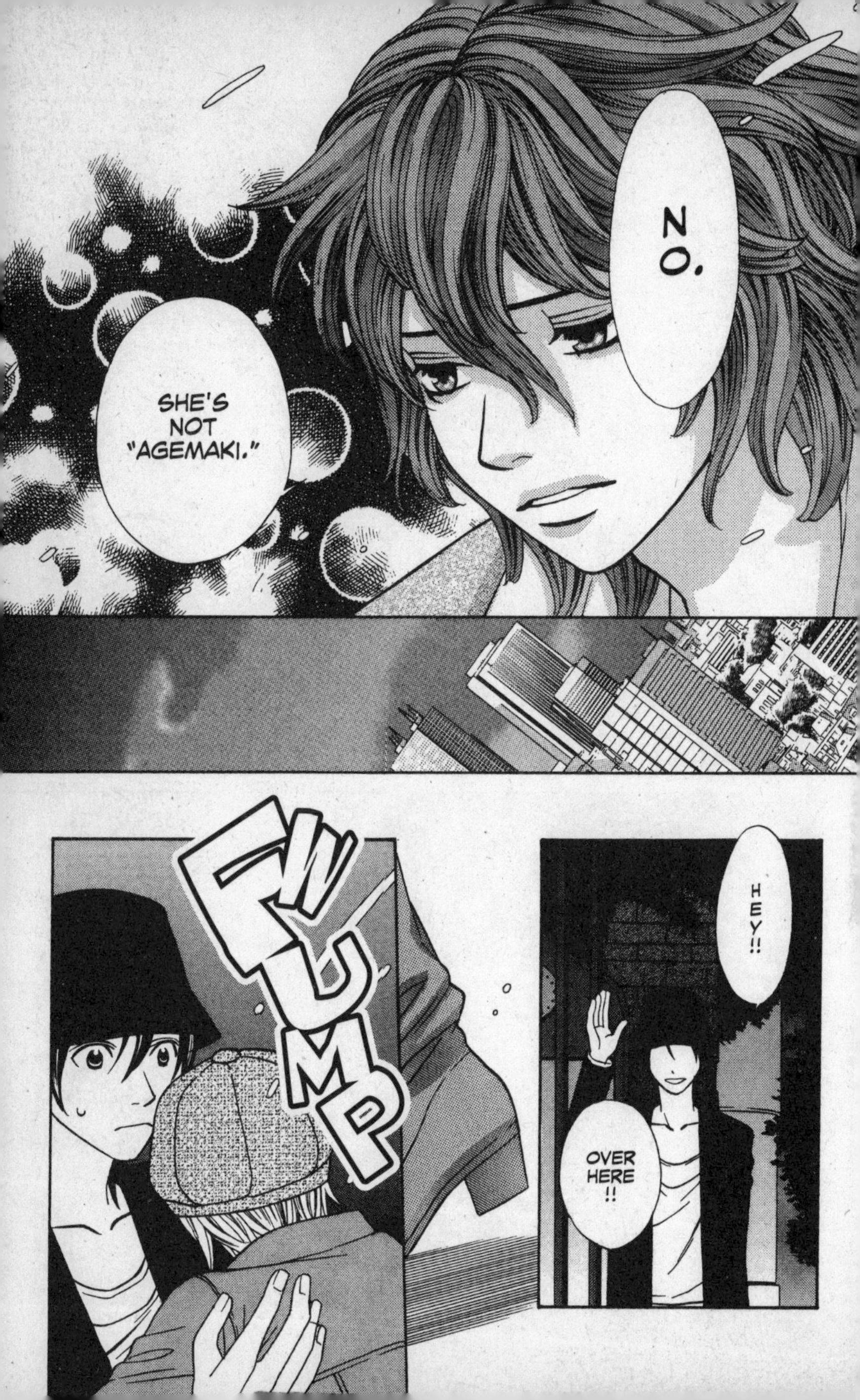
NO.
SHE'S NOT "AGEMAKI."
HEY!!
OVER HERE!!
FWUMP

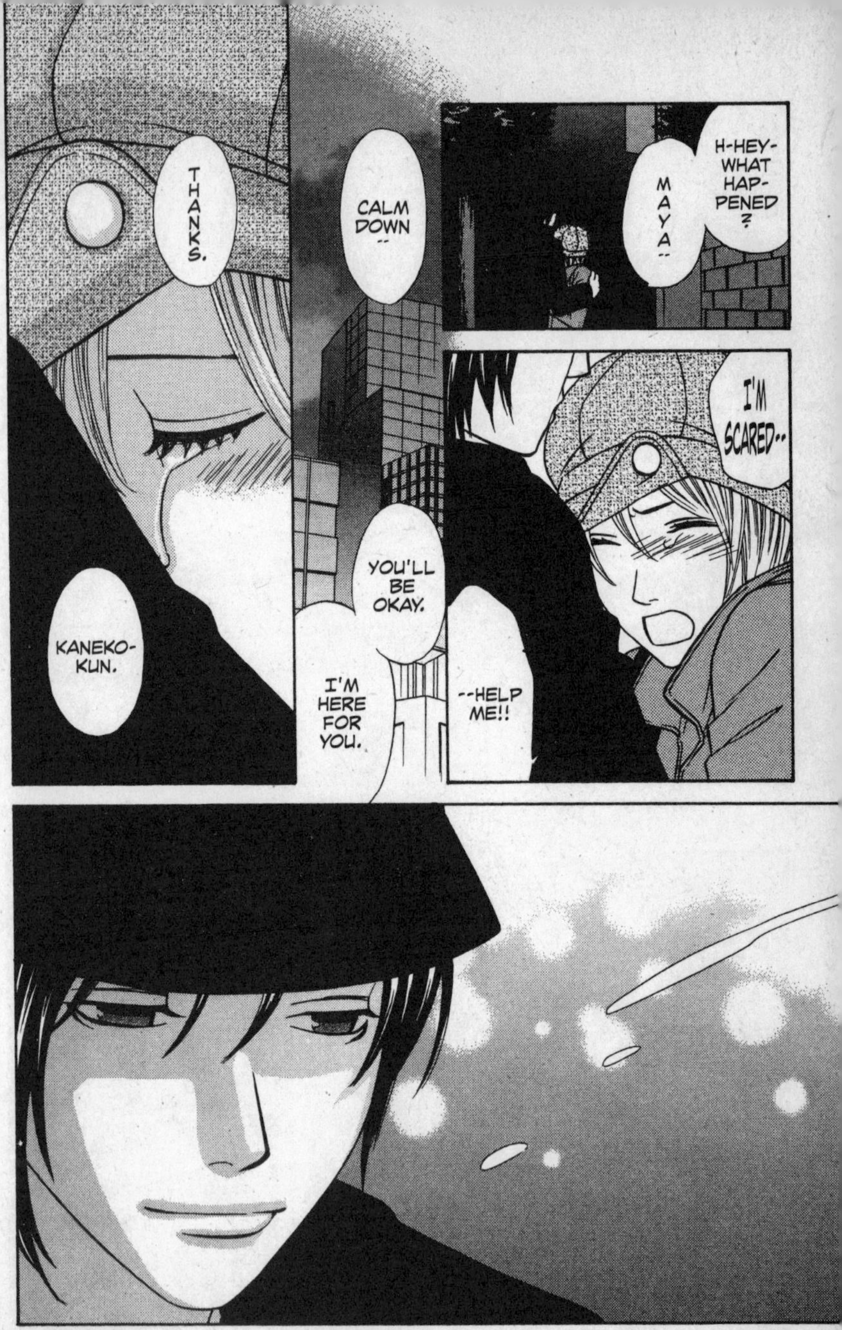
H-HEY-WHAT HAP-PENED?
MAYA--
I'M SCARED--
--HELP ME!!
CALM DOWN--
YOU'LL BE OKAY.
I'M HERE FOR YOU.
THANKS.
KANEKO-KUN.

CHAPTER NINE: END.

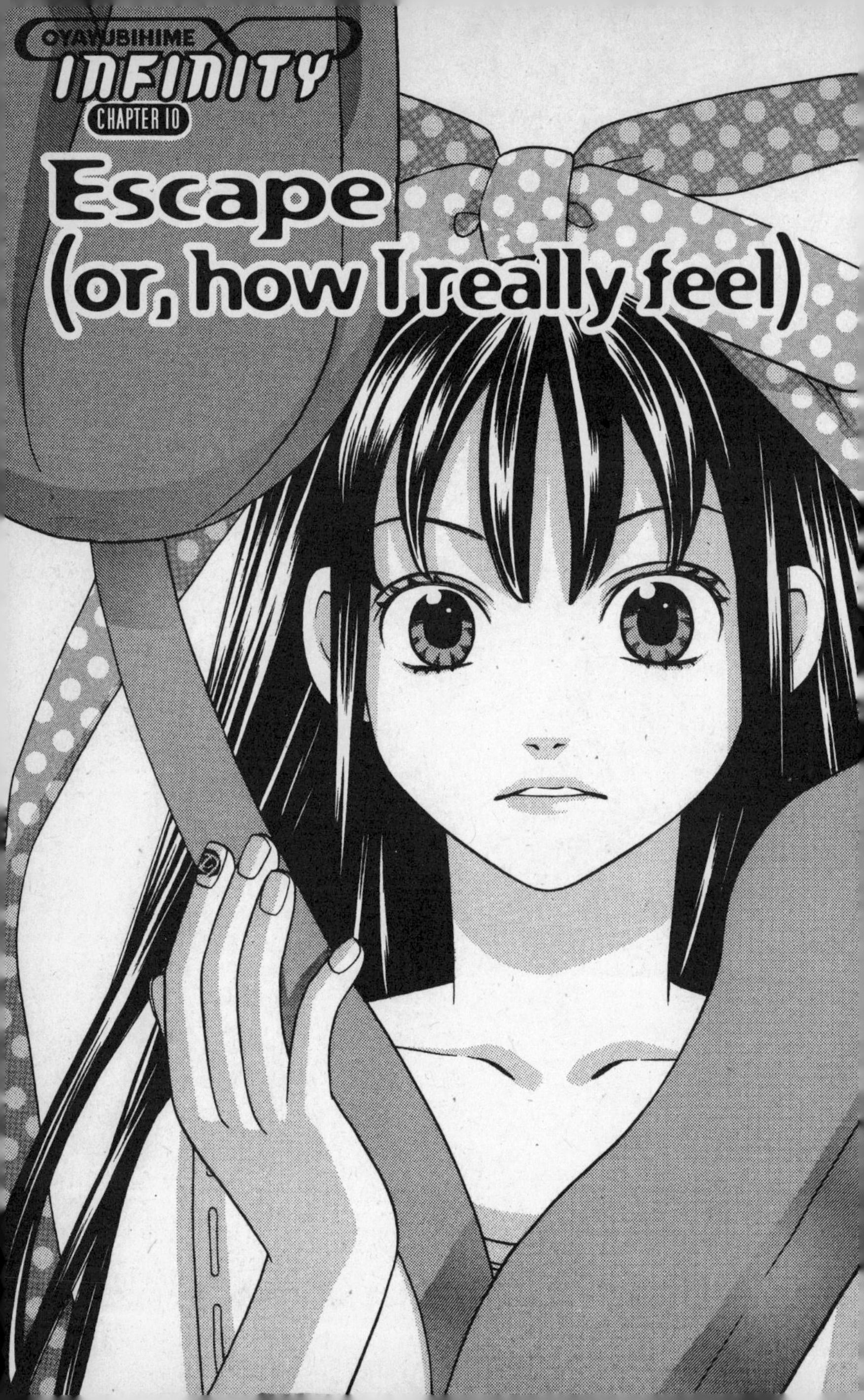
OYAYUBIHIME
INFINITY
CHAPTER 10
Escape
(or, how I really feel)

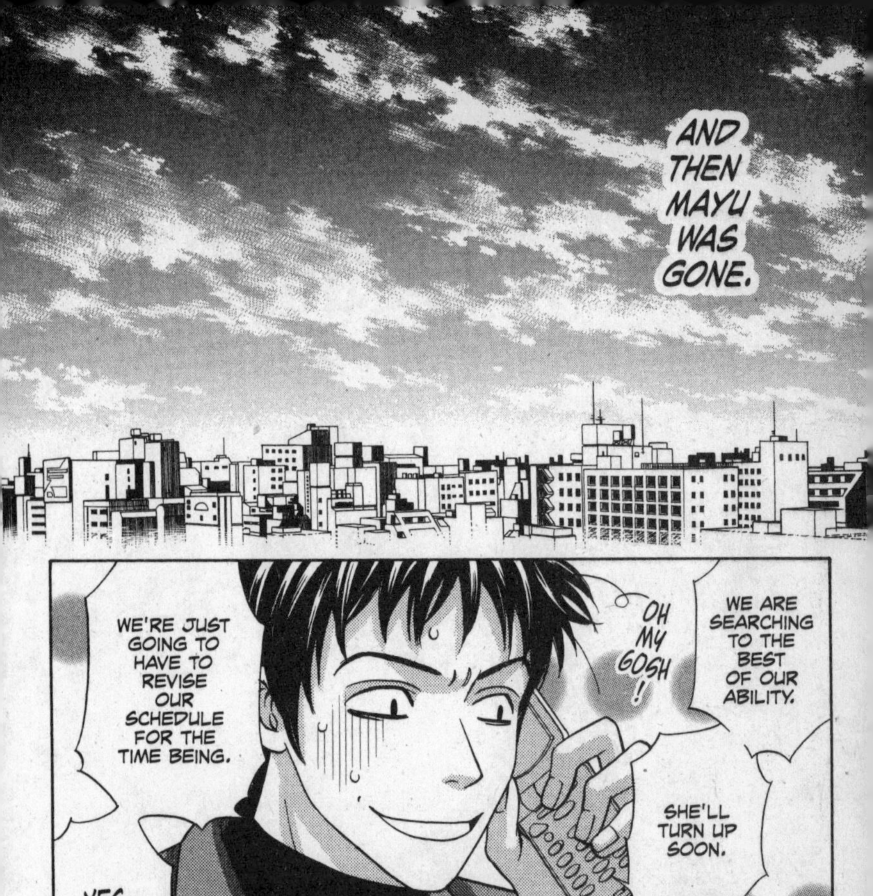
AND THEN MAYU WAS GONE.
WE ARE SEARCHING TO THE BEST OF OUR ABILITY.
OH MY GOSH!
SHE'LL TURN UP SOON.
WE'RE JUST GOING TO HAVE TO REVISE OUR SCHEDULE FOR THE TIME BEING.
YES, YES.

Character Guide: 17

Kameko Yomoyama

Birthday: 3/3

Blood Type: AB

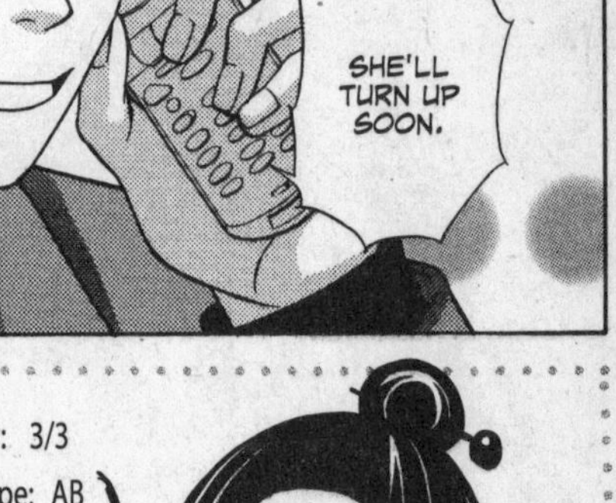
HA HA HA HA

I first drew her without any kind of preconception other than that she was going to be a diligent member of the creative writing club. What resulted was quite wonderful. Might she be a dark horse candidate for a starring role in future stories?

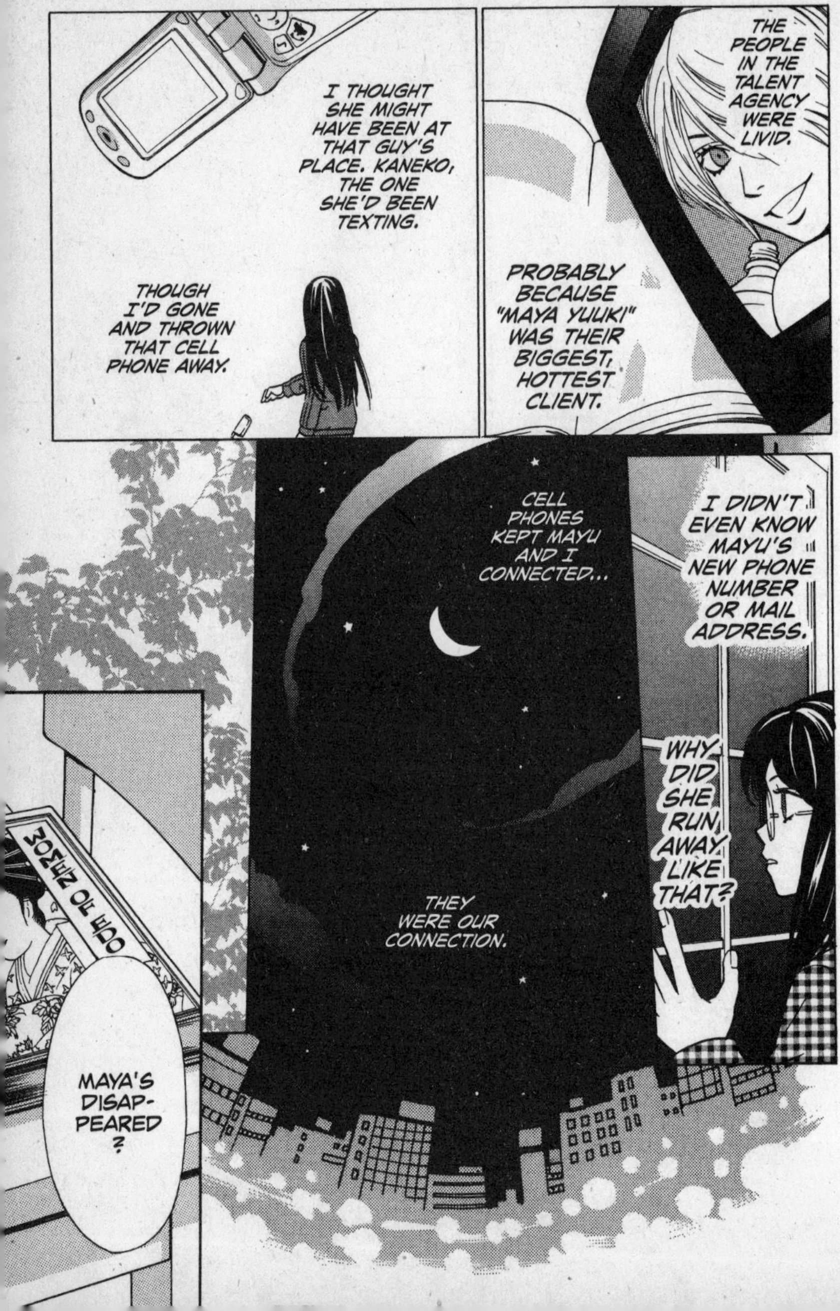
THE PEOPLE IN THE TALENT AGENCY WERE LIVID.
PROBABLY BECAUSE "MAYA YUUKI" WAS THEIR BIGGEST, HOTTEST CLIENT.
I THOUGHT SHE MIGHT HAVE BEEN AT THAT GUY'S PLACE. KANEKO, THE ONE SHE'D BEEN TEXTING.
THOUGH I'D GONE AND THROWN THAT CELL PHONE AWAY.
I DIDN'T EVEN KNOW MAYU'S NEW PHONE NUMBER OR MAIL ADDRESS.
WHY DID SHE RUN AWAY LIKE THAT?
CELL PHONES KEPT MAYU AND I CONNECTED...
THEY WERE OUR CONNECTION.
WOMEN OF EDO
MAYA'S DISAP-PEARED?

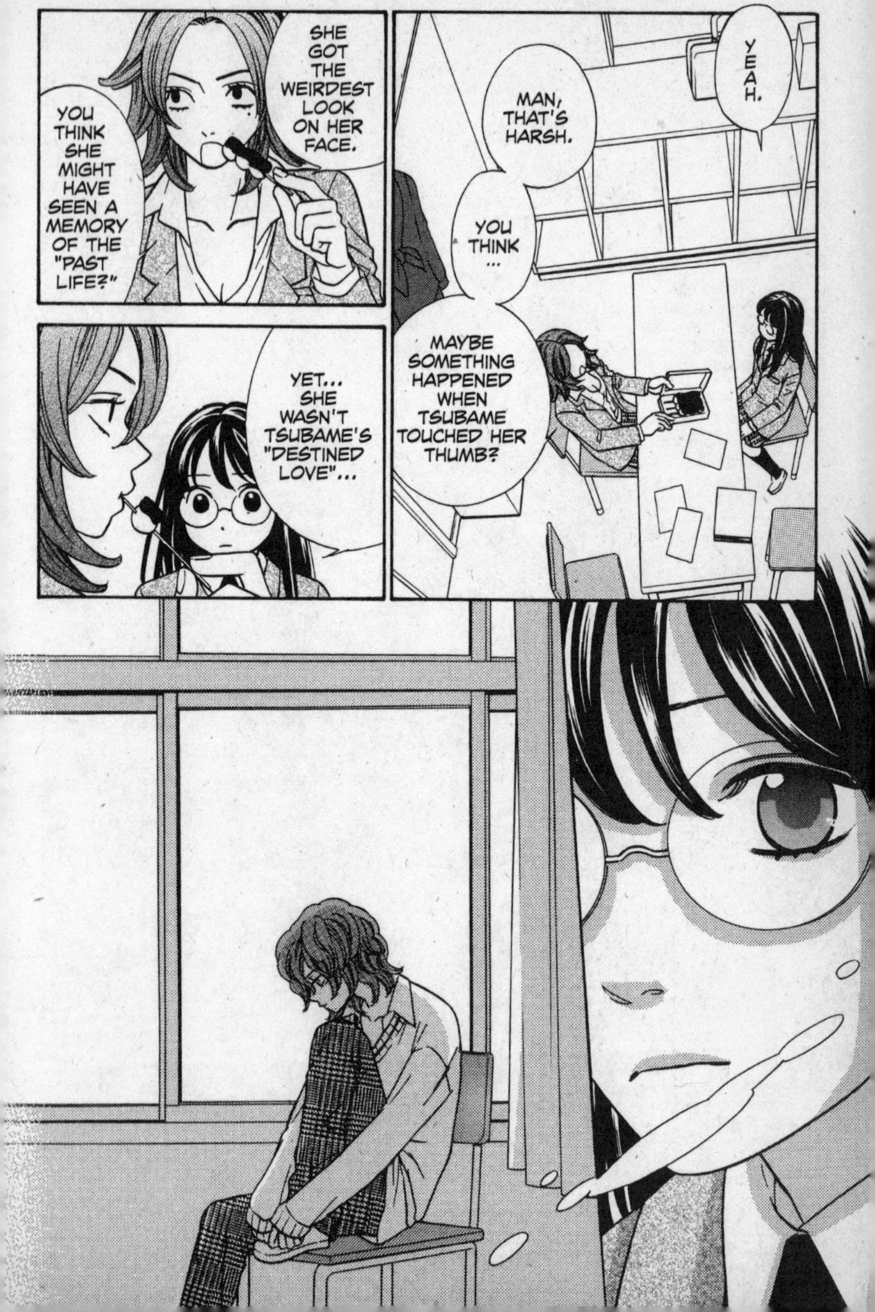
YEAH.
MAN, THAT'S HARSH.
YOU THINK...
MAYBE SOMETHING HAPPENED WHEN TSUBAME TOUCHED HER THUMB?
SHE GOT THE WEIRDEST LOOK ON HER FACE.
YOU THINK SHE MIGHT HAVE SEEN A MEMORY OF THE "PAST LIFE?"
YET... SHE WASN'T TSUBAME'S "DESTINED LOVE"...

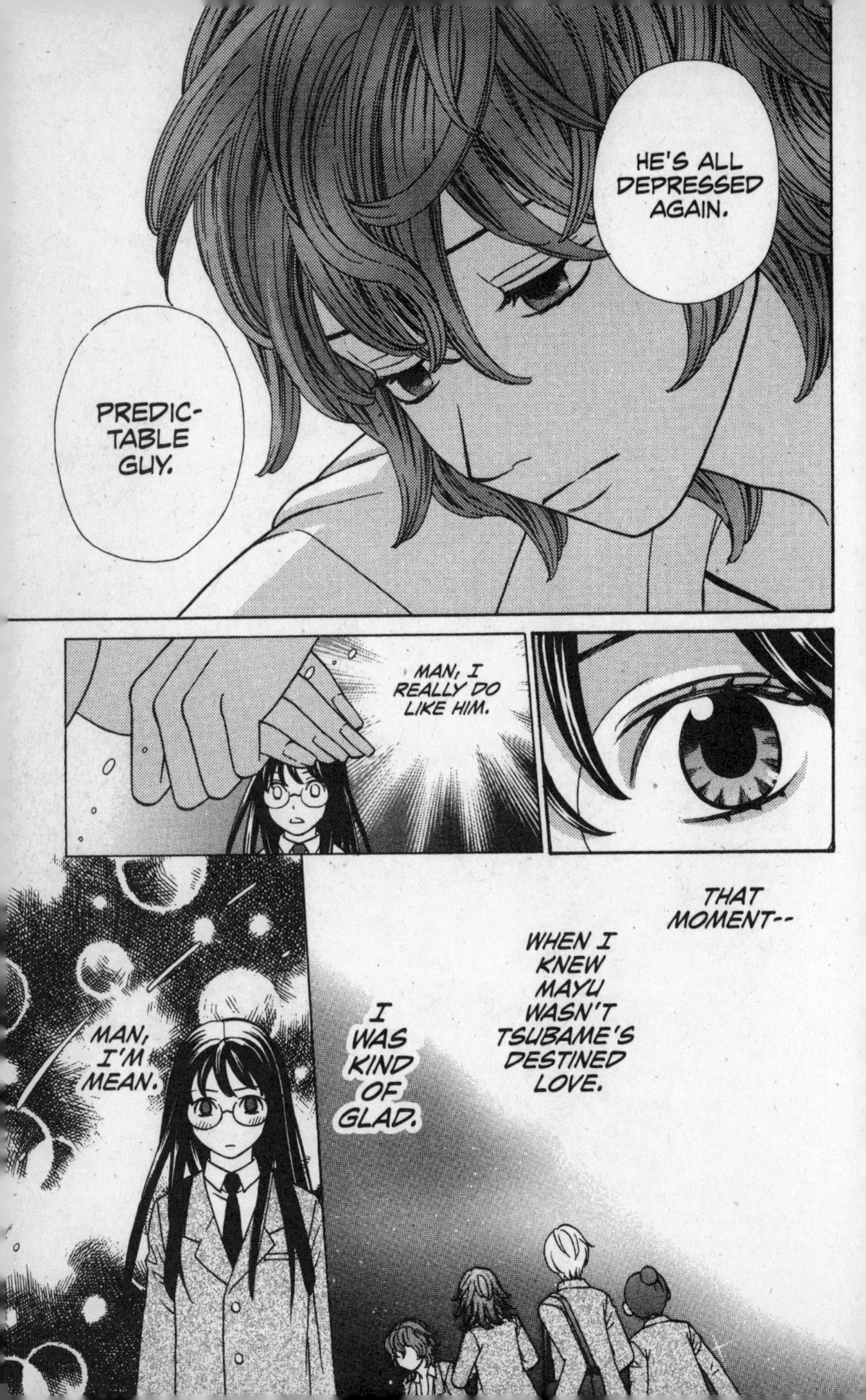
HE'S ALL DEPRESSED AGAIN.
PREDIC-TABLE GUY.
MAN, I REALLY DO LIKE HIM.
THAT MOMENT--
WHEN I KNEW MAYU WASN'T TSUBAME'S DESTINED LOVE.
I WAS KIND OF GLAD.
MAN, I'M MEAN.

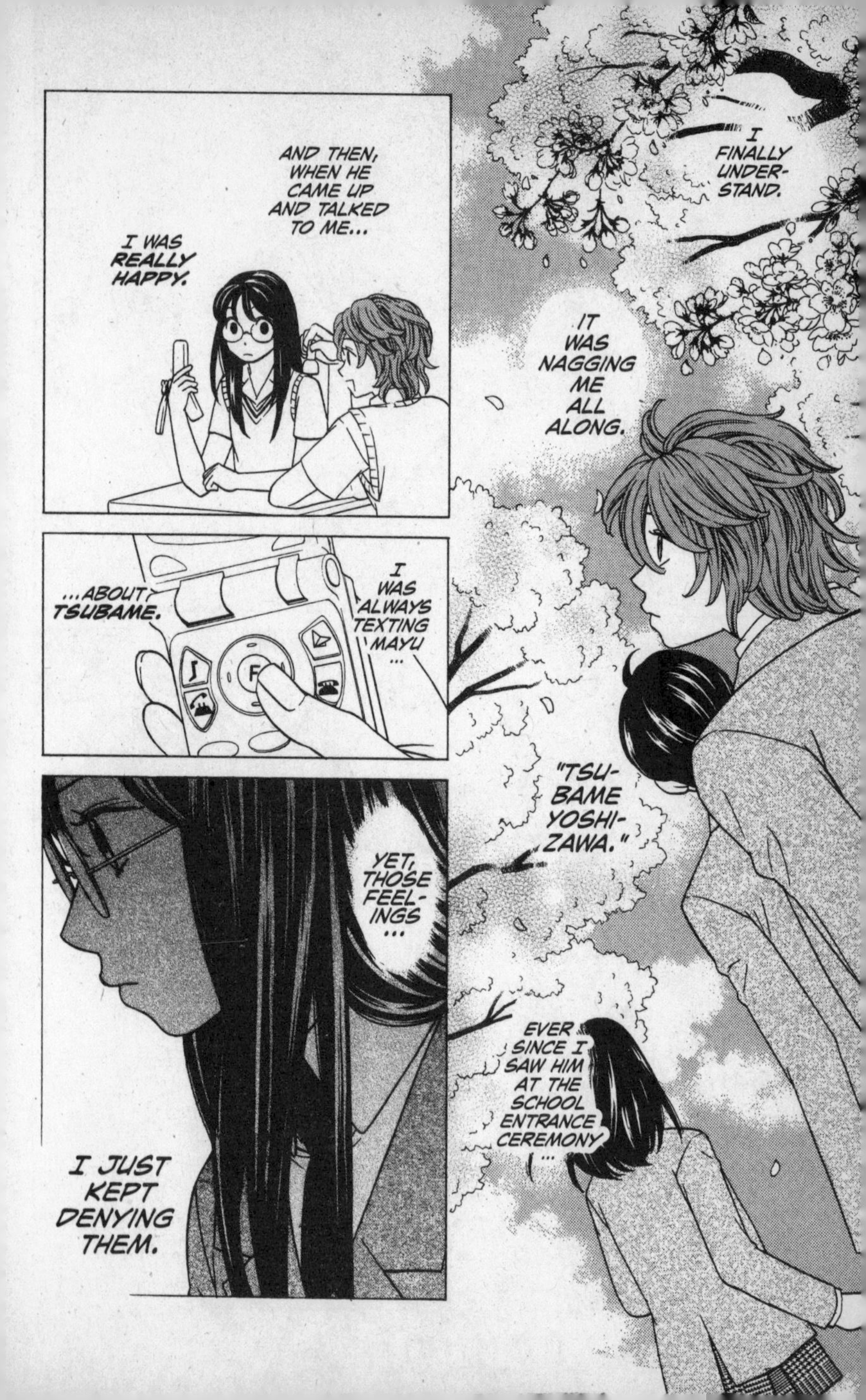
I FINALLY UNDERSTAND.
IT WAS NAGGING ME ALL ALONG.
"TSUBAME YOSHIZAWA."
EVER SINCE I SAW HIM AT THE SCHOOL ENTRANCE CEREMONY...
AND THEN, WHEN HE CAME UP AND TALKED TO ME...
I WAS REALLY HAPPY.
I WAS ALWAYS TEXTING MAYU...
...ABOUT TSUBAME.
YET, THOSE FEELINGS...
I JUST KEPT DENYING THEM.

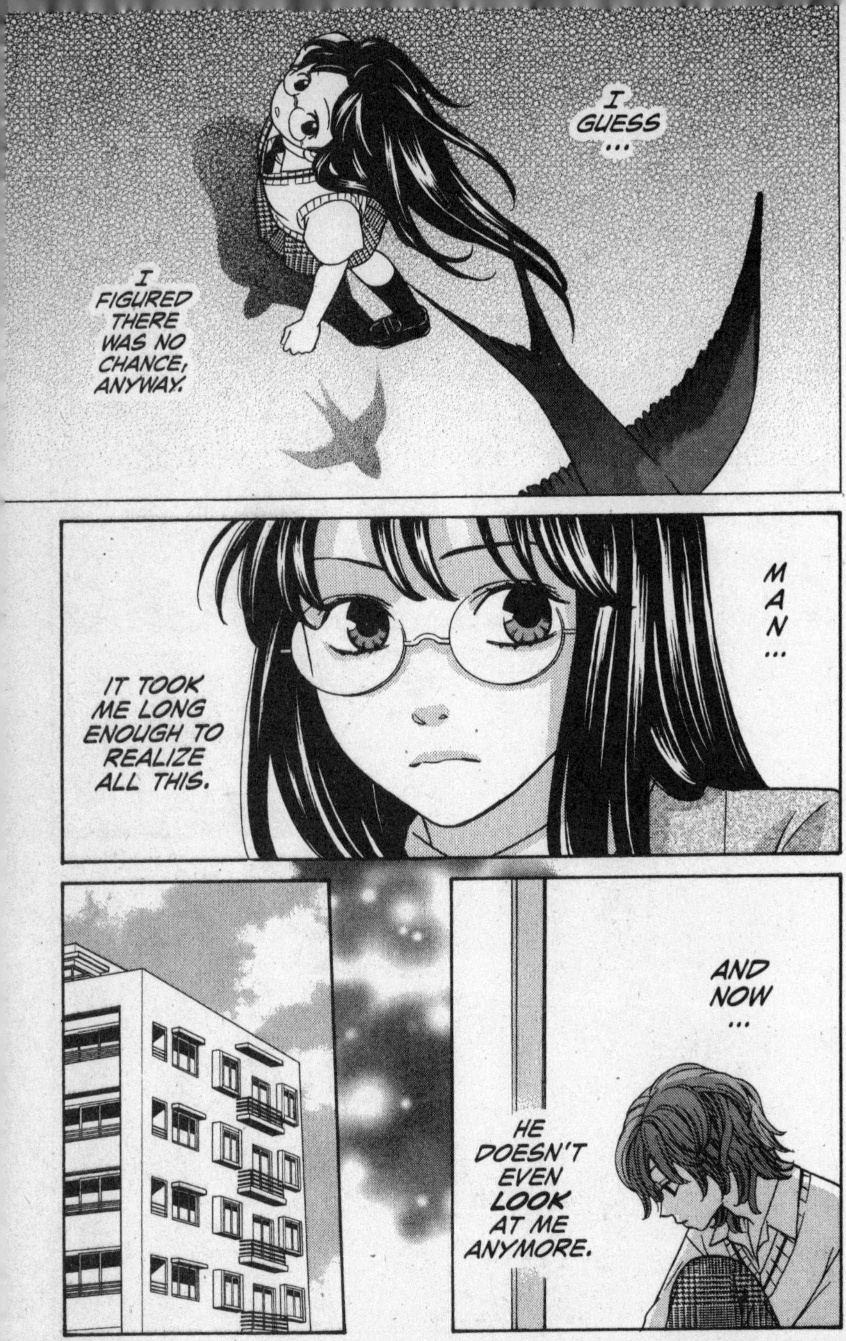
I GUESS ...
I FIGURED THERE WAS NO CHANCE, ANYWAY.
MAN ...
IT TOOK ME LONG ENOUGH TO REALIZE ALL THIS.
AND NOW ...
HE DOESN'T EVEN LOOK AT ME ANYMORE.

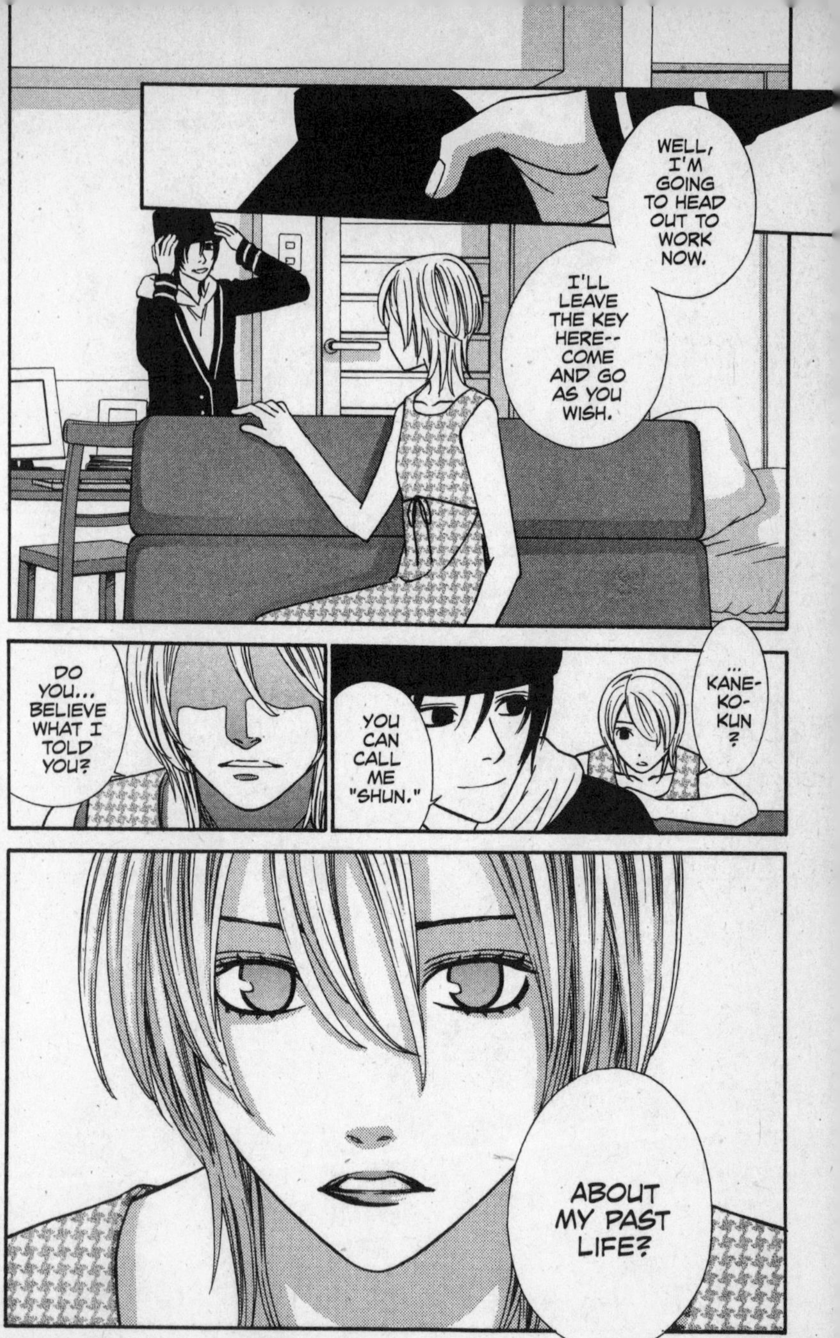

WELL, I'M GOING TO HEAD OUT TO WORK NOW.
I'LL LEAVE THE KEY HERE--COME AND GO AS YOU WISH.
...KANEKO-KUN?
YOU CAN CALL ME "SHUN."
DO YOU... BELIEVE WHAT I TOLD YOU?
ABOUT MY PAST LIFE?

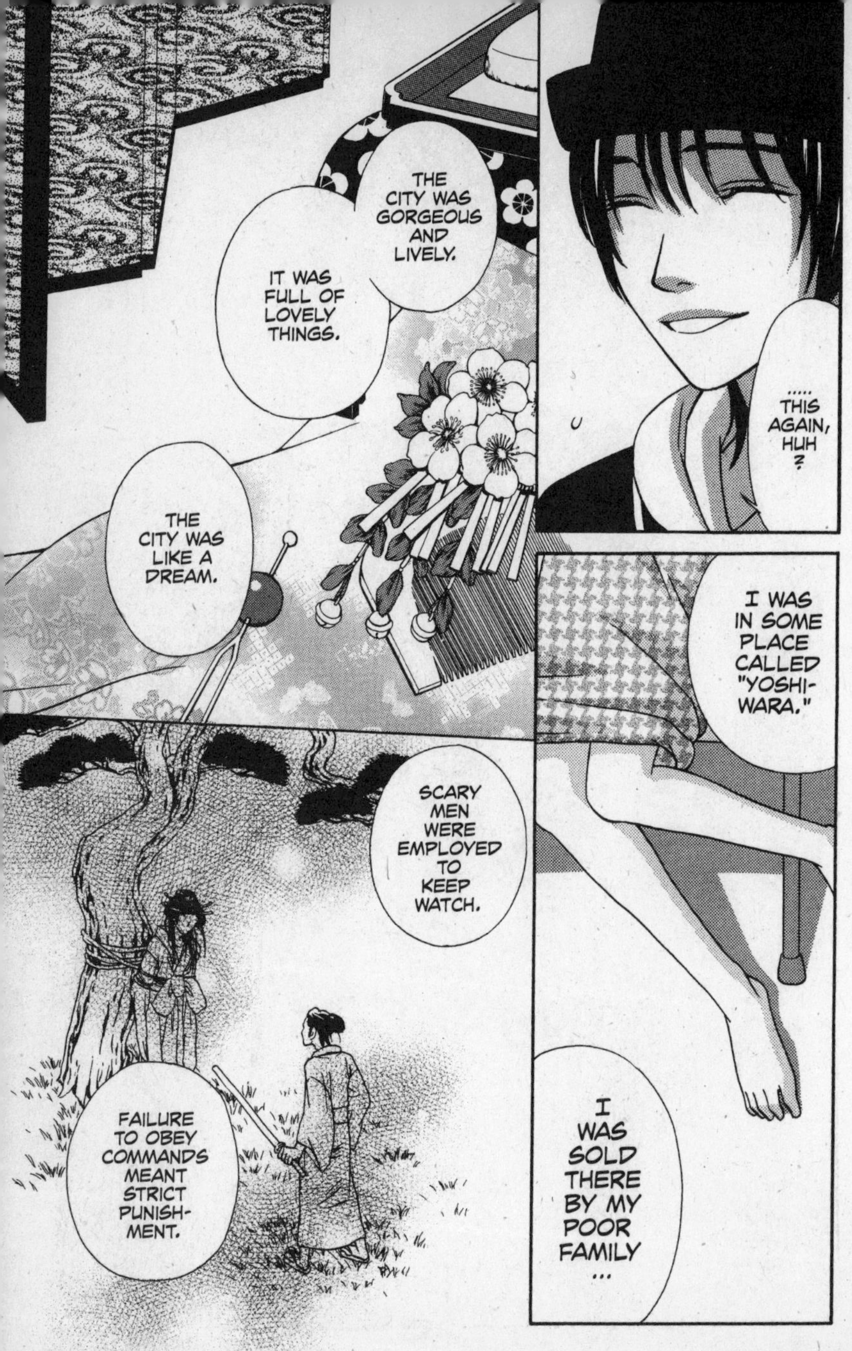
.....THIS AGAIN, HUH?
THE CITY WAS GORGEOUS AND LIVELY.
IT WAS FULL OF LOVELY THINGS.
THE CITY WAS LIKE A DREAM.
I WAS IN SOME PLACE CALLED "YOSHI-WARA."
I WAS SOLD THERE BY MY POOR FAMILY...
SCARY MEN WERE EMPLOYED TO KEEP WATCH.
FAILURE TO OBEY COMMANDS MEANT STRICT PUNISH-MENT.

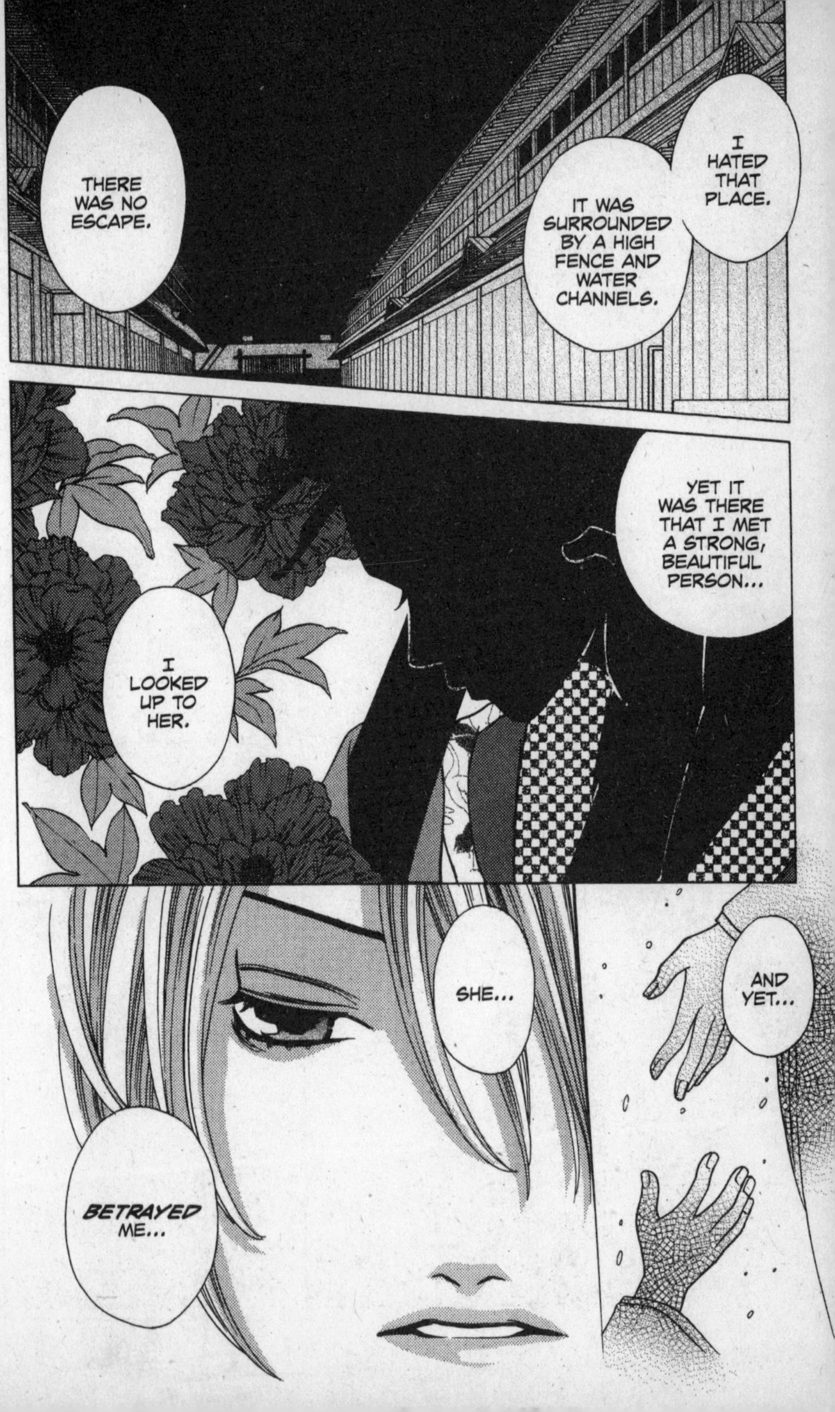
I HATED THAT PLACE.
IT WAS SURROUNDED BY A HIGH FENCE AND WATER CHANNELS.
THERE WAS NO ESCAPE.
YET IT WAS THERE THAT I MET A STRONG, BEAUTIFUL PERSON...
I LOOKED UP TO HER.
AND YET...
SHE...
BETRAYED ME...

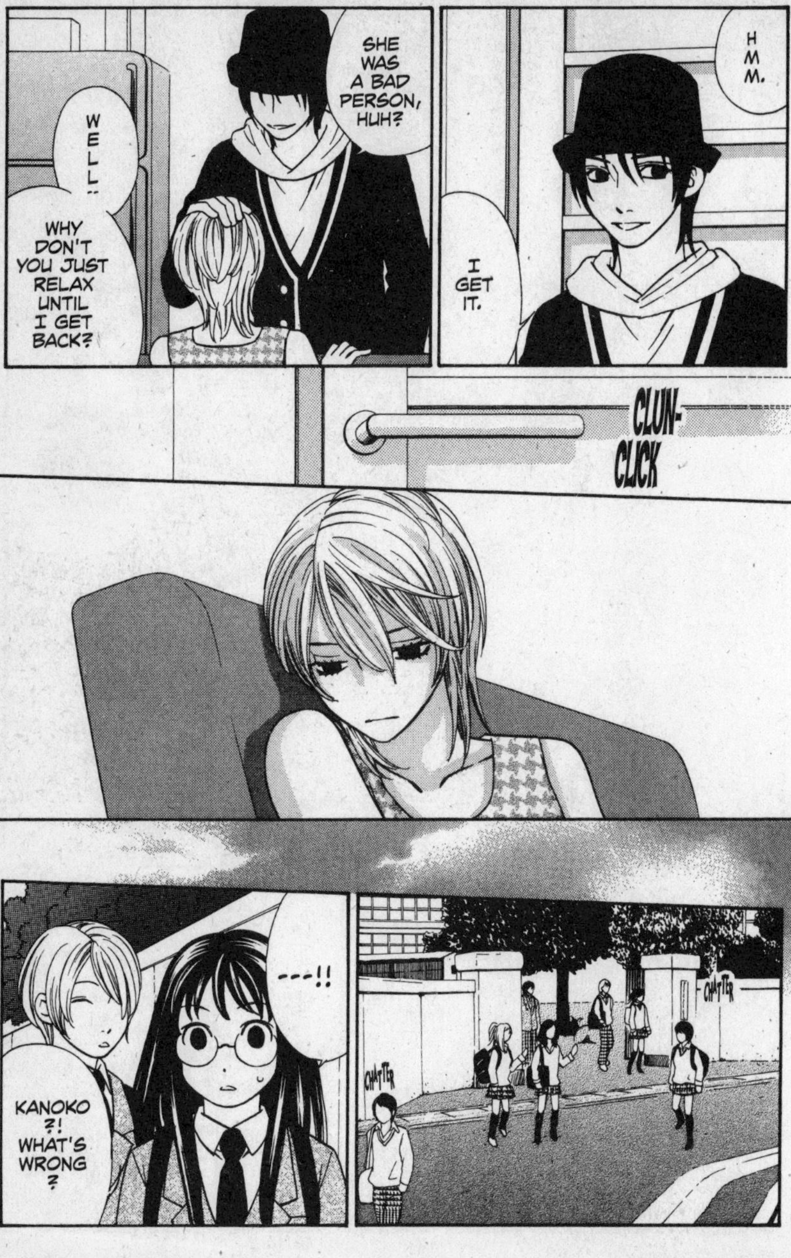
HMM.
I GET IT.
SHE WAS A BAD PERSON, HUH?
WELL...
WHY DON'T YOU JUST RELAX UNTIL I GET BACK?
CLUN-CLICK
CHATTER
CHATTER
---!!
KANOKO?! WHAT'S WRONG?

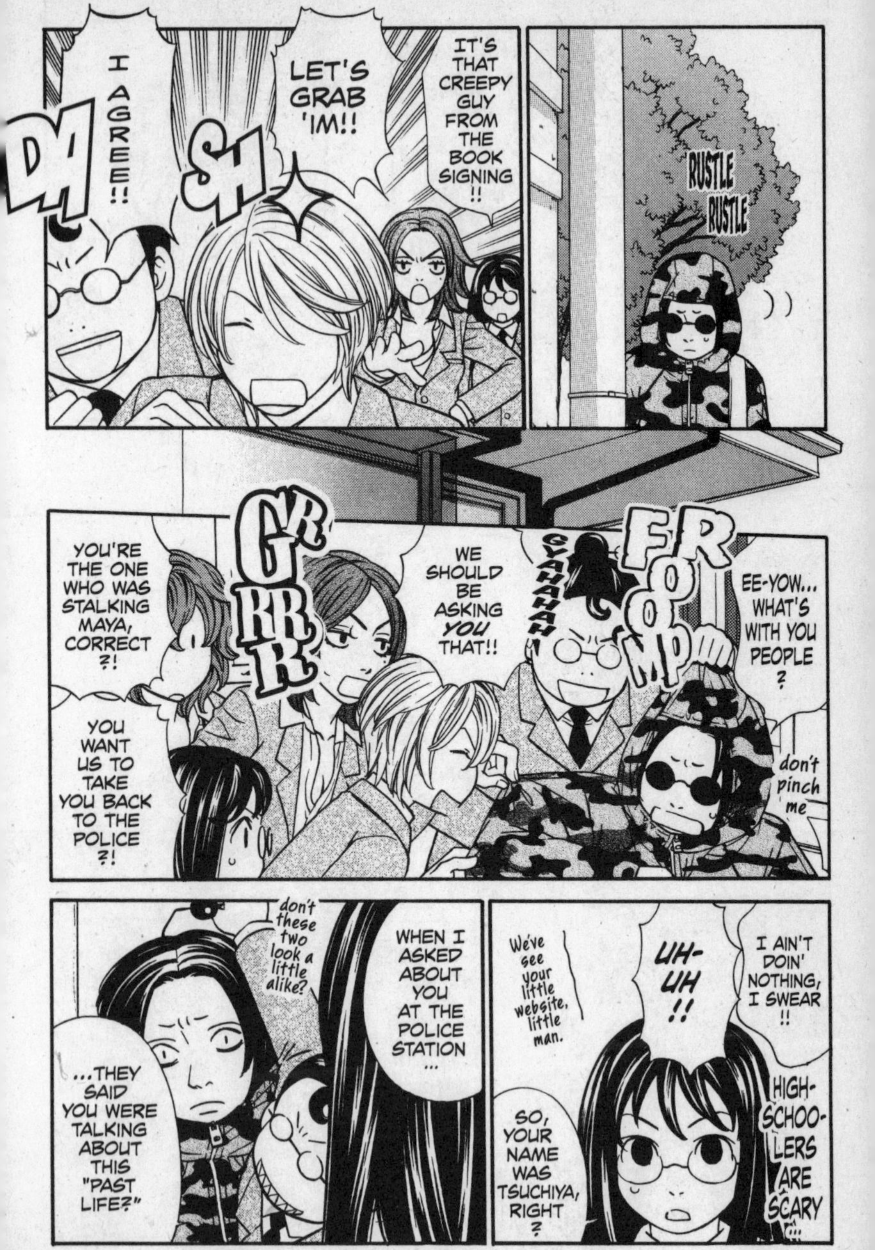
RUSTLE RUSTLE
IT'S THAT CREEPY GUY FROM THE BOOK SIGNING!!
LET'S GRAB 'IM!!
DASH
I AGREE!!
FROOMP
EE-YOW... WHAT'S WITH YOU PEOPLE?
GYAHAHAH
don't pinch me
WE SHOULD BE ASKING YOU THAT!!
GRRRR
YOU'RE THE ONE WHO WAS STALKING MAYA, CORRECT?!
YOU WANT US TO TAKE YOU BACK TO THE POLICE?!
I AIN'T DOIN' NOTHING, I SWEAR!!
UH-UH!!
We've see your little website, little man.
HIGH-SCHOOLERS ARE SCARY...!
SO, YOUR NAME WAS TSUCHIYA, RIGHT?
WHEN I ASKED ABOUT YOU AT THE POLICE STATION...
don't these two look a little alike?
...THEY SAID YOU WERE TALKING ABOUT THIS "PAST LIFE?"

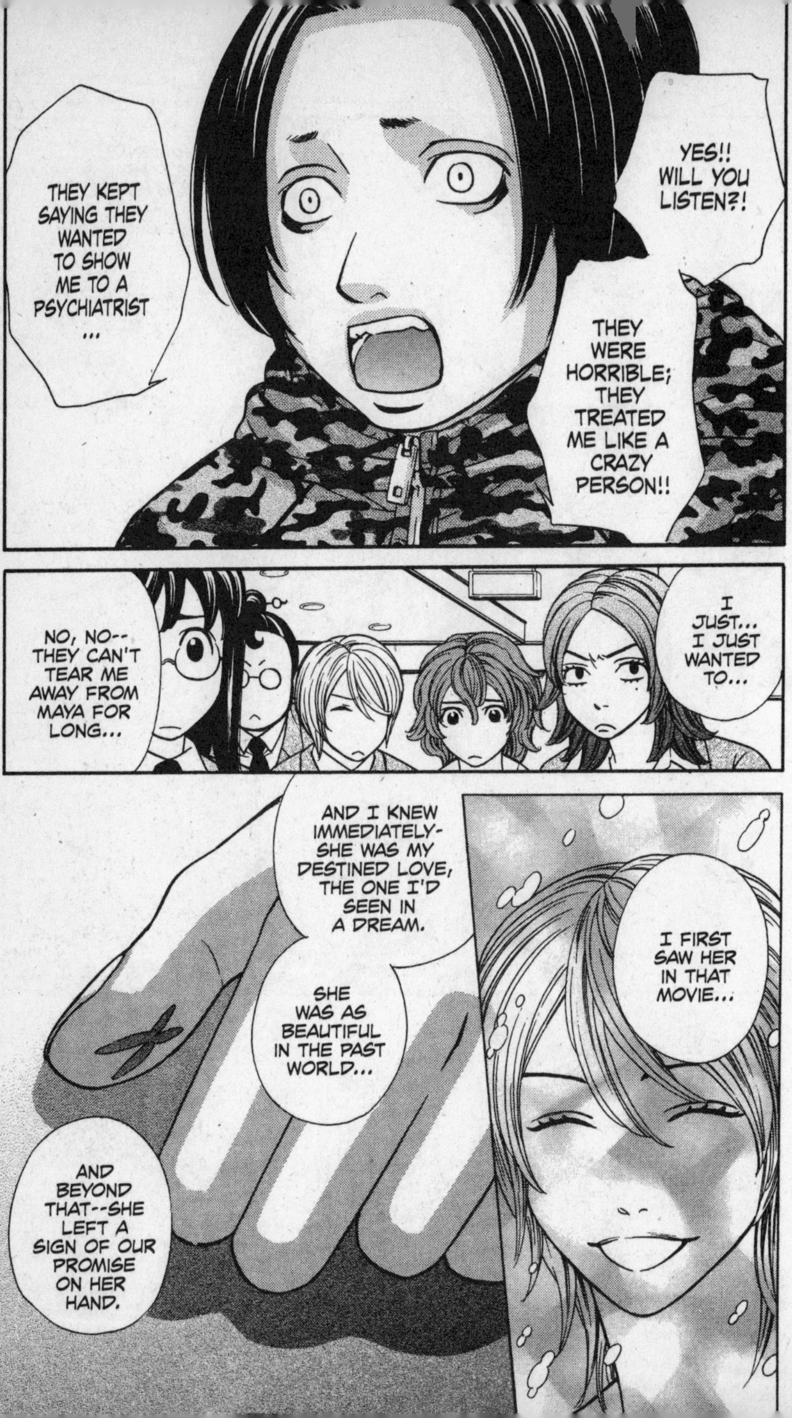
YES!! WILL YOU LISTEN?!
THEY WERE HORRIBLE; THEY TREATED ME LIKE A CRAZY PERSON!!
THEY KEPT SAYING THEY WANTED TO SHOW ME TO A PSYCHIATRIST...
I JUST... I JUST WANTED TO...
NO, NO-- THEY CAN'T TEAR ME AWAY FROM MAYA FOR LONG...
I FIRST SAW HER IN THAT MOVIE...
AND I KNEW IMMEDIATELY- SHE WAS MY DESTINED LOVE, THE ONE I'D SEEN IN A DREAM.
SHE WAS AS BEAUTIFUL IN THE PAST WORLD...
AND BEYOND THAT--SHE LEFT A SIGN OF OUR PROMISE ON HER HAND.

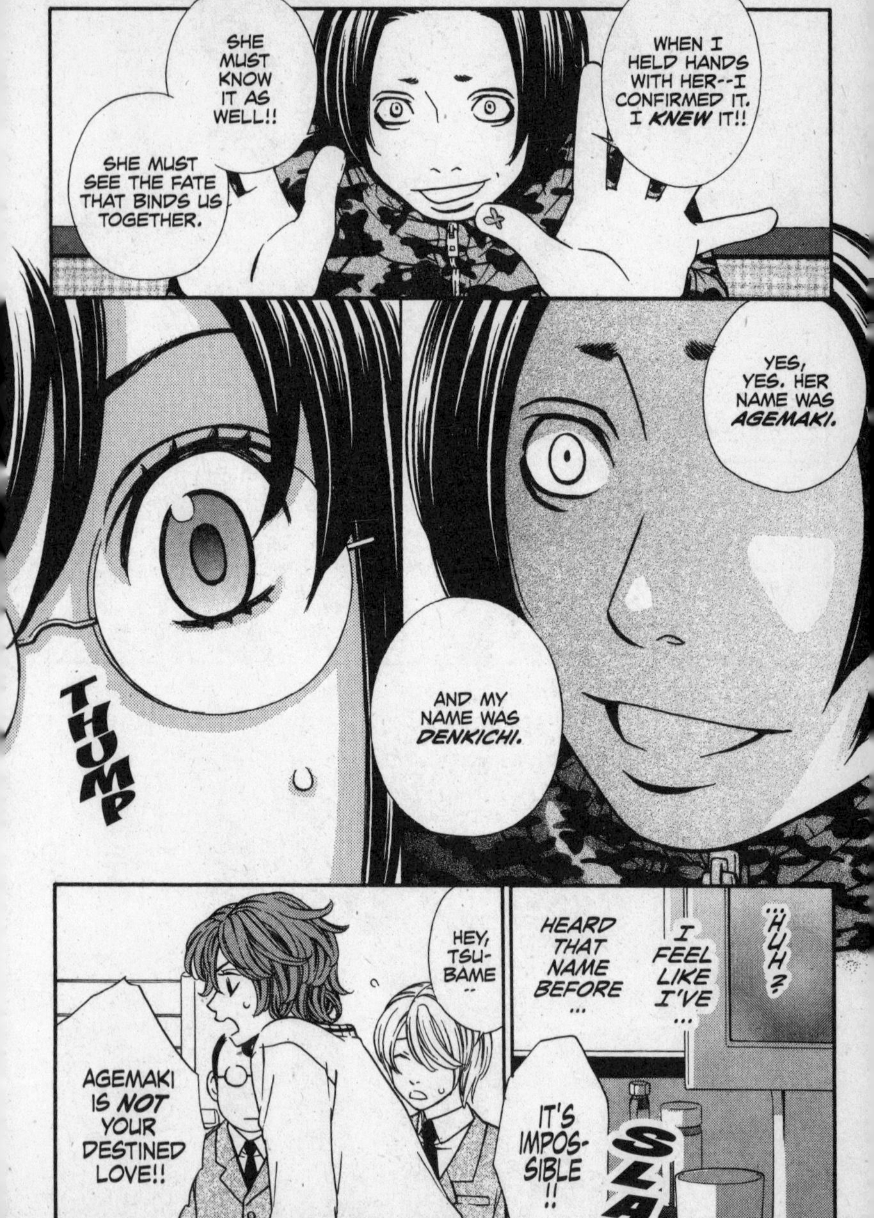
WHEN I HELD HANDS WITH HER--I CONFIRMED IT. I *KNEW* IT!!
SHE MUST KNOW IT AS WELL!!
SHE MUST SEE THE FATE THAT BINDS US TOGETHER.
YES, YES. HER NAME WAS *AGEMAKI.*
AND MY NAME WAS *DENKICHI.*
THUMP
...HUH?
I FEEL LIKE I'VE...
HEARD THAT NAME BEFORE...
IT'S IMPOSSIBLE!!
SLAM
HEY, TSUBAME--
AGEMAKI IS *NOT* YOUR DESTINED LOVE!!

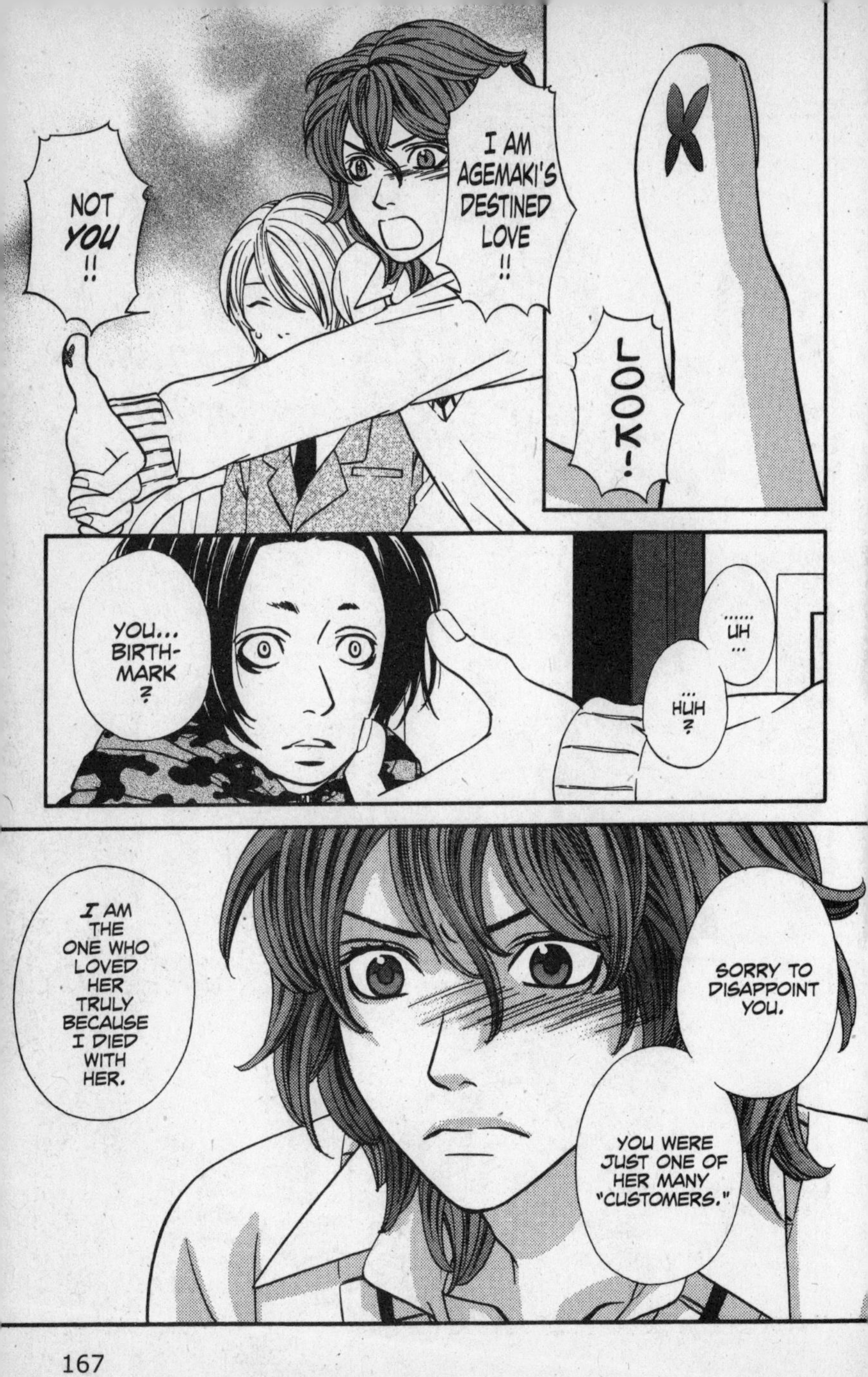
LOOK!
I AM AGEMAKI'S DESTINED LOVE !!
NOT *YOU* !!
......UH ...
... HUH ?
YOU... BIRTH-MARK ?
SORRY TO DISAPPOINT YOU.
YOU WERE JUST ONE OF HER MANY "CUSTOMERS."
I AM THE ONE WHO LOVED HER TRULY BECAUSE I DIED WITH HER.

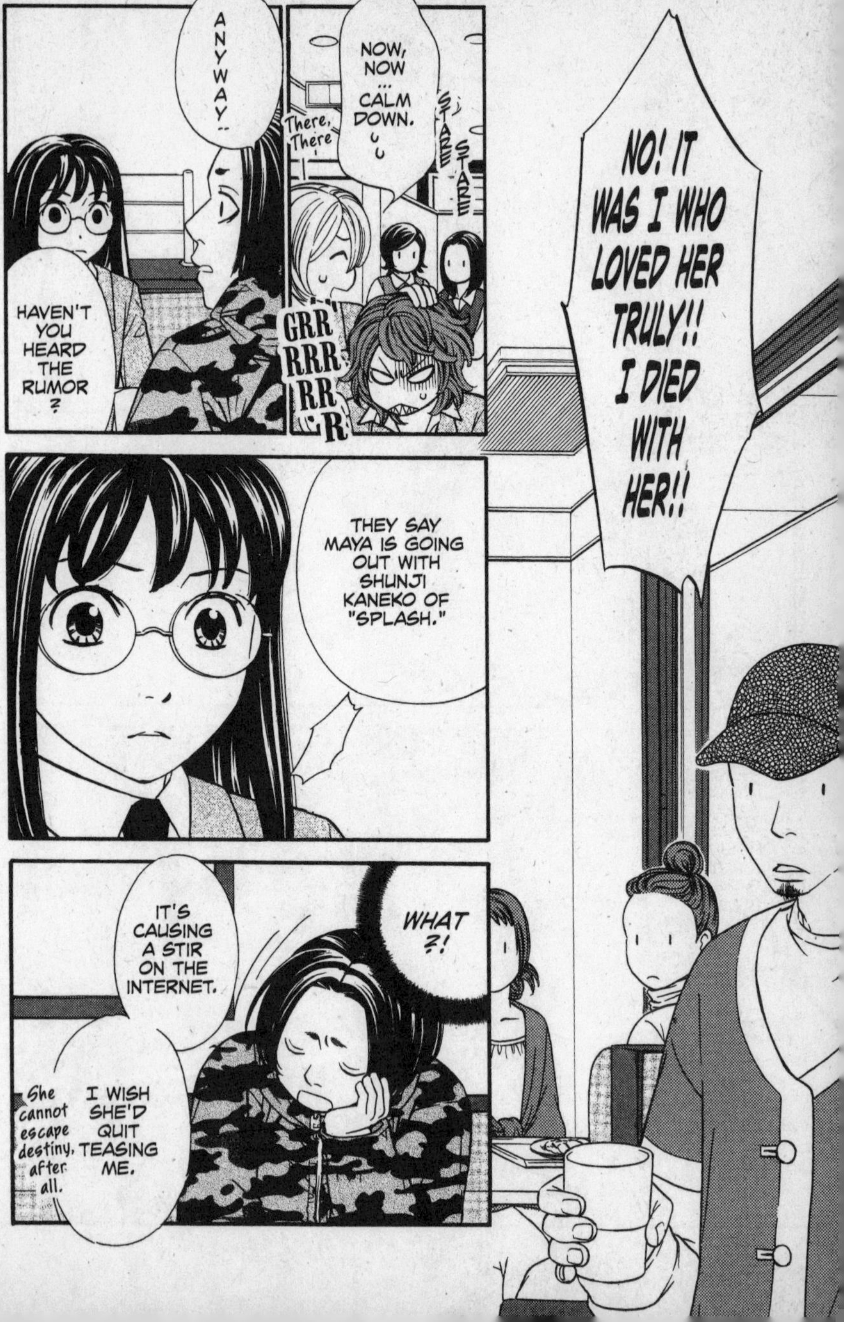
NO! IT WAS I WHO LOVED HER TRULY!! I DIED WITH HER!!
NOW, NOW... CALM DOWN.
There, There
STARE STARE
GRRRRRRRR
ANYWAY..
HAVEN'T YOU HEARD THE RUMOR?
THEY SAY MAYA IS GOING OUT WITH SHUNJI KANEKO OF "SPLASH."
WHAT?!
IT'S CAUSING A STIR ON THE INTERNET.
I WISH SHE'D QUIT TEASING ME.
She cannot escape destiny, after all.

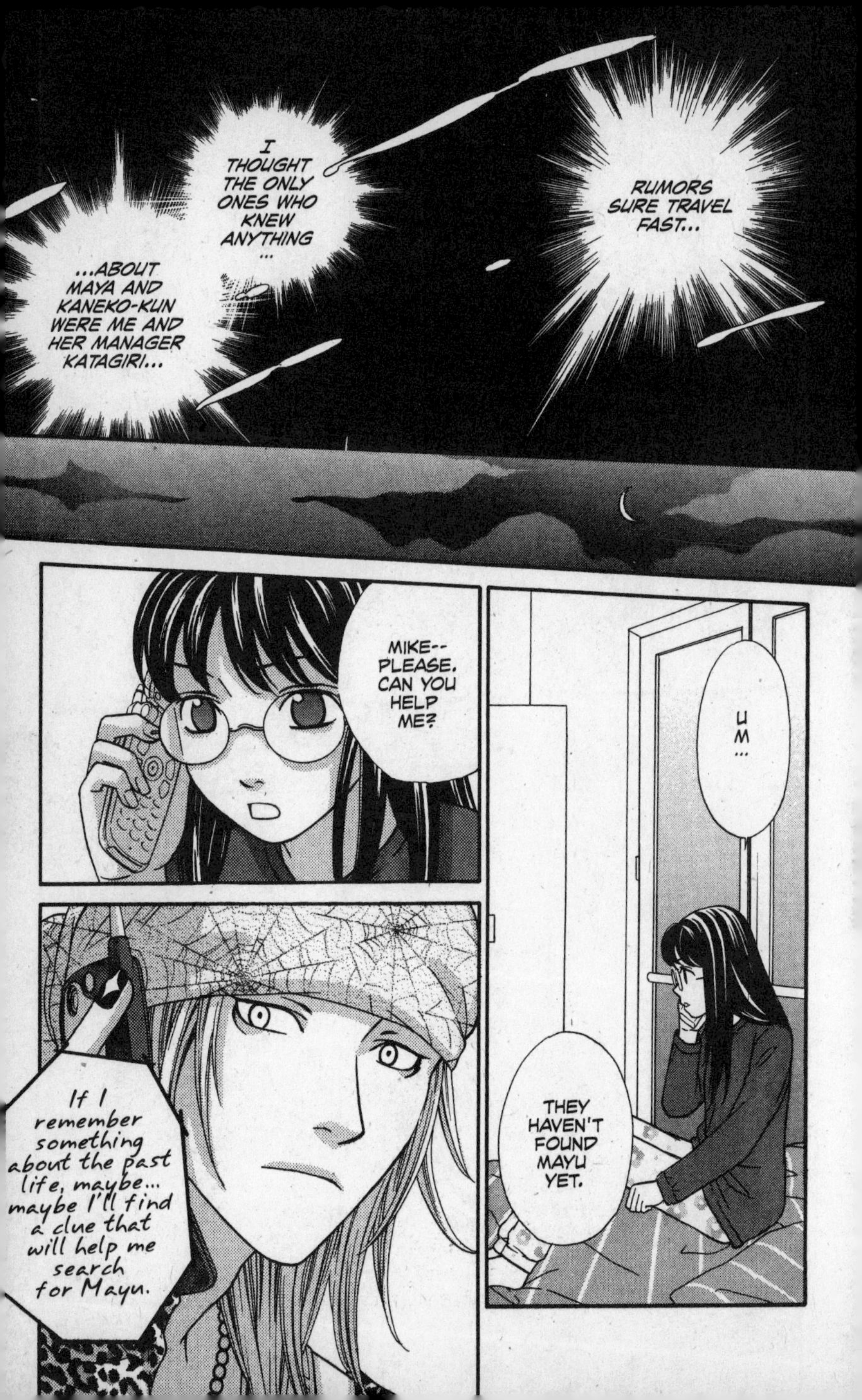
RUMORS SURE TRAVEL FAST...
I THOUGHT THE ONLY ONES WHO KNEW ANYTHING ...
...ABOUT MAYA AND KANEKO-KUN WERE ME AND HER MANAGER KATAGIRI...
UM ...
THEY HAVEN'T FOUND MAYU YET.
MIKE--PLEASE. CAN YOU HELP ME?
If I remember something about the past life, maybe... maybe I'll find a clue that will help me search for Mayu.

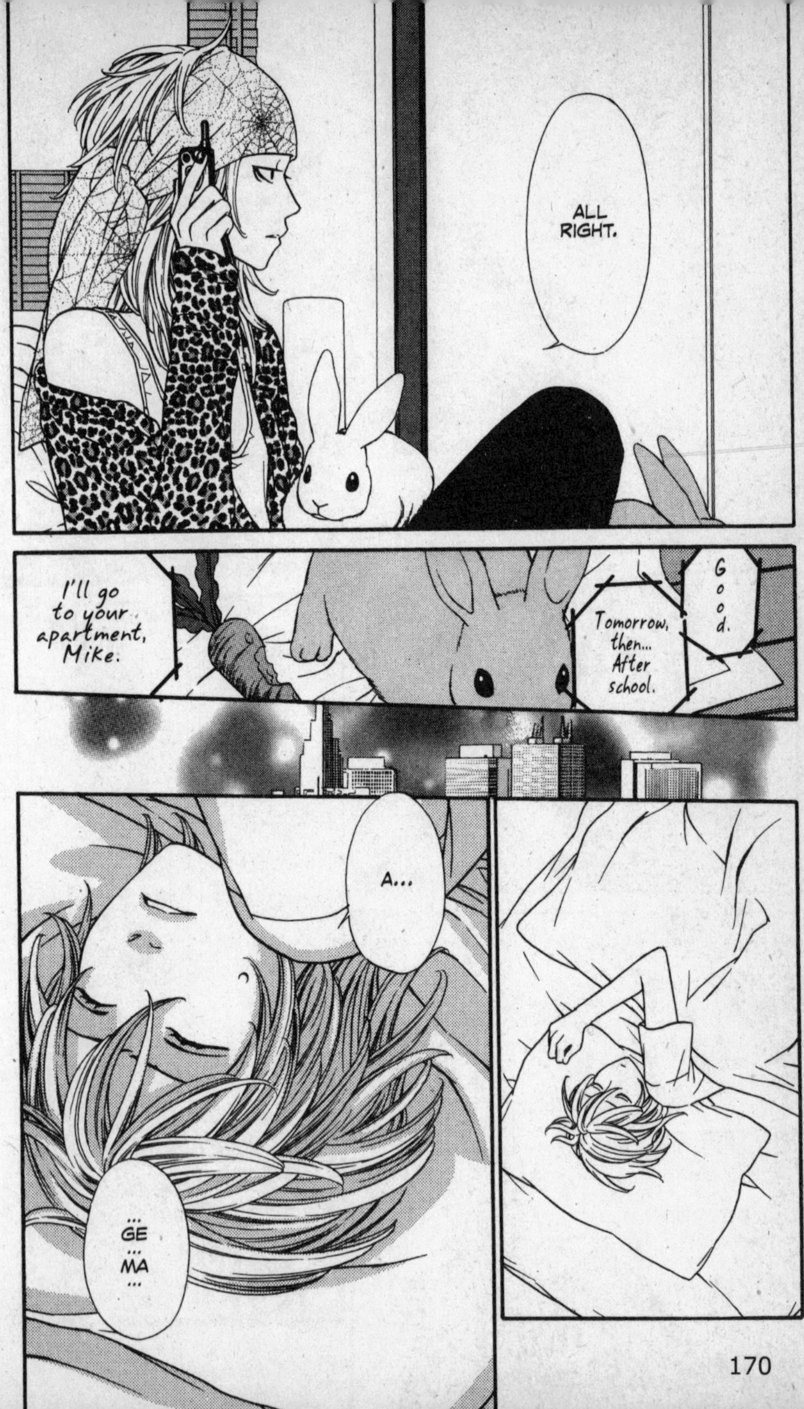
ALL RIGHT.
Good.
Tomorrow, then... After school.
I'll go to your apartment, Mike.
A...
...GE...MA...

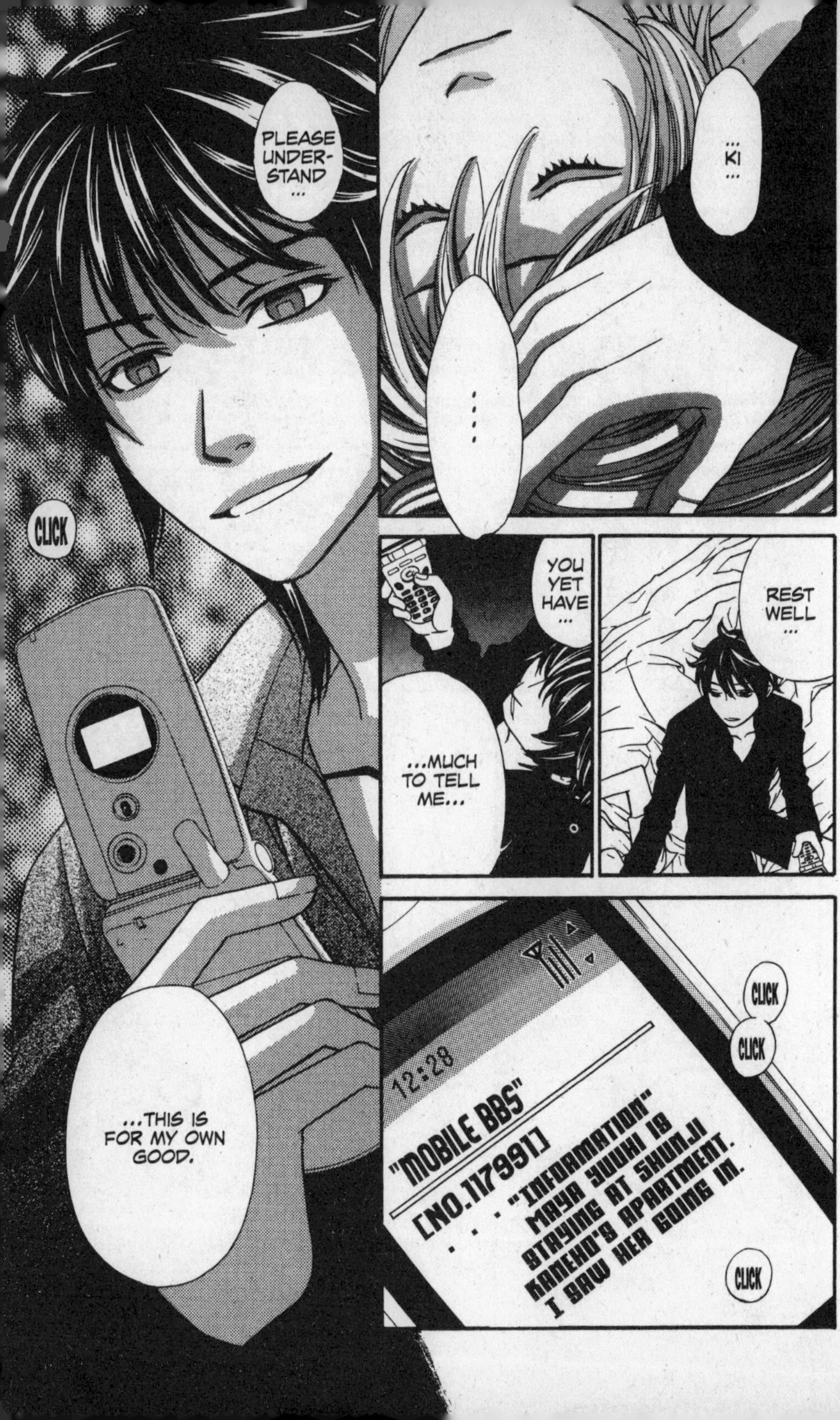

...KI...
....
REST WELL...
YOU YET HAVE...
...MUCH TO TELL ME...
CLICK
CLICK
12:28
"MOBILE BBS"
[NO.117991]
. . . "INFORMATION" MAYA YUUKI IS STAYING AT SHUNJI KANEKO'S APARTMENT. I SAW HER GOING IN.
CLICK
PLEASE UNDERSTAND...
CLICK
...THIS IS FOR MY OWN GOOD.

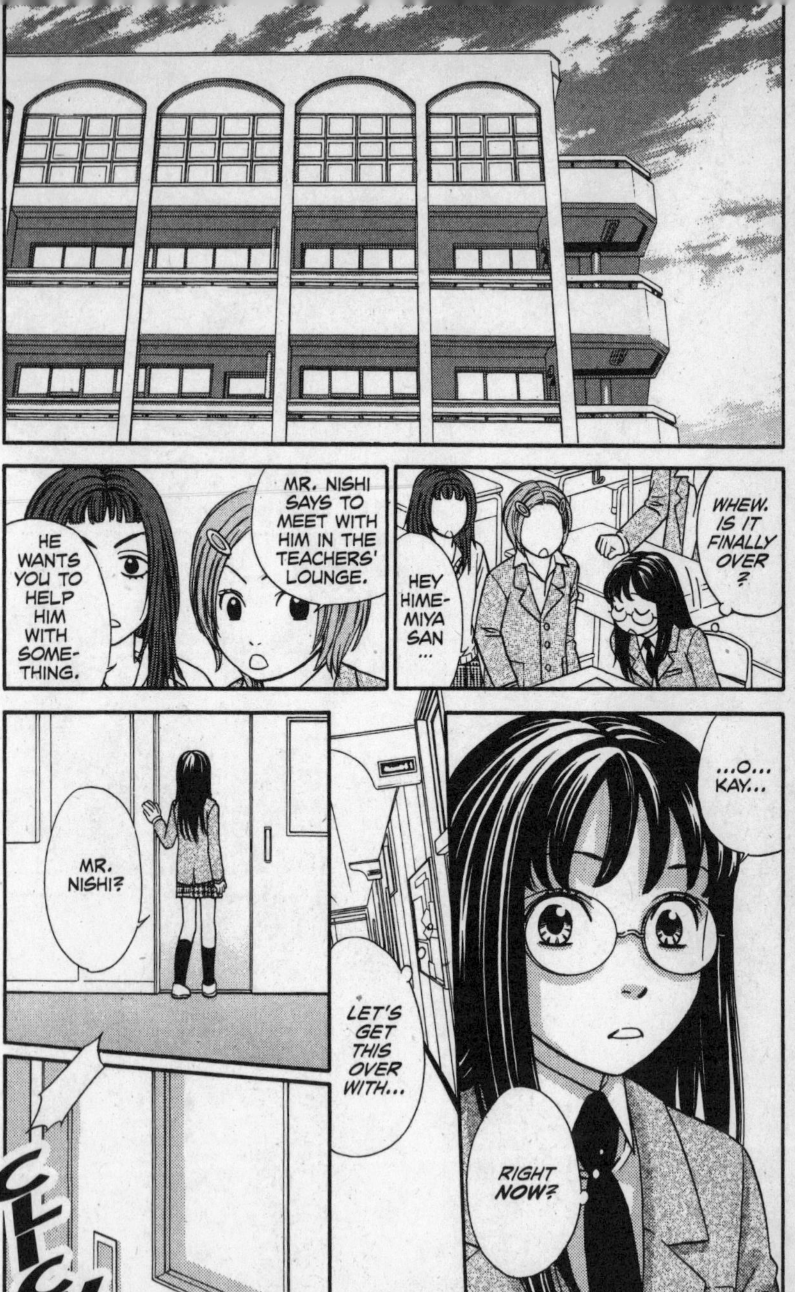
WHEW. IS IT FINALLY OVER?
HEY HIME-MIYA SAN...
MR. NISHI SAYS TO MEET WITH HIM IN THE TEACHERS' LOUNGE.
HE WANTS YOU TO HELP HIM WITH SOMETHING.
...O... KAY...
LET'S GET THIS OVER WITH...
RIGHT NOW?
MR. NISHI?
CLICK

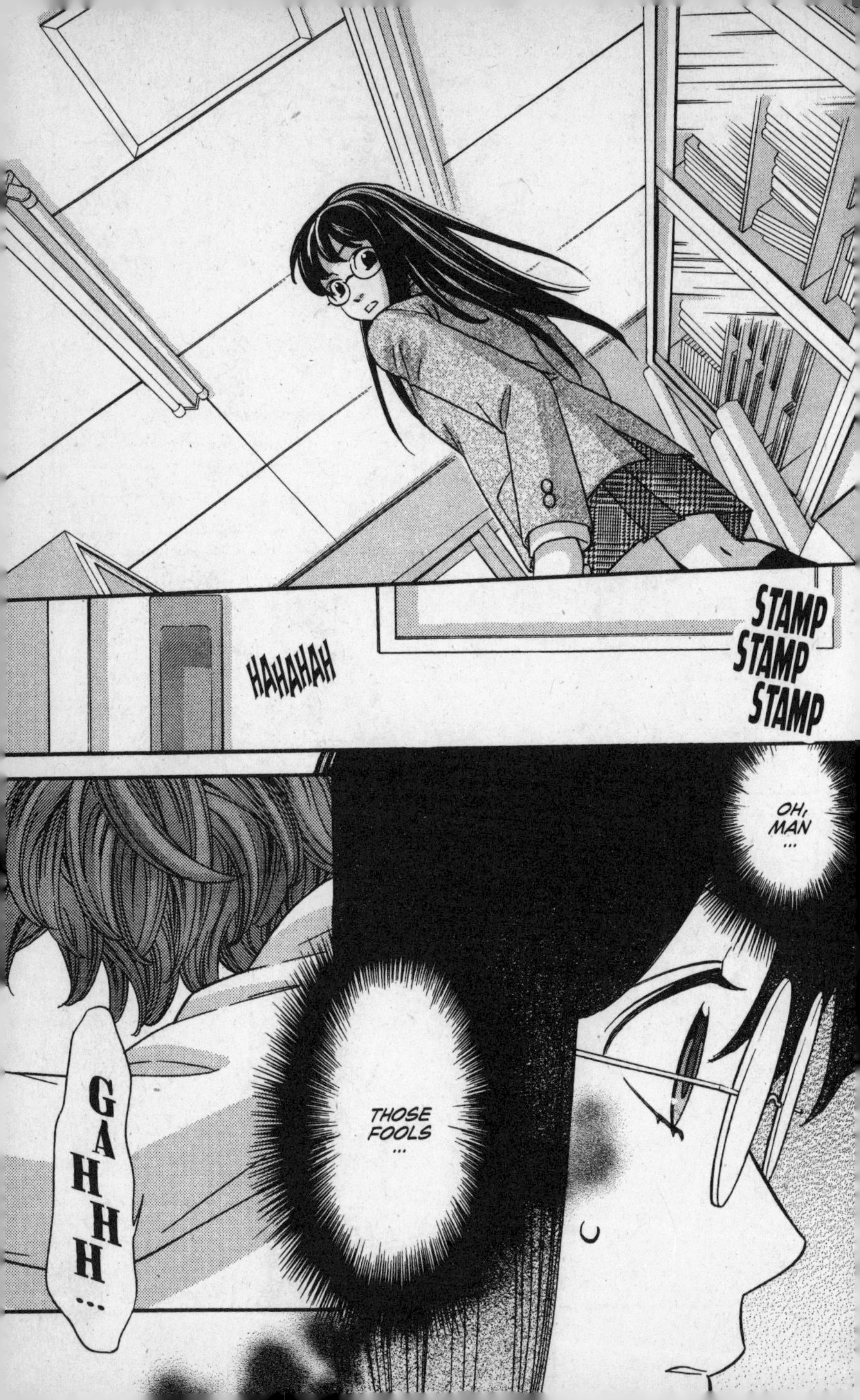
STAMP STAMP STAMP
HAHAHAH
OH, MAN ...
THOSE FOOLS ...
GAHHH ...

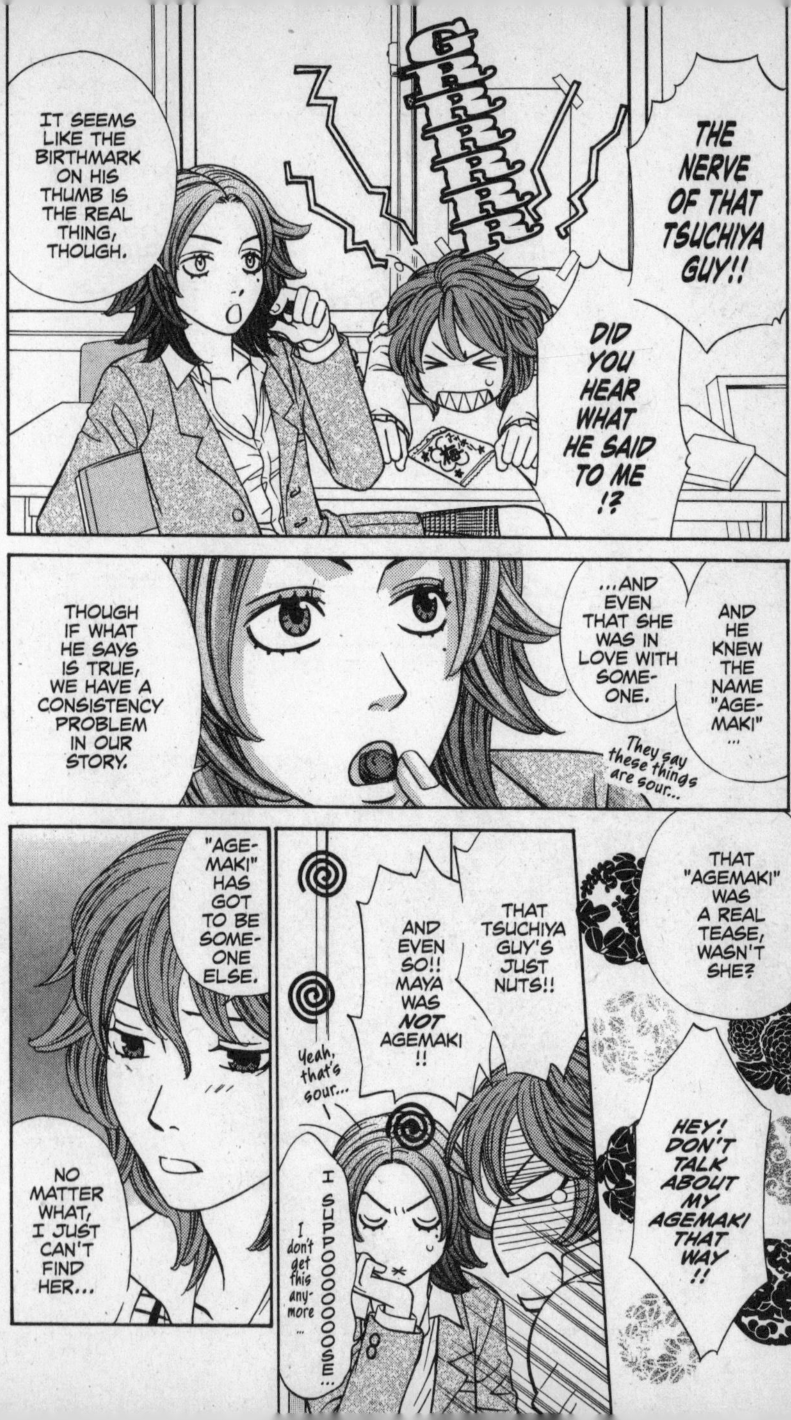
THE NERVE OF THAT TSUCHIYA GUY!!
DID YOU HEAR WHAT HE SAID TO ME !?
IT SEEMS LIKE THE BIRTHMARK ON HIS THUMB IS THE REAL THING, THOUGH.
AND HE KNEW THE NAME "AGE-MAKI"...
...AND EVEN THAT SHE WAS IN LOVE WITH SOME-ONE.
They say these things are sour...
THOUGH IF WHAT HE SAYS IS TRUE, WE HAVE A CONSISTENCY PROBLEM IN OUR STORY.
THAT "AGEMAKI" WAS A REAL TEASE, WASN'T SHE?
HEY! DON'T TALK ABOUT MY AGEMAKI THAT WAY!!
THAT TSUCHIYA GUY'S JUST NUTS!!
AND EVEN SO!! MAYA WAS NOT AGEMAKI!!
Yeah, that's sour...
I SUPPOOOOOOOSE...
I don't get this anymore...
"AGE-MAKI" HAS GOT TO BE SOME-ONE ELSE.
NO MATTER WHAT, I JUST CAN'T FIND HER...

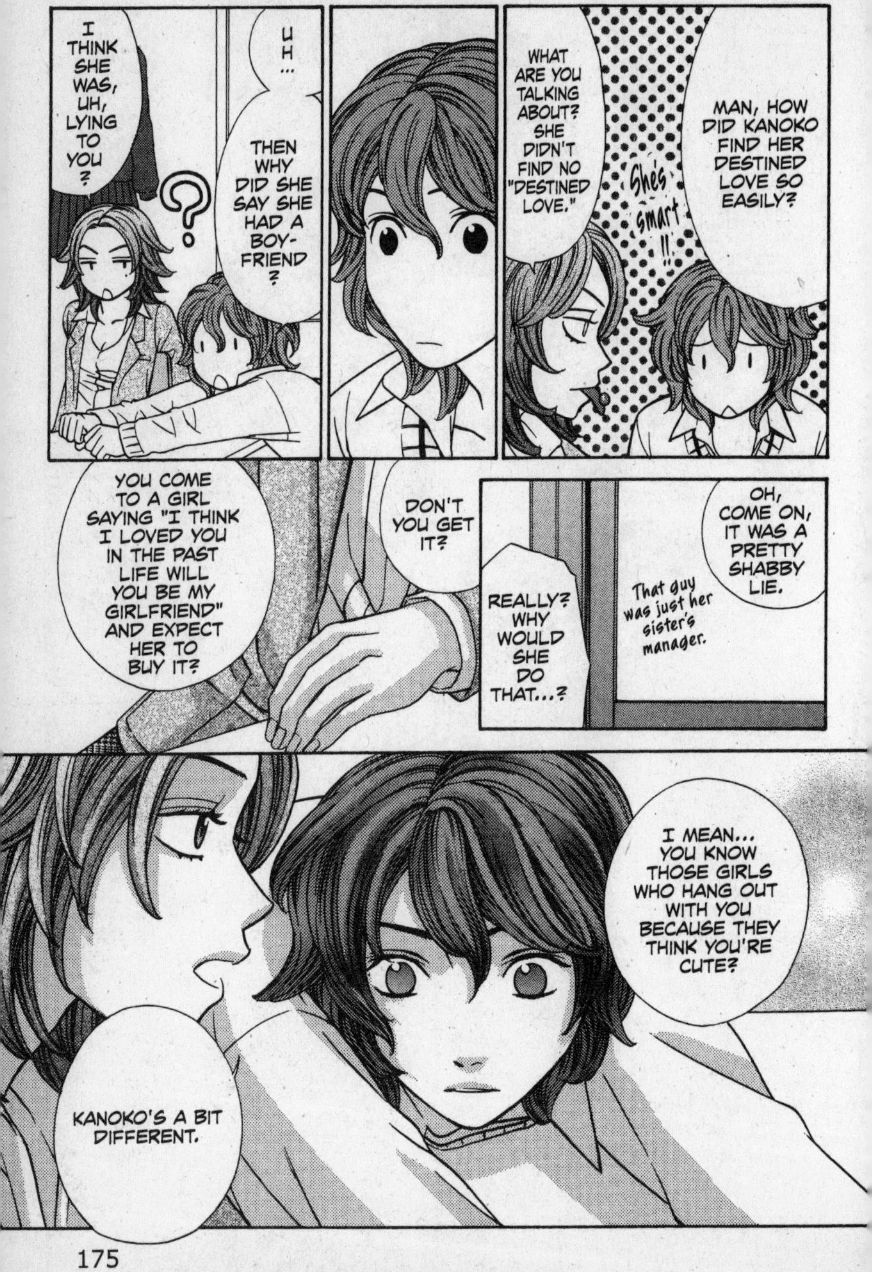
MAN, HOW DID KANOKO FIND HER DESTINED LOVE SO EASILY?
WHAT ARE YOU TALKING ABOUT? SHE DIDN'T FIND NO "DESTINED LOVE."
She's smart!!
UH...
I THINK SHE WAS, UH, LYING TO YOU?
THEN WHY DID SHE SAY SHE HAD A BOY-FRIEND?
OH, COME ON, IT WAS A PRETTY SHABBY LIE.
That guy was just her sister's manager.
REALLY? WHY WOULD SHE DO THAT...?
DON'T YOU GET IT?
YOU COME TO A GIRL SAYING "I THINK I LOVED YOU IN THE PAST LIFE WILL YOU BE MY GIRLFRIEND" AND EXPECT HER TO BUY IT?
I MEAN... YOU KNOW THOSE GIRLS WHO HANG OUT WITH YOU BECAUSE THEY THINK YOU'RE CUTE?
KANOKO'S A BIT DIFFERENT.

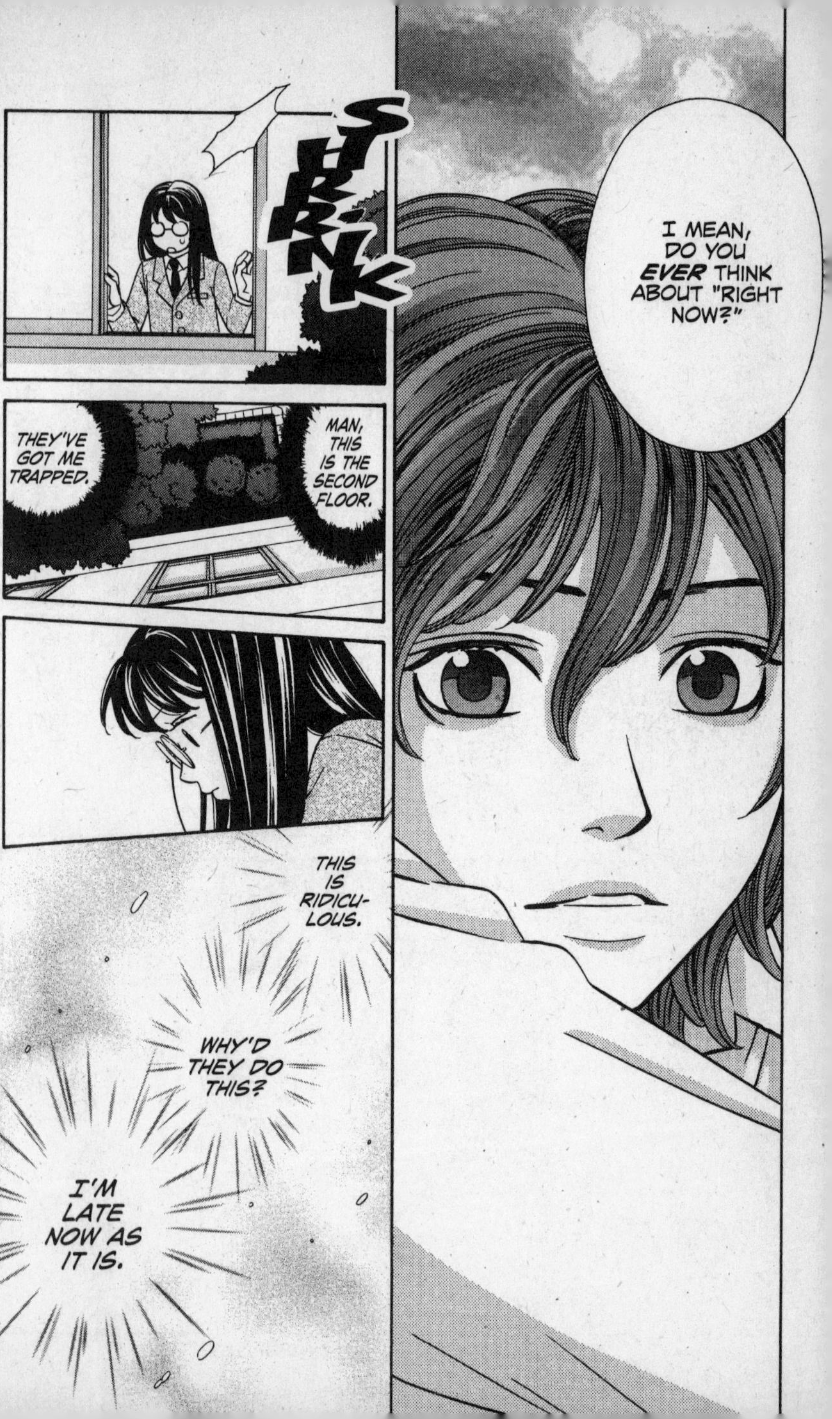
I MEAN, DO YOU EVER THINK ABOUT "RIGHT NOW?"
SHRRNK
MAN, THIS IS THE SECOND FLOOR.
THEY'VE GOT ME TRAPPED.
THIS IS RIDICULOUS.
WHY'D THEY DO THIS?
I'M LATE NOW AS IT IS.

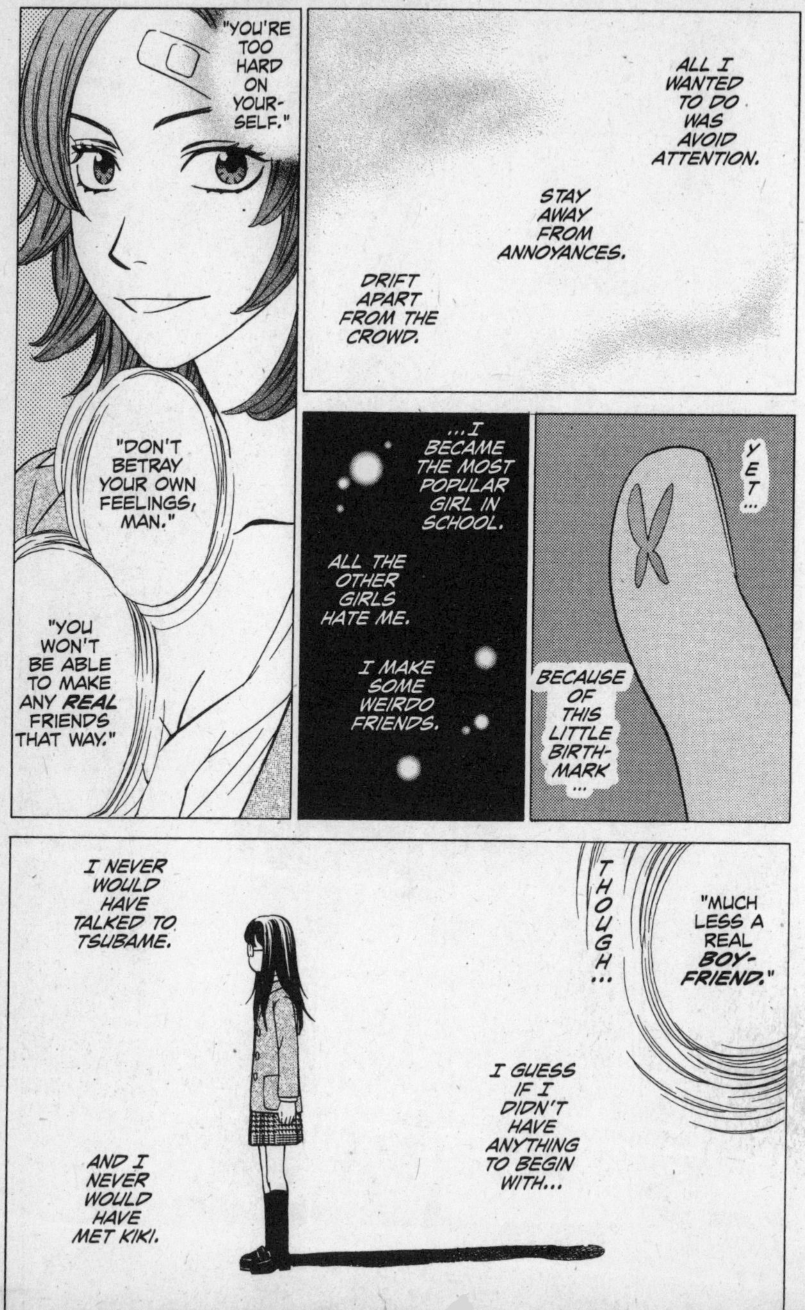
ALL I WANTED TO DO WAS AVOID ATTENTION.
STAY AWAY FROM ANNOYANCES.
DRIFT APART FROM THE CROWD.
YET...
BECAUSE OF THIS LITTLE BIRTH-MARK...
...I BECAME THE MOST POPULAR GIRL IN SCHOOL.
ALL THE OTHER GIRLS HATE ME.
I MAKE SOME WEIRDO FRIENDS.
"YOU'RE TOO HARD ON YOUR-SELF."
"DON'T BETRAY YOUR OWN FEELINGS, MAN."
"YOU WON'T BE ABLE TO MAKE ANY REAL FRIENDS THAT WAY."
"MUCH LESS A REAL BOY-FRIEND."
THOUGH...
I NEVER WOULD HAVE TALKED TO TSUBAME.
I GUESS IF I DIDN'T HAVE ANYTHING TO BEGIN WITH...
AND I NEVER WOULD HAVE MET KIKI.

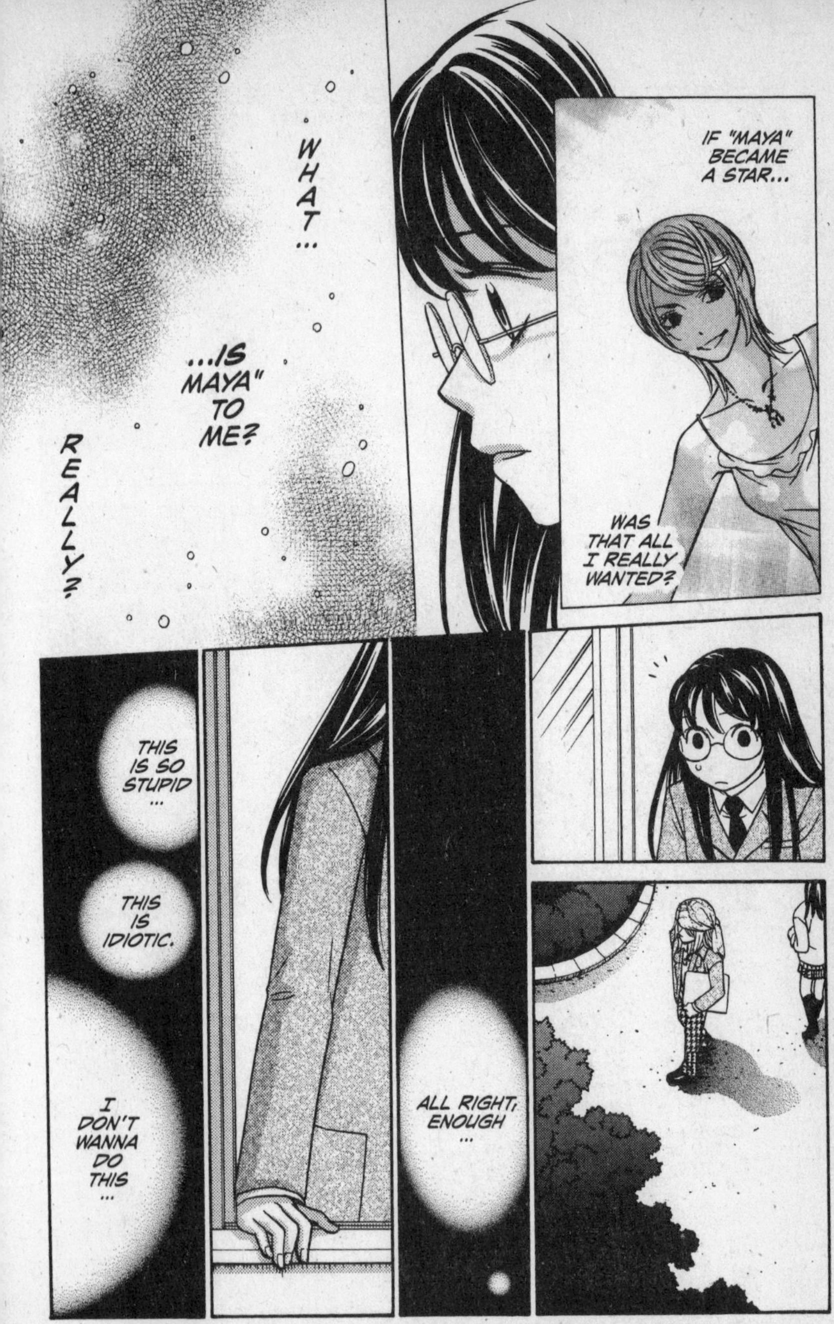

IF "MAYA" BECAME A STAR...
WAS THAT ALL I REALLY WANTED?
WHAT...
...IS MAYA" TO ME?
REALLY?
ALL RIGHT, ENOUGH ...
THIS IS SO STUPID ...
THIS IS IDIOTIC.
I DON'T WANNA DO THIS ...

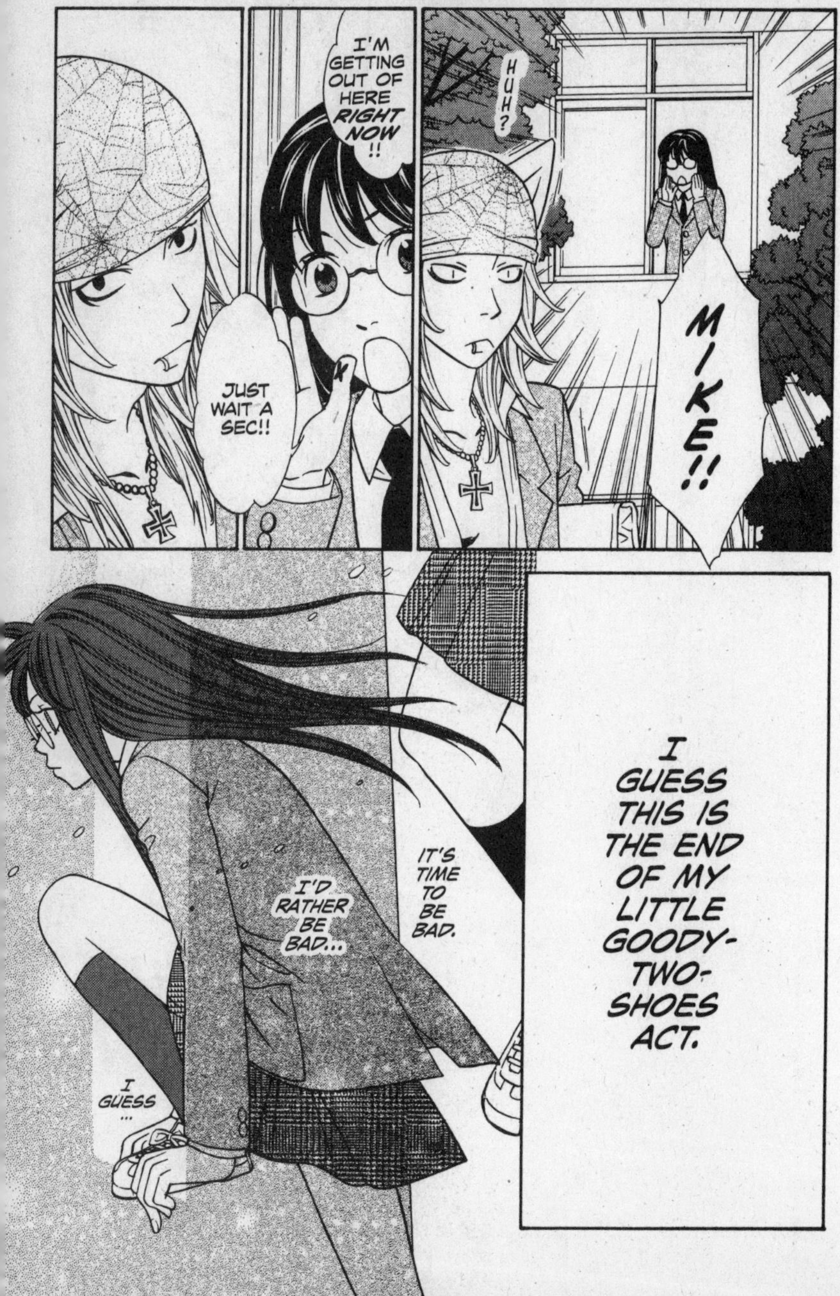
MIKE!!
HUH?
I'M GETTING OUT OF HERE RIGHT NOW!!
JUST WAIT A SEC!!
I GUESS THIS IS THE END OF MY LITTLE GOODY-TWO-SHOES ACT.
IT'S TIME TO BE BAD.
I'D RATHER BE BAD...
I GUESS...

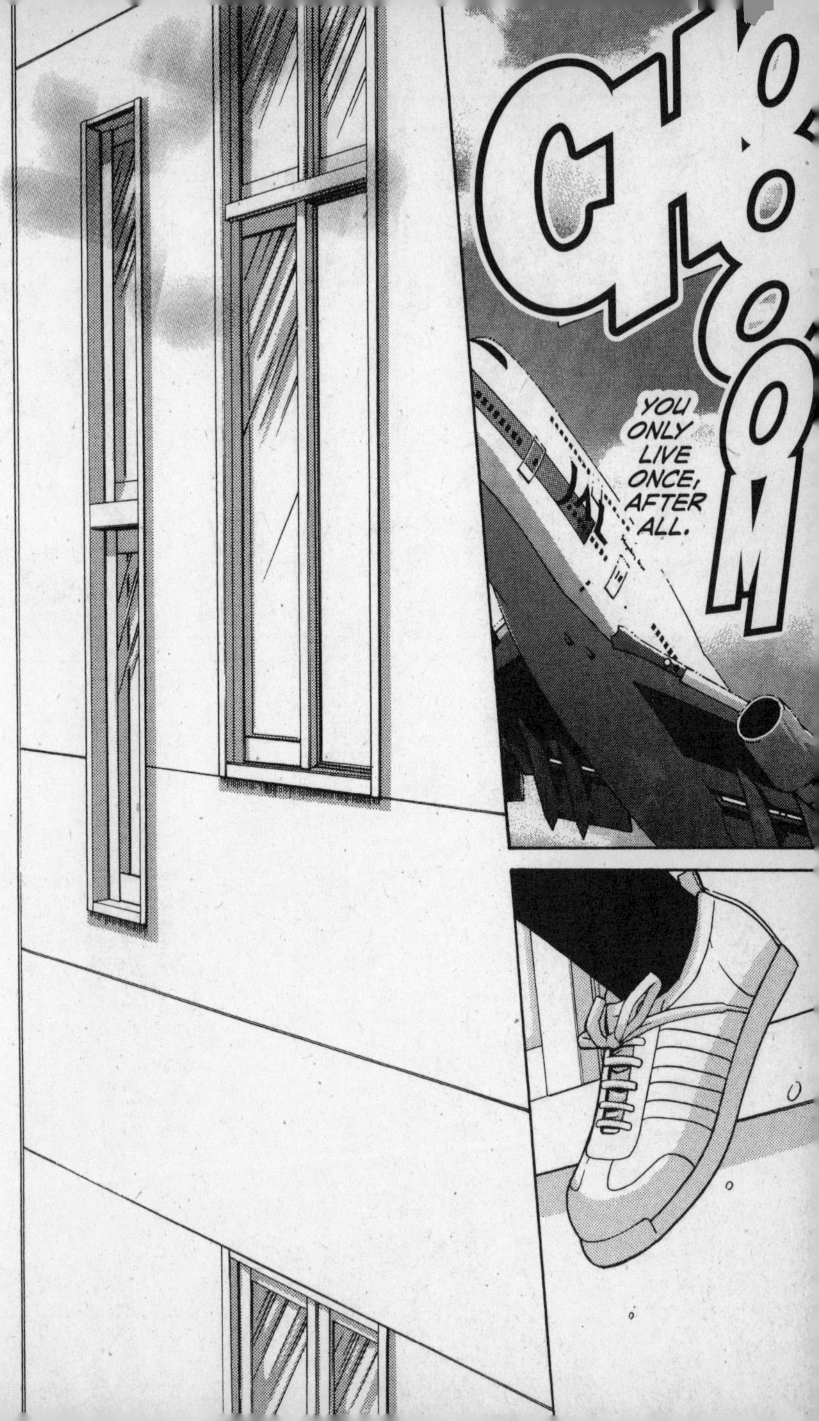
YOU ONLY LIVE ONCE, AFTER ALL.

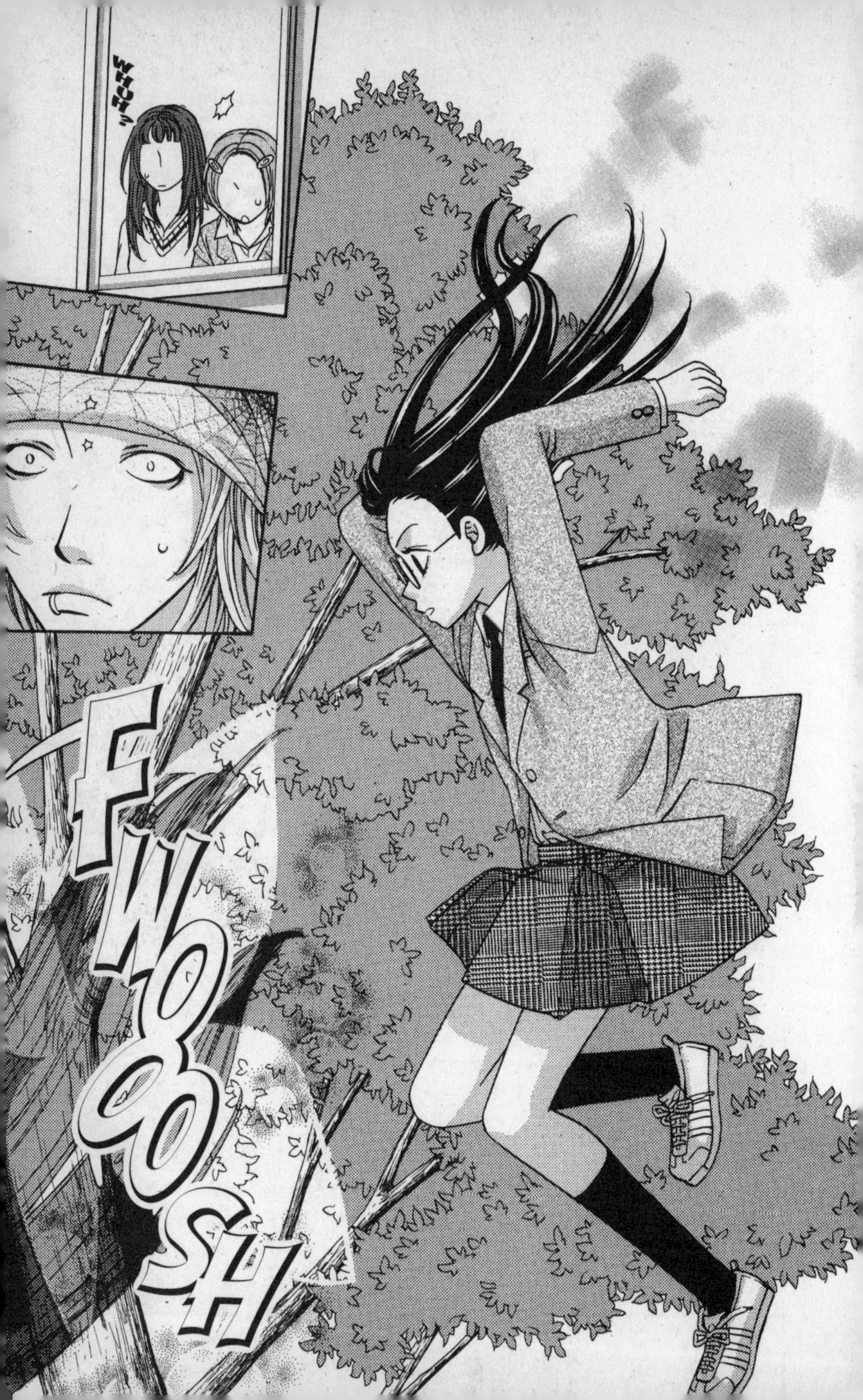
FWOOSH
WHUH?

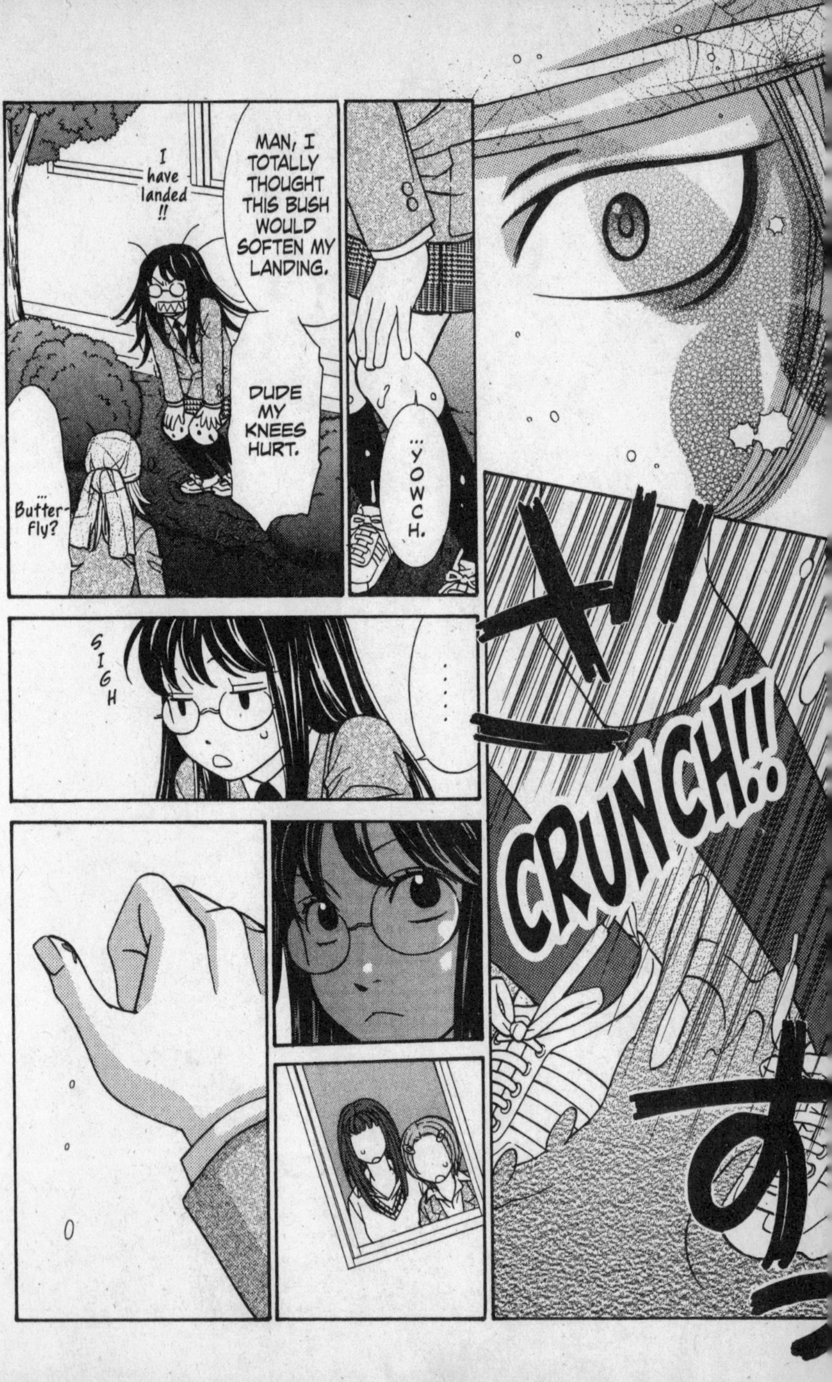
CRUNCH!!
...YOWCH.
MAN, I TOTALLY THOUGHT THIS BUSH WOULD SOFTEN MY LANDING.
DUDE MY KNEES HURT.
I have landed!!
...Butterfly?
.....
SIGH

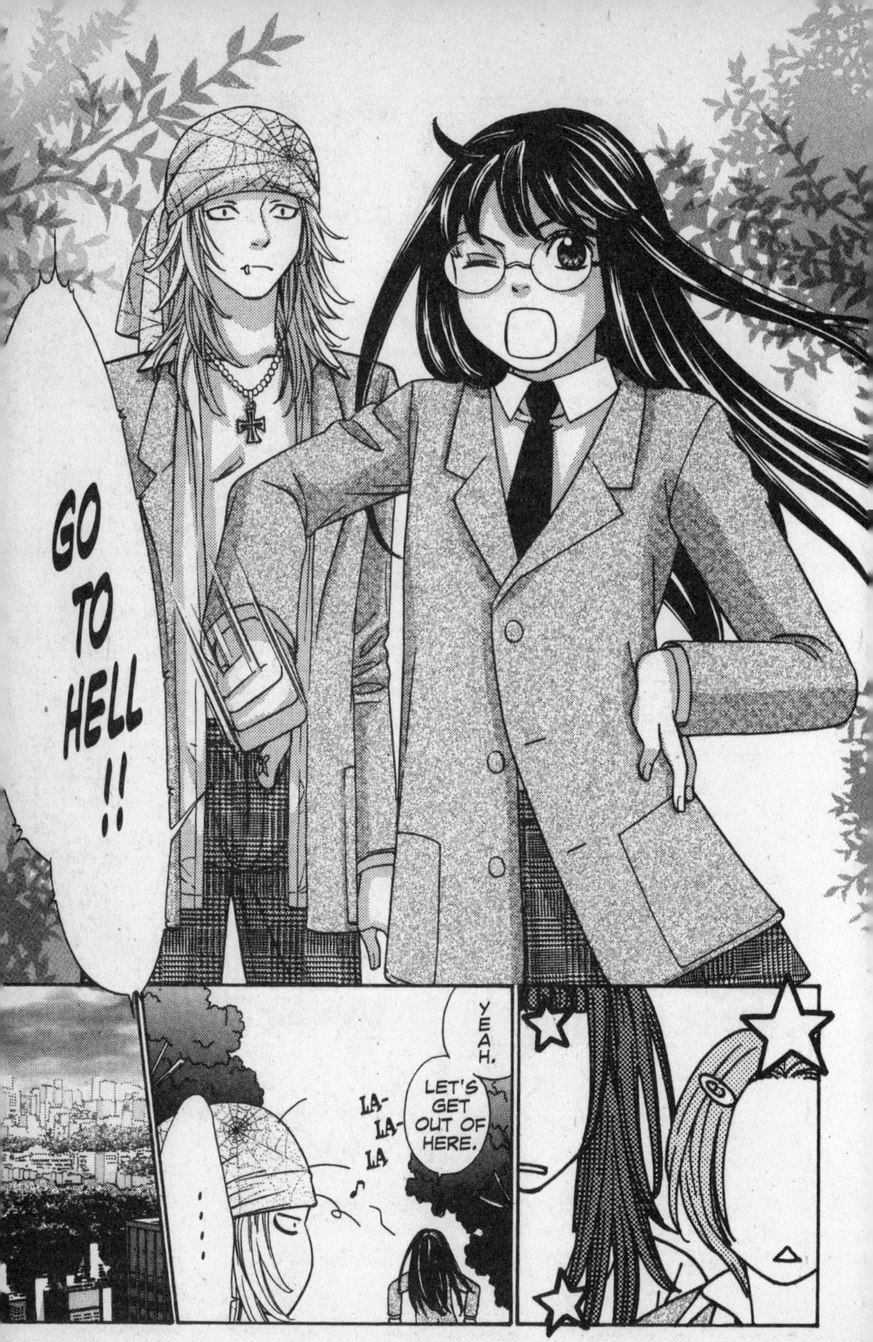
GO TO HELL!!
YEAH.
LET'S GET OUT OF HERE.
LA-LA-LA
...

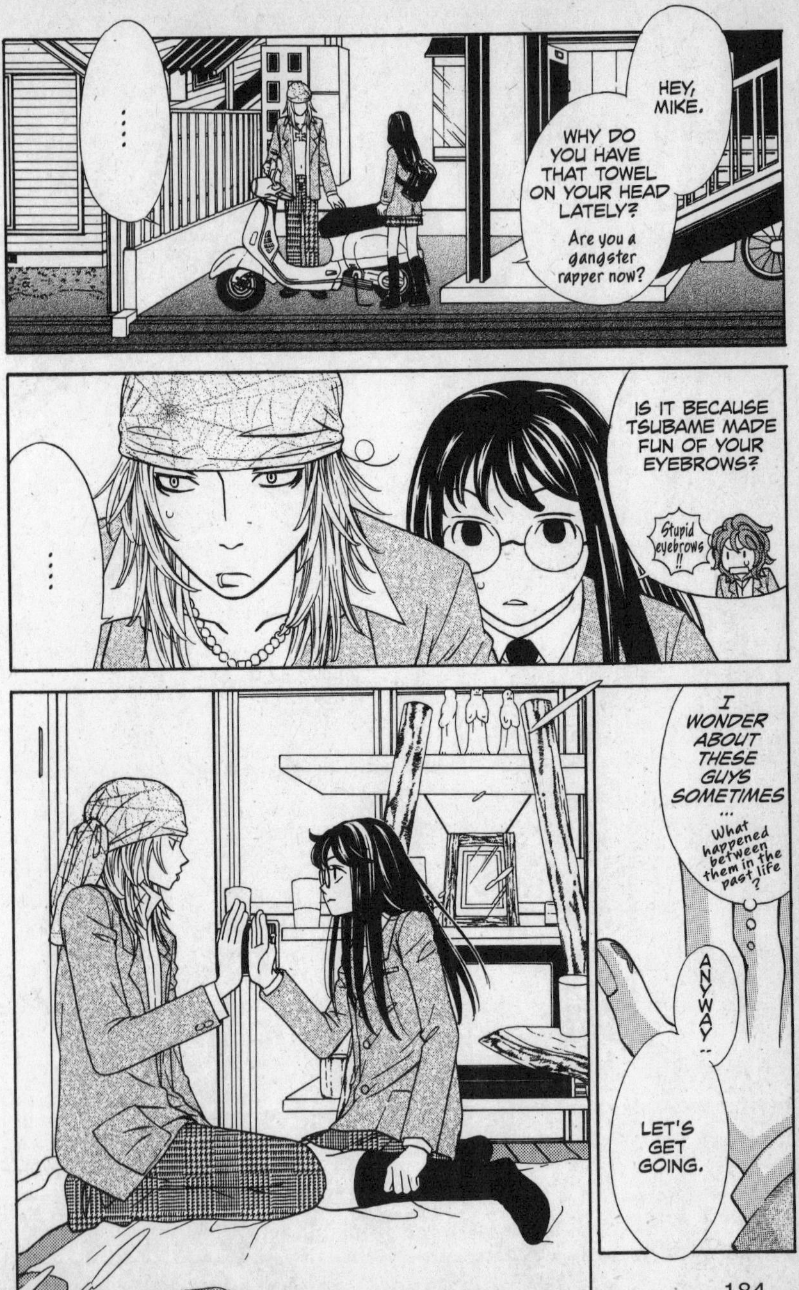
HEY, MIKE.
WHY DO YOU HAVE THAT TOWEL ON YOUR HEAD LATELY? Are you a gangster rapper now?
....
IS IT BECAUSE TSUBAME MADE FUN OF YOUR EYEBROWS?
Stupid eyebrows!!
....
I WONDER ABOUT THESE GUYS SOMETIMES...
What happened between them in the past life?
ANYWAY..
LET'S GET GOING.

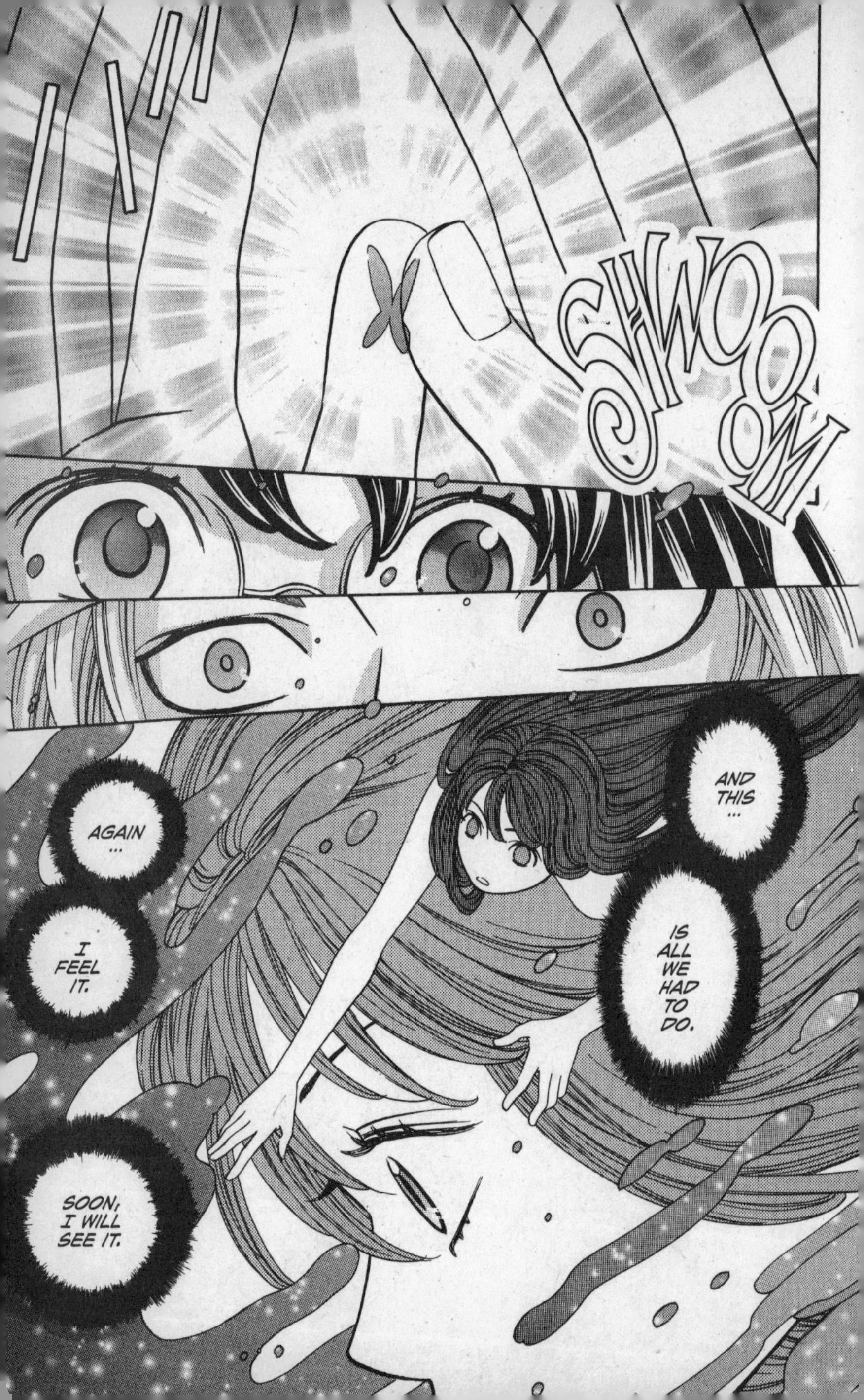
SHWOOOM
AND THIS ...
IS ALL WE HAD TO DO.
AGAIN ...
I FEEL IT.
SOON, I WILL SEE IT.

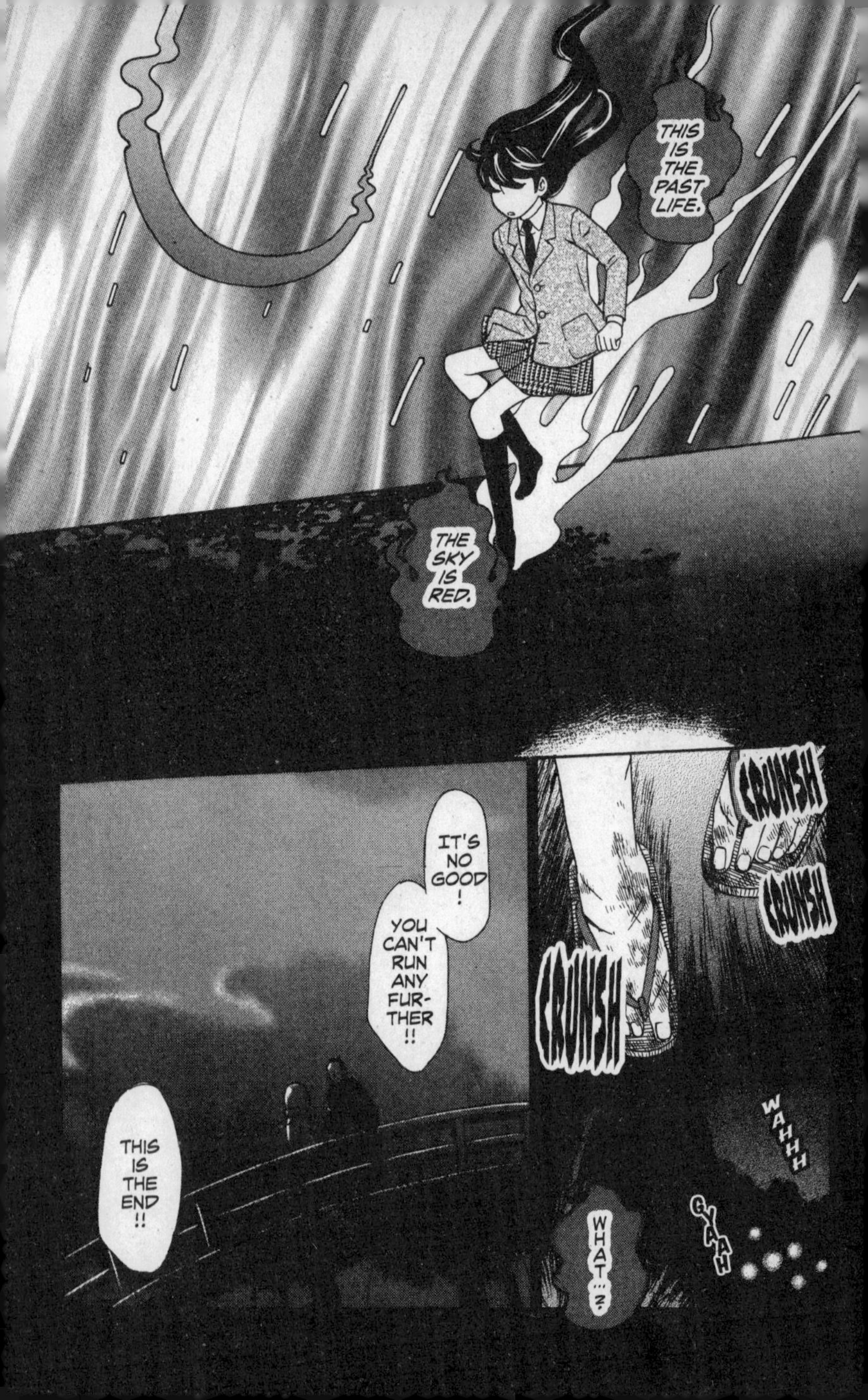
THIS IS THE PAST LIFE.
THE SKY IS RED.
CRUNSH
CRUNSH
CRUNSH
WAHHH
GYAAH
WHAT...?
IT'S NO GOOD!
YOU CAN'T RUN ANY FUR-THER!!
THIS IS THE END!!

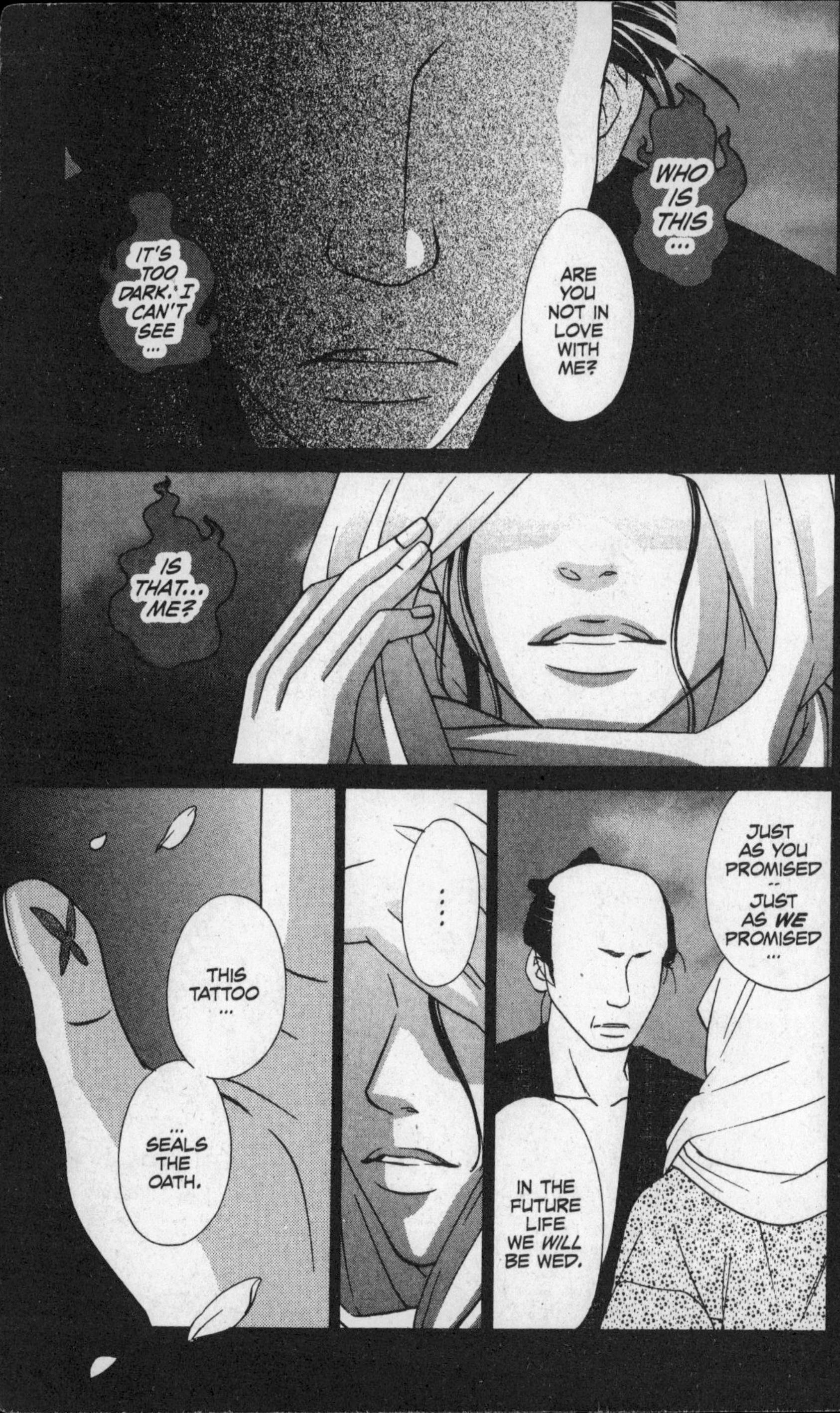
WHO IS THIS...
ARE YOU NOT IN LOVE WITH ME?
IT'S TOO DARK. I CAN'T SEE...
IS THAT... ME?
JUST AS YOU PROMISED -- JUST AS *WE* PROMISED...
IN THE FUTURE LIFE WE *WILL* BE WED.
....
THIS TATTOO...
...SEALS THE OATH.

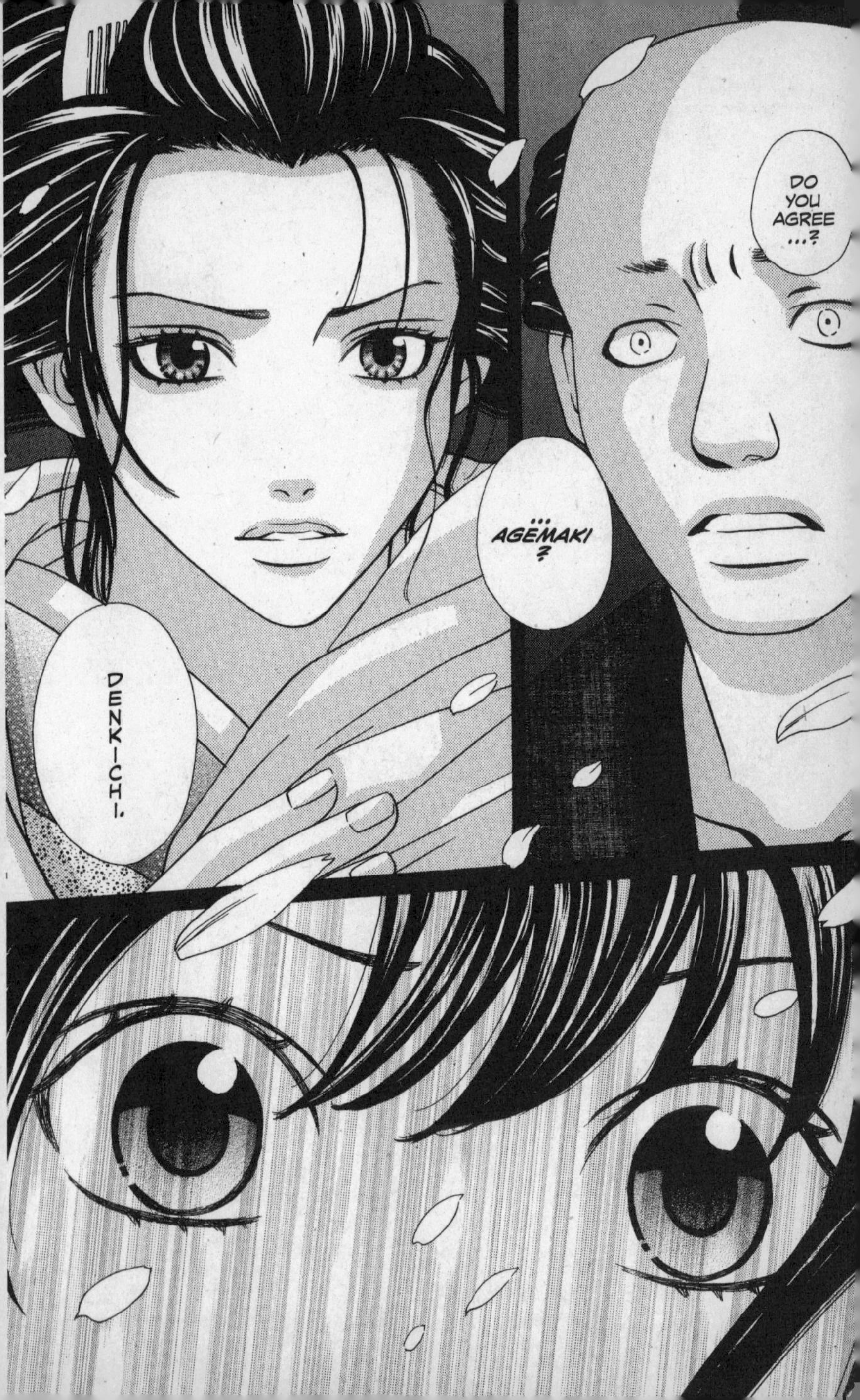
DO YOU AGREE ...?
...AGEMAKI?
DENKICHI.

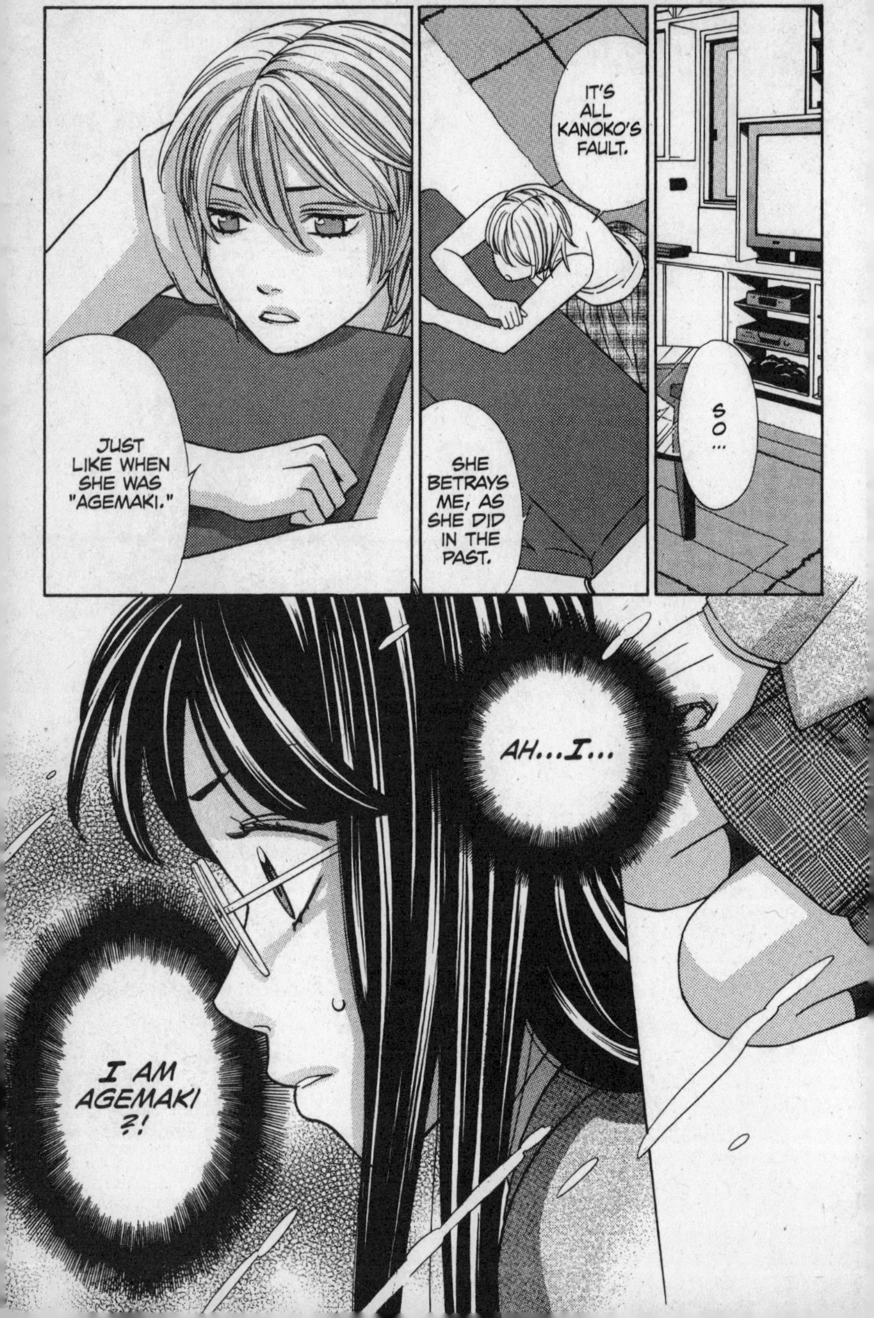
SO...
IT'S ALL KANOKO'S FAULT.
SHE BETRAYS ME, AS SHE DID IN THE PAST.
JUST LIKE WHEN SHE WAS "AGEMAKI."
AH...I...
I AM AGEMAKI ?!

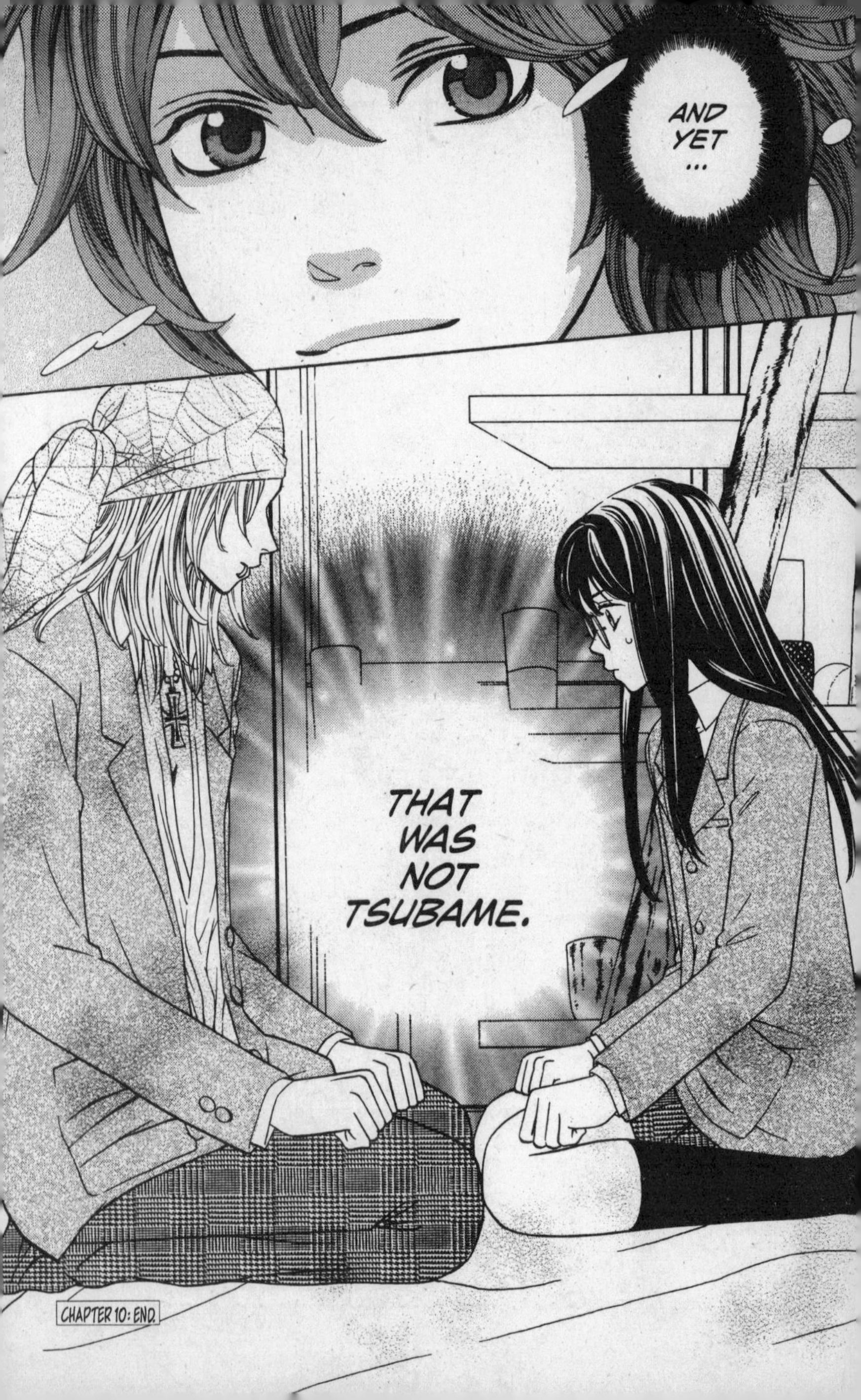
AND YET ...
THAT WAS NOT TSUBAME.
CHAPTER 10: END.

Continued From Page 36

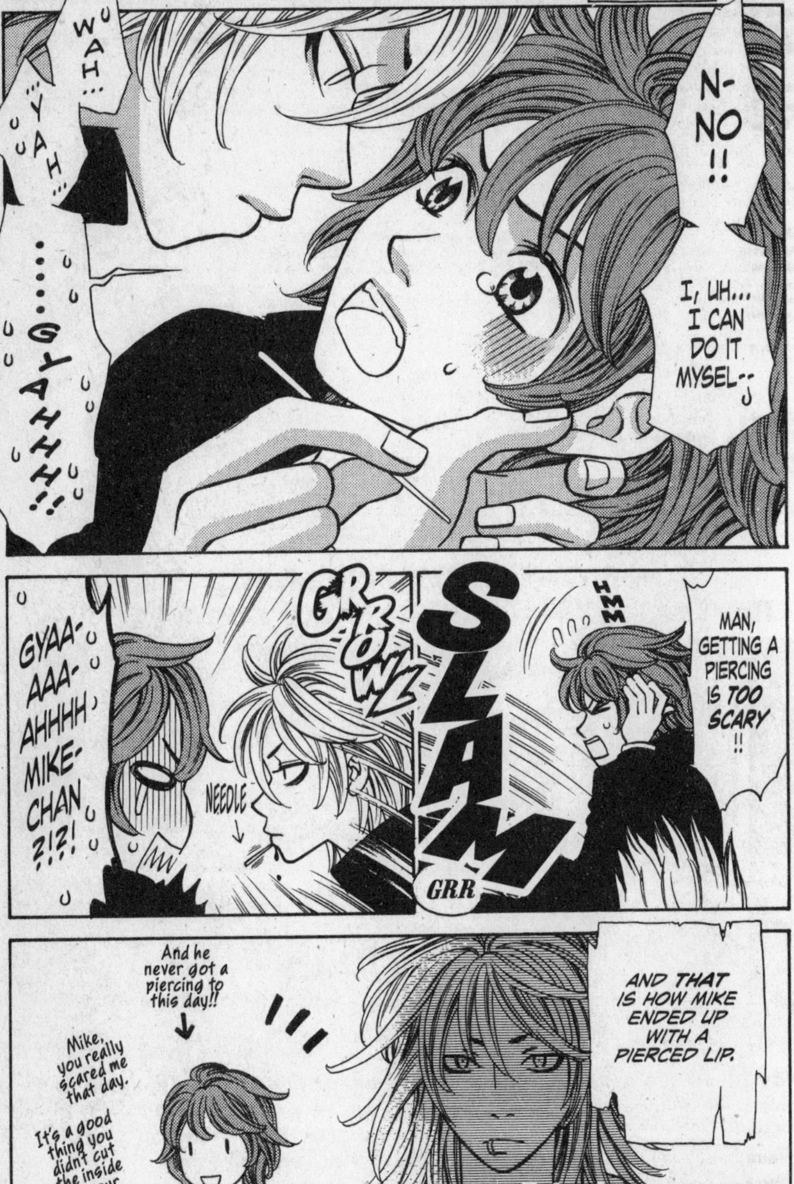
N-NO!!
I, UH... I CAN DO IT MYSEL--
WAH... YAH...
...GYAHHH!!
MAN, GETTING A PIERCING IS TOO SCARY!!
HMM
SLAM
GRR
GRROWL
NEEDLE
GYAA-AAA-AHHHH MIKE-CHAN?!?!
AND THAT IS HOW MIKE ENDED UP WITH A PIERCED LIP.
Readers, please get a professional to do your piercings, okay?!
And he never got a piercing to this day!!
Mike, you really scared me that day.
It's a good thing you didn't cut the inside of your mouth!!

FIN.

"OYAYUBIHIME INFINITY" Volume 2: End.

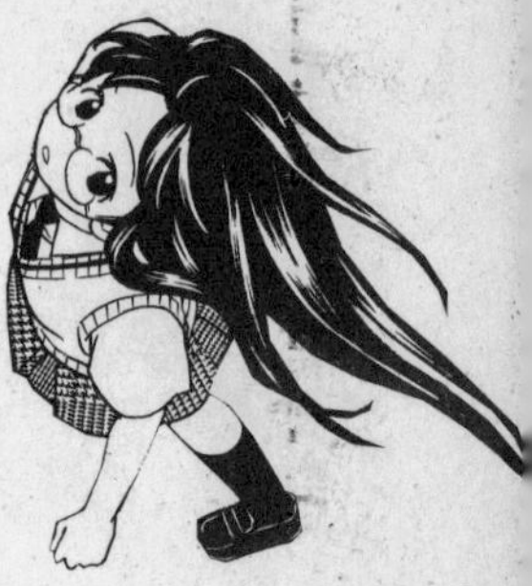

's – Translation and Adaptation
eys' Melanie Olsen – Lettering
ry – Design
wick – Editor

ISBN:1-4012-1076-7
ISBN-13: 978-1-4012-1076-2

COMING IN DECEMBER: MORE NEW EVELATIONS ABOUT KANOKO'S PAST LIFE!

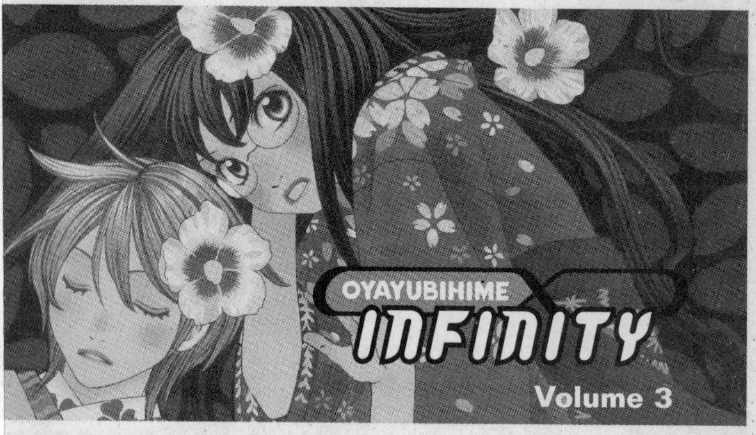
OYAYUBIHIME
INFINITY
Volume 3

Toru Fujieda. So now Tsubame is convinced that Kanoko has betrayed in both their past and present lives. Will he find out the real reason why oko was with Mike? Meanwhile, Kanoko seems to have discovered that ame is definitely not her destined love. (Or so it seems.) If that's the case who are the people they are each supposed to be with? And where does a fit in with all of this?